Tigran Petrosi His Life and Games

VIK L. VASILIEV
With added material by Tigran V. Petrosian
Game annotations by Alexei S. Suetin, Tigran V. Petrosian
Translated and edited by Michael Basman

With a new foreword and games converted
into Algebraic Notation by Sam Sloan

ISHI PRESS INTERNATIONAL

Tigran Petrosian His Life and Games
by Vik L. Vasiliev

With added material by Tigran Petrosian
Game annotations by Alexei S. Suetin
Translated and Edited by Michael Basman
With a new foreword and games converted
into Algebraic Notation by Sam Sloan

First published in 1969 in Russian in Yerevan,
Armenia as *Zhizn Shakhmatista* ("*The Life of a Chess Player*")

First published in the USA in 1974 by R H M Press,
a Division of RHM Associates of Delaware, Inc., as
a "work made for hire".

Current Printing October, 2009 by
Ishi Press in New York and Tokyo

Copyright © 2009 by Ishi Press and Sam Sloan

All rights reserved according to International Law. No
part of this book may be reproduced or otherwise
copied without the written permission of the publisher.

ISBN 4-87187-813-9
978-4-87187-813-5

Ishi Press International
1664 Davidson Avenue, Suite 1B
Bronx NY 10453
917-507-7226
Printed in the United States of America

Foreword by Sam Sloan

Tigran Petrosian His Life and Games

Foreword by Sam Sloan

Tigran Petrosian (**1929-1984**) was **World Chess Champion** from **1963** to **1969** and was one of the strongest players in the world throughout his lengthy career.

His style of play was the opposite of what others said it was. Others characterized his play as "dull" and "drawish". However, statistics prove that while others considered his play to be dull by their standards, it was not drawish.

Petrosian had the lowest percentage of draws of any top grandmaster in the world. Whereas **Tal** is considered to have been the opposite of Petrosian, with daring sacrificial attacks, in reality **Tal** drew more games than Petrosian did. Similarly, **Fischer** whose play was characterized by direct assaults, nevertheless drew more games than Petrosian did.

Petrosian represented the **USSR** in the World Chess Olympiad ten times. His result was **78 wins, 50 draws and only one loss, for 79.8 per cent.**

The most famous instance of this was at the **1966 Chess Olympiad** in **Havana, Cuba**, where he won the **gold medal** on top board with **88.46 percent** vs. **Bobby Fischer's 88.23 percent**.

Petrosian was a **Candidate for the World Championship** on eight occasions (**1953, 1956, 1959, 1962, 1971, 1974, 1977** and **1980**). He won the world championship in **1963** by defeating **Botvinnik**, successfully defended it in **1966** against **Spassky**, and lost it in **1969** to **Spassky**. Thus, he was the defending **World Champion** or a **World Champion Candidate** in ten

Foreword by Sam Sloan

consecutive three-year cycles.

He won the **Soviet Championship** four times (**1959, 1961, 1969,** and **1975**).

In spite of these impressive results, he is perhaps best known for breaking **Bobby Fischer's winning streak of 20 games** by beating Bobby in game two of their **1971 match**.

Why is it then that, in the face of these amazing results, Petrosian is considered to be a dull and drawish player?

It is because of the way that he achieved his results. He did not often launch a direct, immediate attack. Instead, he maneuvered, seeming endlessly. He waited for his opponent to make an error or to attack unsoundly. When the mistake finally occurred, Petrosian exploited it ruthlessly.

In many ways, Petrosian played the way that modern computers seem to play, sometimes making moves that seem pointless and yet winning the game in the end.

An example of this is the **Petrosian System** in the **Queen's Indian Defense**: 1. d4 Nf6 2. c4 e6 3. Nf3 b6 **4. a3**.

The purpose to **a3** is obviously to stop Black from playing **Bb4+**. Yet, Bb4+ is not really a threat or even a very good move. Why waste a valuable move in the opening to stop a non-existent threat?

Petrosian felt that **a3** would turn out to be a useful move later in the game and thus was not wasted. Moreover, a3 was in accordance with his policy of restricting his opponent, thereby causing his opponent to feel frustrated, leading to his opponent making a rash decision which Petrosian could exploit.

Bobby Fischer said that Petrosian *"will smell any kind of*

Foreword by Sam Sloan

danger 20 moves before!"

Tigran Petrosian was born in **Tbilisi, Georgia** on **17 June 1929**. He died of stomach cancer in **Moscow** on **13 August 1984**. The poor quality of the **Soviet Health Care System** may have contributed to his early death at age **only 55**.

Petrosian lived in **Moscow** most of his life. In spite of neither being born nor living in **Armenia**, he has always been considered to be **Armenian** and he is a national hero of the **Republic of Armenia**.

This book was originally published in **Russian** in **Yerevan, Armenia** as *Zhizn Shakhmatista* (*"The Life of a Chess Player"*) by **Viktor Vasiliev**.

It was translated into **English** by **Michael Basman** (who, it is not well known, is an ethnic Armenian and who studied as a college student for several years at the **University in Yerevan**).

Eventually, the rights to this book were acquired by **Sidney Fried** for his company, **RHM Press**.

This **RHM Series** of high quality chess books was the brain child of **Sidney Fried (born 22 June 1919 – died 1 June 1991)**. Sidney Fried was not a strong player but was an **aficionado** or big fan of chess.

Sidney Fried had a lot of money. He had made his fortune in common stock purchase warrants. Then, he made more money writing books and two newsletters about it. His stock market books are still available today, including such works as *"Investment and Speculation with Warrants - Options & Convertibles"* and *"Fortune building in the 70's with common stock warrants and low-price stocks"* by Sidney Fried.

Foreword by Sam Sloan

Fried had a number of unusual habits, one of which was that he owned nothing. He put everything he owned into his corporations, **R H M Press, a Division of RHM Associates of Delaware, Inc.**

Fried was a member of the **Libertarian Party**. Since Fried had no assets, this enabled him to get away with not paying any taxes. However, upon his death it was discovered that he had left no will and therefore nothing, including his New York townhouse, his personal home on Long Island, his yacht and his California estate that were owned by his corporations could be inherited. All of his property went to the state.

This also affected the publication of this book. It appears that all of his RHM books were "**Work Made for Hire**" books, in which he paid the authors in cash rather than signing standard royalty agreements. This certainly simplified matters. It enabled his books to have numerous authors, translators and editors and a chief editor, **Burt Hochberg (1933-2006)**. Hochberg wrote, "*grandmasters were very well paid to write them.*" Imagine the difficulties of dividing royalty payments among the many contributors and the even bigger problems of trying to negotiate royalty deals with different people. (For example, "I demand to be paid as much as Petrosian!!!")

By paying everybody in cash, Fried was able to assemble teams to help him create his works. For example, this book was originally written by **Viktor Vasiliev**. It was translated into **English** by **Michael Basman**. Notes were provided by **Alexei Suetin**, additional material was provided by **Tigran Petrosian** himself. Further notes were by **Liberzon, Boleslavsky** and **Holmov**. **Kevin J. O'Connell** was a proof reader. **Burt Hochberg** probably did some editing although his name is not mentioned in the book. The whole thing was assembled by **Sidney Fried**. I have probably left out somebody.

Eventually, Sidney Fried lost a lot of money the same way he

Foreword by Sam Sloan

had made it, gambling on stock market purchase options and warrants. It is not clear whether he died broke or nearly broke, but in any case he left behind a great series of chess books that we can still read today and remember him by.

This book was originally published in **Descriptive Chess Notation**. Since that time, Descriptive has become almost obsolete. For that reason, all **50 games** in this book have been converted into modern **Algebraic Notation** and are included in an appendix in the back of the book.

Sam Sloan
October 13, 2009

ISBN 4-87187-813-9
978-4-87187-813-5

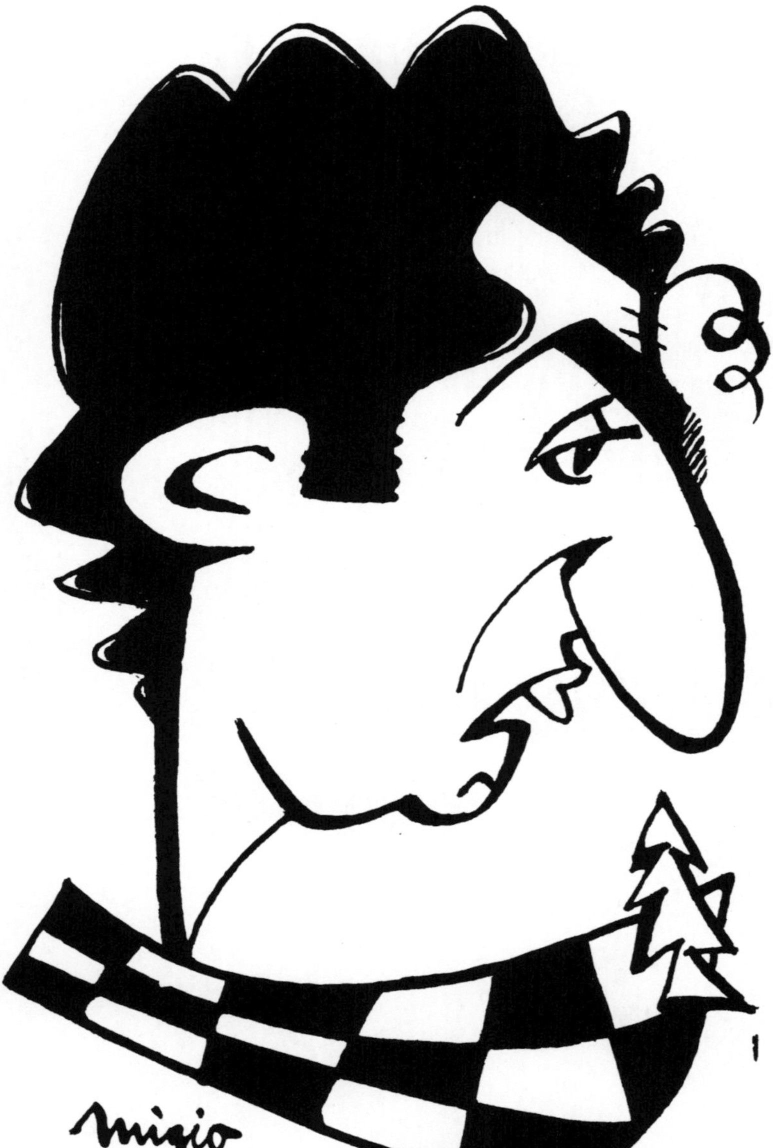
Migio

Contents

	Preface and Acknowledgements	6
	Biographical details	7
	Tournament and match record	7
	Introduction, Ice and Flame	11
1	'I believe only in "correct" play...'	15
2	'A young boy – and he did not lose a single game?!'	23
3	Hallo Moscow!	36
4	Iron Century	43
5	Safety First!	57
6	Prospect Rustaveli	72
7	Tal comes and goes	86
8	At the door of The King	108
9	Ninth Champion	125
10	And everything back to the beginning again!...	155
11	Instead of an Epilogue	201
12	Losing the World Championship	210
13	The candidates' matches as I saw them	220
	Index of Openings	242
	Index of Games	242
	Index – General	243
	Index of Names	245
	Index of Places	247

Illustrations between pages 128 *and* 129

Preface & Acknowledgements

This book is based on the Russian *Zhizn Shakhmatista* (Life of a Chessplayer) by Vik Vasiliev, Erevan 1969.

Vasiliev, one of the Soviet Union's top chess journalists (he is chess correspondent for the Soviet sports newspaper *Sovietsky Sport*), wrote the biographical sections on the basis of information provided directly by Petrosian.

The annotations to the games were by Alexei Suetin, who has long been Petrosian's openings adviser in preparation for matches, thus the notes are largely based on Petrosian's own ideas and impressions about the games.

This edition is different from the Russian in several respects:

1) 10 additional games have been included to up-date the games' section.
2) 2 chapters have been added (12 and 13).
3) Other additions, for which I should like to thank Batsford's Assistant Chess Editor, Kevin J. O'Connell, who also edited the typescript and read the proofs, are:
   a) the most complete tournament and match record of Petrosian's career so far published.
   b) a more detailed index of opponents and openings.
   c) a general index, an index of names and an index of places.

MJB
London, February 1974

Biographical Details

Tigran Vartanovich Petrosian
born Tiflis, Georgia   17.6.1929
began playing chess   1941
1st category   1945
Candidate Master   1945
USSR Youth Champion   1946
Master   1947
Grandmaster   1952
Candidate   1953, 1956, 1959, 1962, 1971, 1974
USSR Champion   1959, 1961, 1969
Master of Sport of USSR   1960
Challenger   1962
World Champion   1963–1969
Editor of *64*   1968–
Master of Philosophical Science   1968
(*degree thesis: Chess Logic, Some Problems of the Logic of Chess Thought, Yerevan 1968*)

Tournament and Match Record

			+	=	–
1944	1st category tournament	1			
	5th Georgian Ch	9–11=			
1945	2 Tiflis Ch	2			
	Junior tournament, Tiflis	1			
	Selection tournament for Yerevan				
	½-final All-Union CM tournament			qualified	
	All-Union Junior, Leningrad	1–3=		(11–4)	
	6 Georgian Ch	1			
1946	6 Armenian Ch	1		(9–1)	
	7 Georgian Ch	5		(12½–6½)	
	All-Union Junior, Leningrad	1	13	2	0
	Armenian Ch match v. Kasparian	Won		(8–6)	
	15 USSR Ch, Tiflis ½-final	16		(6–11)	
1947	7 Armenian Ch	2–4=		(8½–2½)	
	All-Union CM, Tiflis	1	8	7	0

8 Tournament and Match Record

			+	=	−
	16 USSR Ch, Moscow ½-final	5		(8½–6½)	
	Spartak Club Ch	10	6	9	4
1948	USSR Team Ch, Tiflis ½-final	bd. 2	1	2	0
	Trans Caucasian Republics	2	6	6	0
	8 Armenian Ch	1–2=	12	1	0
1949	9 Armenian Ch	2		(12½–2½)	
	17 USSR Ch, Tiflis ½-final	2	7	8	1
	Master & CM tournament	2–5=		(6–6)	
	Uzbekhistan Jubilee	1–2=	11	3	1
	17 USSR Ch, Moscow	16	4	7	8
1950	Moscow Ch	3	4	10	1
	18 USSR Ch, Gorky ½-final	2–3=	8	4	3
	18 USSR Ch, Moscow	12–13=	5	6	6
1951	Moscow Ch	1	7	5	0
	19 USSR Ch, Sverdlovsk ½-final	1	9	9	1
	USSR Team Ch, Moscow	bd. 3	2	1	2
	Master & CM, Tiflis	2–3=	7	5	3
	19 USSR Ch, Moscow	2–3=	8	7	2
1952	Budapest	7–8=	6	7	4
	Interzonal, Stockholm	2–3=	7	13	0
1953	Bucharest	2	7	12	0
	Candidates, Zurich	5	6	18	4
	Austria–USSR (Lokvenc)	bd. 1	2	0	0
1954	21 USSR Ch, Kiev	4–5=	6	13	0
	Argentina–USSR (Pilnik)	bd. 6	1	3	0
	Uruguay–USSR	bd. 5	2	0	0
	France–USSR (Belkadi)	bd. 5	2	0	0
	USA–USSR (Bisguier)	bd. 7	2	2	0
	England–USSR (Milner–Barry)	bd. 6	2	0	0
	Sweden–USSR	bd. 6	2	0	0
	USSR Team Ch, Riga	bd. 1	8	11	1
	Belgrade	4–5=	7	9	3
1955	22 USSR Ch, Moscow	3–6=	4	15	0
	Hungary–USSR	—	4	3	0
	USSR–USA	bd. 6	4	0	0
	Interzonal, Goteborg	4	5	15	0
1956	Candidates, Amsterdam	3–7=	3	13	2
	Yugoslavia–USSR, Belgrade	—	1	6	1
	Moscow Ch	1–2=	6	8	1
	Moscow Ch play-off v. Simagin	Won	2	2	0
	24 USSR Ch, Tiflis ½-final	1	10	9	0
1957	24 USSR Ch, Moscow	7–8=	7	10	4
	USSR–Yugoslavia, Leningrad	(bd. 7)	3	4	1
	Europe Team Ch, Vienna	bd. 6	3	2	0
	25 USSR Ch, Kiev ½-final	1	7	11	1
1958	25 USSR Ch. Riga	2	6	12	0
	USSR Team Ch	bd. 2		(5½–2½)	
	Interzonal, Portoroz	3–4=	6	13	1

			+	−	=
	13 Olympiad, Munich	2nd res.	8	5	0
1959	26 USSR Ch, Tiflis	1	8	11	0
	USSR–Yugoslavia, Kiev	bd. 2	2	2	0
	Moscow–Leningrad (Taimanov)	bd. 2	1	0	1
	USSR Spartakiad, Moscow	bd. 3	3	4	0
	Candidates, Bled–Zagreb–Belgrade	3	7	17	4
1960	Beverwijk	1–2=	4	5	0
	27 USSR Ch, Leningrad	2–3=	10	7	2
	Tunisia–USSR	bd. 2	2	0	0
	Italy–USSR	bd. 2	1	0	0
	W. Germany–USSR, Hamburg	bd. 3	6	1	0
	Copenhagen	1	10	3	0
	14 Olympiad, Leipzig	2nd res.	11	2	0
	USSR Team Ch	bd. 2	4	0	1
1961	28 USSR Ch, Moscow	1	9	9	1
	Yugoslavia–USSR, Belgrade	—	3	2	0
	*Moscow Team Ch	?	—	—	1
	*Spartak Team Ch	?	1	—	—
	Zurich	2	7	3	1
	Europa Team Ch, Oberhausen	bd. 4	4	4	0
	Bled	3–5=	8	9	2
	USSR Team Ch, Riga	bd. 1	1	1	3
1962	Interzonal, Stockholm	2–3=	8	14	0
	Candidates, Curacao	1	8	19	0
	Holland–USSR, Hague (Donner)	bd. 1	1	1	0
	15 Olympiad, Varna	bd. 2	8	4	0
1963	World Championship – Botvinnik	Won	5	15	2
	Los Angeles	1–2=	4	9	1
	USSR Spartakiad	bd. 1	4	3	2
1964	*USSR Team Ch, Tallinn ½-final	bd. 1	2	2	—
	*'Sportivnikh Obshch stv' Ch, Moscow	?	2	—	—
	Buenos Aires	1–2=	8	9	0
	USSR Team Ch	bd. 1	2	3	1
	16 Olympiad, Tel Aviv	bd. 1	6	7	0
	Trades Union Ch, Moscow	1	7	7	1
1965	Zagreb	3	7	11	1
	Europa Team Ch, Hamburg	bd. 1	2	8	0
	Yerevan	2–3=	4	9	0
	Moscow–Leningrad (Korchnoi)	bd. 1	0	0	2
1966	*Moscow Team Ch	bd. 1	1	2	—
	Moscow, Training	1	7	2	1
	World Championship – Spassky	Won	4	17	3
	Santa Monica	6–7=	3	12	3
	USSR Team Ch	bd. 1	2	8	0
	17 Olympiad, Havana	bd. 1	10	3	0
1967	*Moscow Spartakiad	bd. 1	2	2	—
	Moscow	9–12=	3	11	3

10 Tournament and Match Record

			+	=	−
	USSR Spartakiad, Moscow	bd. 1	3	3	2
	Venice	2–3=	7	6	0
1968	Bamberg	2–3=	5	10	0
	Moscow Ch	1–2=	6	9	0
	18 Olympiad, Lugano	bd. 1	9	3	0
	Palma	4	7	9	1
1969	World Championship – Spassky	Lost	4	13	6
	Yugoslavia–USSR, Skopje	bd. 2	1	1	1
	37 USSR Ch, Moscow	1–2=	6	16	0
	Palma	2	6	11	0
1970	37 USSR Ch play-off v. Polugaevsky	Won	2	3	0
	USSR–World, Belgrade (Fischer)	bd. 2	0	2	2
	Rovinj–Zagreb	6	5	11	1
	Europa Team Ch, Kapfenberg	bd. 1	1	5	0
	19 Olympiad, Siegen	bd. 2	6	8	0
	Vinkovci	6–9=	4	10	1
1971	Wijk aan Zee	2–5=	4	11	0
	Candidates ¼-final v. Hübner	Won	1	6	0
	Candidates ½-final v. Korchnoi	Won	1	9	0
	Candidates Final v. Fischer	Lost	1	3	5
	Moscow, Alekhine Memorial	4–5=	4	12	1
	*Moscow Olympiad	bd. 1	2	2	—
1972	USSR Olympiad	bd. 1	2	5	0
	Sarajevo	2	6	9	0
	Yugoslavia–USSR, Okhrid	bd. 1	2	2	0
	20 Olympiad, Skopje	bd. 1	6	9	1
	San Antonio	1–3=	6	9	0
1973	Las Palmas	1–2=	4	11	0
	USSR National Teams	bd. 2	1	3	0
	Europa Team Ch, Bath	bd. 2	2	5	0
	Amsterdam	1–2=	6	8	1
	41 USSR Ch, Moscow	2–6=	4	13	0
	*USSR–Yugoslavia (Gligoric)	bd. 1	1	—	1
1974	Candidates ¼-final v. Portisch	Won	3	8	2

```
                                    1524      597    811    116
                                    87½/136
                                    Total            1090/1660
```

* Indicates that full details could not be traced.

Introduction
Ice and Flame

When after a long and gruelling struggle on the isle of Curacao – that ancient retreat of corsairs and sea warriors – there finally appeared the next opponent to world champion Mikhail Botvinnik, the chess world reacted with a certain reserve. There were quite a few reasons for this attitude. The victory had not been very effective, nor very convincing. Tigran Petrosian had hardly swept the board in Curacao. With his nearest rivals – Paul Keres and Yefim Geller – he had drawn all eight games and only outdistanced them by half a point. For comparison, Botvinnik's previous opponent, Mikhail Tal, had led Keres in the Candidates' tournament of 1959 by 1½ points. At that time, Petrosian, who occupied third place, was 4½ points behind. And Vasily Smyslov, who before Tal twice came out on top in Candidates' tournaments, won the first with a lead of 2 points and the second by 1½ points. . . .

And what about Petrosian's style? It was, of course, extremely reliable. But surely there might be in that some evidence of vulnerability? Was it not significant that it was generally he and not his opponent who had to suffer tests of endurance? Why did he always have to receive blows, but not deliver them? Those who judged in such a way probably overlooked that Petrosian, in suitable moments, was always prepared to seize the initiative and go in for a life or death struggle. It is true that he often saw what to them were 'suitable' moments as unsuitable. Petrosian's sober calculations, his caution, never found sympathy among those people who liked to follow the romantics of the chess world. The chess public did not always like Petrosian's peaceful ways. In the Candidates' tournament of 1956 he drew 13 games out of 18, in 1959 he drew 17 out of 28, and in 1962, 19 out of 27. That was quite a lot, especially in the last one, which he won.

And so, there were quite a few reasons why the chess world reacted coolly to the news of Petrosian's great success in Curacao. Furthermore, at the beginning of the competition very few commentators believed that Petrosian would come out as the victor. What Mikhail Yudovich wrote was typical: 'Nobody doubts that Petrosian will produce a good result, but very few believe that he can win'.

However, the most penetrating, the wisest observers understood the real significance of what had happened at Curacao. Petrosian's victory could not have been accidental: in chess, accidents do not happen. Let it have been by ever so little, let it have been by 'only half a point', but Petrosian had turned out stronger than his opponents. Perhaps an even more important factor was involved: a chess-player had arisen against Botvinnik who appeared down to the very tips of his fingers to have been created for match play.

It had been far harder to obtain the right to a match than to play the match itself – for all Petrosian's characteristics of caution, preparedness to accept draws, which in tournaments could often prevent him from attaining higher than third or fourth place, had a completely different effect in match play. A few superfluous draws in a tournament could quite easily push him back out of the leading group, but a draw in a match never changed anything. It meant he needn't take any unnecessary risks, needn't strain himself nor overtax his resources, but he could carry on in his favourite style, withstand a multitude of attacks and then, finally, choose the most suitable moment to seize the initiative and to launch himself at his opponent. Here especially his chessic and psychological steadfastness was useful, and was to play a decisive role in the match.

After the Curacao tournament had ended, Grandmaster Alexander Tolush wrote an article in which he underlined the general evenness of the successes of the challenger. However, he later mentioned that Petrosian's style was not all that popular with the wide circle of chess lovers who generally prefer sharp combinational struggles. But, as Botvinnik, the World Champion said, style was not that important, strength of play was important. All the same, it was precisely Petrosian's style that Botvinnik had praised. A deeply original manner of play, especially difficult for the opponent to meet.

'The practical strength of Petrosian's style, founded on an original and precise positional understanding,' wrote Botvinnik 'lies in this: that as he gains more experience he becomes all the more dangerous to his opponents and his superiority of positional understanding is a permanent factor by no means accidental. This should some day make itself felt.'

Due to his accumulation of experience, Petrosian became so dangerous to his opponents that he won the right to play a match for the world championship. In this match, as is well known, Petrosian not only fully proved the truth of Botvinnik's words but he also proved that the chess crown had fallen in the hands of a fighter who was completely at home in match situations.

The match with Boris Spassky, which took place three years later once again showed Petrosian's enormous strength. For the first time in thirty-two years (since the match Alekhine versus Bogoljubow) the World Champion had won the world championship match, not his opponent. And surely Spassky, seven years the younger man, had full confidence in himself and the full confidence of the chess world after his crushing victories in match play over Keres, Geller and Tal. But Petrosian excelled his opponent not only in the simplest positions but also in complicated tactical play.

Here then was the World Champion thrust upon an unwilling world. Here was a chess-player of an original, deep and precise style. Very cautious but at the same time decisive. Peace-loving yet nonetheless aggressive. Agreeable to draws but never conciliatory – and always having in him the ability to gain the necessary point at the right time....

Complicated, contradictory, even enigmatic. How had such a chess character arisen? How did such an unusual combination of characteristics come together in one person? How indeed did it happen that flame and ice befriended each other?

1 'I believe only in "correct" play....'

All little boys love to play games. This little boy liked playing, especially, draughts, backgammon and Turkish draughts. Games in which it is necessary to think. His father was the caretaker at the Tiflis officers' home, and elderly Armenians would often gather at his house to talk of this and that, to judge upon the happenings in the world and afterwards play back-gammon or draughts. Old Vartan had no greater pleasure than to watch how little Tigran would beat one and all at his favourite game.

As the youngest son in the Petrosian family, Tigran gladdened the hearts of his mother and father not only by his obvious skill in table games. He also had an irreproachable record at school. Unlike his contemporaries, Tigran went to study as if he was going on a holiday. Sometimes he would get up in the late evening, walk on tiptoe to the wall clock and push the hands of the clock forward in order that he might get to class earlier than usual. When he left the house he would quietly push the hands of the clock back again. His old parents noticed this innocent prank and smiled to themselves with pleasure: such afflictions could probably be survived. What was more, the little boy brought home only 5's (5's – Soviet system of marking in schools and universities. 5 is the highest mark, 4 is good, 3 satisfactory and 2 is a fail in an exam).

However, his brother, Hmayak, and his sister, Vartoosh, also studied very well at school. Their mother went to school only once a year, to receive three excellent school reports.

Old Vartan, who had not yet succeeded in becoming literate himself, never tired of telling Tigran to 'Study, study, study'. Afterwards, when Tigran had already become attracted to chess, his father would say: 'Study! Chess will never earn you a living.'

However, his father pronounced this more as an exhortation which he felt it incumbent on him to deliver himself of from time to time. Tigran always studied very well. He was fortunate in his teachers and this probably helped him a great deal. He went to the Seventy-Third Armenian School in Tiflis. The Director there, Maria Nikitichna Melikian, was a remarkable woman with an extremely generous heart and fanatical devotion to her work and, of course, to her children.

Tigran was also 'her child' and Maria Nikitichna always remained for him a good fairy.

Petrosian would never forget his favourite teacher of mathematics, Solomon Grigorievich Salibegian. Tigran learnt from him not to trust accidental successes which had not been reinforced by fundamental preparation and deep study. If you like, it was precisely Solomon Grigorievich who, with all the characteristics of his mathematical mind, taught Tigran to live 'according to position'. . . .

Tigran became acquainted with chess quite early. But the acquaintance was only passing and it did not develop at once into a friendship. Film shows were often arranged at the officers' home and little Tigran was a constant guest at these. He would appear an hour and a half before the show, listen to the music and read the magazines and always stayed a long time in the foyer watching the visitors playing chess.

There is a legend that Capablanca learnt to play only by watching other people playing and that he never asked anyone to teach him the rules. Petrosian, who so many people were later to compare with that famous Cuban, only watched silently and . . . understood nothing. His inborn modesty prevented him from asking strangers to explain to him. However, one way or another, acquaintanceship with chess did in fact develop and from that moment young Petrosian never lost his delight in the intelligent game, nor his interest in its enigmatic figures. Long before the war, 12-year-old Tigran gained the right to attend the town Palace of Pioneers. Here he entered the chess section and would sometimes sit the whole day at the board. In this same Palace he learnt of the existence of chess books which simply exhilarated him. By a strange trick of fate, the boy whom Petrosian first saw carrying a book of chess games also had a 'chess' surname – Fine. With him and Andro Lekiashvali, Tigran for the first time in his life began to analyse the games of the chess masters.

That summer when Petrosian went on a school excursion he was drawn once again to the chess section. At that moment, a well-known chess player, Nikolai Sorokin, was giving a simultaneous display. Tigran would have liked there and then to have entered the circle of players. However, the excursion passed on. Still, on the following day he realized his intention.

Petrosian threw himself at chess with the eagerness of youth. Chess attracted him in such a way that at home they didn't know whether to be glad or sorry. Tigran lived and dreamed about chess. Backgammon and Turkish draughts fell into the background. His old love of football also waned. Tigran's appetite for chess was insatiable. Fulfilling the norm for a fourth category rating in one tournament, he would straightaway enrol for another and then for a third, until he had ten times over acquired the norm for a fourth category player. And so it was on every rung of the classification ladder.

He now began to get hold of chess books. Tigran stumbled across a shortened version of Maizelis's text book in an Armenian bookshop and gave his breakfast money in order to acquire this book. Once Tigran obtained Nimzowitsch's 'Chess Praxis'. This for him was an important event and about this it is worthwhile to dwell in more detail.

'I analyzed the games and positions of this book innumerable times' Petrosian later wrote, 'and I even liked to read it without a chess set in front of me, so it wasn't surprising that in the end I learnt it off by heart.'

Let a few decades pass and the son of the Tiflis Palace of Pioneers had already become a chess king. And to the question: 'Which chess books had the greatest influence on you?' he would answer: 'The books of Nimzowitsch!'. Sometimes as a young man he would trade in his chess books at the used book shop which was in Rustaveli Street, next to the offices of the newspaper 'Eastern Rally', but he would never trade in his books by Nimzowitsch.

How did this chess sage capture the imagination of the young boy? First of all perhaps in the vivid aphoristic means of expression used in his books. Petrosian knew that it was useful to occupy the 7th rank. He had read about this already in quite a few books but only in Nimzowitsch did he find an exact aphoristic formula: 7th rank absolute. And what of his conviction that the chess pieces strived to give their lives as dearly as possible? And what of his ideas about prophylaxis? Prophylaxis, which later became one of the most 'Petrosian-like' qualities of the future World Champion's play.

But how ever much Tigran was attracted to the language of Nimzowitsch's book, the meaning behind his writings seized him even more strongly. Even though Petrosian at that time did not pay attention to this fact and only guessed the truth later on, he was drawn to Nimzowitsch first and foremost not because he wrote about chess with such enthusiasm – that had been done by many before and after – but because of the fanatical conviction with which Nimzowitsch laid down his principles. Nimzowitsch had a sacred belief in his principles, in his system, in that whole severe logical order which according to his fulsome conviction should rule on the chess board.

Principles, methods of approach, logic – this was the main thing that most attracted Tigran. Logic – this was the factor which later became his personal chess credo.

Thrilled by Nimzowitsch's passionate conviction, by his total commitment to his own theories, the young boy became a faithful apostle to this chess oracle. Later, in his adult years, Petrosian might sometimes disagree with the views of Nimzowitsch, but even when he had learnt to judge critically the inheritance of his teacher, he still retained a deep respect for the system and for the principles, and he was to name Nimzowitsch as his spiritual father.

It might be well to mention also *The Art of Sacrifice in Chess* by Rudolph Spielmann, which Tigran also acquired. The many beautiful combinations in this book were quite sufficient to make the boy hide this book, like Nimzowitsch's book, under his pillow at night. *The Art of Sacrifice in Chess* left a deep impression on Tigran, especially because he found within its pages a theory of combinations and found that the innumerable sacrifices of pieces and pawns which occurred in chess games had an accurate classification.

Besides Nimzowitsch, there was still one more chess player who Petrosian was to call his spiritual father – Capablanca. He seduced Tigran with his style, with his games and chess ideas. Unfathomably deep but crystal clear like the waters of a mountain lake. Here everything was so logical! In every game Capablanca seemed to be building an edifice – first the foundations, then the walls, the roof, then the inside rooms. And everything he constructed was good – the foundations, the firm walls the exquisite rooms.

There was another circumstance which deepened Tigran's love of Capablanca's games. Archil Ebralidze, with whom Tigran was later to study chess in the Palace of Pioneers, was a chess player of severe, even pedantic, positional style. He loved chess completely and in chess he loved Capablanca.

Tigran didn't study very long with Ebralidze; a year and a half, but this study gave the young boy a great deal. At that time, Petrosian's talents had still to be discovered, notwithstanding his obvious enthusiasm for chess. And ten years later Ebralidze somewhat shamefacedly told Petrosian that he had paid more attention to Alexander Buslayev.

He explained it in this way: 'You must understand you were rather modest, rather quiet. But in chess character is necessary. You have to have confidence in yourself. You hid your character rather deeply.'

Ebralidze strengthened Tigran's love of chess and also his respect for chess, for chess theory, for chess books. Everything that the youth at the time dimly guessed himself was to his great joy confirmed by his teacher. Many years later when Petrosian was already the World Champion, he wrote about Ebralidze:

'A man of rare preparedness and spiritual goodness, Archil Silovanovich was a master of great culture. He was completely devoted to chess and he himself worked a lot at the game, widening our already growing interest in its mysteries. . . .

'Ebralidze supported positional play. He believed in the unshakeability of fundamental strategical rules and he would search for hours to find the refutation to some combination, if only in his opinion the position did not permit such a "forced" decision. . . . In disputes with other masters he always took the side of the player who seemed to be following the fundamental principles of chess strategy. . . .'

'I would also add that Ebralidze was a great supporter of Nimzowitsch, Capablanca and . . . of the Caro-Kann Defence.'

And so Tigran studied under a man who valued the logic of chess. He studied books which taught a severely scientific approach to chess play and he himself liked to win with the help of purely positional means. It was hardly surprising that this young player selected openings which were extremely solid and which gave little leeway to fantasy and imagination. It was hardly surprising that he always took the most direct and reliable course to his goal when playing a chess game and avoided dubious combinations and other tactical adventures.

But all the same, this paradox was already noticeable in his play: he was according to his chess nature, by virtue of his enormous natural ability, a typical tactical player and quickly orientated himself in very unclear situations. So it is quite possible that if Petrosian had not met Ebralidze and if he hadn't come across Nimzowitsch's books, his chess development would have taken a very different course.

One way or another, his other chess 'I' always lived with him. Often it lay quiet and concealed in his spirit. In the chess diary which young Petrosian used to keep there once appeared the following remark: 'I beat my nearest rival, Sorokin, in sharp (not typical for me) style.'

He himself considered that risk and danger were not for him. Quite naturally, many of his opponents had that opinion of Petrosian too. And this opinion lasted for many years and was only finally destroyed when 20 years later Boris Spassky tried to lure Petrosian into a tactical fight. He tried and, to his surprise, it was precisely there, in the arena of a tactical struggle, that he suffered crushing defeats. . . .

But this was to happen many years later, and for the time being Petrosian's tactical 'alter ego' was only now and then to make itself felt. For this period of time Tigran appeared as a typical positional chess-player with an extremely solid style.

Sometimes, it is true, he dimly felt that his understanding of chess had a somewhat primitive directness. Once – this was in the winter of 1942 – a tournament was held in Tiflis in which Bronstein and Shamkovich, then young men, took part. These two met in the first round. Playing Black in a Caro-Kann Defence, Bronstein on the fifth move pushed his king's rook pawn forward two squares. Petrosian could hardly believe his eyes. This was ridiculous. He did not doubt that retribution would soon follow. But, strange to say, Bronstein's position soon proved itself to be in no way inferior! A shadow of doubt stirred in Petrosian's heart as to the correctness of his beliefs. But he pushed away these seditious thoughts. As to what had happened, the time for deep understanding of chess had not yet come.

During that period, autumn and winter 1942, Petrosian often met Bronstein, though not generally at the chess board. Tigran liked to walk through a smallish park on his way to school. He would always find Bronstein there. Striving not to fall into the trenches which had been dug all over the park, David would wander along the paths, analyzing some position or other with the help of his pocket chess set. He was then emaciated and pale, dressed in a cotton jacket from the pocket of which protruded a piece of black bread.

The war continued. The front slid slowly closer towards Tiflis and everyone felt the uneasiness in the air. Life became crueller and at this point the Petrosian family suffered a misfortune: their mother died. Old Vartan, who was already 70 years old, was prostrate with grief and everything slipped from his fingers. On top of that, Tigran became seriously ill himself and he couldn't attend school for six months. Tigran began to work first as a time-board keeper and then as a film mechanic's apprentice, striving to help his father at home.

They – old Vartan, Tigran and Vartoosh (Hmayak was in the army) – had a hard time without their mother. And Tigran's future would have been very uncertain had it not been for the steadfastness of his great-aunt, who devoted the remainder of her life to the family. She joined the family and shouldered all their cares.

When Tigran was finally able to return to his lessons and to chess, the family suffered a new misfortune – father died. Tigran had to take over his father's difficult job. The 15-year-old boy became a caretaker.

As one can see, fate dealt cruelly with Tigran. He was bereaved, deprived of the joys of a carefree adolescence. Yet he did not lament but began to look at life without illusion. Nimzowitsch had been right when he said: 'strategically important points must be defended more than usual – must be defended in excess. . . .' Petrosian would always defend his strategic points thus.

The winter of 1944–45 brought heavy falls of snow. Unusually for Tiflis snow drifts altered the normal profile of the city. A thin, dark skinned youth, holding his school books under his arm hurries along Rustaveli Prospect. His serious eyes, out of place for one of his years, gaze at the falling snow with unconcealed distaste. Reaching home, he has a quick meal and, armed with a spade, goes out to clear away the snow. Finishing his work, he hurries off to do his lessons and afterwards he has to go and play the next round in the Georgian Chess Championship. After playing he goes home immediately and tries to get to sleep as quickly as possible: tomorrow early in the morning he has to go to work.

All this, to say the least, hardly facilitated the achievement of sporting successes. But at the same time the long interval had not brought any great damage: Tigran had grown hungry for chess and played with rapacity. The Georgian Championship was preceded by a tournament of first category players. Formally Petrosian did not have a first category rating but his strength was well-known and the Director of the Chess Circle at the Palace of Pioneers, Alexander Blagidze, allowed him to play in the tournament. He fully justified this faith shown in him: he not only occupied second place but also received the 'bal' for a candidate master title ('bal' – soviet system of sporting awards. Two qualifying bals make one title).

The Georgian Championship was the first tournament in which Petrosian came up against masters, with Mikenas and Kasparian. Strong candidate masters also played in that tournament – Sorokin, Shishov and others. Tigran occupied 9-11th places in a field of 18 players. In general, it wasn't a bad result but Petrosian could, even then, have reckoned on a higher placing. What had hindered him?

'In chess there is only one mistake – overestimating the opponent,' Tartakower had said at some time. In the paradoxes of this 'Oscar Wilde' of chess the truth is sometimes difficult to perceive. But as regards the reserved and even tremulous Petrosian of those years, this aphorism has a real ring of truth.

Believing 'according to Nimzowitsch' in a just scientific order on the chess board, Petrosian was terribly afraid of appearing in the eyes of his experienced opponents as a self-confident, disrespectful ignoramus. In his diary the same remark appears four times: 'I resigned this game prematurely, imagining that my position was lost.' This touching and oft-met 'imagining' best sums up the young Petrosian. With his natural abilities he could calculate variations in a flash and play, as it were, for two people. Having thought out his plan, Tigran would immediately start to look (and what was worse – would find!) the plan for his opponent. When his opponent's plan turned out to be stronger, Petrosian would throw in the towel. It never entered his head that quite likely his opponent had never even suspected the existence of such rich possibilities in the position. But even if Petrosian sometimes guessed that his opponent wouldn't find the best continuation, he would nonetheless always look for the strongest continuation for him in his analysis. He prized the sacred immovability of principles higher than anything else.

Some decades later, quite soon after the world championship match with Spassky, Petrosian gave an interview to the newspaper *Sovietsky Sport*.

'Could you perhaps, as short as possible, formulate your chess credo? What do you value most of all in chess?' That was one of the questions given to him.

'Logic!' answered Petrosian. 'I deeply believe that in chess, even though it is only a game, there is nothing accidental. That is my credo. I like only such games where I have played in accord with the demands of the position. . . . I believe only in logical, "correct" play. . . .'

However, the striving (and ability) to play for his opponent, to see sometimes more than he would see himself, not only saved Petrosian in difficult moments but also explained his amazing capacity to sense approach of danger from afar.

For the present, this shackled him, prevented him from being brave and resolved. In general old beyond his years, he was in chess as well old for his years. Prophylaxis! Who thought of that at the age of 15? Petrosian thought of it. Petrosian was concerned at the slightest whiff of danger, even when there was no danger whatsoever. To strengthen his advanced posts, to deepen his points of occupation, to repair his lines of communication. He never burned his bridges, his rear was always in excellent condition!

2 'A young boy – and he did not lose a single game!?'

'This tournament proved to be a watershed in my career,' wrote Petrosian in his diary about the Georgian Championship. 'The tournament strengthened my belief in my powers. Masters and candidate masters beat me when they could but they did not outplay me.'

Since they had not outplayed him, but since he had committed, in most cases due to lack of experience or to tiredness, obvious errors, it meant that he could have achieved a higher sporting result. Petrosian made this completely correct conclusion after the Georgian Championship. However, others had come to the same conclusion, more experienced and more impartial. Once Petrosian was returning home by night with Mikenas after one of the rounds had ended 'If you work,' said Mikenas 'after two years, no later, you will become a master. And a good master.'

He was, in fact, already a strong chess player. Inexperienced, tremulous before authority, but all the same a strong player. In 1945 Petrosian gained second place in the Tiflis championship, behind Kasparian but in front of Ebralidze. He won both his games against these masters who each in his way had been a teacher to him. Afterwards, he won every game in a junior tournament. And in a selection tournament he gained the right to play in the Yerevan semi-final for an all-union tournament of candidate masters.

This semi-final coincided with an all-union junior tournament which was beginning on 1st August in Leningrad. Petrosian decided to go to Leningrad.

Even though Petrosian lived in a large, very beautiful city, at the time of this journey he felt himself something of a provincial. The prospect of meetings with chess players from Moscow, Leningrad and Kiev did not fill him with exhilaration. Always modest and self-critical, Petrosian did not rate his chances against his opponents. He had already heard conversations about his future rivals in Tiflis. Soloviev was particularly praised and great hopes were placed on Reshko, the Leningrad player. Reshko, playing in the City Championship for the Dynamo Club, beat all and sundry. Tigran heard about this success when he got to Leningrad, where he was met by Master Lisitsin who gave him short and rather fanciful reports about the participants in the tournament on the road to the hotel. Tigran listened to Lisitsin and grew cold. He felt that it would be ridiculous to try and fight against such people as Reshko and Soloviev.

Naturally, the lottery cast Petrosian and Reshko together in the first round!

Tigran made his first moves with trembling hands. Afterwards, he took himself in hand. After all, wasn't he almost a candidate master? He had two 'bals' whereas Reshko didn't have any yet. What was there to be afraid of? He got angry with himself and beat Reshko. This success proved useful to him at the end of the tournament, for he shared first place with Reshko and Vasilchuk.

Probably, Petrosian was the only participant who was surprised by this result, considering himself to have been extremely fortunate.

Even when Petrosian became the Georgian champion, which happened in that very same year, he was still loth to believe in the 'lawfulness' of his success. His talent was strong and his understanding of positions became daily more subtle, but for the present he considered himself to be a fortunate provincial.

On one side, Petrosian soberly weighed the results of every tournament in which he took part and came to the conclusion that by the class of his play he could have occupied even higher places. On the other side, it always seemed to him that he could not truly count upon success. Here we come across, once again, the contradiction in Petrosian's style, in his evaluation both of himself and of his opponents. A reserved young man, afraid to believe in his own gifts, timid before established chess-players – this was how Petrosian was at that time.

It is curious that in the next Georgian Championship he, though winner of the previous year's competition, played like a shamefaced debutante. It was true that this time he had some justification for this: masters Vladas Mikenas, Alexander Zagoriansky took part, and the famous grandmaster Paul Keres, hors concours.

Paul Keres himself. He who had played in tournaments with Alekhine, Capablanca(!). However, Botvinnik had played with them and had even outdistanced them. And now he, young Tigran, would be playing with Keres face to face. Throughout the whole tournament Petrosian could not quite get over his surprise at this (what was more, that he managed to draw his game with the grandmaster) and gazed at Keres with quiet, far-off hero worship.

Petrosian did not play badly in this very strong tournament and gained 5th place, behind Keres, Mikenas, Zagoriansky and Ebralidze. Even though he was a great way behind Keres (18 points to 12), he was only ½ point behind Archil Ebralidze who became the Georgian champion for that year. By itself, the sporting result had not been at all bad, but what Tigran valued far more was his ½ point in the game with Keres. (Only two players out of the 20 participants managed to draw with Keres, the other was Ebralidze.) As white, Tigran played a variation of the Grünfeld Defence, which involved the sacrifice of a pawn, such as had been played in the Alekhine–Bogoljubow match. As it turned out, the variation had long ago gone out of currency and Keres employed a new (for Petrosian!) plan of development, by means of which he maintained his pawn and a good position.

But Petrosian was determined not to bite the dust. He sacrificed the exchange and obtained an equal position and then plucked up his courage to offer a draw. Keres, not suspecting that before him sat the future 'iron Tigran', that great master of defence, declined this peaceful suggestion. (Later on he was many times to remember this episode with a smile.) But afterwards he was forced to recognize the incorrectness of his decision. This was an enormous moral success for Petrosian. He carried the score sheet with the moves of this game everywhere, trembled before it – and finally lost it. In 1964 Keres presented this historic game to the world champion. The venerable grandmaster has retained all his games, even that one with 'someone called Petrosian. . . .'

In that same year, 1946, Petrosian took part again in the all-union Youth Tournament which once again took place in Leningrad. Petrosian did not suffer a single defeat even though such talented players as Korchnoi, Krogius, Nei, Vasilchuk, Zurakhov and Kotkov took part. This result called forth a surprised remark bordering on a reprimand from the veteran player Duz-Hotimirsky.

'What – a young boy and he did not lose a single game?'

Duz-Hotimirsky could be understood. But it was also necessary to understand something else: that it took a very strong player to outshine his contemporaries so completely. Yes, Petrosian had not lost any games and had only allowed two draws. His superiority had been so enormous that for the first and last time in his life, probably, he allowed himself a not very modest remark in his diary: 'The young first category players could put up no resistance to my experience and strength.'

However, Petrosian had an extremely authoritative witness in such a severe judge as grandmaster Levenfish. 'Petrosian's success,' he wrote, 'is a just consequence of the gradual development of his young talent. . . . In the region of opening play Petrosian has a command which even experienced masters might envy. He has a good feel for the position and in most of the games he strategically outplayed his young opponents and then finished them off with a few tactical blows. He has quite a good eye for combinations and rarely makes errors of calculation. Petrosian's vulnerable spots appear to be the endgame and defending difficult positions. . . . In any event, this 18-year-old has every chance of obtaining the title of master in the very near future.' A rather curious description. Note only that young Petrosian was regarded as having a good eye for combinations but his defence and endgame play, that is, those parts of the game which were later to be regarded as his strongest points, were taken to be his weaknesses...

In this evaluation of Petrosian, Levenfish had quite probably been correct. The great defender was still only beginning to awaken in Petrosian, and at 17 years probably nobody has a very deep penetration of the mysteries of the endgame. He was also correct in noting Petrosian's tactical awareness. Petrosian could very quickly find combinational possibilities, calculate them in seconds without error, and therefore give the impression of an energetic, aggressive chess playing manner. Add to that a good understanding of positions and strategical preparedness, and Petrosian became a many sided chess player. All the same, it was very typical of Petrosian, now on the threshold of masterhood, that he should have occasioned an evaluation of his play which after the passage of years was to prove incorrect or at least disputable. Even then, when Petrosian was being formed as a chess-player, his style differed in its complexity and contradictions. Levenfish didn't notice Petrosian's remarkable ability to sense danger far in advance. But all the same, this capacity was developing and from time to time revealed itself. His conviction that if you achieve a positional advantage in the opening it definitely should lead to victory was also becoming stronger. And for that reason he felt it was unnecessary to take any risks.

The following expressions now begin to appear in Petrosian's diary: 'I won this game in a lawful manner – obtained an advantage in the opening and then pressed it home.' This oft repeated phrase 'lawful manner' held within itself the seeds of danger. Chess laws had unnoticeably become dogmas for Petrosian. He now felt the creative ideas of Capablanca and Nimzowitsch even more strongly. He often used their favourite opening systems, carried out his strategical plans in the spirit of Nimzowitsch, and tried to imitate Capablanca in his endgame play. He developed a useful quality for a young chess player: technique. He would only have to weaken his opponent's pawn formation, then begin a siege, after which he would no doubt win a pawn and then force a general capitulation.

It may seem surprising that one reason for this approach may have been that Petrosian achieved great successes very early. He twice running gained first place in the All-Union Youth Championships. People began to write about him, even such authoritative writers as Romanovsky and Levenfish. Many looked upon him as a rising star, even though at that time it was not usual to speak extravagantly about young talents. But the formal title of USSR Youth Champion showed that he was first among his contemporaries.

Let us remember that Tigran's childhood had been spent during the war years, that he had lost both his parents early. It wasn't surprising that he placed a high value on his chess successes and regarded them as life successes. Nor could he, careful and reserved by nature, persuade himself to take risks where he could obtain his goal by quieter and more reliable methods.

So a style was gradually being formed, by which he was later to be called impenetrable, 'the iron Tigran'. A style which above all guaranteed safety. However, in forming this style Petrosian still had to suffer many disappointments. A time approached where he realized that the means upon which he relied were completely insufficient. This period began when Petrosian qualified for the first time to play in the semi-finals of the Soviet Championship, where he came up against far more experienced opponents. This semi-final took place in the autumn of 1946 in Tiflis. Petrosian came to Tiflis as a guest. A few months before the tournament began he had transferred his living quarters to Yerevan.

Tigran got acquainted with Yerevan in May, when he was invited to play, hors concours, in the Armenian Championship. He had studied in Tiflis in an Armenian school. Armenians would often gather at his house. Tigran had always been interested in the history of his people and their ancient traditions and customs. His visit to Yerevan left a tremendous impression on him. Later he recalled that on leaving the station he was suddenly moved to see that the signs were written in the Armenian language. A detail which the people of Yerevan had long since forgotten to notice. . . .

Playing in the Championship, Tigran was pleasantly surprised to see that many of the Yerevan chess fans supported him. At the beginning of the last round Petrosian was lying first equal with Henrikh Kasparian, many times champion of Armenia and a famous chess study composer. Kasparian was extremely popular among the Yerevan chess public. But as is well known, youth also has its rights. In the last round so many fans for both the leaders appeared that the tournament hall was packed tight.

The game took a dramatic course. Tigran played Black. When he had managed not only to equalize the game but even to get a slightly more promising position, he offered a draw. Kasparian rejected the offer. Tigran then began to force the combination which should have led straight to a draw. Kasparian still had faith in himself; at one time he left the main line of play and sacrificed a piece. White's attack seemed to be extremely dangerous, but Petrosian calculated all the variations and managed to hide his king in a safe place.

When Kasparian resigned, Tigran blushed from embarrassment and joy: everybody in the tournament hall applauded him. This was the second time he had been applauded in his life. The first time had been when he made a draw with Keres. Tigran was extremely touched. So when, after the tournament had ended, they suggested that he should come and live in Yerevan, he agreed instantly.

Nonetheless, Tigran was sorry to leave Tiflis. This had been the city of his childhood and youth. He had been educated in the Tiflis Palace of Pioneers and had begun to study chess there. And there he had achieved his first successes. Tigran had gained experience playing in Tiflis chess tournaments. He had learned much from his meetings with Ebralidze, Sorokin, Shishov, Pirtshalova, Blagidze, Sereda, Sinsads and other Tiflis chess players.

Tournaments of the war years had a peculiar character. Often games were played by the light of kerosene lamps. Once during the 1944 Georgian Championship, which took place on the stage of the trade union house, the lights went out and candidate master Sereda went to the grand piano and played a then popular song in the darkness – 'Dark Night'. Then there were the adventures with the food vouchers which were handed out to all the participants. The restaurant where they were meant to have their evening meal closed early and often on making a move the players would scamper off to the restaurant, push the food in their mouths, and hurry back.

Yes, he liked Tiflis, but he could not remain indifferent to the warm welcome given to him by his new Yerevan friends. Tigran became particularly friendly with three youths – Karen Kalantar, Emile Tatevossian and Voloda Asadoorian. These were all competent chess players and helped Tigran to get accustomed to his new home. At the beginning, he lived with the Kalantar family who were very fond of chess. Karen's brother, Alexander Kalantar, was champion of Armenia. Kasparian had great sympathy for Petrosian. He never regarded Tigran as an opponent or a rival, though it was obvious that with Petrosian's arrival the veteran would have to give up his title of republic champion. This may have been because Kasparian gained his main creative satisfactions not in practical play but in composing studies. At any rate, Kasparian greeted him very warmly, often inviting him to his home, where he would show him his studies, prepare with him and give him advice.

Andro Hagopian, one of the founders of chess in Armenia and then the Director of the Chess Club, took great interest in Tigran. Hagopian got him a job as an instructor, tried to help him obtain an apartment sooner and took pains to see that Tigran ate well and went to bed early.

Loris Kalashian became a lifelong and faithful friend of Petrosian. He was the future Director of the Armenian Physical Culture Institute. But at that time he was a student of philosophy. Once in the championship of the republic, Kalashian managed to beat Tigran. Hardly concealing his joy, Kalashian began to set up the pieces intending to analyse the game with his partner, when suddenly Tigran leapt from the table and rushed towards his own room. (He lived in a small room in the same building where the tournament was taking place.) Kalashian followed him and found his friend in tears. He was bewildered and didn't know how to console Tigran, but he suddenly exclaimed: 'Aren't you happy that your friend has now become a candidate master?'

This proved the strongest argument. Tigran smiled and the friends went off to spend the evening in Yerevan.

The two would often go walking together and argue about chess. Tigran was convinced that a talented chess player would undoubtedly show his gifts in other fields. Kalashian thought that chess was a specific gift. Tigran stood firm in his opinion. He believed that if he had been fanatically devoted to science as he was to chess, he would have undoubtedly achieved much. Kalashian listened to this with surprise. Of course Tigran's knowledge lacked system but he was very well read and had a lively natural intelligence. In any event, these discussions already gave indication of that deep psychology which Petrosian revealed in his two matches for the World Championship.

There were, therefore, quite a lot of people who could help Tigran to feel himself at home in Yerevan. Tigran could repay his friends in only one way – by successes in competitions. He began by taking first place in that junior tournament where, as has been said, he allowed only two draws. When he returned from Leningrad, he played a match with Kasparian for the title of Champion of Armenia. Petrosian won by a score of 8–6. On the basis of this success, the Armenian Chess Federation asked that he be awarded the title of master. But the All-Union Qualifications Commission (which Petrosian was later to head) showed reserve and refrained from satisfying this request. The results of Petrosian's performance in his next tournament – the Tiflis semifinal for the Soviet Championship – seemed to show the correctness of this decision.

Petrosian had never played in a tournament like this in his life before. Out of 18 participants only 4, including himself, were candidate masters, and among the remaining 14 masters there were such strong chess players as Aronin, Makogonov, Mikenas, Lisitsin, Vasiliev, Zagoriansky, Ufimtsev, Veresov, Sokolsky.

Petrosian was lost in such company. In some of the games he even managed to get into time trouble which before hardly ever happened to him. Though he realized that among such players he could not hope for any particular success, he nonetheless had faith in himself and in his knowledge of the laws, and he hoped that he could at least fulfil the requirements for a master title. He called all his abilities to his aid, and played in his tried and reliable style – ('Advantage in the opening and subsequent realization of the advantage gained'. . .) In a word, he tried his very hardest.

Unfortunately, Petrosian had to suffer a great disappointment – he occupied next to last place. Perhaps he had played too much in that year. Perhaps he had been intimidated in the company of such famous masters. But all the same, he never expected that he would go to the very bottom of the table.

For anybody else this would have been a blow to his vanity. For Tigran it was above all a signal for unease. Something was going rotten in the state of Denmark. Petrosian now had to listen to reproaches about the dryness of his play, about the lack of practicality in it. Before he had always had a complete answer – sporting success. Now his main trump had been beaten.

Analyzing his games very carefully after the tournament had ended, Petrosian came to an undisputable conclusion: it seemed that he believed too much in 'laws'.

Take for example his game with Ufimtsev. Petrosian played it brilliantly and achieved a very strong advantage. Shortly before the adjournment he won a pawn. An extra pawn with the better position – this surely meant a clear win. Petrosian, hardly the most confident of players, did not even bother to analyse the position. Why? The position was won and that meant he had to win.

Ufimtsev, who had his own share of chess rules, had another opinion. It was, objectively speaking, a lost position. But besides the very important objective points in a game there are also very important subjective ones. One of these was precisely that his young opponent had a rather simple, even naive approach to positional problems and to chess in general.

Ufimtsev came to the adjournment not only armed to the teeth with variations discovered with the help of analysis at home, but also psychologically prepared for a stubborn resistance. With the help of surprising tactical blows, he placed before his opponent one complicated problem after another. Petrosian was not prepared for this 'unlawful' attack. This was hardly right – this scrambling and cunning. Surely the position was lost . . . The time came when Petrosian began to scold himself severely for so easily believing in his position. Ufimtsev not only got back on even terms, but even managed to seize the initiative. Demoralized by this sudden change of roles, Petrosian didn't manage to put up a decent resistance and suffered a horrible defeat.

Chess had taught him a hard lesson. And Petrosian understood that he had to be thankful to Ufimtsev for the service. 'This tournament gave me a great deal,' Petrosian wrote in his diary. 'I understood that to achieve success not only talent but also persevering work, especially in the field of complicated and double-edged middle-games, was necessary. It is necessary to conduct a game not only positionally but also to play for the attack even though this might involve some risk, for the world belongs to the brave.'

It should be recalled that this 'cognition' came from a youth. At 17 years chess-players are generally noted for their daring. Good sense usually comes later. But Petrosian was trying to persuade himself that 'the brave inherit the earth'.

These were not just words. Tigran had discovered some important chinks in his chess armour. He did not lose faith in Nimzowitsch and Capablanca, but he realized that they had revealed to him only certain areas of chess creativity and without understanding other areas he could not go forward. He once again returned to his studies and the era of Chigorin and Alekhine began. Petrosian began to swim in a sea of romanticism, in a limitless ocean of complex combinations. This sea was not completely unsuited to him. He was a fine tactician already and calculated variations easily and without error. (In later years he was to have no equal in blitz games.) When already a powerful grandmaster, he also noticed a tendency in himself to seek tactical decisions in simple positions, even though the position itself called for a non-tactical approach.

In combinational play chess draws closest to art. There imagination, fantasy are paramount. Petrosian lived and suffered with this art. He would secretly have longed to exchange many of his technical masterpieces for one game embroidered with the many colours of combinational play. But drawing his tactical sword from its sheath, admiring its sheen, Petrosian then, with a sigh, returned it to its previous place in a dusty corner. No, these joys were not for him. In his essence, temperament, chess understanding, natural ability, tastes, customs, in short in that extreme complex of characteristics which we designate by the one word 'style', Petrosian the man came into conflict with Petrosian the chess player, Petrosian the realist with Petrosian the romantic. And in this conflict, which often reached powerful internal proportions, the scales generally tipped in favour of Petrosian the realist, Petrosian the pragmatist.

Tigran liked and understood sharp combinative play. He saw that Chigorin and Alekhine were also close to him in spirit. He tested himself and became convinced that he could play in this way too. But, always cautious, he could not bring himself to strain himself. He could not become friends with danger and risk, if there were a quieter course, even whereby the game might trickle into a draw.

This unceasing struggle between his two 'I's' was to give Petrosian's play a remarkable character. Afterwards, when he was already a grandmaster, a German chess magazine remarked that 'Petrosian is a complete romantic whose distinguishing creative strength lies in his fantasy and intuition.' Whereas at the same time ex-World Champion Max Euwe wrote that 'If Petrosian could begin to combine a little, nobody would be able to play chess with him any more.' Both of these judgements were correct, but surely they contradict one another?...

Mikhail Tal perhaps spoke best when he said that Petrosian himself never started an argument but always gave as good as he got.

'Yes, indeed, I do prefer defence to attack, but who has proved that defence is a less dangerous and risky procedure than attack? In defence one mistake is enough. Surely when a chess-player is defending his castle from storm he is balanced on the edge of disaster? Surely such play also requires courage? And surely many games have enriched chess art precisely because of the virtuosity of the defence?'

This and similar passionate monologues Petrosian used to deliver in favour of his defence, in favour of his method of 'giving as good as he got', but never beginning the offence himself. There is a weak point in the argument, however, for if both players strive to attack then you generally get an interesting battle, but if both of them think only about safety then the game generally peters out to a bloodless draw. The attacker by virtue of the very fact that he begins the struggle should be given the preference. But, 'everyone plays according to his nature'. Petrosian, the would-be dangerous tactical player employed these weapons normally only in defence and only when the position forced it upon him.

Petrosian, therefore, came to some serious conclusions regarding his first real failure and deepened his chess understanding, sharpened his play and re-trained his natural combinative ability. All this was bound to tell in his future performances, not of course immediately but after a certain passage of time.

In 1947, Petrosian took part in the Tiflis group of an all-union tournament for candidate masters. Hearing that he was to be invited to the tournament, Petrosian hesitated. He was still able to play in the all-union junior tournament, where he had every chance of repeating his success of the previous two years. But grandmaster Bondarevsky, playing hors concours in the Armenian Championship, advised him to play in the stronger candidates' tournament. Tigran would have liked very much to taste an almost certain victory, but he took the advice of Bondarevsky and went to Tiflis.

It is true that Petrosian didn't follow the grandmaster's second piece of advice. In an article devoted to the Armenian Championship (where Tigran occupied 2nd–4th places) Bondarevsky wrote: 'Candidate master Petrosian, who will soon be 18 years old, is certainly a chess player with a great future. He only needs to find the correct course of development for his talents. Playing in positional style and selecting his opening repertoire accordingly, Petrosian, in my opinion retards his creative development. Such a young chess-player should play rather more aggressively. Petrosian has limited himself rather early to the Catalan opening. It would be much better for him if he were to play the King's Gambit!'

Petrosian could not agree with this advice. He had by this time made quite a few alterations in his creative approach to tactics, to combinational methods of playing, but he had no intention of making a complete change in his style. So whenever he heard such advice or reproaches, he kept silent. He would never change his style, but only try to make it more flexible and universal. And the Tiflis tournament showed that he was right.

In this tournament Petrosian played like a new man. The young candidate master found, understood and remembered (and his memory was phenomenal) an enormous quantity of games played by masters with sharp styles. Quantity gradually became quality and this transposed into experience. Petrosian didn't lose a single game, took first place and secured the right to participate in the semi-final of the Soviet Championship. The Moscow semi-final of the 16th Championship took place in late autumn of 1947 in the club of the 'Gosnak' factory – not far from the house in Piatnitskaya Street where the World Champion was later to live. Surprisingly enough, after 11 rounds Tigran had altogether 1½ points. He had not, however, suffered a collapse – he had simply accumulated no less than 8 adjourned and postponed games.

In the last round Petrosian had to play Simagin. A lot depended on this game: if he drew he would achieve the long awaited title of master, and if he won he would be able to take part in the final of the championship. Petrosian achieved an almost won position and . . . proposed a draw. As it turned out, Simagin didn't have much faith in the strength of his opponent and declined the proposal. Any other might have been spurred on by such a refusal, but Petrosian's patience did not give way to emotion – to him a bird in the hand was always better than two in the bush. The young chess-player, realizing that without undue risk he could play for the win, once again proposed a draw and . . . once again received a rebuff! At last Petrosian became irritated. But, nonetheless, after a few more moves he once again offered a draw. And only then Simagin agreed.

In this curious episode Petrosian remained true to himself as he had been and as he always would be. But in many of the games of this tournament his chess creativity had a different, less rigid aspect. An example of this was his game with Kamishev. The opponents played the Queen's Gambit. But suddenly, when they were not even out of the opening, Kamishev, playing Black, began to move forward his pawns on both flanks! Petrosian knew Black was playing 'incorrectly' and began to consider how he could punish him immediately. Immediately – here Petrosian's previous orthodoxy was speaking:

Kamishev's risky play had a certain point to it and it wasn't definitely necessary to try and refute it. But all the same, Petrosian was determined to refute Black's play, and at this moment he demonstrated a somewhat different approach to his chess problems: he sacrificed a piece.

As it turned out, the sacrifice was reckless and unfounded. He didn't get a serious attack going and Black retained his material advantage. Petrosian then saw he had nowhere to retreat and started a few more sacrifices, and after many adventures the game went into an endgame where White's knight and five pawns fought against a rook and three pawns. During the adjournment Petrosian analysed the position with Kasparian and managed to find a way to victory. He was extremely excited. It was true that Kamishev had brought on the tactical battle, but he, Petrosian, had accepted the challenge and with a few sacrifices had sharpened the play even more.

There was another game with Podolny where Petrosian took his king from the centre without castling, making the monarch, as it were, march on foot to his permanent place of refuge. Before, such a manoeuvre had never entered his head. Petrosian, now a master, had returned to battle and he wanted to play and play again. But in 1948 he only managed to take part in two competitions, a trans-Caucasian tournament and the championship of Armenia, in both of which he took second place. In the first tournament Makogonov won, in the second Kasparian. These results were not bad, but two tournaments a year was rather meagre.

All the same, this had its advantages. Tigran studied theory throughout the year and he especially concentrated on the games of the match tournament for the world championship. This was the year when Mikhail Botvinnik, first among Soviet chess-players, became World Champion.

Tigran worked as an instructor in the 'Spartak' club and lived in a room nearby the Committee of Physical Culture. Sometimes he wouldn't leave the house for days on end and would simply sit over the chess board, where friends would bring him his food. In the spring of the following year, once again in Tiflis, the semi-final of the 17th championship of the country took place. At last Tigran had managed to take part in a strong tournament where he could test himself and all the knowledge he had gained in the previous year. In this tournament Petrosian's games were distinguished by accurate strategical planning. In the summarizing article the sturdiness and reliability of his style was emphasized.

There were, nonetheless, other opinions. Ratmir Holmov, who took third place, declared in an interview: 'The second finalist – young master Petrosian – plays very freely. His play perhaps isn't sufficiently deep yet but he is very competent in tactical complications.' Both these opinions, as we know, were true. Petrosian's play was gradually acquiring a complex, many-sidedness, which allowed different and even sometimes contradictory evaluations. That Petrosian was being formed who 'never begins an argument but is always ready with an answer'.

3 Hallo Moscow!

Petrosian took second place, ahead of many well-known masters. This was already a great success. The World Champion, Botvinnik, praised his play. Making a few complimentary remarks about the winner of the semi-final, Yefim Geller, Botvinnik then declared: 'Much the same can be said about young Petrosian and Holmov. All three have one thing in common – they are continually perfecting their play.'

Continually perfecting... Tigran often thought about how he might perfect his play in Yerevan, where there was already nobody to offer him equal opposition. Sometimes he caught himself thinking that he should leave Yerevan even though he realized that not everybody there would approve of that step. But his friends, his most faithful and trusting friends, would understand him. Petrosian didn't doubt that.

Once Tigran had a long conversation about this with Ratmir Makogonov. Makogonov made a remark about Kasparian. If Kasparian had lived in Moscow, said Makogonov, he would have become a great chess player. Suren Abramian simply tried to persuade Tigran to go to the capital. Nature has given you a talent, he said, and you don't have the right to waste it.

It was easy to say 'go to Moscow and get to the centre of chess life'. But how could this be done if nobody invited him? But as it turned out some people were prepared to invite Tigran. After the semi-final Petrosian went to a coastal resort near Riga. He had to rest before the final. In Moscow he wanted to get to see a football match – football was his strongest passion after chess, but here it is true he was only a spectator. At that time it was difficult to get hold of tickets and Tigran went to the Central Committee of the 'Spartak' club. He spoke with two deputy chairmen – Moiseev-Cherkasky and Goldsberg. They were not only great chess fans, they were also fans of Tigran. After that Tigran could always rely on obtaining tickets for football matches.

The conversation touched upon the fact that it was difficult to prepare for the final in Yerevan and difficult to improve one's play whatsoever there.

'If you lived in Moscow, we could help you,' said Moiseyev-Cherkasky. 'But surely you wouldn't be prepared to leave Yerevan?'

Surprising himself, Tigran answered immediately. 'Of course I would. Surely I have to. . . .'

So he took a very important decision and came to Moscow at the end of 1949. He was dressed in a light coat, summer shoes and had a few chess books under his arm – these were all he owned. The chess Rastiniac had come to take Moscow, never considering that one day he would own the whole world. He still didn't have much faith in his future, specially since his debut in the final could hardly be called successful – Petrosian was 16th out of 20 participants.

However, the beginning foreshadowed an even more disastrous outcome. The tournament took place in the Central Home of Culture for Railwaymen. Tigran sat on the stage and wandered about. It seemed to him that all the spectators were looking at him, the youngest of the players. But then he grew petrified with fright when he saw Keres, Flohr, Bronstein, Smyslov, Boleslavsky, Levenfish, Lilienthal, Kotov, all sitting on the same stage as him . . . to think that he was accepted in such dazzling company as an equal. . . .

It was still necessary, however, to prove that he was an equal. Strong grandmasters only recognize 'their own' among those who can return their blows. In this tournament Petrosian at first only 'received'. Tigran could not believe inside himself that he had the moral right to play in the final of the Soviet Championship together with grandmasters.

His first opponent was Kotov. Tigran was so agitated that he made an extremely simple error in the opening of the kind that he had many times corrected among young players at the Yerevan Palace of Pioneers. Kotov didn't have to make the slightest effort to achieve victory – Petrosian did it for him. Making his 12th move, Petrosian resigned. He could have just as easily done so on the 7th move.

In the next round he came up against Smyslov. The same grandmaster who one year before had occupied second place in the match tournament for the world championship. After the confusion of the first round, Petrosian was still rather groggy. For this game, nonetheless, he did receive a good lesson in positional play. Playing White, Petrosian saddled Smyslov with a backward pawn in the centre, and began to lay siege to it. This was fully correct. Tigran based all his calculations on the fact that the pawn was a chronic defect in Black's position.

Suddenly, this weak pawn moved forward! It turned out that there was a concealed dynamic in the position. Such strategy was an eye-opener for Petrosian. He had rather mechanically evaluated these positions, and had not paid enough attention to their potential energies. He later recalled what Nimzowitsch had taught: in the event of an incorrect positional siege the opponent will break the front precisely at the strongest point of siege.

Petrosian's third opponent, Flohr, did not show any mercy either. Generally peaceful and unambitious, he, once Tigran had committed a strategical error in the opening, turned his guns upon the black king and won in attacking style. Tigran's only success in this game was that he managed to adjourn it. He did not succeed in resuming play.

Petrosian prayed to fortune for a breathing space, and it seemed he might get one – in the fourth round he had to play with Geller. But Geller, after suffering defeat in the first two rounds, began to set a tremendous pace.

How self-confident that young player from Odessa was! And how Tigran envied that unshakable conviction that he, Geller, a debutant in the championship, had all moral prerequisites not only to fight on equal terms with famous grandmasters but also to aim at no less than the title of champion. Crossing his hands behind his back, Geller walked confidently about the stage as if he owned it, leaving the impression of unshakable strength on all who beheld him. It was amazing that Geller, who had taken part in the semi-finals as a candidate master, was ahead of everybody up to the last day. And if in the last round he had shown one iota of that caution and common sense which Petrosian knew, Geller could have shared first place and become a grandmaster on his first attempt.

At that time in the fourth round nobody knew of this, but Geller began his run of victories with this game. Once again, Tigran committed a positional error and Geller finished him off in 27 moves.

Four losses in four rounds! But Petrosian's luck was still out and he was fated to lose a fifth game. This time Keres performed the role of executioner. Playing White, the grandmaster obtained slightly freer play out of the opening. Afterwards he reduced the activity of his opponent's pieces and wound it up with an attack on the king. Oof! – after five rounds Tigran had moved into clear last place. Most of the commentators mentioned that the youngest master, due to a quite natural agitation, had not yet revealed his full possibilities. However, realizing the uselessness of struggle and the hopelessness of his situation, Tigran suddenly calmed down and his normal soberness of thought returned. In the sixth game with Lilienthal he obtained a good position and was about to offer a draw – he wanted at all cost to break the chain of defeats. Only the thought that with five losses it was incorrect to make such a suggestion to a grandmaster prevented him from taking this step. So he won the game, his first win in his first final.

After that everything was much simpler. As it turned out, Petrosian was not the only one who made errors and terrible blunders as a result of 'quite natural agitation'. He no longer committed crude errors and played soberly to the end. After five losses in the first five rounds, he gained 7½ points out of the remaining 14 rounds, and occupied 16th place, which after such a terrible beginning was perhaps the best that he might have hoped for.

He ended the competition by no means crushed. The championship had taught him a lot, had enabled him in part to overcome his fear of grandmasters, but, most important, had shown him his need for experience – experience of practical play with the very strongest opponents and experience of continually living in the society of grandmasters and masters. In the years that he had lived in Yerevan, Tigran had accumulated great creative reserves but for practical purposes he remained a raw chess-player. Now he had to turn this reserve into practical strength. And for this his coming to Moscow could hardly have been more timely.

Petrosian is not generally regarded as a theoretician. At the same time, the conduct of the opening and transference to the middle-game is one of the strongest sides of his game. Here games 1 and 2 are characteristic examples.

1 **Dubinin-Petrosian**

18 USSR Ch, ½ Final, Gorsky 1950

French

1 P-K4	P-K3
2 P-Q4	P-Q4
3 N-QB3	B-N5
4 P-K5	N-K2
5 P-QR3	B×N+
6 P×B	P-QB4
7 Q-N4	N-B4

Nowadays, 7...P×P or 7...Q-B2 are more commonly played, permitting 8 Q×NP R-N1 9 Q×RP, which leads to a sharp strategical struggle over the whole board.

8 B-Q3	P-KR4
9 Q-R3	P×P
10 P-N4	

More promising was 10 B×N P×B 11 Q-N3 with pressure on the black squares.

10 ...	N-K2
11 BP×P	Q-B2
12 N-K2	N1-B3
13 0-0	B-Q2
14 P×P	0-0-0
15 B-KB4	

Routine move. White does not sense the hidden strength of Black's counterplay. B-Q2-N4 was possible, aiming at Q6, or offering an exchange of pieces on QN4.

15 ... QR-N1

Going over to the attack.

16 K-R1 P-KN4!

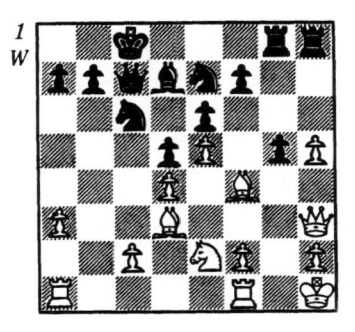

1
W

An excellent plan. With his next moves, Black limits the scope of his opponent's pieces. The 'advantage of the two bishops' has no significance.

Though Petrosian has never been a fanatical supporter of the French defence, his games have had great theoretical value, especially his ability to counter-attack in complex situations. White's pawn wedge at K5, and space advantage would seem to give him a monopoly of action on the K-side; however, Petrosian has demonstrated quite a few exceptions to this general rule. For example, in the game Sakharov–Petrosian, 25 USSR Ch, ½-Final, Kiev 1957, after 1 P–K4 P–K3 2 P–Q4 P–Q4 3 N–QB3 B–N5 4 P–K5 P–QB4 5 B–Q2 N–K2 6 P–QR3 B×N 7 B×B P×P 8 Q×P N–B4 9 Q–KN4 (9 Q–KB4 was more accurate) 9... P–KR4 10 Q–KB4, Black began a sharp counter-attack: 10... P–KN4! 11 B–N5+ N–B3 12 Q–Q2 P–Q5! 13 B–N4 Q–Q4! After 14 Q–K2 Q×NP 15 Q–B3 Q×Q 16 N×Q B Q2 17 N×NP N×P, Black had a strategically won game, which he carried to victory after a sharp struggle.

17 B–N3   R–R3
18 P–KB4 P–N5
19 Q–N2   N–B4
20 Q–B2   R×P

Petrosian's plan has already brought dividends. White's black-square bishop is completely suffocated. While White can do little on the queen's side, Black has every hope of success on the king's.

21 R.B1–QB1 N–R4
22 P–B4?

A despairing sacrifice.

22...   P×P
23 P–Q5   P×P
24 Q×P   N–B3
25 Q–R8+   Q–N1
26 Q×Q+   K×Q

The game has transposed into an endgame which is easily won for Black. White resisted for another 20 moves, but without success.

2 Petrosian–Bondarevsky

18 USSR Ch, Moscow 1950

Dutch

1 N–KB3	P–K3
2 P–KN3	P–KB4
3 B–N2	N–KB3
4 0–0	B–K2
5 P–Q4	0–0
6 P–B4	P–B3
7 Q–B2	Q–K1
8 QN–Q2	P–Q4
9 N–K5	

A good plan, which involves an original placing of the knights, on Q3 and KB3. White simultaneously presses on K5, and holds up Black's K-side advance. On the other side of the board, White plans a general pawn storm, which will be very hard to meet.

This was one of the first games where this particular plan was employed. Now it is regarded as one of the most dangerous plans against Black's system; Petrosian's games have done a great deal in forming this opinion.

9...	QN–Q2
10 N–Q3	N–K5
11 N–B3	N–Q3

A rather suspect manoeuvre. However, practice has shown that counter-attack by 11... P–KN4 or 11... Q–R4 does not offer Black much.

12 P–N3	P–QN4
13 P–B5	N–B2
14 P–QR4	

An important link in White's plan,

Hallo Moscow! 41

for Black threatened to play...
P–QR4, making it difficult to open
up lines on the Q-side.

  14 ...   **P × P**

Bad was 14 ... P–QR4 15 P × P
P × P 16 B–Q2, as was 14 ... P–QR3
15 P × P BP × P 16 B–Q2 with
B–N4 or B–R5 to follow.

  15 R × P   **B–B3**
  16 B–N2   **P–QR3**

Black could have tried to free his
game with 16 ... P–K4, though after
17 P × P N.B2 × P 18 R1–R1
N × N.Q6 19 P × N B × B 20 Q × B
N × P 21 R × P or 17 P × P N.Q2 ×
KP 18 R1–R1 White retains the
initiative on the Q-side.

  17 N.B3–K5   **N.B2 × N**
  18 P × N   **B–K2**
  19 P–B4   **R–N1**

Attempting to enliven play on the
K-side would have led to White's
advantage after 19 ... P–N4 20
P × P B × NP 21 B–B1!

  20 R1–R1   **R–N4**
  21 P–QN4

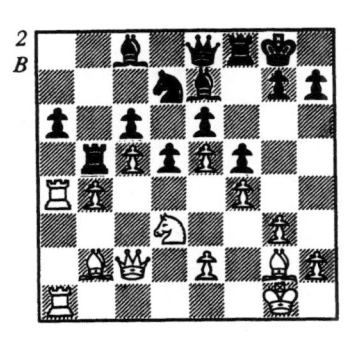

The accuracy of White's play is
instructive. It appears that 21 B–Q4
would be strong here, but White is
planning to put a knight on that
square.

  21 ...   **P–KR4**

  22 B–QB3   **P–R5**
  23 P–K3   **N–N1**

Black, in difficulties, does not play
actively enough. 23 ... P × P followed
by a later ... P–N4 was a better
chance.

  24 N–K1   **R–N2**
  25 P × P   **B × RP**
  26 N–B3   **B–Q1**
  27 P–R4!

A good block, finally eliminating
Black's possibilities of playing ...
P–N4.

  27 ...   **Q–R4**
  28 B–K1   **B–Q2**
  29 Q–KB2   **K–B2**

The exacting, and thankless defensive tasks prove too much for Black,
and he drops a pawn. If he had
played 29 ... B–B1, it would still
have not been easy for White to
organize a decisive infiltration.

  30 B–B1   **R–R1**
  31 B × P   **N × B**
  32 R × N   **B–K2**
  33 R–R7

Winning the QRP not only gives
White a material advantage, but
also allows him to invade down the
QR-file.

  33 ...   **R1–QN1**
  34 R × R   **R × R**
  35 N–Q4

The white knight arrives at the
Q4 square 14 moves after the
instigation of White's plan. Here he
strikes at the weak points K6 and
QB6. Black's game is already hopeless.

  35 ...   **Q–R1**
  36 Q–N3   **Q–QN1**
  37 P–R5   **R–R2**
  38 R–B1

Avoiding a trap: 38 R × R Q × R
39 Q–N6+ K–B1 40 N × KP+ B × N

Hallo Moscow!

41 Q×B Q–R8   42 Q–B8+ K–B2
43 Q×KBP+ K–N1, when White
has to take perpetual check.

38 ...   **Q–N1**
39 Q–N6+   **K–B1**

40 P–N5   **Q–B2**
41 P×P   **1–0**

After 41 ... B–B1   42 Q×Q+
K×Q 43 N–N5 R–R1 44 N–Q6+
K–B1 45 P–B7, White wins easily.

4 Iron Century

Petrosian had finally reached the centre of chess activity in the USSR. He took part in various tournaments, both team and individual, or as a last resort played friendly games. He was always at the chess club, sat too long with the editors of the chess magazine, or simply spent his time chatting with some of the chess-players. He immersed himself in all possible chess impressions, beginning with the conceptions of chess theory, and ending with the anecdotes of master players.

At the same time Petrosian acquired a trainer – Grandmaster Andre Lilienthal. Lilienthal was a fine chess-player, with a deep understanding of chess strategy, and Tigran benefited much from their association.

Gradually Petrosian's 'iron century' approached, when in a remarkably short period of time he developed from a not very strong master into one of the candidates for the world title. The jump was fairy-tale like, few wished to believe in it, but with every new tournament Petrosian demonstrated the reality of what had passed.

Failures fell away from him – the 'iron' Tigran never knew disappointment, hardly even knew defeat. His deep understanding of position, quick eye for combinations, intuitive ability to sense the approach of danger, easiness of play – all this, combined with a burning desire to play and win, made Tigran one of the strongest of tournament fighters.

He began his 'iron century' in 1951, when he became Moscow champion. Later he won the Sverdolovsk semi-final, and finally, won a prize in the Soviet Championship. His semi-final victory was significant in itself, for he came above Geller, Averbakh, and Boleslavsky. The last named had one year previously shared first place with Bronstein in the Candidates' tournament. Tigran here displayed a universality of style, but with a clearly aggressive tendency.

After the tournament, Boleslavsky wrote: 'in this tournament Petrosian and Geller played in ways which we had not seen before. The impression was created that they had exchanged styles with each other. Petrosian was known up till now as a positional chess-player, not avoiding sharp play, but preferring the safe draw to unclear complications . . . here Petrosian won eight games, six of them by an attack on the king. . .'.

The high-point of the year was, of course, the 19th Soviet Championship where Petrosian, like Geller two years before, had great chances of sharing first place but due to inexperience did not manage it.

This championship was of record strength: Botvinnik, Bronstein, Smyslov, Keres, Flohr, Geller, Averbakh, Taimanov, Bondarevsky, Kotov, Simagin, Aronin, Lipnitsky, and quite a few strong masters. But the time had long passed when Petrosian felt himself misplaced in the company of grandmasters. This was already his third appearance in the championship (he shared 12–13th place with Bondarevsky in the 18th championship), and he was tremendously calm. This was mainly because he had nothing to lose, and had not yet begun to think of his possible gains. The tournament was to show that he could already set his sights on the grandmaster title.

Those years were very joyful. Petrosian was later to remember them as the happiest of his life. He was young, healthy, and felt unusually self-confident. He could experiment, even allow himself to slip into the lower half of the tournament table – no one would reproach a young master for that. Petrosian was experiencing such an uplift that from time to time he even forgot his ordinary caution. A little before the start of the championship, Flohr wrote in an article for *Ogonyok*: 'Petrosian ... is always prepared to take any risk'. Indeed Petrosian's tactical mastery did not only appear in retaliation, for at this period he often 'began the quarrel'.

Petrosian began the tournament with two defeats, and those against masters. In the first round he lost to Kopylov, in the second to Aronin. But the sensation of strength and confidence allowed him to overcome these setbacks easily, which at another time might have depressed him. In the third round he drew with Geller, then scored victories over Bondarevsky and Kotov. Afterwards draws with Averbakh, Moiseyev, Flohr and Botvinnik.

His game with the World Champion was the only time when Tigran felt himself in the role of the bashful youngster. This did not prevent him, however, from playing with energy and perseverance. Realizing that he could not attempt to rival Botvinnik in the realm of opening erudition, he, playing White, selected a little played continuation and ... obtained the worse position.

Here is how Master Alatortsev annotated the further course of the struggle: 'For five hours Botvinnik energetically pursued a decisive advantage, having the two bishops and the rather freer position, but by means of a tactical stroke Petrosian created a dangerous passed pawn. The game continued through the adjournment, but after seven hours play a result had still not been reached. The game was adjourned a second time, and though the World Champion refused Petrosian's offer of a draw, during the resumption he was nonetheless forced to agree.' The game lasted in all eleven hours.

Petrosian could well be pleased with this meeting, though for the time being he had not passed the fifty per cent mark. In the 9th round he beat Lipnitsky, drew with Bronstein in the 11th, and six rounds before the end was sharing 7th place with Simagin and Kotov. He had still given no indication that he might be in the running for the champion's title. He was 1½ points behind Botvinnik, Smyslov, and Geller, a point behind Keres and half a point behind Averbakh and Taimanov. At the finish he put on a remarkable spurt: he scored 5½ out of his last six games. The only game he did not win, he should have done, and the fact that he did not was due no doubt to youth: at the time of the tournament Tigran was only 22 years old.

In the twelfth round he demolished Novotelnov in 27 moves, and moved into sixth equal place. Next round he came up against Smyslov.

The events of this game require particular attention. In the event of a draw, coming in between a series of victories, Petrosian would have shown that he was still, after all, a youth; but the victory over one of the strongest players in the world, and achieved in such a manner bore witness to the growth of his powers. In those days Tigran was very friendly with Geller. Though the two young men were rivals in tournaments, they often prepared for matches together, and kept no secrets from each other. Petrosian had White against Smyslov in the 13th round, and Geller was also White, against Flohr. The friends decided to try the very same variation out – an extremely sharp and risky one, which involved the sacrifice of a pawn in the Queen's Gambit. The author of this idea was Geller, but he did not have to spend long persuading Tigran.

On the seventeenth move – an unusual situation – two identical positions appeared on two different demonstration boards. But then a crisis developed; at the same moment both Geller and Petrosian came to the sorrowful conclusion that their experiment could bring them nothing good. For the sacrificed pawn White did not get any attacking chances, and what was worse, the black pawns on the queen's side were threatening to move forward. 'White hasn't the vestige of an attack' said Flohr, 'Black is attacking'.

Geller, the inventive tactician, seeing the threatening phalanx of black pawns lost control and went over into defence. This amounted to moral capitulation, an admission of the incorrectness of his strategy. Neither was it in the spirit of the position, which required courageous, energetic action if one was to fight to retain the initiative.

Tigran thought for a long time over his seventeenth move. The decision he took was risky and paradoxical, but nonetheless in harmony with the logic of the position, since it forced Black onto the defensive.

Two years previously, in the seventeenth championship, Smyslov had shattered Petrosian's position by advancing an apparently hopelessly weak pawn. This time Petrosian scored his revenge: his undefined pawn moved forward onto a square attacked by no less than four black pieces. It was a purely positional sacrifice, though if Black had continued correctly, the course of the struggle would not perhaps have been changed.

Beside its basic chess value, the move had also psychological strength. Smyslov was so stunned by the move that he immediately committed an error and allowed Petrosian to develop a strong attack. The game was adjourned in a hopeless position for Black. . . .

As for Geller, he did not even succeed in adjourning the game. On move 34 the advancing black pawn mass had already forced his resignation. These two results were very important, for two of the tournament leaders suffered defeat, which had its effect on the tournament table. Keres and Botvinnik both won in the thirteenth round, so there were now four people at the top with $8\frac{1}{2}$ points – Botvinnik, Smyslov, Keres and Geller. Half a point behind were Petrosian and Averbakh. The next day saw another reshuffle at the top: Geller beat Botvinnik, Keres beat Smyslov and Petrosian beat Simagin. Averbakh lost to Taimanov. The tournament's youngest contestant was now in third place, ahead of the future combatants for the world title – Botvinnik and Smyslov. All the leaders moved a point ahead in the next round and in the penultimate round the game was played which showed that Petrosian still had to gain experience, not only in chess but speaking generally.

Tigran was White against Keres. Keres was playing magnificently in this tournament and for the second time running won the championship. But in this game with Petrosian he was close to defeat, which might have deprived him of the victor's laurels. Petrosian got the advantage in the opening, and soon both his knights had penetrated to the rear of Black's position. Keres was forced to give up an important pawn.

It seemed that the white knights were hopelessly surrounded by enemy pieces, but Petrosian continued to manoeuvre calmly with his light pieces. Black's position was objectively lost . . . but suddenly Tigran began to hear the applause, with which the spectators greeted his almost every move. The young master, playing boldly and inventively, had from the middle of the tournament attracted their sympathies. Chess fans, as indeed fans of any sport, crave excitement. None of the warnings of the judges present for 'Silence' had any effect on the public. Petrosian became an unwilling victim of the enthusiasm of his supporters. Distracted, he committed an inaccuracy, and Keres redressed the balance. . . .

A victory in the last round over Terpugov allowed Petrosian to share 2nd–3rd places with Geller. He was half a point behind the winner.

This was a great sporting and creative success. Petrosian received a special prize, for the most successful performance against grandmasters. He had beaten three – Smyslov, Bondarevsky and Kotov, and drawn with the remaining four – Botvinnik, Keres, Bronstein and Flohr. Five out of seven against grandmasters – this was an even greater success, perhaps, than the sharing of second prize, and showed that Petrosian was already playing with the strength of a grandmaster.

Evaluating Petrosian's performance Panov wrote: 'fully mastering the art of positional manoeuvring, he strives to found his refined strategical conceptions on accurate and deep calculation. Besides this, Petrosian unflaggingly pursues the initiative in every game.' Referring to his game with Terpugov, Panov stated that this showed 'the Moscow champion's extreme cool-headedness even in the most complicated positions'. Note well: no reproaches for excessive caution or peacefulness!

The 19th Championship was practically a zonal tournament, though it did not have that name at the time. As a prize-winner, Petrosian received the right to play in the Interzonal tournament. Furthermore, the first five in that competition would play in the Candidates' tournament, and, which was more important to Petrosian, would automatically become grandmasters.

Tigran travelled to Sweden in high spirits. He was playing easily, and was experiencing a creative upsurge. He was pleased that Yefim Geller and Yuri Averbakh came with him, who were his especial friends at that time. (Besides these three, Mark Taimanov and Alexander Kotov also represented the Soviet Union).

Before this tournament began, the USSR chess federation gave Petrosian the chance to get acclimatized to playing abroad: he took part in a strong tournament in Budapest and shared 7th-8th places.

In the Interzonal tournament at Saltsjöbaden, a fashionable resort not far from Stockholm, many leading players took part. In comparison with such grandmasters as Szabo, Gligoric and Stahlberg, the young Soviet players looked fairly unimpressive. Even ex-World Champion Euwe erred in his forecasts. Evaluating the chances before the tournament, he declared that Gligoric, Szabo and Stahlberg would undoubtedly prove stronger, and that Matanovic and Unzicker would not prove weaker than the Soviet players. However the decisive voice in this tournament belonged not to the young, but to 40-year-old Kotov: in the first eight rounds he won all his games, and at the end scored $16\frac{1}{2}$ points out of 20.

In these circumstances it was meaningless to try for first place, and Petrosian had not set himself such a task in the first place. He had his target – to get in the top five, so whether it was second or fifth place was not important.

The rest of the participants had more or less the same intention. But for Petrosian this was his final aim. The Candidates' tournament interested him only insomuch as it gave him the title of grandmaster. This was a serious psychological error, which was to lead to others. But of that later.

All the young Soviet players, though differing so greatly in style and temperament, adopted the same tactic in this competition. Against the players who occupied the top ten places, Averbakh, Taimanov and Petrosian each won one game, agreeing the remainder drawn. Geller would probably have been happy to achieve such a result himself, but he was 'forced' to win one game more.

Tigran realized to his surprise that even in such an important competition he could still be master of his fate. He won seven games, did not lose any, and drew 13 – this was quite enough to share 2nd and 3rd places with Taimanov. Geller took fourth place, and Averbakh divided 5th to 8th place, though he had the preferable coefficient over his rivals.

In three years, therefore, Petrosian had made his leap – from a timid debutant in the Soviet Championship, to a contestant for the throne of the World Champion. Even during the course of the tournament Petrosian noted a definite change of attitude toward him. The roles had reversed – now others trembled before him. In round eleven Petrosian was playing white against the Colombian master Sanchez. The Colombian was a competent player but extremely nervous. The game took a quiet course, Petrosian did not obtain any advantage and proposed a draw. Sanchez did not comprehend and looked enquiringly at him. At length the meaning reached him and he leapt up in his chair, released a joyful cry, and began to shake hands. Tigran himself did not understand and looked at Sanchez as if he had gone mad. Finally, the meaning became clear: Sanchez was happy because he, Petrosian, had offered him a draw. . . .

3 **Lipnitsky–Petrosian**

19 USSR Ch, Moscow, 1951

Hungarian

1 P–K4	P–K4
2 N–KB3	N–QB3
3 B–B4	B–K2
4 P–Q4	P–Q3
5 N–B3	N–B3
6 P–KR3	0–0
7 0–0	P–QR3

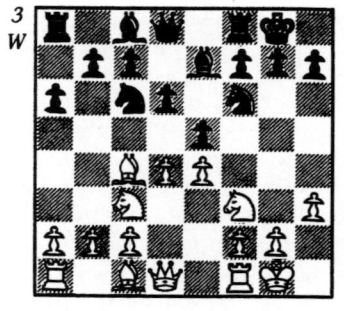

This type of position is instructive,

because it quite often turns up. Black has the opportunity here of freeing his game by the combination 7 ... N × KP 8 N × N P–Q4. Opening books often recommend such simplifying manoeuvres for the second player, since they diminish the tension in the centre, yet retain a symmetrical pawn formation. However, the opening up of the game is to White's advantage, since his pieces are better developed, and Black often gets into difficulties as a result. After a likely continuation 9 B × P Q × B 10 N–B3 Q–R4 11 N × P N × N 12 P × N Q × KP 13 R–K1 Q–Q3 14 Q–B3, Black would find it very hard to complete the development of his Q-side, and meanwhile White is threatening to unleash devastating 'fire' down the central files.

Even the most famous grandmasters sometimes demonstrate surprising lapses of memory; for example, the identical error was committed by A. Rubinstein in the Carlsbad variation of the Queen's Gambit, in his games with Euwe (Kissingen 1928) and Alekhine (Sam Remo 1930).

From his earliest days, Petrosian has always shown the ability to learn from personal experience, even the most painful experience. Immediately after this game he turned to me and said: 'You know, during the opening I remembered our game from the previous year's final, and refrained from capturing on K5.' In that game, where Petrosian had also been Black, the moves were: 1 P–K4 P–K4 2 N–KB3 N–QB3 3 B–N5 P–QR3 4 B–R4 N–B3 5 0–0 B–K2 6 P–Q4 P × P 7 R–K1 0–0 8 P–K5 N–Q4 9 N × P N × N 10 Q × N N–N3 11 B–N3 P–Q4 12 P × Pep Q × P 13 Q–K4! B–B3 14 N–B3 R–N1 15 B–KB4 Q–B4 16 Q–K3! after which Black had a very difficult position.

Even though these games arose from different openings, Petrosian was able to divine their underlying similarity, and this helped him to make the correct strategical decision in the present game.

8 P–QR4   P × P
9 N × P   N–QN5

Black is now threatening to open the centre by 10 ... P–Q4, or even by 10 ... N × KP 11 N × N P–Q4. White's decision on the next move is completely justified.

10 N–Q5   N5 × N
11 P × N   N–Q2
12 P–R5

Otherwise Black would play 12 ... P–QR4 and install his knight on ... QB4.

12 ...   B–B3
13 P–QB3

If White wishes, he could force drawish simplifications by 13 N–K6 P × N 14 P × P K–R1 15 P × N B × QP, but he shows a natural desire for a full-blooded struggle.

13 ...   N–K4
14 B–N3   R–K1
15 B–B2   B–Q2
16 P–KB4   N–N3

White has driven the black knight back, but at the same time hemmed in his own queen's bishop.

17 Q–Q3   P–B4

A responsible decision. Black obtains active play in the centre, accepting pawn weaknesses in return. There was no other sensible course of action. It is impossible to play chess without undertaking some strategical risks, especially as Black!

18 P × Pep   P × P

19 N–B5　　　B×N

A necessary exchange. On 19...P–Q4, 20 N–Q6 could be played, followed by N–N7, heading for the important QB5 square.

**20 Q×B　　　P–Q4
21 B–Q2　　　N–B1
22 Q–Q3　　　P–B4**

Black continues with the plan begun on move 17. He intends... P–B5, blocking the attack on the QRP, and in turn creating counterplay against the pawns on QR5 and QN2.

23 R.B1–K1

During the game, Black considered that 23 B–R4 would have been more unpleasant. Against this he intended to play 23...R–K3　24 P–B5 P–B5 25 Q–B3 R–K5　26 B–K3 N–Q2! with sufficient counterplay.

**23...　　　　R×R+
24 B×R　　　P–B5
25 Q–K2　　　Q–B2
26 Q–B3　　　R–Q1
27 B–B2　　　P–Q5
28 Q–K4**

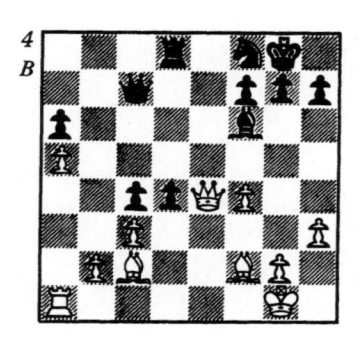

A critical point in the struggle. 28...P–Q6 is answered by 29 B–N6, but an exchange sacrifice was worth serious attention: 28...P×P　29 B–N6 P×P　30 R–K1 Q–B1　31 B×R Q×B　32 Q×BP Q×P　33 R–K8 Q–N3+!　34 K–R2 B–Q5! and Black at the worst has equal chances.

28...　　　　P–N3

This slip was the result of time-shortage, which affected both players. The remainder of the game is characterized by tense positions and ...blunders by White, which eventually decide the outcome of the struggle.

**29 P×P　　　R–N1
30 P–Q5**

The pawn could have been held only by 30 R–R2. White pins his hopes on his passed pawn, but the cost of advancing it proves rather dear....

**30...　　　　R×P
31 R–Q1　　　P–B6
32 P–Q6**

In the heat of the battle, White forgets about his pawn on QR5. Correct was 32 B–N6.

**32...　　　　Q×RP
33 P–Q7　　　Q–B2
34 Q–K8　　　B–Q1**

But not 34...R×B　35 P–Q8=Q B×Q　36 R×Q R–B8+　37 K–R2 Q×P+　38 B–N3 Q–QN5　39 B–Q6, when White wins.

**35 Q–K4　　　B–B3
36 Q–K8　　　R–N1
37 K–R1**

This loses quickly. White could have offered stiffer resistance by 37 B–QN3 R×B　38 P–Q8=Q B×Q 39 R×B Q×R 40 Q×Q P–B7 41 B–K3 R×B　42 Q–Q2 R–K7!, though here too Black has every chance of winning. (variation shown by T. Petrosian).

**37...　　　　R–Q1
38 B–QR4　　P–B7**

39 R–QB1	Q×BP
40 B–K3	Q×B.5

0–1

Both sides were in good form in this game.

4 Petrosian–Kotov

19 USSR Ch, Moscow, 1951

King's Indian

1 P–Q4	N–KB3
2 P–QB4	P–Q3
3 N–QB3	P–K4
4 N–B3	QN–Q2
5 P–KN3	P–KN3
6 B–N2	B–N2
7 0–0	0–0
8 P–K4	P×P

Prematurely ceding the centre. Nowadays, 8 ... P–B3 9 P–KR3 Q–N3 or 9 ... Q–R4 would be played, leading to complex tactical play.

9 N×P	P–QR4
10 P–KR3	N–B4
11 R–K1	R–K1
12 Q–B2	P–R5
13 B–K3	P–B3
14 QR–Q1	Q–R4

A typical manoeuvring position has come about, where White has a space advantage, and obvious pressure against Q6. Black has a variety of dynamic counter-chances at his disposal, and the struggle is very lively. It could be said that White's position is more 'weighty', but that the 'monarch's crown is very heavy'!

15 B–B4

The most natural decision. If White wants to keep the initiative in the middle-game, then he must create threats.

15 ...	B–B1
16 B–KB1	N–R4

16 ... N3–Q2 17 B–K3 N–K3 18 N×N R×N 19 P–B4 R–K1 was worth considering. In that event, Black would have retained an active position.

17 B–K3	N–B3
18 B–B4	N–R4
19 B–B1	N–N2
20 K–R2	B–Q2
21 P–R3	

A committal, but correct decision. White denies Black the ... QN4 square, and once and for all eliminates the threat of ... P–R6. In the present case, the weakness on QN3 is not significant.

21 ...	N2–K3
22 B–K3	N×N

Perhaps 22 ... QR–Q1, followed by ... B–QB1 and ... B–KN2 would have been better. It would then have been difficult to locate vulnerable spots in Black's position.

23 B×N	N–N6
24 B–K3	B–K3

This move is a definite error. Black should have played 24 ... P–QB4! here, taking control of the ... Q5 square.

25 P–B4	QR–Q1

Now 25 ... P–QB4 would be too late. After 26 P–B5 B–Q2 27 N–Q5 B–N2 28 P–B6, White would have strong threats on the K-side. However, the move played has its drawbacks too; the lesser among evils was 25 ... P–KB4, striving for counterplay in the centre.

26 Q–B2

5 B

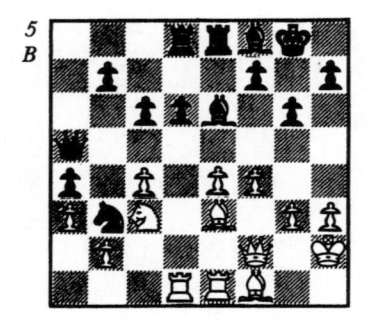

It is instructive to watch how White's initiative grows into a mighty 'overloading' combination.

26 ...   Q-R3
26 ... R-Q2 27 P-KB5! P×P 28 B-N6 Q-K4 29 P×P was no improvement. The best chance was 26 ... N-B4.

27 B-N6   R-Q2
If the rook moves off the Q-file 28 P-QB5! followed by P×P is very strong.

28 P-QB5   B-B5
Another forced reply. On 28 ... Q-R1 29 P-B5! NP×P 30 KP×P B-Q4 31 R×R Q×R 32 N×B P×N 33 B-N5 decides.

29 B×B   Q×B.5
30 P-K5   P-Q4
31 N-K4!

Black has to give up the exchange, in view of the threats N-B6+ and N-Q6.

31 ...   P×N
32 R×R   B×P
33 B×B   N×B
34 R-Q4   Q-K3
35 Q-B2!   P-N3
36 R-Q6   Q-B1
37 Q-B4

White has achieved both material and positional advantages. This game is a fine example of an 'overloading' combination.

Objectively, Black's position is lost. His blunder on the next move hastens the end. **37 ... P-R4? 38 R×NP+ K-B1 39 R-B6 Q-Q2 40 R-Q6 Q-B4 41 R-B6 Q-Q2 42 R-Q1 Q-B2 43 Q-K2 P-R5 44 Q-N4 R-Q1 45 R×R+ Q×R 46 R-Q6 P×P+ 47 K×P Q-B2 48 Q-R4 K-K1 49 Q-R8+ K-K2 50 Q-B6+ K-K1 51 R×P Q-Q2 52 Q-Q6 1-0**

5 Petrosian-Smyslov

19 USSR Ch, Moscow 1951

Slav

1 P-Q4	P-Q4
2 P-QB4	P×P
3 N-KB3	N-KB3
4 N-B3	P-B3
5 P-K4	P-QN4
6 P-K5	N-Q4
7 P-QR4	P-K3
8 P×P	N×N
9 P×N	P×P
10 N-N5	B-N2
11 Q-R5	P-N3
12 Q-N4	B-K2

This sharp variation was at the time hardly analyzed. This game, along with Geller-Flohr, which took place on the same stage on the same evening, was one of the first times it was tried out in practice. The game also serves to illustrate young Petrosian's style, and contradicts the general opinion that he was an extremely conservative and cautious strategical player.

On the contrary, Petrosian was never lost in sharp positions, even if he had not already prepared for them in home analysis. The further course of the struggle amply demonstrates Petrosian's lively practicality and inventiveness. It was precisely in this way that the many-sidedness of his play was developed.

13 B–K2　　N–Q2
14 P–R4

This move has the appearance of improvisation. Such double-edged strategical positions demand very accurate and concrete analysis. A year later, in the game Geller–Unzicker (Stockholm 1952) a satisfactory continuation was found for White: 14 B–B3! Q–B2　15 N–K4 N–N3　16 B–R6 R–KN1　17 B–N5! and White demonstrated that the initiative and pressure on the black squares more than compensated for the pawn. But for the time being Geller also went on a false trail. . . .

14 . . .　　P–KR4
15 Q–N3　　N–N3
16 0–0　　P–R4

Simple and strong. Seeing that White has no direct threats, Black goes over to the attack on the Q-side. The strength of this plan was shown clearly in the game Geller–Flohr, which continued: 17 R–N1 P–N5 18 P–B4 Q–Q2　19 R–R1 P–N6! and Black won without too much difficulty.

Petrosian's next decision was both unexpected and courageous, but also correct practically.

17 P–Q5!?

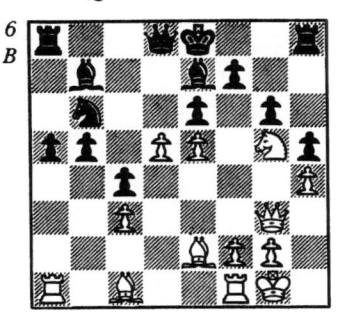

White places his central pawn under the attack of no less than four enemy pieces aiming above all else to suddenly alter the course of the game. And in fact this moment proves a decisive turning point; Black, though one of the candidates for the world title, does not subject the position to concrete analysis, and acts out of 'general considerations'.

17 . . .　　N × P

17 . . . B × P was correct, retaining control of the . . . K5 square, and preventing the manoeuvre N–K4.

18 R–Q1　　Q–B2
19 N–K4　　0–0–0

Black's possibilities are already strictly limited. After 19 . . . 0–0, for example, 20 B × RP is strong. Perhaps 19 . . . K–B1 was best, intending to put the king on . . . KN2.

20 B–N5

Very strong. By exchanging the black-squared bishops White manages to start an attack on the king, by means of the weakened dark squares.

20 . . .　　B × B
21 Q × B　　P–R5

Now this advance has no real force, and does not deflect White from the prosecution of the attack.

22 Q–N3　　P–B4
23 N–Q6+　　R × N

It was very difficult to bear such a knight. Now Black has two pawns for the exchange, but White retains a strong initiative, and gives Black no respite.

24 P × R　　P–B5?

This only makes matters worse; in a difficult position, mistakes are the easiest moves to find.

25 Q × NP　　Q × P
26 B–B3　　B–B3

27 R–K1	R–K1
28 B×N	Q×B
29 QR–Q1	

White continues to play accurately. The ending turns out to be hopeless for Black.

29 ...	Q–KB4
30 Q×Q	P×Q
31 R×R+	B×R
32 P–B3	K–B2
33 K–B2	K–N3
34 K–K2	K–R4
35 R–QN1	

A necessary provision. ... P–N5 could not be permitted.

| 35 ... | P–R6 |
| 36 K–Q2 | P–N5 |

If instead 36 ... K–R5 37 R–N4+ K–R4 38 K–B2, White also wins.

37 P×P+	K–R5
38 K–B3	P–R7
39 R–QR1	K–R6
40 K×P!	

An elegant finish. White sacrifices the rook, but wins forcibly. 40 ... K–N7 41 R–K1 P–R8=Q 42 R×Q K×R 43 P–N5 B–Q2 44 P–N6 B–B1 45 K–Q4 K–N7 46 K–K5 K–B6 47 K×P.4 K–Q5 48 K–N5 K–K4 49 K×RP K–B3 50 P–N4 B–N2 51 K–R6 1–0

6 Szabo–Petrosian

Interzonal, Stockholm 1952

Sicilian

1 P–K4	P–QB4
2 N–KB3	P–Q3
3 P–Q4	P×P
4 N×P	N–KB3
5 N–QB3	P–QR3
6 P–B4	Q–B2
7 B–K2	P–K4

The Najdorf variation, very fashionable at the time. Present-day players prefer to avoid it as White. Practice has shown that Black gets good counterplay in the centre and on the Q-side.

| 8 N–B3 | B–K3 |

Since this was a relatively new variation, even the best players often played it by ear. It is now recognized that the white-squared bishop is best developed on the long diagonal, creating pressure against the point ... K5. For this reason, 8 ... B–K2 and 9 ... 0–0, completing K-side development, would have been more elastic.

9 P–B5	B–B5
10 B–N5	QN–Q2
11 N–Q2	B×B

11 ... P–N4 was an interesting possibility.

| 12 Q×B | R–B1 |
| 13 P–QR3 | |

Unnecessary prophylaxis. More logical was 13 B×N N×B 14 0–0–0, intending N–B1–K3, with the initiative to White.

| 13 ... | Q–N3 |
| 14 0–0–0? | |

14 R–QN1 would have been more circumspect. White underestimates the coming positional sacrifice.

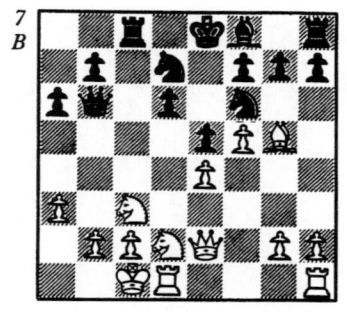

| 14 ... | R×N! |

A good, though not automatic

move; Black has still to complete his development. Nonetheless, the perspectives are promising for Black.

15 P×R   P–Q4!
16 N–N1   N×P?

Correct was 16...P×P, which Petrosian had originally planned. However, he was attracted by the variation 16...N×P 17 R×P N×B, but 'forgot' White's 18th move.... The game was played at one of the most decisive stages of the Interzonal tournament, so agitation on the part of a recent debutant in the Soviet Championship is quite understandable!...

17 R×P   N×B
18 P–KR4!   B–B4

Black's position is becoming critical. Bad was 18...B–K2 19 R1–Q1 N–B3 20 R×P N4–K5 21 R×N N×R 22 Q×N or 19...N–B4 20 Q×KP, when White's threats are too strong.

19 P×N   B–K6+
20 N–Q2   B×P
21 Q–Q3

White plays perseveringly and increases his advantage. 21 Q–B4 Q–QB3 22 Q×Q P×Q 23 R–R5 K–K2! would have given Black chances of a successful defence.

21 ...   Q–B2
22 K–Q1   B×N
23 K×B   P–B3
24 K–B1   N–N3
25 R–Q6

Starting from now, White begins to lose the thread of the struggle, even though Black was now in terrible time-trouble. Petrosian thought that 25 R–Q1 would be the most dangerous move. After 25...N×R 26 Q×N R–B1 27 Q–K6+ Q–K2 28 Q–B8+ K–B2 29 Q–B4+ K–K1 30 R–Q5

White has a strong threat in R–B5! If 26...Q–B1 27 Q–Q6, and White has a variety of threats (for example, transferring the rook to B5).

25 ...   0–0
26 R–Q1

A further slip, which appreciably alters the course of the battle. 26 R–R4! was best, in order to answer 26...Q–B4 by 27 R–QN4.

Now the advantage passes to Black.

26 ...   Q–B4
27 R–Q8   Q×RP+
28 K–N1   P–KR4!

A fine move. The immediate threat is 28...N–R5! Besides this White's KB and KN pawns are now split, and the black king is given a bolt hole.

29 R×R+   Q×R
30 Q–K4

White is surrounded by errors. The lesser evil was 30 Q–Q8.

30 ...   Q–K2
31 Q–QN4   Q–QB2
32 Q–Q6?

After the queen exchange White's game is hopeless. Quite probably, White was by now banking on Black's time-trouble ... and little else.

32 ...   Q×Q
33 R×Q   N–B5!

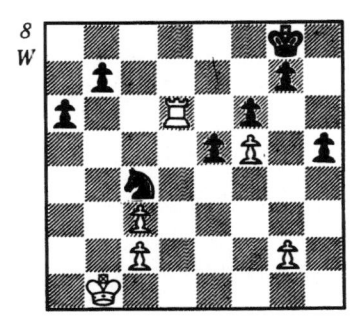

Black's knight becomes remarkably active.

34 R–Q7	P–QN4
35 R–R7	N–K6
36 R×RP	N×NP
37 K–B1	

White also wins by force after 37 R–N6 P–R5 38 R×NP P–R6 39 K–R2 P–K5 40 P–B4 P–K6 41 P–B5 P–K7 42 R–N1 P–K8=Q 43 R×Q N×R 44 P–B6 P–R7. Nor is 39 R–Q5 P–K5 40 K–B1 P–K6 any improvement.

37 ...	P–R5
38 K–Q2	P–R6
39 R–R1	N–R5
40 P–B4	P×P
41 R–R1	

41 K–B3 N×P 42 K×P N–N6 43 K–Q5 P–R7 44 P–B4 P–R8=Q 45 R×Q N×R 46 P–B5 N–N6 47 P–B6 N–B4 was insufficient to save the game.

41 ...	N×P
42 K–B3	N–Q3
43 R×P	K–B2
44 R–R7	P–B4
45 K–N4	P–B5
46 K–B5	P–KB6!
47 R–R1	P–K5
0–1	

A game full of drama. The victory assured Petrosian of a place in the Candidates' tournament.

5 Safety First!

Preparing himself to play in the Candidates' tournament, Petrosian was in no way prepared to play for first place. Nor for second. Nor even perhaps for third. It was all the same to him how he played there. And that was a serious psychological error, since it led to a period of creative and sporting limbo. The tactic employed, which was fully justified in competitions where it was necessary to obtain no lower than fifth place, was now employed by Petrosian in tournaments where he should have been fighting for first place.

Tigran's iron century, when he rarely lost but was able also to win, when he did not fear complications, but even took risks himself, came to an end. In its place there appeared a lengthy period during which Petrosian acted, always and in everything, according to the motto 'Safety First'.

The cause of this lay in Petrosian's conviction that he had gone rather far in his chess development. Like a war commander who has penetrated deep into enemy territory, but who declines further advances in order not to be cut off from his rear, Petrosian too felt the need to replenish his stocks, before seeking further conquests. It seemed to him that, becoming a grandmaster, he had achieved all that he might sensibly dream of, and now his thoughts turned to only one aim – preserve what had been acquired.

Playing according to this motto, Petrosian achieved a very high and extremely level series of results. He was concerned only to fulfil his minimum programme, a 'maximum' programme did not exist. It was considered that he lacked the thirsting ambition of Geller, and his friend often showed him an example. Now even if Tigran took third or fourth place in a powerful tournament, hardly anyone praised him. He was like an acrobat who, achieving the most difficult manoeuvres, was not applauded; his audience considered him capable of even more complex feats.

It became fashionable to criticize Petrosian. Once he was even called a tiger in a rabbit's skin. According to an original inertia, he was even cursed for draws in games where he had fought for victory until the last move. But though the criticisms were sometimes excessive, on the whole they were justified; for Petrosian as a beginner had valued the aesthetic in chess, as a youth had shone in tactical play, but now commonly sacrificed the artistic side of the game to the demands of practicality.

His striving to avoid defeat reached such heights that his occasional defeats became sensations. Petrosian was remarkably persevering and impenetrable in defence. His tactical weapons fell further into disuse; sometimes he might use them in positional, sometimes in defensive battles. Many of his colleagues strove to obtain good positions, in order to finish off their opponents by tactical blows; Petrosian could, with the help of small tactical strokes, achieve a powerful position. In the 22nd championship, for example, Taimanov felt the strength of such a strategy. By a series of combinations, Petrosian achieved complete positional superiority. Black's pieces were suffocated. Seeing that he did not have a sensible move, Taimanov resigned, although most of his army still remained on the board.

But such games became all the more infrequent. Petrosian produced these masterpieces as if to say, 'See what I can do?' And then went back to his boring wood-chopping.

The beginnings of this ill-starred era took place in the autumn of 1953 in Zurich. Tigran deliberated as follows: as the youngest and most inexperienced participant, I can have few hopes of first place, therefore it is not sensible to play for it. At first sight a fully logical conclusion, but how it contradicts the spirit of chess struggle! Petrosian himself later regretted that he did not show full opposition to his rivals in this tournament . . . it was indeed too early to think seriously of becoming the challenger, but the subconscious act of excluding himself from the circle of possible pretenders greatly retarded his further chess development.

In Saltjöbaden, Tigran had drawn 13 games out of 20; in Zurich the quantity of drawn games reached 20 out of 28. Petrosian was the youngest player, he was modest and knew his place. He threatened no-one, was a real domesticated tiger. . . Smyslov tenderly called him 'Tiggy', for the rest of the participants he was 'Tabby'.

There were nine Soviet grandmasters at Zurich – Smyslov, Bronstein, Keres, Petrosian, Geller, Kotov, Taimanov, Averbakh, Boleslavsky, and also Reshevsky (USA), Najdorf (Argentina), Szabo (Hungary), Gligoric (Yugoslavia), Euwe (Holland), and Stahlberg (Sweden).

Tigran began the tournament with four draws. Then he lost two games running – to Taimanov and Najdorf, and in the following round drew a quick game with Averbakh. After 7 rounds he had collected 2½ points, and only Kotov had less than him. Draws were quite in order, but last place did not fit in with his intentions, so he won three games running, over Szabo, Euwe and Stahlberg. A few draws later and he ended the first cycle with 7½ points, sharing 5th-7th places with Euwe and Boleslavsky. He acquired the same number of points in the second cycle, losses to Keres and Taimanov and wins against Szabo, Gligoric and Stahlberg. He took fifth place behind Smyslov (18 points), Bronstein, Keres and Reshevsky (16 points).

Immediately on his return from Sweden he took part in the 21st championship of the country. He shared 4th to 5th places, without losing any games, but drawing 13 out of 19 games. Commenting on this flood of draws Konstantinopolsky ventured the opinion that Petrosian 'seemed slightly wearied after the tournament in Zurich.' However, Petrosian's subsequent appearances cast doubt upon the validity of this point of view.

Throughout the whole tournament Petrosian was among the leaders. After five rounds he shared 3rd-4th places, after eight – first to fifth, after twelve – fifth to sixth, after fifteen, fourth to fifth, which position he retained at the end of the tournament, alongside master Lisitsin, and behind Averbakh, Korchnoi and Taimanov.

This was not the stamp of weariness, but the absence of sporting ambition. He seemed to be playing in a qualifying tournament where he must not fall below fifth place. Even though he was in the lead after eight rounds, together with Averbakh, Korchnoi, Furman and Lisitsin, he never attempted to put on a spurt, or even reinforce this position: he drew the next four games, in 23, 27, 31, and 28 moves. Throughout the tournament he never won two games in a row. The contrast with the 19th championship was impressive, where, as a promising master he had spread-eagled the field in a finishing burst of 5½ out of 6.

Tigran's play in the 22nd championship was even more passive. In many ways this tournament resembled the 19th championship. First of all it was unusually strong – Botvinnik, Smyslov, Keres, Geller, Taimanov, Kotov, young Korchnoi and Spassky took part. In the second place, it was a zonal tournament – the four winners (not counting, of course, the World Champion himself, Smyslov and Keres) had the right to play in the Candidates' tournament.

This was perhaps the most circumspect, the most bloodless tournament of Petrosian's life. Naturally, he did not lose a game – this surprised no-one. But out of 19 games he drew 15! Only Flohr, the recognized king of draws, managed to equal this. Not one of his drawn games went beyond 20 moves, and, excluding his game with Taimanov, all his games with the first fifteen players were drawn. Still only 26 years old, such sobriety, such creative asceticism was something to be marvelled at.

The tournament had not passed the half-way mark when Petrosian began to hear some disgruntled comments about his play. P. Romanovsky, a passionate and irrepressible popularizer of chess as an art form, wrote an article in the bulletin of the event entitled 'On draws'.

'The 22nd USSR championship, now in progress, had produced a whole crop of games full of great creative inspiration . . . the deplorable run of draws by Petrosian and Flohr scarcely harmonize with the general impression given to millions of chess fans of our leading players.'

Before the end of the tournament, Panov gave Petrosian's play a pitiless valuation:

'Real chances of victory, besides Botvinnik and Smyslov, up to round 15, are held by Geller, Spassky and Taimanov. I deliberately exclude Petrosian from this group, since from the very first rounds the latter has made it clear that he is playing for an easier, but also honourable conquest – a place in the interzonal quartet.'

Finally, there was the opinion of Bronstein, delivered before the end of the competition: 'Tigran Petrosian, the youngest and for his years the most circumspect grandmaster, did not display his chess gifts in this tournament'.

The most discordant comment on Petrosian came once again from Romanovsky, in his article in the tournament book. Saying nothing directly about the frank pragmatism of Petrosian's play, the chess veteran was nonetheless unable to conceal his disappointment. Speaking of Korchnoi, who occupied next to last place, Romanovsky said that from the creative aspect, his games were hardly inferior to Petrosian's. At the end of the article he named eight players who had proved their ability to occupy the forefront of soviet chess artistry (here among others he singled out the young players Geller, Spassky, Taimanov and Furman) but omitted Petrosian's name.

All this was very distressing, and more so because Petrosian, in his heart of hearts, agreed with the opinions delivered. But he nonetheless continued on his chosen path. Once before he had taken the advice of Bondarevsky, and played in a candidate master tournament. But he had ignored Bondarevsky's second piece of advice, and declined to alter his style fundamentally. Here he had decided to be cautious and avoid risks, and he was standing by his decision even if it should cause him certain discomfort.

Deeper reasons may lie in his character, and in the character formed in the environment of his childhood. Life had not dealt kindly with young Tigran. He could never forget the war years, or how difficult it had been without his mother and father. For that reason he valued his success in life very highly. It appeared to him very important for his reputation to qualify for the Candidates' tournament, and even more important, not to disgrace himself there. He considered that by careful play he could definitely come third or fourth, and this was all that he aimed for.

Petrosian conducted the Göteborg interzonal tournament in his favourite manner: no losses, draws with the top ten and five wins, mainly against the tail-enders. In all, 15 draws and 5 wins was fully sufficient for him to occupy 'his' fourth position, and qualify for the

Candidates' tournament. Once again, these tactics seemed uncalled for; no less than nine players qualified from this tournament for the challengers', so Petrosian could have played more freely without risking anything. At the same time it was not difficult for him to carry out this tactic; most players were only too happy to split the point with him, and if any demurred he would use his immense skills to force immediate simplification. His simplifying technique was on a very high level.

Despite these negative features, many people continued to believe in his star. After the USSR–Hungary match, where Petrosian played brilliantly, and scored 5½ out of 7, the veteran Hungarian master Asztalos declared that Botvinnik's next opponent would be Petrosian.

All this, and all that was happening around him, seemed to leave little impression on Petrosian. At Göteborg, when Geller and Bronstein registered 10 draws, and Keres and young Spassky 8, Petrosian had 15. At the same time Bronstein conducted his games in such an inspired fashion that it seemed he was not after a place in the Candidates' tournament, but a prize for creative achievements.

In appearance unaffected, in reality time and other factors were wearing away Petrosian's mask of passivity. Eventually he grew tired of the criticisms, grew tired of receiving letters like the one sent by an exasperated Yerevan supporter: 'When' came the direct question, 'are we to see the last of your draws?'. Tigran asked himself the same question. This was the second time running he had qualified for the Candidates' tournament, and by virtue of this he could now consider himself a serious challenger for the world title. For the time being he did not dream of first place, but he wanted to allow himself a little excitement. 'In the candidates' tournament I decided to "play some chess".' – he wrote at the end of the competition. 'To play each game without reference to the strength of the opposition, without anxiety as to the result, or its effect upon the tournament table.'

Such a sudden change of approach had its effect – his old striving for the quiet life was a habit not so easy to discard. The iron Tigran, in learning not to lose games, had in the meantime forgotten how to win against his equals. He began the Amsterdam tournament optimistically, but the experiences of the first few games soon quenched his fervour. In round 1 he played black against Geller. In one way or another the two friends had always managed to draw most of their games with each other, so, after obtaining the better position out of the opening, Petrosian played a few insignificant moves and began diplomatic overtures. This time, however, Geller was in a very aggressive mood, and declined the offered draw. Petrosian was taken aback by this unexpected turn of events and lost quickly.

He had grown accustomed to tournaments without defeat, but here was a loss in the first round. There was worse to come. The next opponent was Bronstein. Petrosian, according to the opinion of Bronstein himself, conducted the game 'in grandiose style'. Making use of a few inaccuracies in the opening, Petrosian established full positional superiority. White's pieces occupied all the valuable strategical points, whereas up until the very end of the game, black did not manage to develop his queen's rook and queen's bishop. Black was so tied up that he could not undertake even the most modest manoeuvre to improve his position, and in fact the last eight moves of the game Bronstein spent mechanically moving a knight back and forth. On the eighth move the knight happened to attack the white queen, and Petrosian, distracted by the approaching end of the struggle, neglected to move the queen away. Shrugging his shoulders, Bronstein captured the queen.

'I will never forget the look of horror with which Petrosian greeted the departure of his queen from the board. With an expression of hopeless resignation, he silently stoped the clocks. A tragic end to what might have been the game of his life. . . .'

This episode had a surprising sequel. At a dinner held in honour of the players by the people of Leuwarden, the cooks prepared ice-cream in the shape of chess pieces. Bronstein took the queen and offered it to Petrosian:

'Now we're quits! . . .'

Tigran smiled wordlessly. He could not even offer his opponents a pawn. . . .

On the evening when Petrosian lost to Bronstein, he walked for long hours with Keres around the streets of Amsterdam. Neither spoke more than three words to the other. Petrosian was not in a talkative mood, and Keres, always tactful, realized that any words of consolation would be misplaced.

The adventures were not quite over. In the third round Petrosian played black against Smyslov, who was then at the height of his powers, and indeed won the world championship a year later. Playing very energetically, Petrosian obtained a clearly won position. However, trying to win the game in the most 'comfortable' fashion, he allowed Smyslov to slip out.

In the fourth round, Petrosian's won position came against Spassky, and the story was repeated: Spassky got a draw. Petrosian nonetheless managed to finish the first cycle with fifty per cent, since he won against both Filip and Pilnik. In the second cycle, Petrosian was already a changed man – Tigran had devolved back into 'Tiggy'. He completed his 'vendetta', winning against Geller, but then drew all his remaining eight games. His final score was $9\frac{1}{2}$, $1\frac{1}{2}$ points behind Keres, and 2 points behind the winner, Smyslov. He shared 3rd to 7th places with Bronstein, Geller, Spassky and Szabo.

For an unsuccessful tournament, which had begun with two defeats this did not appear a bad result. But Petrosian was dissatisfied, not so much with the result, nor with the disastrous outcome of his new tournament strategy. He felt uneasy, and his uneasiness was directed at his now regular policy of taking points from the weak and sharing them with the strong. He had to conclude that his unsuccessful games against Bronstein, Smyslov and Spassky were only in appearance accidental. . . .

He need not, of course, have left his queen en prise against Bronstein, but perhaps the circumstances of the game had weakened his attention somewhat? After obtaining a won position, he was not disposed to find an immediate win, but prepared to manoeuvre quietly to the adjournment, when he could work out the win in comfort. Perhaps too, the striving, which Abramov was to call 'love of strengthening the position' had prevented him from finding an easy win against Smyslov. And his 37th move – a king move, dictated by his desire for 'the quiet life' – hadn't that given Spassky the chance to escape?

There was much food for thought in this, especially since these clearly psychological loopholes had led to tactical failures. Petrosian was not even cheered by complimentary remarks on his play, such as those made by Euwe at the end of the first cycle of the tournament: 'Petrosian's play made a very favourable impression on the spectators, and on me personally. Thanks to his positional understanding he can exploit the tiniest positional advantage . . . if Petrosian could only begin to combine a little, no-one would be able to play chess against him!'

A similar opinion of Petrosian's tactical awareness was given by assistant arbiter Heidenfeld: 'Though it may seem hard to credit, since we are speaking about a tournament of the strongest chess players in the world, one of the players, Petrosian, several times running achieved winning positions, and each time proved incapable of finding the decisive continuation. One clearly superior and three won positions secured him a total of 1 point. One alternates between admiration of such strategical mastery which enables him to outplay opponents of the calibre of Bronstein, Smyslov and Spassky, and disappointment with his tactical weakness which denies him the fruits of his previous work. . . .'

Finally here is Abramov writing in the Amsterdam tournament book: 'We come now to Petrosian. It must be recognized, that he did indeed have real chances of victory in this tournament. He was aided in this by his delicate positional understanding, thanks to which he never once had a bad position. What is more, in a good half of his games he outplayed his opponents, and obtained won positions. But then something inexplicable happened to him: blunder after blunder, and eventual dissipation of the advantage. . . .'

Opinion on Petrosian became sharply divided. There were the

optimists who considered that he 'only needed to start to combine a little' and the pessimists who felt that Petrosian would never be able to overcome the limitations of his own nature, or find it in him to make a real bid for the world championship. As to which of these viewpoints correctly divined his future course, Petrosian was to give an answer in the following year, when he participated in the 24th Soviet championship. With this tournament a new period begins in the biography of the future world champion.

7 Reshevsky–Petrosian

Candidates', Zürich 1953

Nimzo-Indian

1 P–Q4	N–KB3
2 P–QB4	P–K3
3 N–QB3	B–N5
4 P–K3	0–0
5 B–Q3	P–Q4
6 N–B3	P–B4
7 0–0	N–B3
8 P–QR3	B×N
9 P×B	P–QN3

Practical tests of this variation have been relatively few, though White has so far been unable to demonstrate a clear advantage. In practice, Black has a rather cramped position to defend, and this type of game is not to every chess-player's liking. Petrosian is one of the few players who believe in the resilience of Black's game, and can blunt the opponent's initiative.

10 BP×P	KP×P
11 B–N2	P–B5

Parrying the positional threat to open the centre with 12 P–B4! The strategical contours of the game are now defined: Black tries to limit the scope of White's bishops, and White tries to open the centre, and then transfer the weight of the struggle to the K-side.

12 B–B2	B–N5
13 Q–K1	N–K5

13 ... B×N 14 P×B N–KR4 was worth considering, beginning a complex positional duel of knights against bishops.

14 N–Q2	N×N
15 Q×N	B–R4
16 P–B3	B–N3
17 P–K4	Q–Q2
18 KR–K1	P×P
19 P×P	KR–K1

With his last two moves, Black finally reveals his plans for piece action against the central squares. The main struggle centres round White's K4 square.

20 Q–B4

20 P–QR4 could be met by the simplifying manoeuvre 20 ... N–K4 21 B–R3 N–Q6.

20 ... P–N4

Threatening an eventual Q-side advance, and fixing the pawn on QR3. Black is conducting the defence very coolly, even though White appears to have made definite progress. Petrosian is here playing according to Steinitz's principles: the defence is allowed to retreat, but it must be an economical retreat!

21 B–Q1	R–K2
22 B–N4	Q–K1
23 P–K5	P–QR4
24 R–K3	R–Q1
25 R1–K1	R–K3!

Safety First! 65

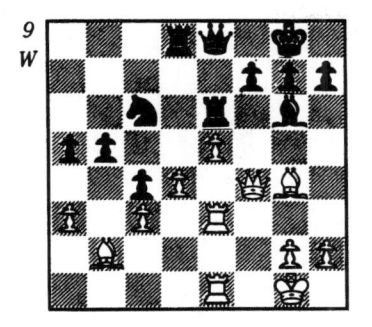

**9
W**

A remarkable defensive idea. The fundamental idea is to establish a blockade on the white squares. White would probably have done best to ignore the rook, and try to start an attack on the K-side, by means of R–N3, P–KR4 and so on.

26 P–QR4

A cunning move. On 26 . . . P–N5 White plays 27 P–Q5 R × QP 28 B × R P × B 29 Q × P with advantage. But Black is consistent.

26 . . .	N–K2
27 B × R	P × B
28 Q–B1	N–Q4
29 R–B3	B–Q6

Black's pieces unexpectedly come to life, and White's material advantage becomes . . . immaterial.

30 R × B

There was nothing better.

30 . . .	P × R
31 Q × P	P–N5
32 P × P	

White could have tried more complicated variations with 32 P–B4 N–N3 33 R–QB1 N × RP 34 B–R1 Q–B3 or 33 P–Q5 P × P 34 P–B5 N × P 35 B–Q4 R–B1 36 Q–KB3 Q–K3, but here too Black's position is hardly inferior; so White's decision to follow a quiet line was fully justified.

| 32 . . . | P × P |

32 . . . N × P 33 Q–QN3 N–Q4 or 33 Q–N5 Q × Q 34 P × Q N–Q6 35 R–K2 R–N1 36 R–Q2 R × P 37 R × N R × B 38 P–Q5 was also sufficient to draw (variation shown by Bronstein).

33 P–R5	R–R1
34 R–R1	Q–B3
35 B–B1	Q–B2

Black could have sacrificed the exchange here by 35 . . . R × P 36 R × R Q × B+; he would still not have been risking losing.

36 P–R6	Q–N3
37 B–Q2	P–N6
38 Q–B4	P–R3
39 P–R3	P–N7
40 R–N1	K–R1
41 B–K1	½–½

A fine example by Black of defence in a strategically difficult position. In Bronstein's opinion, this was one of the best games of the Candidates' tournament.

8 Nezhmetdinov–Petrosian

21 USSR Ch, Kiev 1954

Sicilian

1 P–K4	P–QB4
2 N–KB3	P–Q3
3 P–Q4	P × P
4 N × P	N–KB3
5 N–QB3	P–QR3
6 B–KN5	QN–Q2
7 Q–B3	

This variation was enjoying a certain popularity at the time. The present game contributed to the fall from favour of White's 7 Q–B3. Nowadays 7 B–QB4 is reckoned a more energetic alternative.

7 . . . **P–R3!**

Forcing White to declare his

intentions regarding the positioning of his queen's bishop. If 8 B–R4, then 8... P–KN4 9 B–N3 B–N2. Probably the best retreat was to Q2. White's actual decision, a very natural one, meets an energetic refutation.

8 B–K3   P–K4

This is the 'salt' of Black's idea. The weakening of the central squares is not important here, but the harmonious interaction of White's pieces is hindered, since he can no longer play N–B5–K3!

9 N–B5

9 N–N3 was a slight improvement.

9 ...   P–KN3
10 N–N3   P–QN4
11 P–KR4   P–KR4

Another finely judged move; the weakness on Black's KN4 is not dangerous.

12 B–N5   B–K2
13 0–0–0   B–N2

10
W

Black's pieces are very harmoniously placed, something which cannot be said of White's congested array. White's K4 square is indeed weak; the initiative clearly belongs to Black.

14 K–N1   R–QB1
15 B–Q3   N–B4
16 N.N3–K2 P–N5

Forcibly bringing about exchanges favourable to Black.

17 B×N   B×B
18 N–Q5   B×N
19 P×B   Q–K2

But not 19... B×P 20 P–N4!

20 N–N3

20 Q–R3 could be answered by 20... 0–0 21 P–KB3 P–K5! 22 P×P Q–K4, when Black has a powerful initiative.

20 ...   B×P

Now this capture is quite in order.

21 N–K4   B–N4
22 P–KN3   P–R4
23 R.Q1–K1 N×N
24 B×N   P–B4
25 B–Q3

White's game is lost. He could try to confuse the issue at this point by sacrificing a piece: 25 B×P P×B 26 Q×BP R–B4 27 Q–N6+ K–Q1 28 R×RP R×R 29 Q×R K–B2. He chooses a less extreme method, but the outcome is equally bleak.

25 ...   B–B3
26 B–N5+   K–B2
27 Q–N3   K–N2
28 P–KB3   P–KR5
29 P–N4   P×P
30 P×P   B–N4
31 B–Q3   P–R6
32 B–R6   R–R1
33 R×RP   B–R5!

The simplest. If instead 33... R×B 34 R×R K×R, 35 Q–Q3! hits rook and KNP simultaneously.

34 R1–R1   R×B
35 P–N5   Q×P
36 Q–B4   R–R2

White has managed to regain the material, but his position is still terrible. The remaining moves were:

37 R×B R×R 38 Q×R Q×Q 39 R×Q R–QB2 40 R–R1 P–N4 41

K-B1 R-B4 42 R-Q1 K-N3 43 R-Q2 P-N5 44 K-Q1 K-B4 0-1.

Nezhmetdinov is one of the most original attacking players of the Soviet school, and has even managed to defeat players like Tal and Spassky in sharp positions; but against Petrosian his score is almost zero. Petrosian may indeed be one of the leaders of the positional school of chess-players, but he combines this with a remarkable invulnerability against the most uncompromising and dashing attacking masters.

9 **Petrosian–Taimanov**

22 USSR Ch, Moscow 1955

Slav

1 P-Q4	P-Q4
2 P-QB4	P-K3
3 N-KB3	N-KB3
4 N-B3	P-B3
5 P-K3	QN-Q2
6 B-Q3	B-N5
7 0-0	0-0
8 Q-B2	B-Q3

A strange decision. The usual continuation here is 8 . . . Q-K2. The move played amounts to a loss of time, which is not compensated for in other ways.

9 P-QN3	P × P
10 P × P	P-K4
11 B-N2	R-K1
12 N-K4	N × N
13 B × N	P-KR3?

Another inaccuracy, which enables White to develop a strong attack on the K-side. Better 13 . . . P-KN3, though after 14 B-Q3! Q-K2 15 P-B5 B-B2 16 B-B4! White has the advantage.

14 QR-Q1   P × P

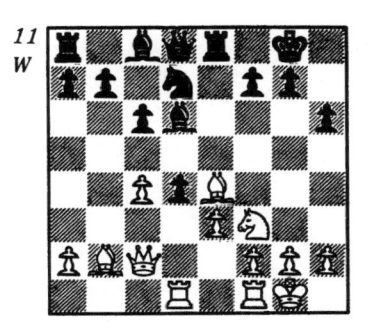

11 W

15 B-R7+!

From this point, White plays the attack brilliantly. 15 R × P at once would be answered by 15 . . . N-B3!

15 . . .	K-R1
16 R × P	B-B4

16 . . . Q-K2 17 R-K4 Q-B1 18 R-R4 N-K4 was a little better. White would have very good attacking chances here too: 19 N-N5! P-KB4 (19 . . . P × N 20 B-N8+!) 20 B-N6 N × B 21 R × P+ K-N1 22 R × N. (variation pointed out by O'Kelly).

17 R-B4	Q-K2
18 R-K4!	

The movements of the white rook are very curious. It is not often you see such a 'heavy' piece move so lightly in the middle game!

18 . . .	Q-B1
19 R-R4	P-B3

Forced, otherwise 20 R × P.

20 B-N6	R-K2
21 R-R5	

Completing the journey (R-Q4-B4-K4-R4-R5). There is no defence against N-R4.

21 . . .	B-Q3
22 R-Q1	B-K4
23 B-R3!	P-QB4
24 N-R4	1-0

Black has no defence against the threat of 25 B–R7 with 26 N–N6+ to follow. If 24 ... Q–Q1 25 B×P, and if 24 ... Q–N1 25 B–R7! Q×B 26 N–N6+.

10 Petrosian–Geller

Candidates', Amsterdam 1956

Tarrasch

1 P–QB4	P–QB4
2 P–KN3	N–QB3
3 B–N2	N–B3
4 N–KB3	P–K3
5 O–O	P–Q4
6 P×P	P×P
7 P–Q4	

By transposition of moves, the game has entered the Rubinstein variation of the Tarrasch defence. The ensuing positional struggle revolves around the central black pawn, and the square upon which it stands.

7 ...	B–K2
8 N–B3	O–O
9 B–B4	

9 P×P or 9 B–N5 are more frequently played. The text move is less analyzed, but also logical, and corresponds to the spirit of the position.

9 ...   P×P

Defining the central configuration. On 9 ... P–B5, 10 N–K5 and P–QN3 is possible. Black could also play 9 ... B–K3, as occurred in the game Moiseyev—Bonch–Osmolovsky, Moscow 1949. That game continued 10 P×P B×P 11 N–K5 Q–K2 12 R–B1 QR–B1 13 N–R4 B–Q3 14 N×N R×N 15 R×R P×R 16 B×B Q×B 17 Q–Q4, with a small, but very clear advantage to White. After 10 P×P, 10 ... P–Q5 would be risky: 11 N–QN5 B×P 12 R–B1 Q–N3 13 P–QR4, with the unpleasant threat of 14 B–B7.

10 N.KB3×P   Q–N3
11 N×N

White relieves Black of his weakness on Q4, but creates a new, and perhaps even more serious one on Black's QB3; since the defensibility of the pawn on ... Q4 is ultimately connected with that of the ... QB3 pawn, we might say that White is now attacking two weaknesses instead of one. However, White's own QNP may become a target for Black.

11 ...	P×N
12 Q–B2	B–K3
13 B–K3	

A slight inaccuracy. 13 QR–B1! was more natural.

13 ...   Q–R4

Petrosian pointed out that 13 ... P–B4! should have been played here, and if 14 N–R4 Q–N4 15 B×BP QR–B1 16 P–QN4 B×B 17 P×B B–Q2! with very good play for Black.

14 Q–R4   Q×Q

It might have been wiser to avoid the exchange of queens and retreat to QB2. In the endgame especially, Black's pawn weaknesses begin to tell.

15 N×Q	N–Q2
16 KR–Q1	KR–N1
17 P–N3	

In order to take advantage of weak pawns, it is first necessary to blockade them, that is limit their mobility. In this respect White aims his fire at the black Q4 square first, indirectly preventing ... P–QB4.

17 ...   B–QR6
18 B–Q4

A cunning manoeuvre, tempting

18 ... P–QB4. After 19 B–QB3!, Black's QP would be defenceless.

18 ...   B–KN5

Black does not manage to find a good plan. Petrosian recommended 18 ... P–KB4 followed by bringing the king to Q3, setting up a solid central position.

**19 R–Q2   R–K1
20 P–K3   B–KB4
21 B–N2   B × B**

From the positional point of view, not an inviting decision. But on 21 ... B–B1 22 R–QB1 QR–B1 23 B–B1 with B–R6 to follow, Black is very uncomfortable; 21 ... B–QN5 22 R–Q4 B–Q3 23 P–K4! is also bad.

**22 R × B   N–N3
23 N–B5   P–QR4
24 R–QB1   R.K1–QB1**

Bad was 24 ... P–R5   25 N × P N × N   26 P × N R.K1–QB1   27 R–N6 R × P   28 R6 × P R × R   29 R × R R × P   30 B × P!

25 P–K4!

The signal for the advance on the Q-side and in the centre. It is very difficult for Black to find satisfactory counterplay.

25 ...   B–N3

After 25 ... P × P 26 N × P, Black loses the pawn on his QB3.

26 P–B4   P–B3

26 ... P × P was the lesser evil. Now White creates a passed king pawn.

27 B–R3   R.B1–N1

Bad was 27 ... R–K1 28 B–K6+ B–B2 29 B × B+ K × B 30 N–N7!

28 P–K5!

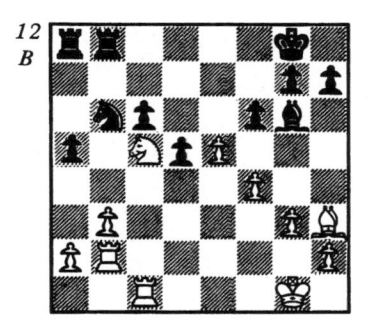

*12
B*

Weaknesses are weaknesses, but new trumps (here the passed KP) have to be created. Black now stirs out of his defensive pattern and initiates active counterplay.

**28 ...   P × P
29 P × P   P–R5**

29 ... N–B5 is easily parried by 30 R–K2.

**30 P × P   N–B5
31 R × R+   R × R
32 P–K6   R–N8**

White's passed pawn is extremely unpleasant, and it is difficult to suggest other defences for Black. If for example 32 ... R–R1   33 P–K7 R–K1   34 R–K1 K–B2   35 B–Q7 R × P 36 R–KB1+ K–N1 37 B–K6+ B–B2   38 R × B R × R   39 N–Q7 P–N3   40 P–R5 N × P   41 N–K5 K–N2   42 B × R K–B3   43 N × BP N × N   44 B × QP and White has a clearly won endgame.

**33 R × R   B × R
34 B–B1   N–Q3**

The QR2 pawn is invulnerable to capture. If 34 ... B × P?   35 B × N P × B   36 K–B2 White wins easily. 34 ... N–R4   35 N–N3 N–B5   36 P–R5 B × P   37 B × N P × B   38 P–R6! is also bad.

**35 P–QR3   K–B1
36 P–R5   N–B1
37 K–B2   K–K2**

38 K–K3	K–Q3
39 K–Q4	B–B4
40 B–K2	N–R2
41 P–R6	

41 P–N4 B–N3 42 P–KR4 P–R3 43 P–R5 followed by B–Q3! was worth consideration.

41 ... B–R6

Black defends very stubbornly. 41 ... B×P? 42 N×B K×N 43 K–B5 K–Q2 44 K–N6 N–B1+ 45 K–N7 N–Q3+ 46 K–N8! would have lost.

42 P–R4 N–B1

Alternatively 42 ... P–N3 43 P–N4! B–N7 44 K–K3! N–B1 45 K–B2 B–R8 46 K–N1 B–K5 47 N×B P×N 48 B–B4 and White wins.

43 N–N7+

Beginning forced manoeuvres. Black's game is hopeless.

43 ... K×P

43 ... K–B2 is answered by 44 K–K5!

44 K–B5	K–Q2
45 N–R5	

White might have effectively finished off the game by 45 N–Q6! N–R2 46 N–N5! P×N 47 P×P.

45 ... K–B2

Or 45 ... N–R2 46 N×P!

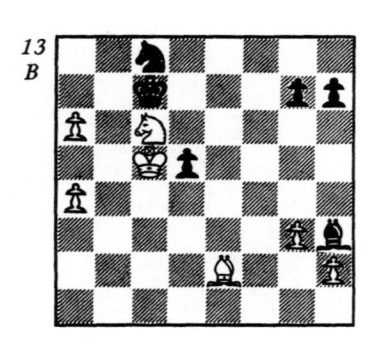

46 N×P

It seems that everything is over. But chess games demand colossal attention right up to the last move, and at this point tiredness after a long struggle has its effect.

46 ...	N–N3
47 B–N5	N–Q2+
48 K×P?	

48 K–Q4 would have won. Now White's task is unexpectedly complicated.

48 ...	B–N7+
49 K–K6	B×N
50 B×B	K×B
51 P–R7	N–N3

Black misses a study-like salvation: 51 ... N–B4+! 52 K–B7 K–N2 53 K×P N–K5! 54 K×P N–Q7! and now if 55 P–N4, 55 ... N–B6, or if 55 P–R3 N–K5! and so on.

52 P–R5	N–R1
53 K–B7	

53 P–KR4! would have been more accurate.

53 ...	P–N4
54 K–B6!	

54 K–N7, though natural, is worse: 54 ... K–N2 55 K×P N–B2 56 K–N6 N–K3 57 K–B5 N–Q5+, after which the win is problematical.

54 ...	P–N5
55 K–N5	K–N2
56 K×P	N–B2
57 K–N5	N–Q4
58 P–R3	N–B6
59 P–N4	N–K5+
60 K–B5	N–N6+

White also wins after 60 ... N–Q3+ 61 K–K5 N–B2+ 62 K–B6 N–Q3 63 K–N7 N–K5 64 P–R4 K×P 65 P–N5!

61 K–B4	N–K7+
62 K–K3	N–B6
63 P–N5	N–Q4+

64 K–K4	N–K2	70 ...	K–R3
65 K–B4!	N–Q4+	71 K–B4	K×P
66 K–B3	N–K2	72 K–K5	K–N3
67 P–R4	K×P	73 K–K6	1–0
68 K–B4	N–N3+		
69 K–N4	N–K2		
70 P–R5			

Now the knight is unable to attack the pawns from the rear. The game is over.

White's last move could still have let the win slip! If 73 K–B6? N–Q4+ 74 K–N7 N–B5 75 P–N6 N×NP!

Hardly a faultless game, but a fascinating episode in the struggle for world championship honours.

6 Prospect Rustaveli

Petrosian, despite the initial setback in the Candidates' tournament, was still prepared to continue his attempts to increase the dynamic element in his play. His next tournament was the 24th Soviet championship, perhaps one of the hardest tournaments in the world, and marked by its gladiatorial contests. In the 21st and 22nd championships Petrosian had gone through without defeat – in many ways a remarkable feat – but this had earned him few cheers from his supporters, and a steady flow of adverse criticism in the bulletins. Two years later, in the Candidates' tournament, Petrosian was to state: 'Grandmasters are not gladiators', but here in Moscow the opposite had to be the case. In fact in the present championship the play was even sharper than usual, and its composition was impressive. In order of finishing the players were: Tal, Bronstein, Keres, Spassky–Tolush, Holmov, Korchnoi–Petrosian, Boleslavsky, Aronin–Taimanov, Furman, Bannik–Klaman–Nezhmetdinov, Antoshin, Stoliar, Mikenas, Aronson–Gurgenidze–Tarasov–Hasin. Here Tal made his staggering debut, and grandmaster Tolush delivered his swan song.

In the first four rounds Tal collected 4 points. In the sixth round he was caught by Tolush, in the eighth Spassky replaced Tolush; from the ninth to the eleventh Tolush again led. In the twelfth Petrosian and Korchnoi were leading, in the thirteenth it was Tolush and Holmov, but a round later the leader became . . . Keres! In the sixteenth both Tal and Bronstein overtook him, to be joined a round later by Tolush. Tolush then dropped back again, and after nineteen rounds Tal was alone in the lead. After the twentieth it was again a threesome – Tal, Bronstein and Tolush, and finally a victory in the last round over Tolush allowed 20-year-old Tal to become champion of the Soviet Union!

For long stretches Petrosian was well up among the leaders, but he could not match the final spurt of Tal, Keres, Bronstein, Spassky and Tolush. It seemed that the competitors had thrown all caution aside. Tolush managed to draw only seven games out of 21. Tal was even more daring. In his games with the top ten players he gained 7 points. He altered the regular formula of 'draws with the strongest and wins against the tailenders', and attacked his main rivals. He beat five grandmasters – Bronstein, Keres, Tolush, Petrosian, and Taimanov – quite a considerable selection.

In this atmosphere of high excitement Petrosian found it relatively easy to 'change his skin'. He willingly entered into complicated situations, some of which went in his favour, some of them not. He was effectively routed by Bannik, and in the time scramble against Holmov he even managed to get mated, but he continued to play with appetite and enjoyment. His efforts did not go unnoticed in the bulletins. V. Panov wrote at the end of the first half of the tournament: 'Grandmaster Petrosian, who specialized in short draws in previous championships, seems to have completely changed his style, and notwithstanding his defeat in the first round against Furman, strives to create sharp and complex positions.' L. Abramov was even more enthusiastic: 'If Petrosian had conducted this tournament in his "1955 style", he would have had, after 15 rounds, at least three victories, and no defeats, a minimum of 9 points. Here he hasn't even reached that "Petrosianic" minimum. But all the same no-one would reproach him for this. Six wins, four losses, five draws – this result shows the grandmaster's desire to break away from his previous lethargy. Both his wins (for example, against Tolush), and losses (against Bannik) bear this opinion out.

'It may only be remarked that Petrosian has not chosen an opening repertoire with the black pieces corresponding to his new approach; but on the whole his new creative profile is very welcome to chess lovers. . . .'

Perhaps the most pleasant evaluation came from the tournament winner, Tal: 'The tournament was exceptionally lively. Everyone played with great sporting "malice", and willingly strove to sharpen the conflict. It is very pleasant to play in such competitions. Tolush, Bronstein, Petrosian and Nezhmetdinov did much to raise the temper of the struggle.'

Apart from these critics, there was the distant, but far more numerous chess public. For Petrosian this was, first and foremost, the people of Armenia. Though he had now a good ten years left Yerevan, the Armenians still considered him a representative of the republic. Petrosian was extremely unambitious, but the temper of his people was quite the opposite, and when he noticed the unflagging interest with which they followed – and still follow – his almost every move, this gave him an added spur to his efforts. It was particularly they who were delighted by his new approach, delighted – but not satisfied; he had to win.

The following, 25th Soviet championship, was at the same time a zonal tournament. Even though the sporting aims – a place in the top four – impelled Petrosian to avoid too much risk, he was still contesting for first place throughout the tournament.

The championship took place in Tal's home city, Riga, at the beginning of 1958. Up until the fourteenth round Petrosian was in the leading group, then he drew level with the leader, Spassky, and after sixteen rounds he was alone in first place. For a while he retained this position, but in the eighteenth, penultimate round, Tal caught him up. On the last day Petrosian played black against Averbakh, and Tal, also black, played Spassky. Tal and Petrosian had $11\frac{1}{2}$, and Spassky and Averbakh had $10\frac{1}{2}$ points (Bronstein had 11). The game with Averbakh was drawn in 22 moves, but full of concealed tensions. At one point Petrosian offered the sacrifice of a rook, but this was declined, and the game went back to equality. Since Bronstein had decided not to tempt fate, and agreed a draw with Korchnoi, there remained only one game outstanding – Spassky–Tal. The position there arrived at approximate equality, and black proposed a draw, which would have allowed him to share 1st-2nd places with Petrosian. However, Spassky declined, and the game was later adjourned with winning chances for him.

On his way to the tournament hall the following morning, Spassky met Petrosian, and with a smile said: 'Today you will become champion.'

Petrosian did not reply, nor even return the smile.

For most of the second session Spassky energetically pursued the black king, and at one point could have played a decisive combination. But overlooking this possibility, he gradually lost the initiative. He nonetheless continued to play for the attack, and very soon black was attacking. Spassky went down to defeat. Thus Petrosian was not even able to share first place, let alone become sole champion. And Spassky deprived himself of a place in the interzonal tournament. . . .

The evaluation of Petrosian's play was this time given by Bronstein: 'Tigran Petrosian – one of the most talented grandmasters, prize winner in two interzonal tournaments, competitor in two Candidates' tournaments. Even from his youth his play was distinguished by its maturity and deep penetration to the essentials of a position. It is practically impossible to win against Petrosian – he was the only undefeated player, while his rivals lost at least two games each. Petrosian has never taken first place in a strong tournament, but at the same time rarely falls below third–fourth, and fifth place would be considered an unsuccessful performance. This time, however, he really was close to first place, so it must be hoped that this success marks a new epoch in his creative and sporting results. If he had before more or less consciously limited the activity in his play, and cloaked his exceptional combinative abilities in order to preserve solidity, he has now become noticeably more aggressive, and his results are beginning to reflect this change.'

There was also noticeable the intrusion of a new element besides in

Petrosian's play. This was the admission of psychological factors. Previously, with his belief in principles, in the over-riding logic of the game, he had always regarded such matters with deep suspicion. A few years later he was to give the following answer to the question 'How much importance do you think psychological factors have in the chess game?' 'As much as they should have. In clashes between players of equal strength, the psychological moments can be very important sometimes. However, I would like to say that, in my opinion, the attention given to this aspect of chess has grown to unnecessarily large proportions. Psychology has become very fashionable, a magical approach, with which it is possible to explain everything with remarkable ease.'

This was, so to speak, theory. In actual fact Petrosian was to rely to an increasing degree on psychological devices. A case in point was his game with Tal in the 25th championship. Petrosian had to find a suitable opening system as black, to somehow combat Tal's effervescence. He might have been expected to choose one which would allow him to keep an active position, with ample manoeuvring space, and the possibility of easy transference of pieces from one wing to another. Petrosian actually chose something very different. Realizing that Tal liked to drum up crises hardly out of the opening, Petrosian chose a variation of the Ruy Lopez which leads to a very constricted position for black. But here the pawn chains, like a whole row of trenches, divided the two armies. Positional warfare. White enjoyed greater command of space, and wide manoeuvring possibilities; perhaps even his game was strategically won. But – and herein lay the psychology behind Petrosian's choice of opening – the position demanded long, patient work, which was contrary to Tal's temperament.

Having secured an excellent attacking position, Tal did in fact act hastily! He accepted Petrosian's offer of the exchange, but instead of ceding the initiative for a while to consolidate his material advantage, he himself gave up a pawn and unwisely opened up the position. When the game was adjourned, Petrosian had a great advantage, but during the second session Tal nevertheless managed to save the game.

This game attracted the attention of the World Champion. A little while later, in an article published in *Ogonyok*, entitled 'On the style of a chessplayer', Botvinnik wrote: 'It appeared that Tal had obtained an obvious positional advantage out of the opening, but Petrosian managed to uncover the shady side of White's position with a clever sacrifice, and Tal, now a little unsettled, was forced to find salvation himself. . . .'

Even though Petrosian had almost accidentally missed first place at Riga, he could hardly have justly laid claim to this position. Tal had won 9 games, and Spassky, who shared 5th–6th places, won 7 games, whereas he, Petrosian had beaten only five of his opponents. This was, speaking frankly, a somewhat miserly figure. Still there was always next year.

In the Interzonal tournament at Portoroz, in Yugoslavia, Petrosian once again gave evidence of his quickening ambitions. For most of the time he was in the lead, but at the finish Tal once more outstripped him. Petrosian, with 12½ points shared 3rd–4th places with Benko, Tal was first with 13½, and Gligoric scored 13.

For the second time running, the daring Rigan chess-player had snatched victory from his grasp. At the back of his mind a thought was assailing Petrosian: in the coming Candidates' tournament it was unlikely that Smyslov could manage a third time to overcome his rivals and emerge as Botvinnik's challenger, so the most likely winners on the basis of previous results, were he and the eternally youthful Keres. Were it not for Tal. . . . Tigran was determined to beat Tal in a tournament, and the scene of the next duel was in his home town, Tiflis. Here, in the town of his youth, Petrosian was for the first time to become champion of the Soviet Union. In the second half of the tournament he set such a pace that even Tal with his traditional final spurt was unable to catch him, sharing 2nd-3rd places with Spassky, a point behind.

The new champion did not lose a game, but with that managed to secure eight victories – a result which spoke for itself. The sporting rivalry in the tournament took an original course. At the beginning Spassky went ahead, scoring 6½ out of eight. Taimanov had 5½ points, Bronstein 5, and Tal 4½ (out of seven). As for Petrosian he had a total of 3 points, though no catastrophe had occurred; he had simply fallen ill and postponed three games. In the ninth round he beat Krogius, and of his main rivals only Tal took a step forward, winning against Nezhmetdinov. Petrosian then took another point, against the same Nezhmetdinov, and Tal beat Averbakh. The remaining contenders suffered fiascos: Spassky lost to Taimanov, and Bronstein to Keres.

Petrosian was satisfied; while the main contenders fought it out among themselves, he moved silently forward. After nine rounds he had 5½ points out of eight (he had drawn his postponed game against Keres). In the eleventh round the situation improved still more: Petrosian beat Averbakh, and Tal was unexpectedly routed by the debutant of the championship, Gufeld. On the following day Petrosian scored his fourth victory in a row, over Gufeld. Four wins in as many rounds – this was as much as he had registered in the whole 19 rounds of the 22nd championship!

After 12 rounds Petrosian had 7½ (out of ten), and shared second place with Tal (who had postponed one game), and Spassky. Half a point ahead was Taimanov. In the next round Spassky replaced

Taimanov, but after 14 rounds Petrosian, winning against Vasiukov and drawing his postponed game against Bronstein, went into the lead, which position he held until the very end of the tournament.

After all the adjourned and postponed games had been played off, Petrosian had 10½ points, Tal 10, and Spassky and Taimanov were on 9. In the next two rounds Petrosian collected 1½ points, and after 16 rounds had 12 points, Tal 11, Spassky 10½. Practically, only Tal and Spassky could still catch him, but in the 18th round Tal lost to Korchnoi, and at the end Spassky could do no more than cut down the lead to ½ a point. In the last round Petrosian only needed a draw to become champion, and needless to say, though he was faced by a difficult (for him) opponent – Korchnoi – he proved equal to the task.

Up to now this was Petrosian's greatest triumph, and it was achieved only nine months before the start of the Candidates' tournament. It is well known that the Soviet championship, with its strong and even composition, is the best criterion for judging the real strength of a player. Before playing Botvinnik for the world championship, Bronstein had twice been Soviet champion, and two years before his 1957 match Smyslov had shared first place. Not every Soviet champion becomes World Champion, but each future World Champion does his preliminary sparring in this tournament.

Petrosian's play in Tiflis showed a remarkable universality of style. He seemed to have found the ideal mean between sharpness, risk and caution. This harmony of style was noted by the World Champion. In the aforementioned article, 'On the style of a chessplayer', published just after the Tiflis championship, Botvinnik wrote:

'Petrosian's style, to a large degree, recalls the style of Capablanca, of Flohr, and perhaps even of Smyslov. What is the common stylistic denominator of these players? Chessplayers of this type generally seek to employ their main weapon – superiority of positional understanding; for that reason they aim for positions where elements of time and tactics do not have decisive importance ... chessplayers like Alekhine and Tal force "everything" to depend on dynamics, where the decisive factor is time and combinative vision. "Everything" has been placed in quotation marks deliberately, since a player of the second type could not be successful without having a good positional feel and technique, just as a player of the first type could not succeed without a strong command of tactics.'

Further on: 'Doubtless, if Tigran Petrosian were only a specialist in the field of positional struggles, and were not at the same time a cunning tactician, he would not have been able to score such a convincing victory in Tiflis!'

Reading these lines the 'cunning tactician' felt happy....

11 Petrosian–Trifunovic

USSR–Yugoslavia, Leningrad 1957
Ruy Lopez

1 P–K4

This game begs for inclusion, if only because of its first move. 1 P–K4 is as much a favourite move of mine as it is unusual for Petrosian. I imagine it is largely a matter of habit. At any rate, in this game Tigran hardly performs worse than the most devoted 'Spaniards'.

1 ...	P–K4
2 N–KB3	N–QB3
3 B–N5	P–QR3
4 B–R4	N–B3
5 0–0	B–K2
6 R–K1	P–QN4
7 B–N3	P–Q3
8 P–B3	0–0
9 P–KR3	N–QR4
10 B–B2	P–B4
11 P–Q4	Q–B2
12 QN–Q2	B–N2

A relatively new line in the Chigorin system. 12 ... N–B3, with central simplification, is the older move.

13 N–B1	BP×P
14 P×P	QR–B1
15 B–Q3	P–Q4
16 QP×P	N×P
17 N–N3	B–N5

This position was met for the first time in the game Bronstein–Panov (Moscow 1946), when White energetically demonstrated the weakness of Black's bishop attack. Afterwards Panov strengthened Black's play, suggesting a variation involving a pawn sacrifice: 17 ... P–B4 18 P×Pep B×P 19 B×N P×B 20 N×P B×N 21 R×B Q–B7. Practice has shown that this variation too is insufficient, though it is not an easy task for White to exploit his material advantage.

Dr Trifunovic, probably banking on Petrosian's inexperience in the Ruy Lopez, employs a discarded variation. As it turns out, an unsound calculation.

18 R–K2	P–B4
19 P×Pep	N×N
20 P×N	Q×P
21 B–B5!	

The game has become very tactical, and White cannot afford to lose time in the battle for the initiative.

21 ...   **P–Q5**

21 ... R–QB2 would have been more cautious. Now White gets a material advantage by force.

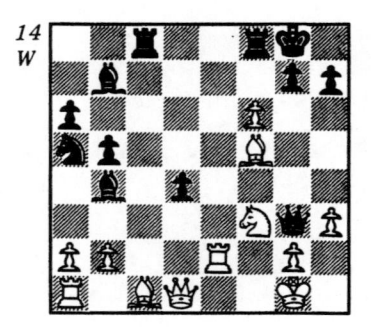

14 W

22 B–K6+!

22 B×R R×B! is less clear. 22 ... B×N? is inferior: 23 B–K6+ K–R1 24 Q–Q3! R×P 25 B–N4! or 24 ... B–Q3 25 Q×B Q–R7+ 26 K–B1 R×P 27 B–B5 P–N3 28 B–R6!, and White wins.

22 ...	K–R1
23 B×R	B×N
24 Q–Q3!	

Destroying Black's hopes. He has to resign himself to the loss of the exchange.

24...	R × B

24... R × P is answered by 25 B-N4!

25 Q × B	Q × Q
26 P × P+	K × P
27 P × Q	

The outcome of the middle-game skirmishes have brought no joy to Black. Resistance continues, but without the possibility of avoiding defeat.

27...	P-Q6
28 R-N2+	K-B3
29 B-N5+	K-B4
30 R-Q1	R-B7
31 P-KR4!	

White easily parries his opponent's threats. The remainder of the game does not require commentary. 31... P-Q7 32 B × P R × P 33 R-N5+ K-K3 34 R-K1+ K-B3 35 B × B R × B 36 R-K4 R-N7 37 R-KB4+ K-K3 38 R-K4+ K-B3 39 R-N2 R-N8+ 40 K-R2 N-B5 41 R2-K2 P-QR4 42 R-B4+ K-N3 43 R-KN2+ K-R4 44 R-B5+ K-R3 45 P-B4 N-K6 46 R-B6+ K-R4 47 R-N5+ K × P 48 R-KR6 mate.

12 **Petrosian–Matanovic**

Interzonal, Portoroz 1958

Nimzo-Indian

1 P-QB4	N-KB3
2 N-QB3	P-K3
3 N-B3	P-Q4
4 P-Q4	B-N5
5 P × P	P × P
6 B-N5	P-KR3
7 B-R4	P-B4
8 P-K3	0-0

Black could well have gone into the main variation 8... P-KN4 9 B-N3 N-K5 10 Q-B2 Q-R4, when White has to give up a pawn.

9 P × P	QN-Q2

9... N-B3 10 B-K2 B-K3 11 0-0 B × P was definitely more energetic. Now White takes over the initiative, whereas Black lags behind in development.

10 B-K2	Q-R4

Continuing along his unprofitable course. 10... N × P 11 0-0 B × N 12 P × B N4-K5 was still better, with chances of equality.

11 0-0!	B × N
12 P × B	Q × BP.4
13 R-B1	P-QN3

Another small inaccuracy. Fianchettoing his bishop on N2 weakens the KB4 square. 13... Q-K2 was comparatively better, following up with... N-QN3.

14 P-B4	B-N2
15 N-Q4	QR-B1

Black's position is already very difficult. He should here have continued 15... P × P 16 B × P (16 R × P Q-Q4) 16... Q-QR4. White would still have maintained a strong advantage, but its concrete realization would not have been easy.

16 B-B3

Directly threatening 17 N-B5 or 17 P × P.

16...	Q-N5

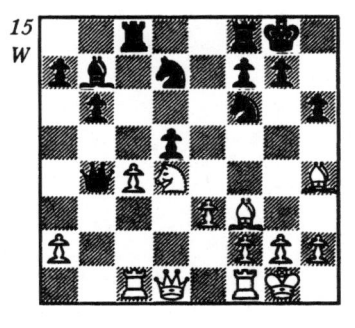

17 P-QR3!

A quiet, but extremely dangerous move. Black's choice is very restricted; he has to accept the pawn sacrifice, for on 17 ... Q-R4 comes 18 N-B5! and the threats of N-K7+ and N-Q6 force Black to part with his important QP.

17 ...	Q×RP
18 R-R1	Q-B4
19 R×P	

As a result of the operation begun on move 17 White's rook has reached the seventh rank. Black's position is hopeless. White finishes the game off with some very accurate strokes.

19 ...	B-R1
20 Q-R1!	K-R2
21 R-Q1!	

The threats are mounting. Both 22 P×P B×P 23 R×N N×R 24 N-B5 and 22 N-K2 Q×BP 23 B×N N×B 24 R-QB1 are 'on'.

21 ...	Q×P
22 B-K2!	

Wins immediately. On 22 ... Q-B4 or 22 ... Q-N5, 23 B-Q3+ K-R1 24 B-B5 is decisive. 22 N-B5, though attractive, would be answered by 22 ... Q-B7.

22 ...	Q-B6
23 R×B!	1-0

13 **Petrosian-Suetin**

25 USSR Ch, Riga 1958

King's Indian

1 P-Q4	N-KB3
2 P-QB4	P-KN3
3 N-QB3	B-N2
4 P-K4	P-Q3
5 B-K2	0-0
6 N-B3	P-K4
7 P-Q5	QN-Q2
8 B-N5	

As far as I can establish, this was the first game in which Petrosian tried out this system, one of his finest creations. The plan is extremely deep. In order to free himself from the pin, which hampers his counterplay on the king's wing Black sooner or later has to play ... P-KR3 and ... P-KN4. But this weakens the squares ... KB4 and ... KN5, thus giving White a foothold for neutralizing Black's play on that wing. At the same time White has very good opportunities for a pawn storm on the other wing.

8 ...	P-KR3
9 B-R4	P-KN4

It is difficult to suggest any other reaction on Black's part. Practice has shown that the alternative plan, connected with 9 ... P-QR3, ... Q-K1, ... N-R2, and ... P-KB4 is extremely dubious. As a rule, Black's counterplay in these cases loses its force.

10 B-N3	N-R4
11 0-0	P-QR4
12 N-K1	N-B5
13 N-B2	

White's plans are developing. He ignores the black knight's invasion on KB4 and continues to increase the grip on the KB5 and KN4 squares, simultaneously hemming in the bishop on KN7.

13 ...	N-B4

A small but significant error. Correct was 13 ... P-KB4 14 P×P N×B+ (14 ... N-B3 15 B-N4!) 15 Q×N N-B3 followed by ... B×P.

In that event Black could have fought more or less successfully for equal chances. Now White gradually takes over the game and achieves his positional aims.

14 N–K3　　　N×KP

Black did not like the look of the positional threat 15 B–N4. However, the exchange combination, initiated by him, does not alleviate his game much.

15 N×N　　　N×B+
16 Q×N　　　P–KB4
17 P–B3　　　P–B5

17... P×N 18 P×P R–B5 19 B×R KP×B 20 N–B5 is no better, since Black has no compensation for the exchange.

18 P–B5

16 B

White plays extremely energetically. Black should here have played 18... P–N3, when it would have been more difficult to open up the game on the Q-side.

18...　　　P×N

After 18... P×B there would come 19 RP×P, followed by P–KN4, when White's knights would be clearly better than Black's bishops.

19 Q×P　　　B–B4
20 QR–B1　　Q–Q2
21 R–B4　　　P×P

Otherwise White captures on Q6, and then invades with his queen on QN6.

22 Q×BP　　　P–N3
23 Q–K3　　　Q×P

A considerable tactical error, which helps White's invasion down the QB-file. 23... R–B2 offered more resistance, covering the QB2 square, and having an eye on counter-attacking against the pawn on Q5.

24 R×P　　　Q–Q5

24... Q×P 25 N–Q6 Q–Q4! 26 R–K1! would be very dangerous, after which 26... Q–Q5 or 26... Q×N are answered by 27 R×B+!

25 B–B2!　　　Q×Q

An unsuccessful decision. The best chance was probably to go into complications by playing 25... Q×P. Here 26 N×NP P×N 27 Q×KNP is answered by 27... P–K5!

26 B×Q　　　B–K3
27 P–QR3　　P–N4
28 B–Q2!

White is already well on the way to the win. He transfers his bishop to QB3, his rook to K1, intending the manoeuvre N–N3–R5.

28...　　　KR–Q1
29 B–B3　　　P–R5
30 R–K1　　　QR–B1
31 R–N7

Naturally, White wants to keep his rook on the seventh rank. If 31... R–N1 White replies 32 R×B+ K×R 33 B×P+ winning a pawn.

31...　　　R–Q4
32 R–N6　　　B–B2

There is no satisfactory defence. 32... B–Q2 is met by 33 R×RP!, 32... R–K1 by 33 N–Q6.

33 N–Q6　　　R–Q1
34 N–B5

Even more accurate than 34 N×P In any case, Black cannot escape material losses.

34...　　　K–R2
35 R–N7　　　R1–Q2
36 R×R　　　R×R

37 N×B   K×N
38 R×P   K–N3
39 R×QNP

In his path White has collected yet another pawn. The endgame is won for him, notwithstanding the bishops of opposite colours.

39 ...   R–Q8+
40 K–B2   R–QB8

In difficult positions it is not easy to give good advice. It would have been better to keep the rook at home. Now White's difficulties are lightened.

41 R–N6+   K–R2
42 P–KN4   R–KR8
43 P–R3   B–Q4

The pawn is untouchable. On 43 ... R×P comes 44 K–N2 R–R5 45 B–K1. The rest of the game needs no commentary. **44 R–Q6 R–Q8 45 R–Q7+ K–N1 46 K–K3 B–N6 47 R–KN7+ K–B1 48 R–N6 B–B7 49 R×RP R–Q6+ 50 K–K2 R–Q4 51 P–R4 P×P 52 R×P K–B2 53 P–B4 B–Q8+ 54 K–K3 K–N3 55 P–N5 B–R4 56 B–B6 R–QB4 57 K–Q4 R–N4 58 K–K4 B–Q8 59 P–B5+ K–B2 60 B–K5 B–B7+ 61 K–B4 1–0.**

14 **Petrosian–Yukhtman**

26 USSR Ch, Tiflis 1959

King's Indian

1 P–Q4	N–KB3
2 P–QB4	P–KN3
3 N–QB3	B–N2
4 P–K4	P–Q3
5 B–K2	0–0
6 N–B3	P–K4
7 P–Q5	N–R3
8 B–N5	P–R3
9 B–R4	P–KN4
10 B–N3	N–R4
11 N–Q2	N–B5
12 0–0	N–B4
13 B–N4	

At the time this game was played, the 'Petrosian system' had not been sufficiently well analyzed, and play here follows the 'last word of theory' for the given moment of time.

13 ...   P–QR4

A stereotyped reply. Correct was 13 ... P–QB3 followed by ... Q–N3 after which Black has very good counterplay. It is not accidental that in recent years Petrosian has preferred 11 P–KR4! to 11 N–Q2, aiming for sharp play on the king's wing.

Now White obtains a favourable strategical position. 13 ... B×B 14 Q×B P–KR4 15 Q–B5 P–R5 16 B×N KP×B 17 N–B3 would also have been to White's advantage.

14 P–B3!

An excellent reply. White not only frees his queen, but also strengthens the position of his bishop on KN4. 14 ... B×B 15 P×B is bad for Black, since ... P–KB4 is ruled out completely, and White soon takes over the key squares.

14 ...   N4–Q6?

A blow in the wind! 14 ... P–QB3 was correct here too, letting the queen into the game.

15 Q–B2

15 Q–N1 was rather more precise, threatening 16 B×N N×B 17 P–KN3 with definite advantage on the white squares. Now 16 B×N is not a threat, since Black can interpose 16 ... N–N5 before playing ... KP×B.

15 ...   P–QB3
16 K–R1   P–R4

17 B×B	R×B
18 P-QR3	

18 B×N N-N5 19 B×NP N×Q 20 B×Q N×R 21 B-K7 KR-K1 22 B×P N-B7 23 P-B5 is unclear. Here too the advantage is with White, but Petrosian did not want exchanges.

18...	P×P
19 BP×P	

White could also have kept the advantage playing 19 N×P N×N 20 KP×N N-B5 21 Q-B5, but he is playing in purely positional style.

19...	N-B4

Black had to play 19... Q-N3, meeting the positional threat 20 B×N N×B 21 P-KN3, which would be answered by 21... N-K7! followed by 22... N-Q5! In other variations Black would be threatening to bring his queen to Q5. Now Black is positionally doomed.

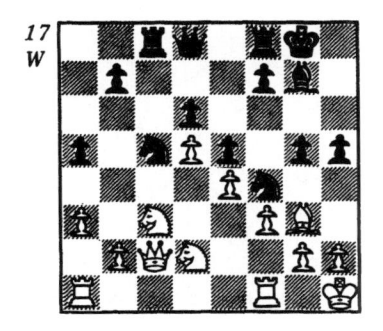

17
W

20 B-B2	P-N5

Black's nerves give way. Opening the KB-file only plays into White's hands.

21 P-KN3	N-N3
22 P×P	P×P
23 B-K3	P-N4?

Time-scramble fever. Obviously White's faultless strategy has used up all Black's time and energy!

24 N×P Q-N3 25 P-QR4 Q-R3 26 N-B4 P-B4 27 R×P R×R 28 P×R Q-N2 29 Q-N2 N-N6 30 N4×QP Q-Q2 31 R-KB1 1-0.

15 **Petrosian-Lutikov**

26 USSR Ch, Tiflis 1959

King's Indian

1 N-KB3	N-KB3
2 P-QB4	P-KN3
3 N-B3	B-N2
4 P-K4	0-0
5 P-Q4	P-Q3
6 B-K2	P-K4
7 P-Q5	N-R3
8 B-N5	P-R3
9 B-R4	P-B4
10 N-Q2	B-Q2

An inaccuracy. Better was 10... N-B2 immediately.

11 N-N5	B-K1

A forced retreat. Naturally, 11... B×N 12 P×B would have been positionally unjustified, since Black's light squares would then have been fatally weak. 11... Q-K2 also had its drawbacks: it would then have been difficult for Black to relieve himself of the pin along the KR4-Q8 diagonal.

12 P-QR3	Q-Q2

A clumsy manoeuvre. 12... N-B2 was preferable, even though after 13 N-QB3 P-R3 14 P-QN4! White would have a definite initiative on the queen's wing.

13 P-KN4

White refrains from castling, and intends a general pawn advance on both flanks. By playing 13 P-KN4 he appreciably limits Black's counterplay on the K-side, bringing KB5 under fire.

This game, by the way, is an example of Petrosian's great mastery of play with ... pawns. It appears that Petrosian has yet more deeply inspired the humble pawn – the 'soul of chess'.

13 ...　　　　N–B2

13 ... N–R2 was possible, intending ... B–B3–N4. Petrosian intended to reply 14 B–N3.

14 N–QB3　　P–R3
15 P–R4　　　Q–B1
16 P–R3!

Accurately played. White strengthens the important KN4 square, and in case of ... P–KB4 will exchange off on the KB5 square and place his bishop on KN4. At the same time he intends the manoeuvre N–Q1–K3.

16 ...　　　　R–N1
17 Q–B2　　　B–Q2
18 P–N3　　　P–N3
19 N–Q1　　　P–QN4
20 P–R5!

Another very instructive moment. White's pawns constitute a blanket, smothering the life out of Black's position. The black knight on QB2 has no future.

20 ...　　　　K–R1

At first sight it appears that 20 ... P×P　21 P×P　R–N5 was quite promising. But then, playing 22 N–N2 and 23 N–Q3 White would have altered the route taken by his knight, in the meantime threatening P–KB4! For the time being ... P–N5 is not advisable, since Black would then be forced to withstand a long siege on the K-side.

21 B–N3　　　N–N1
22 N–K3　　　N–K2

Black's position gets steadily worse. It might have been best to try 22 ... P×P　23 P×P　R–N5　24 Q–B3.

Here White would continue with N–B2 and retain a good position.

23 B–R4!

A necessary preliminary to opening up play on the queen's wing. If at once 23 P–N4!? then 23 ... P–B4 24 QNP×P P–B5 25 BP×QP P×N 26 P×P N.B2×P 27 KP×N N×P with very unclear play. So White first transfers his bishop to the KR4–Q8 diagonal, calculating that Black cannot afford to play ... P–N4 in reply, which would irretrievably weaken his king's wing.

23 ...　　　　Q–K1

23 ... N–N1 was slightly better, when White was intending to continue 24 O–O B–KB3 25 B×B N×B 26 P–B4! (26 P–N4! is also good) 26 ... Q–K1 27 P–B5 P–N4 28 P–N4.

24 P–N4!

18
B

A timely blow, asserting White's superiority. On 24 ... BP×P follows 25 P–B5! R–B1 26 P–B6 (26 B×N Q×B 27 P–B6 B–K1 gives Black defensive chances) 26 ... N×BP 27 P×N B×BP and White has a clear advantage.

Petrosian analyses an extremely unclear variation in 26 P×P (instead of 26 P–B6!) 26 ... N.B2×P 27 QP×N R×Q 28 P×R=Q+ Q×Q 29 N×R N–B5 or 27 ... N×N 28

P × R = Q+ Q × Q 29 Q × R Q × Q
30 P × N. All this demonstrates how deeply White calculated before playing 24 P–N4!

24 ...	N–B1
25 NP × P	QP × P
26 P × P	N × NP

If 26 ... B × QNP then 27 Q × P

| 27 B × N | R × B |

27 ... B × B was slightly stronger, striving for counterplay on the white squares. In that event, White has the pleasant choice between 28 Q × P and 28 N2–B4, with a clear advantage in each case.

| 28 0–0 | P–B4 |
| 29 P–B3 | R–B2 |

29 ... P–R4, trying to create some play on the K-side, would have set White more problems.

| 30 N2–B4 | R–N5 |

After this Black's task is practically hopeless. 30 ... P–B5 was more stubborn.

31 B–K1!

White wins a very important tempo for the transference of his bishop to the QR1–KR8 diagonal.

31 ...	R–N2
32 B–B3	P–R4
33 NP × BP	P × P
34 P × P	P–K5

A harmless attempt to muddy the waters.

35 K–R2

The most accurate. White clears the way to the KN-file for his rooks. The end is easily understood.

35 ... P × P 36 R × P B–Q5 37 Q–Q3 B–KB3 38 R–KN1 K–R2 39 B × B R × B 40 Q–B3 Q–B1 41 R–N6 R–KB2 42 R–N5 1–0

On 42 ... Q–R3 there can follow 43 R–N6 Q–B1 44 N–K5, winning quickly.

One of Petrosian's best achievements in the 26th Championship.

7 Tal comes and goes

The Tiflis championship finally convinced Petrosian that he had every right to try for the world championship. Preparation went forward on all fronts. Rona, his wife, relieved him of the everyday cares of life, and brought strict order to the household. The only thing that remained inviolate – that was his passion for watching sport, in particular football. The Moscow 'Spartak' team had always been his pride and sorrow. Later, ice hockey was to join football. Tigran never considered time spent in the stands as wasted, especially if his favourite team won. . . .

His style required a certain degree of modernization. As we know, Petrosian had always been a staunch supporter of Capablanca and Nimzowitsch, believed in the unshakeability of certain chess principles, and tried to carry them out in practice. Particularly, none of the World Champions after Capablanca – Alekhine, Euwe, Botvinnik, and Smyslov – notwithstanding the individual stylistic differences, had placed in doubt the fundamental laws of positional play, though they 'constructed' their game on different lines. The fifties had been almost totally dominated by the classic positional styles of Botvinnik and Smyslov. It was especially in these years that Petrosian's style had been formed. Perhaps it was, sensing 'his own', that Botvinnik came to Petrosian's defence, even when the latter was earning stern rebukes from the chess press. Once again quoting from Botvinnik's article of 1959 in *Ogonyok*:

'Four years ago, referring to the current Soviet championship, the reporter was extremely courteous to all the participants, excepting one, Tigran Petrosian. The young grandmaster was reproached for superfluous draws, even, if my memory serves me right, of being in danger of creative malformation. . . .

'In all fairness, it should be remarked that one of the contestants spoke out in defence of his modestly silent colleague. In the opinion of this – clearly to all – chess fighter, it was incorrect to so categorically criticize a developing chess-player. And indeed, surely it is the right of every grandmaster to independently determine his chess style, if that style is capable of bringing him success? One player may like courageous attacks, another may strive to stun the opponent by a dazzling sacrifice, a third, by setting cunning traps, may be able to catch his opponent in the time scramble; and there are players who, not attracted by chance factors, try to penetrate to the essence of a situation, play "according to position", and if the position demands a peaceful outcome, do not try to avoid it.

'This last style is not a popular one. It seems too circumspect, cautious, even cowardly. Whenever a lively struggle is in progress, you will always find someone there to praise it to the skies! Perhaps I am in error, but I feel that a modest, careful, but nonetheless militant style has just as much right to existence as a more striking style, based on combinative vision and tactical calculation.

'The practical value of Petrosian's style lies in this, that as he acquires more experience he becomes all the more dangerous to his rivals, and that his superiority of positional understanding is a continually acting, not an accidental factor. . . .

'By the way, which is better, two draws or one win? From the creative point of view, the difference is not great; what is important is how the game is played. . . . If the draw is colourless, if the player sidesteps (without real basis) a struggle, then this is bad, and bad especially for the player himself! If these draws were the result of a delicate, albeit short struggle, then in my opinion from the creative aspect these games are preferable to a win and a loss, if the "fighting" results were achieved through taking advantage of some or other obvious error. . . .'

In this heartfelt monologue a certain contradictoriness strikes the eye. Emphasizing that if a chess-player avoids face-to-face combat this 'is of course bad', Botvinnik at the same time comes out in defence of Petrosian '1955 model', when the latter quite frequently refrained from giving battle, and 'created,' not, it is true, without the help of his partners, quite a number of colourless draws. However, this is a fully comprehensible result of a polemical outburst. In the present context, the important thing is that Petrosian belonged to the 'positional' school of players.

At first sight there seems little remarkable in this. People always have and always will play positionally, and if one side consistently breaks the positional laws of the game, he will undoubtedly, if his opponent plays the right moves, suffer defeat. In fact it is not so simple. The great Emanuel Lasker, who held the world championship for more than a quarter of a century, quite often played not according to position, but according 'to the partner'. In other words, seeing the chess struggle as a battle between individuals, a clash of differing characters, even world outlooks, Lasker often chose what was objectively not the strongest, but subjectively the most likely continuation. Here the important factor for him was not so much the position, as the character of the player seated before him.

Many masters to a greater or lesser degree make use of psychological ploys (Botvinnik is one such player), but among the players of the past only Lasker, with his philosophical bent, made continuous recourse to psychological moments in his play, made it in fact, his trade-mark. Extremely individualistic, he founded no school, nor did he have a successor.

Eventually, talented chess-players began to unearth this style again. Here is what L. Abramov wrote during the 24th Soviet championship:

'Many very highly qualified chess masters concur in my impression of Korchnoi's play, and declare that they simply do not understand it. Sometimes his play is extremely deep and far-sighted. But the question arises, has not Korchnoi's striving to depart from the laws of positional play become an end in itself? Doesn't he sometimes ignore possibilities of resolving simply the problems of the chessboard?

'Korchnoi himself must answer this question, but it is very clear that the question requires answering, by reason of the marked difference between the results and the potentialities of this very talented and single-minded chess-player.'

Korchnoi's answer is now well-known: 'not an iota will I change myself, my creative individuality, my style'. Korchnoi managed to become Soviet champion quite a few times, and three times qualified for the Candidates' tournament. Explaining his reasons for breaking the rules, Korchnoi wrote:

'Emanuel Lasker in his time remarked that with equality of strength games rarely have content, and often end in draws. The chess-player who does not like draws (and I belong to this number) must somehow destroy this equilibrium. Either he sacrifices, and thanks to this seizes the initiative, or he allows his opponent to attack, creating a few weaknesses, which he hopes to exploit later, by way of compensation.'

Korchnoi's play, with which Petrosian had first become acquainted in the all-union youth tournament of 1946, caused him considerable cogitation. After all, there must be something in it if Korchnoi nonetheless had successes. But it occasioned no more than that – Petrosian had no intention of following Korchnoi, or altering his chess principles. It required yet another player to unsettle Petrosian's faith in the infallibility of his convictions, to cause him to make a definite stylistic alteration. There was a wind of change coursing through the cathedral of chess art, penetrating its silent halls. This wind, entering with an almighty crash and a disrespectful slamming of doors, was the play of Tal. From the years 1957–60 he lived a fantastic career; twice champion of the Soviet Union, best result at the 13th Olympiad, Munich 1958, with $13\frac{1}{2}$ out of 15, winner of the Interzonal, of the Candidates' tournament, victor at the Zurich international tournament, and finally, World Champion.

Here there could be no talk of 'accidents', and yet Tal often played not 'according to position'.

It must be realized, first of all, that Tal did not become a chess rule-breaker from the beginning. In the 24th championship, when Tal contrived his grandmasterly 'massacre' he was comparatively rarely at odds with the position. But trying once or twice to crash the barriers, and seeing how quickly his opponents lost their bearings in the changed circumstances, he began to make the destruction of the equilibrium his creative method. In this approach to the game, Tal came very close to Korchnoi (though it is true that these two fine players also have many antagonistic features). Here is how Tal explained why he sometimes consciously destroyed the balance of the position, if the logic of the struggle demanded such a course:

'If both sides do not burn with the fierce desire to win at all costs, they play correctly (in the best, and perhaps very worst meaning of the word). The possibility of error is reduced to a minimum, and the partners play very easily; everything goes very smoothly, very correctly, and after eighteen or nineteen moves, this "genuine faultless game" ends to the mutual satisfaction of both players.

'What is to be done, when you have to win? Try to give mate? But the opponent foresees the attack while it is still in the cradle, and takes the necessary precautions. Exploit positional weaknesses? The opponent has no intention of creating them! Precisely for this reason, in many games today one of the players, and sometimes both, deliberately depart from the established canons of play, and enter a "dark forest" of unknown chess variations, where there is room only for one. Far too many nowadays know not only the chess multiplication tables, but also chess logarithms, so to be successful you often have to prove that two and two make – five. . . .'

Two and two make five? This was not a formula that Petrosian would have concocted. Once, towards the end of the Botvinnik–Tal match, when it was clear that the colossus had fallen, I asked Petrosian if he didn't think that the laws of chess needed some revision, now that Tal was champion?

'No' he said, 'No. Because sooner or later a chess-player of the style of Capablanca will become World Champion, who will bring order to chess.'

Petrosian's belief that two and two would always make four was supported by the knowledge that, if he wished to avoid the sameness of 'correct' play, he had no need to destroy the balance of the position, or take any extraordinary measures. He had his own personal weapon, such as belonged to no-one else, not even Botvinnik himself. This weapon was the Petrosianic art of manoeuvring.

In the chess dictionary, the word 'manoeuvring' is described as 'a series of movements by various pieces of a more or less extended character, but not always having a clear, concrete aim'. In this last mentioned quality is concealed the complexity, and also the strength of manoeuvring.

Quite probably every chess-player prefers clear positions to unclear. Unclear positions somehow ask to be clarified. All the same Petrosian liked unclear positions. In such situations his opponent felt uncomfortable, uncertain as to where the next diversion was to come from. Petrosian sensed danger in advance, and had already taken measures against it. The players were as in a deep fog, but one saw through the fog, the other no further than his hand.

Here was an extremely dangerous weapon. Petrosian would form a striking force behind his lines, disband them, gather them together in one area of the board, then another, and when the opponent's vigilance weakened, or simply he lost the ability to evaluate the position, he would suddenly begin an unexpected advance. The manoeuvring was over, the position had been clarified. . . .

A great deal has already been written about Petrosian's manoeuvring ability. It is a subject which touches on the indefinable, such as questions of positional understanding, of intuition, and the most inexplicable – talent. For if Tal's talent was displayed in the creation of bewildering complications, in driving attacks with piece sacrifices, Petrosian's gifts lay in the quiet dance of the pieces, imbued with inner energy and hidden dynamism.

At the same time Petrosian could never help but feel exhilaration as he viewed another Tal kamikaze attack, or a cliff-hanging escapade by Korchnoi; the same exhilaration which he felt in the stadium, when the Moscow 'Spartak' team came through to score a goal. Reserve is not a quality called upon in a spectator.

Once Lasker wrote of Capablanca: 'The depth of his play, is the depth of a mathematician, not of a poet. . . .'

Petrosian, who had frequently been compared with Capablanca, considered that there was less in common between them than was generally thought. Probably this was because at heart he considered himself more of a poet than a mathematician. '. . . in thought and aim deep, secretive, "adventurous" middle-play. . .' as such he had been appraised by one German commentator.

An additional factor that was impelling Petrosian to assume one pole of the contemporary, intuitive or psychological style (a precise nomenclature evades us) was that for all the 'adventurism', 'incorrectness' of his play, Tal nonetheless swept aside all obstacles in his path. In the final count, one does not argue with success!

Petrosian travelled to the Candidates' tournament in Yugoslavia with every intention of fighting for first place. But he was still out of step. Tal and Keres set such a tremendous pace that he could do little more than spectate, less than exhilarated, and draw conclusions.

At the start of the tournament, however, Petrosian played very successfully, and fully achieved his aims; out of the first four games he scored $3\frac{1}{2}$: wins against Olafsson, Fischer and Keres, and a draw with

Smyslov. In a 'normal' Candidates' tournament, this would mark the beginning of a long spell in the lead, but here it was just a modest episode in the struggle. For the moment Fischer was a point behind, and Tal, Keres and Smyslov were on 2. In the fifth round he made a short draw in 22 moves with Tal, drew a complicated struggle with Benko in the sixth, and in the seventh lost to Gligoric. Tal and Keres had already caught him up! And the most remarkable thing was that both his rivals had only drawn one game each – four wins and two losses. A chess wind was raging through Bled!

It was precisely the uncompromising vigour of his rivals which troubled Petrosian. He realized that one of the two might not withstand the tension, but he could not suppose that this might happen to both. He began to reckon his chances of success as extremely small; and to act on the off-chance of success had never been a particular trait of Petrosian. He was prepared to re-align his style to a certain degree, but not to the extent that he could no longer recognize himself therein. In the second cycle (the tournament comprised eight grandmasters – Smyslov, Tal, Keres, Petrosian, the Yugoslav Gligoric, the Americans Fischer and Benko, and Olafsson from Iceland. The players met each other 4 times, making 28 rounds in all) Petrosian collected 4 points (wins against Benko and Fischer, loss to Olafsson) and had, for a tournament of this calibre, a very good score, $8\frac{1}{2}$ out of 14. But here it was only sufficient for third place, behind Keres, 10, and Tal, $9\frac{1}{2}$ in the second cycle Keres had scored $5\frac{1}{2}$, Tal 5!

In the third cycle Tal broke Keres' record – he acquired no less than 6 points (drawing only two games, with Petrosian and Smyslov). Meanwhile Keres had come unstuck; in round 15 he put a bishop en prise to Fischer. But for Petrosian this was neither hot nor cold. He was irreparably distant from both Tal and Keres. The final result was: Tal 20, Keres $18\frac{1}{2}$, Petrosian $15\frac{1}{2}$, Smyslov 15, Gligoric and Fischer $12\frac{1}{2}$, Olafsson 10 and Benko 8.

Third place could hardly be reckoned a failure; at Amsterdam he had been 3rd-7th, at Zurich fifth. All the same, there was a circumstance which spoke against the worth of his achievement; in the first Candidates' he had been three points behind, in the second, two points. Here the difference was $4\frac{1}{2}$ points!

Petrosian returned from Yugoslavia, his head filled with Tal's play. The new challenger had given him much to think about. For instance, in two games with Smyslov, Tal beyond all shadow of doubt incorrectly sacrificed pieces. One of these games Tal won, the other ended in a draw. $1\frac{1}{2}$ points from two lost games! By sacrificing these pieces Tal created, admittedly at great risk to himself, positions where everything was 'hanging', where threats blossomed now on this part of the board, now that; positions which Smyslov did not enjoy playing in. It was a case of an irresistible force against an immovable object, and the immovable object had not learnt to step lightly! Nor did Tal wait for these positions to arise, he created them at the first opportunity. It was as if he were saying, 'We cannot expect kind gifts from Mother Chess – we must seize them ourselves!'

Previously Petrosian had acted otherwise. In the days when he was playing under the motto 'Safety First!', he would often deliberately avoid any sharpening of the conflict, and choose a less promising but more reliable line. Afterwards he began to play 'according to position', and went into complications when this was necessary. Now it appeared this was also too little! Now he had to create these positions himself, with all the manifold risks involved.

On occasion Petrosian had acted in this manner; for example, his choice of opening against Tal in the championship at Riga. But at that time this was the exception. In Tiflis he began more and more to play according to this style. Stahlberg commented accurately on the Bled Candidates' tournament:

'Petrosian has strong nerves, and makes mistakes very rarely. It is far more difficult to win against him than against the other contestants. Besides this, the Soviet champion is a very good tactician, and combines well, if the opportunity presents itself. . . .' Henceforth Petrosian would not wait for the opportunity to present itself. . . .

In the next two Soviet championships, the 27th, which took place in Leningrad, and the 28th held in Moscow, Petrosian was fighting for first place from the very beginning to the end of the tournaments. He developed the ability to risk in consecutive games, not just the odd one. Here is how he ended the Leningrad championship: loss, win, loss again, win, draw, win! In order to create the type of positions he wanted, he began to make appreciable changes in his opening repertoire. In his last round game against Krogius at Leningrad, he chose a variation which saddled him with an isolated pawn from the start, but for which he received no real compensation. In the further course of the game he repeatedly avoided simplification, confused his opponent and finally worked up an irresistible king side attack. There had been a time when Petrosian would have considered the game over as soon as an isolated pawn appeared on the board.

In the Moscow final, playing against Polugaevsky, Petrosian removed his knight to edge of the board at the beginning of the game, then cut off its avenue of re-entry with a pawn move. Here he calculated that his attacking possibilities were enhanced by the manoeuvre, notwithstanding the obvious positional defects.

In the 27th championship Petrosian led from the start, but in the end had to be satisfied with sharing 2nd-3rd places with Geller, half a point behind Korchnoi. In the 28th he was sharing the lead in the 5th, 10th, 11th and 12th rounds, and from the thirteenth to the end maintained sole leadership. In this tournament he managed (together with Korchnoi) to win the greatest number of games – 9. The temper of his play can be understood from the following statistics: he scored 7 points against the top 9 players, and 6½ out of 9 against the grandmasters. He overcame his single defeat of the tournament, to Stein, by scoring 4½ out of his next five games! The triumph was complete, both sporting and creative.

'The prediction, that Petrosian would be among the victors, was an easy one to make.' – wrote M. Yudovich at the end of the tournament 'He has great virtuosity in technical play, evaluates positions very deeply, calculates accurately. Petrosian has a sharpened ability to sense danger. . . . Naturally, it is very hard to beat a player of such class. His defeats in the last few years can be counted on the fingers of one hand.

'But in order to achieve great sporting success, it is not enough to avoid defeat, you have to be able to win . . . for the highest achievements, it is necessary to play with added verve particularly against your main rivals. It is very gratifying to see that in the last few years Petrosian has chosen the difficult path of a real chess fighter. It is characteristic that in this tournament he inflicted the most crushing defeats on his two most dangerous rivals – Korchnoi and Smyslov. . . .'

Here is how the rivals themselves commented on his play.

Korchnoi: 'Before the tournament began, I considered the only "certain" candidate for a place in the interzonal was Petrosian. Now I am satisfied that I was not in error.'

Geller: 'Petrosian's first place was fully deserved. In my opinion, he is now one of the strongest players in the world.'

The chess 'wind' of struggle now beckoned to a lonely island in the Caribbean sea – Curacao. Here the next Candidates' was to take place. But the winds are always changing, and the tournament could not be like its predecessor. This time the battle was not for points, but for half points, and it was not decisive who won, but who lost. Tal had landed up in hospital, and shortly before the beginning of the tournament underwent a difficult operation.

First, however, a stopover had to be made in Stockholm, for the Interzonal tournament. In this competition, alongside many experienced grandmasters, many players of very ordinary strength took part. In such circumstances, Petrosian's tried tactics for selection tournaments were in order, especially since he flew to Stockholm with angina. Playing quietly, he was undefeated and shared 2nd-3rd places with Geller, 2½ points behind Fischer.

Somewhere at the bottom of his heart, he was glad that another player had taken first place; as never before in his life, Tigran Petrosian was prepared to fight for victory in the Candidates', and he did not wish to reveal his intentions prematurely.

16 Keres–Petrosian

Candidates', Bled 1959

Sicilian

1 P–K4	P–QB4
2 N–KB3	N–QB3
3 P–Q4	P×P
4 N×P	P–KN3
5 P–QB4	B–N2
6 B–K3	N–B3
7 N–QB3	N–KN5
8 Q×N	N×N
9 Q–Q1	N–K3

Besides this move, 9 ... N–B3 and 9 ... P–K4 are also played. So far practice has failed to establish which of these continuations is the stronger. The selecting of a plan in this position is, first and foremost, a matter of taste.

10 Q–Q2	P–Q3
11 B–K2	B–Q2
12 0–0	0–0
13 QR–B1	B–QB3
14 KR–Q1	N–B4

14 ... B×N 15 Q×B B×P 16 P–B5 is too dangerous. White has a strong initiative for the pawn.

15 P–B3	P–QR4
16 P–QN3	Q–N3

The contestants are playing their men in a manner typical of closed positions. A complex manoeuvring battle is in prospect. Here 16 ... P–N3 might have been more exact. Now White develops some activity, at the same time forestalling the advance ... P–R5.

17 N–N5!	KR–B1
18 B–B1	Q–Q1
19 Q–KB2	Q–K1

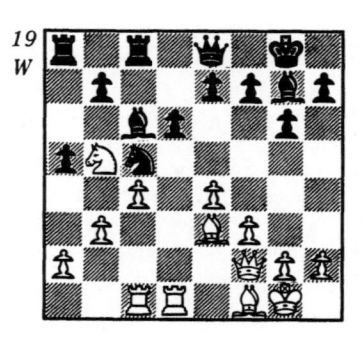

19
W

19 ... B–Q2 or 19 ... P–N3 was more circumspect, for White could here have gone in for an endgame where he has two pawns for the exchange: 20 B×N P×B 21 Q×P B–N7 (21 ... B×P 22 N–B7 B–B4 23 Q–N6) 22 N–R7! P–N3 (22 ... B×R 23 N×R) 23 Q×NP R.B1–N1 24 Q×B B×R 25 R×B R×N 26 Q×Q+ R×Q. At first sight it appears that White has an advantageous position, but deeper investigation reveals that it is by no means easy to get the pawns moving. For example: 27 P–B5 R–N1! 28 P–B6 K–B1, and Black is ready to surround the far advanced white pawn.

20 N–B3	P–N3
21 R–B2	Q–B1
22 Q–Q2	B–Q2
23 N–Q5	QR–N1
24 B–N5	R–K1
25 R–K1	R–N2
26 Q–B2	B–QB3
27 Q–R4	P–B3
28 B–K3	P–K3
29 N–B3	R–Q2
30 B–Q4	P–B4

The play finally enlivens. For the time being White retains his space advantage, but Black has noticeably developed his game on the K-side. Strange as it may appear, White, without making any obvious error, finds himself in the role of the defender.

A characteristic of Petrosian's play is his rare ability, move by move, to outplay even the most experienced opponent.

31 P×P	NP×P
32 R–Q2	B×B+
33 R×B	R–KN2
34 K–R1	

Defending against 34... B×P.

34...	R–N3
35 R–Q2	R–Q1

35... Q–N2 was worth considering, with the double threat 36... Q×N and 36... B×P. Here 36 N–N5 B×P 37 N×P R–KB1 is in Black's favour.

36 R.K1–Q1	R–Q2
37 Q–B2	Q–Q1
38 Q–K3	P–K4
39 P–B4	P–K5

Petrosian has conducted the manoeuvring stage of the game with great artistry and gradually assumed the initiative. But now in time-trouble he commits a definite mistake. By playing 39...Q–R5! he could have developed powerful threats against White's king, in connection with the manoeuvre ... R–R3.

Now Black has to think of defence once more.

40 N–K2	R2–KN2
41 N–Q4	B–Q2
42 P–QR3	

White seems to have 'programmed' himself to conduct the game at a slow pace. 42 N–N5 B×N 43 P×B was rather more energetic.

42...   **Q–R1!**

Starting from this point, Black leads a brilliant attack against the white king.

43 K–N1	P–R4
44 R–N1	

44 P–QN4, though a natural move, is refuted by 44... P×P 45 P×P N–Q6! 46 B×N P×B 47 N–B3 Q–K5! 48 Q×Q P×Q 49 N–N5 B–B4.

44...	P–KR5
45 R1–N2	R–N5
46 R–KB2	Q–Q1!

Preparing the combination. White is hard pressed to find a reasonable defence.

47 P–N4

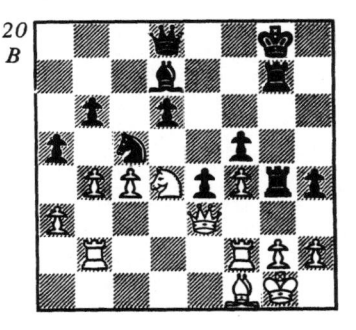

20
B

47...   **R–N6!!**

A brilliant sacrifice, which was published in the chess magazines throughout the world. White can hardly refuse the offer. On 48 Q–K2, 48 Q–K1 or 48 Q–B1 comes 48... N–Q6! 49 B×N R×B and White stands badly.

48 P×R	KRP×P
49 R.B2–Q2	

Black wins forcibly after 49 P×N Q–R5 50 B–Q3 Q–R7+ 51 K–B1 Q–R8+ 52 K–K2 P×R 53 R–N1 P×B+ 54 Q×QP Q×P 55 R–KB1 NP×P 56 N–B2 B–B3.

49...	Q–R5
50 B–K2	R–R2
51 K–B1?	

This allows Black an immediate win. 51 B–R5 R×B 52 K–B1 was best, though after 52 ... P×P 53 P×P N–Q6 54 R×N (nothing better) 54 ... Q–R8+ 55 Q–N1 P×R 56 R–Q2 R–R5 57 R×P R×P+ 58 N–B3 Q×Q+ 59 K×Q R×P 60 K–B1 B–N4! 61 K–K1 R–B8+ 62 K–Q2 B×R 63 K×R B–B8 64 N–R4 P–B5! Black has every chance of victory.

51 ...   Q×P+!!
0–1

The final blow is very striking.

17 Petrosian–Gligoric

Candidates', Belgrade 1959

King's Indian

1 P–Q4	N–KB3
2 P–QB4	P–KN3
3 N–QB3	B–N2
4 P–K4	P–Q3
5 N–B3	0–0
6 B–K2	P–K4
7 P–Q5	QN–Q2
8 B–N5	P–KR3
9 B–R4	P–R3
10 N–Q2	Q–K1
11 0–0	N–R2
12 P–QN4	N–N4
13 R–B1	P–KB4

Black chooses a very double-edged plan of counterplay on the K-side. Practice has shown that here White's chances are better, though the play takes on a very complicated appearance.

14 P–B3	Q–K2
15 K–R1	N–B3
16 P–B5	N–R4
17 P–B6!	

An excellent strategical idea. It is more energetic than 17 BP×P P×QP, as was played in the game Olafsson–Gligoric from the same tournament.

17 ...   P–N3

Accepting a blocked-in queen's bishop. There was little choice in the matter, since after 17 ... NP×P 18 QP×P White obtains the square Q5, and allowing an exchange on ... QN2 would considerably weaken Black's Q-side.

18 P×P	P×P
19 P–N3	B–B3
20 P–B4	

Questionable. 20 P–R4 was probably stronger, bringing the QN5 square under control. In that case 20 ... P–B5 would be answered by 21 P–N4! N–N2, when White has the K4 square, and the bishop on Black's QB1 is still inactive.

20 ...   N–N2
21 N–B4

21 P–R4 was again worth considering. Black's threats on the K-side are in no way dangerous. He is, after all, playing without the rook on QR1.

21 ...	P×P
22 P×P	P–N4
23 N–Q2	N–K5
24 B×B	R×B
25 B–B3	P–QR4!

Black defends with gusto. Sacrificing a pawn, he finally activates his queen's rook.

26 P–QR3	P×P
27 P×P	R–N3!

With an unpleasant threat: 28 .. Q–R5!

28 N2×N	P×N
29 B×P	B–B4
30 B×B	N×B
31 Q–R5	

White in turn plays with maximum energy. With this manoeuvre he counters Black's growing K-side initiative.

31 ... R-B3
32 R-KN1+ K-R1

32 ... K-R2 33 R.B1-K1 Q-B2 34 N-K4! would have brought material losses. (if 34 ... Q×P 35 Q-B3!).

33 R.B1-K1 Q-B2
34 Q×Q R×Q
35 R-K4

35 N×P R-QN1! was inferior, since White has to defend the QNP.

35 ... K-R2

Accurate defence. After 35 ... R-QN1 36 R1-K1 K-R2 37 R-K8 R-N3 38 R-Q8 White has winning chances in view of the threat 39 R-Q7! So Black strengthens his king's position.

36 N×P R-R7
37 N-Q4 N×N
38 R×N R-K2

Black is two pawns to the bad, but his rooks have managed to penetrate to the seventh rank, and this gives him real chances of a draw.

39 P-B5 R2-K7
40 R-R4 R-KB7
41 P-N5

White has only one winning chance left – to deflect one of the rooks from the second rank by a pawn sacrifice.

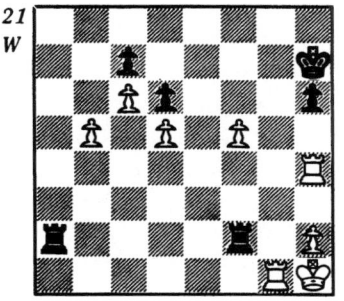

21
W

41 ... R.R7-N7

The move after the time control – and Black throws the game away. It seems natural to put the rook in the rear of the advancing pawn, but this leads to immediate defeat. On the other hand, 41 ... R.R7-B7! would have saved the game. For example: 42 P-B6 R×KBP 43 R4-KN4 R-B2. The game continued: **42 P-N6! R×NP 43 R4-KN4 R-N1 44 R-N7+K-R1 45 R7-N6 1-0**

18 **Petrosian-Larsen**

Copenhagen 1960

Old Indian

1 P-Q4	N-KB3
2 P-QB4	P-Q3
3 N-KB3	B-N5
4 N-B3	QN-Q2
5 P-K4	P-K4
6 B-K2	B-K2
7 0-0	0-0
8 B-K3	

A comparatively little studied variation of the Old Indian defence. Black appears to have solved the problem of the development of his queen's bishop. But modern opening theory long ago discarded 'narrow', formalistic solutions of Black's opening problems. The important thing is to have a concrete plan of counter-attack. And from this point of view Black's prospects are far from rosy. He finds difficulty in obtaining counterplay in the centre, and this is the root cause of his later problems.

8 ... B-R4

8 ... P-B3 was more logical, instead of wasting time on pretentious manoeuvres.

9 N-Q2 B×B

9 ... B-N3 was uninviting. White

would then have to choose between 10 P-Q5 and 10 P-B3 maintaining a clear advantage in the centre.

10 Q×B   P×P

Black does not fancy the positional threat 11 P-Q5, which gives a position in White's favour due to the absence of his king's bishop.

11 B×P   R-K1
12 P-B4   B-B1
13 QR-Q1

Not simply a developing move, but a necessary centralizing preliminary to the coming K-side advance.

13 ...   P-QR3

The simplifying combination 13 ... N×P 14 N2×N P-KB4 15 Q-B3 is in White's favour.

14 Q-B3   P-B3

Move by move Black's position worsens, which is a consequence of his unsuccessful opening strategy. By itself the absence of weaknesses does not guarantee safety to the defending side!

15 P-KN4

Energetic and fully correct. With a firm centre and absence of any Black counter-play, White's K-side attack plays itself.

15 ...   N-B4
16 B×N.5   P×B
17 P-K5!   N-Q2

17 ... Q-Q5+? 18 K-R1 N-Q2 19 N2-K4 brings no relief.

18 N2-K4   Q-B2
19 R-Q3   N-N3
20 P-N3   QR-Q1
21 R1-Q1   B-K2

If Black tries to simplify by 21 ... R×R 22 Q×R B-K2 23 N-Q6 B×N 24 Q×B Q×Q 25 R×Q the endgame is still in White's favour.

22 P-N5!

Beginning the decisive onslaught against the black king.

22 ...   N-B1
23 Q-R5   R×R
24 R×R   R-Q1

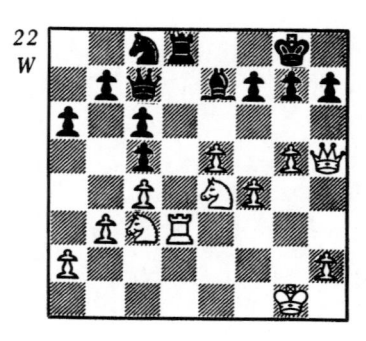

22 W

25 N-B6+

A beautiful combinative stroke. Black has no satisfactory defence.

25 ...   P×N

After 25 ... B×N 26 NP×B R×R 27 Q-N5 K-B1 28 P×P+ K-N1 29 N-K4! Black is defenceless.

26 R-R3   K-B1
27 Q×RP   K-K1
28 P-N6!

The most energetic. If now 28 ... P×NP 29 P-K6 B-B1 30 Q×P+ K-K2 31 Q-B7+ gives mate.

28 ...   B-B1
29 P-N7   B×P
30 Q×B   Q-K2
31 N-K4   R-Q8+
32 K-B2   P-B4

Black could have resigned here, but continues to resist through inertia.

33 N-B6+   K-Q1
34 R-R8+   1-0

On 34 ... K-B2, 35 R-K8 is simplest.

19 Bronstein–Petrosian
27 USSR Ch, Leningrad 1960

Caro-Kann

1 P–K4	P–QB3
2 N–K2	P–Q4
3 P–K5	P–QB4

A correct rejoinder to the slightly pretentious opening system chosen by White. Black relinquishes his Caro-Kann set-up, and goes into a French type formation.

| 4 P–Q4 | N–QB3 |
| 5 P–QB3 | P–K3 |

5 . . . B–B4 might have been played, but Black wanted a 'true French' game.

6 N–Q2	KN–K2
7 N–B3	P × P
8 N2 × P?	

Surely 8 P × P was more natural, establishing a firm central structure. Now Black puts the . . . K4 square under attack and takes the initiative

8 . . .	N–N3
9 N × N	P × N
10 B–Q3	Q–B2
11 Q–K2	P–B3!

Courageous and timely. Black does not fear losing castling rights, since White has no advantage in development, nor central footholds. At the same time Black's pawn phalanx threatens to roll into action.

12 P × P	P × P
13 N–Q4	K–B2
14 P–KB4	P–QB4

Much stronger than taking the 'bait' offered on KB5. If now 15 P–B5 P × N 16 P × N+ RP × P and Black has a clear advantage in view of the threat 17 . . . R × P. If 15 N–B3 P–B5 16 B–B2 N × P, and on 15 N–B2, 15 . . . P–B5 forces the exchange 16 B × N+ P × B. The lesser evil was perhaps 15 N–N5 followed by P–B4. White, however, is diverted into tactical adventures.

15 Q–R5

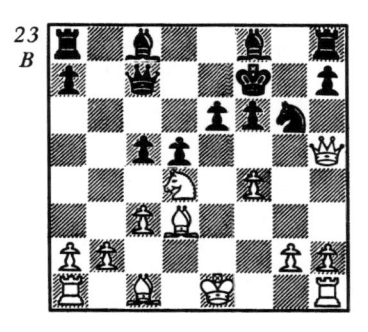

23 B

| 15 . . . | P × N! |

A decisive counteraction. White's attack vanishes without a trace, and his material advantage has only formal character.

| 16 B × N+ | P × B |
| 17 Q × R | P × P |

A 'thematic' position has been reached, featuring an attack on a defenceless king with the queen shut out of play.

| 18 Q–R7+ | B–KN2 |
| 19 B–K3 | |

If 19 P–B5 simplest is 19 . . . Q–K4+ followed by 20 . . . BP × P or 20 . . . Q × BP+, depending on which way the white king goes.

19 . . .	P × P
20 R–Q1	B–QR3
21 P–B5	

Despair.

21 . . .	KP × P
22 Q–R3	Q–B7!
23 Q–B3	B–B5
0–1	

20 Petrosian–Smyslov

28 USSR Ch, Moscow 1961

Queen's Indian

1 P–QB4	N–KB3
2 N–QB3	P–K3
3 N–B3	P–QN3
4 P–Q4	B–N2
5 P–QR3	

One of Petrosian's favourite opening plans. White endeavours to limit the black king's bishop, at the same time avoiding well-trodden paths. Objectively, too, the continuation 5 P–QR3 is quite playable.

5 ...	P–Q4
6 P×P	N×P

6 ... P×P is preferable here.

7 P–K3	B–K2
8 B–N5+	P–QB3
9 B–Q3	P–QB4
10 N×N	Q×N

This and Black's next move show that he is unaware of possible danger. Petrosian recommended the passive, but solid 10 ... P×N.

| 11 P×P | Q×P |

Here he should have played 11 ... B×P or even 11 ... P×P. Now the black queen comes under fire from White's pieces. Black apparently is playing according to general considerations, relying on the symmetrical pawn structure.

12 B–Q2	N–B3
13 R–QB1	Q–Q3
14 Q–B2	R–QB1
15 0–0	

How often such developing moves are made almost automatically! And yet in the present case it was the outcome of definitely concrete consideration. Black had two possible knight moves in reply – 15 ... N–Q5 and 15 ... N–K4 – which had to be taken into consideration. In both instances the reply would be 16 Q–R4+! For example: 15 ... N–K4 16 Q–R4+ B–QB3 17 B–N5 N×N+ 18 P×N B×B 19 R×R+ K–Q2 20 Q×B+ K×R 21 R–B1+ followed by 22 B–N4 with a strong attack. Meanwhile White hinders Black's castling and gains a vital tempo.

15 ...	P–KR3
16 KR–Q1	0–0
17 B–B3	Q–N1

Shutting the queen out of play. The lesser evil was 17 ... Q–B4 followed by 18 ... Q–KR4.

18 Q–.R4!

A very strong manoeuvre. Transferring his queen to the K-side, White builds up an irresistible attack

| 18 ... | KR–Q1 |

18 ... P–N3 might have offered more resistance. Then White could have either continued with 19 Q–KN4, or played 19 B–K4, intending to bring the rook to Q7.

19 Q–K4	P–N3
20 Q–KN4	P–KR4

20 ... K–R2 would allow a beautiful finish in 21 B×P+! P×B 22 Q×KP R–B1 23 R–Q7 R–QB2 24 N–K5! or if 23 ... QR–K1 24 N–N5+ P×N 25 Q–R3+ K–N1 26 Q–R8+ K–B2 27 Q–B6+ and mate next move.

| 21 Q–R3 | P–B4 |

The threat 22 P–KN4 forces a new weakening. If 21 ... R–Q3, then 22 P–KN4 (on 22 ... R–Q4, 23 B×P followed by 24 P×P is decisive) 22 ... R1–Q1 23 P×P R×B 24 R×R R×R 25 P×P P×P 26 Q–R8+ K–B2 27 N–K5+ and White wins.

22 B-B4	R×R+
23 R×R	K-B2
24 P-K4!	

Simple and convincing. White opens up the lines and diagonals for the attack.

24...	Q-B5
25 R-K1	Q-N5
26 P×P!	Q×B
27 P×NP+	K-K1

27...K×P 28 R×P+ K-B2 29 R×N loses.

28 P-N7!

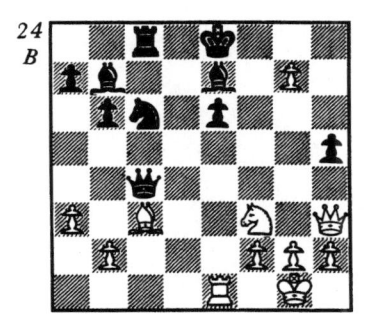

24 B

It doesn't often happen that on the 28th move the game is already decided by a passed pawn on the seventh rank!

28...	P-K4
29 Q×P+	K-Q2
30 R-Q1+	B-Q3
31 B×P	N-Q5
32 N×N	1-0

21 Gurgenidze-Petrosian

'Spartak' team Ch, Moscow 1961

Caro-Kann

1 P-K4	P-QB3
2 N-QB3	P-Q4
3 N-B3	B-N5
4 P-KR3	B×N
5 Q×B	N-B3
6 P-Q3	P-K3
7 B-K2	

A more promising plan is 7 P-R3 followed by 8 P-KN4.

7...	QN-Q2
8 Q-N3	P-KN3

A subtle positional decision. The sieve-like arrangement of Black's pawns is ugly only in appearance. Black's black-square bishop and his other pieces swim comfortably through the matrix.

9 P-KR4

In the first game of the revenge match Smyslov-Botvinnik, 1958, the game continued 9 0-0 B-N2 10 B-B4 Q-N3! and Black seized the initiative. In the present game White attempts to enliven the play on the K-side, though here too Black's defensive reserves are quite large. As it turns out, the plan is also very committal.

9...	P-KR4
10 0-0	Q-N3

10...N-R2 was also possible, since after 11 P×P KP×P (11...BP×P 12 N-N5!) 12 R-K1 B-K2 13 B-R6 N.R2-B1! Black has a good game, despite his king being in the centre.

11 R-N1   B-R3!

This manoeuvre has a paradoxical appearance. It is typical of Petrosian that, when there is an absence of direct tactical threats, he strives to resolve the cardinal strategical problems of the position at the first opportunity. Here the exchange of the black-squared bishops increases the activity of the black queen, as well as the knights.

12 B-N5

A dubious answer, which only weakens White's pawn structure.

Better was 12 B×B R×B 13 Q–B4, to be followed by P–K5 and P–Q4, establishing the central pawns on white squares, and releasing the white-squared bishop.

12...	B×B
13 P×B	

13 Q×B was probably better, though 13...Q–Q5 gives Black good play.

13...	N–R2
14 P×P	KP×P!

14...BP×P is answered by 15 P–Q4, when White has the threat N–N5!

15 K–R1	0–0–0
16 P–B4	QR–K1
17 Q–B2	

White has a lack-lustre game, and the threats of 17...R–K6 followed by...KR–K1 are very apparent. But the endgame, too, is hardly strewn with flowers.

17...	Q×Q
18 R×Q	N.R2–B1

The knight is aiming at...Q5.

19 B–B3

19 P–B5 is answered by 19...N–K4, with 20...N–N5! to come.

19...	N–K3
20 N–K2	P–B3!

Very strong. Static pawn positions need not only serve as objects of pressure. A timely exchange can often create new outposts for pieces.

21 P×P	N2×P
22 P–QN4	

In difficult positions the possibility of error increases! Pawn advances, which leave new weaknesses in the position, are often particularly suspect. Here the patient move was 22 R2–B1, preparing for a lengthy siege.

22...	N–N5
23 R2–B1	

The exchanges 23 B×N P×B+ 24 K–N1 N–N2 25 N–N3 N–B4! 26 N×N P×N are also in Black's favour. Now it becomes clear why 22 R2–B1 was the better move. In that case the variation 22...N–N5 23 B×N P×B+ 24 K–N1 N–N2 25 N–N3 N–B4 26 N×N P×N loses its force, as White could play 27 K–B2! equalizing.

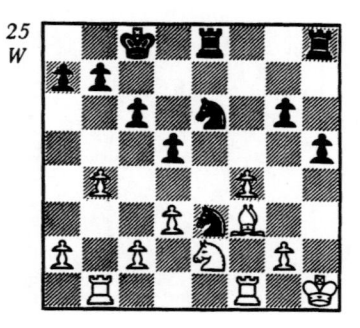

23...   N–K6!

25
W

From this moment White begins to suffer from...very restless knights.

24 R.B1–B1	P–KN4
25 P×P	N3×P
26 N–Q4	P–R5

White's king unexpectedly falls into a mating net. Petrosian himself shows an interesting line: 27 K–N1 P–R6 28 P–N3 P–R7+ 29 K–R1 KR–B1, and White is defenceless. If 27 R–K1, then 27...P–R6 28 K–N1 R–R5! 29 P–B3 P×P 30 B×NP N–R6+ 31 B×N R×B or 29 K–B2 P×P 30 R×N N–R6+ 31 K×P R–N1+ 32 B–N4+ R1×B+ 33 R–N3 R×N, when Black has very good winning chances.

Though these variations are forced, in practice, there are many under-water obstructions to be surmounted by Black. Now he wins quickly and elegantly.

27 N-B5   **N × B**

The simplest. After 27 ... N × N 28 B-N4 KR-B1 29 R-B1 R-K4 30 P-Q4 K-Q1 31 P × R N-N6+ 32 K-N1 White could still offer staunch resistance.

28 N-Q6+	K-N1
29 N × R	N-Q7
30 R-K1	N × BP
31 N-Q6	N × R.N8
32 R × N	R-KB1!
33 P-N5	K-B2
0-1	

22 Petrosian-Najdorf

Bled 1961

King's Indian

1 P-Q4	N-KB3
2 P-QB4	P-KN3
3 N-QB3	B-N2
4 P-K4	P-Q3
5 P-B3	P-K4
6 KN-K2	P-B3
7 B-N5	

Every player has his own beloved openings, plans, even moves. Similar bishop moves against the King's Indian defence are a favourite with the World Champion in a great number of systems. White tries to muffle Black's counterplay on the king's wing, pinning the knight and holding up the advance ... P-KB4.

7 ...   **QN-Q2**

7 ... P × P 8 N × P Q-N3 would have led to more lively play. Now White closes the centre, and the struggle is transferred to the wings.

8 P-Q5   **N-N3**

On 8 ... P × P White intended to play 9 N × P with a firm hold on the Q5 square.

9 N-B1	P × P
10 BP × P	0-0
11 P-QR4	

Another typical Petrosian decision. He is not concerned by the temporary lack of development on the K-side, rather he is interested in creating play on the queen's wing and taking the initiative there. Meanwhile the queen's bishop keeps a lonely watch on the K-side.

11 ...	P-QR3
12 N-N3	B-Q2
13 P-R5	N-B1
14 B-Q3	P-N4

Black does not intend to give up the Q-side for nothing, and here activates his pawn. Now after 15 P × Pep Q × P followed by ... N-R4 and ... P-B4 Black obtains good counterplay.

15 N-R2

A move earlier White was intending the manoeuvre N-R4. Now in the changed circumstances he finds another manoeuvre for the same piece, this time bringing the points QR6 and QB6 under fire.

15 ...   **N-K2**
16 N-N4

Absolute accuracy in chess still does not exist – even among the very finest players. Here White commits a small error, allowing Black to become active on the king's wing. 16 P-N4! was correct, hindering Black's counterplay.

16 ...   **N-R4!**
17 P-N3

Petrosian considers that 17 Q-Q2 N-B5 18 0-0-0 was better, putting up with the knight.

17 ...	P-B3
18 B-K3	P-B4
19 R-QB1	

Needless to say, Petrosian was loth to leave his king exposed in the centre. But, according to the demands of the position, he is always ready to enter the most precarious situations.

19 ...	Q–K1
20 R–B7	N–KB3
21 Q–Q2	P×P
22 P×P	B–R6
23 B–N5	R–B2
24 B×N!	

A brave decision. If the knight is left on the board Black's attack becomes very dangerous.

24 ...	R×B
25 B–B1	B–N5
26 B–K2	B–R6
27 B–B1	B–N5
28 B–N2	

White decides to play for the win, though Black's threats appear to be very powerful.

28 ...	Q–KB1
29 P–R3	

29 R–KB1? R×R+ 30 B×R Q–B6 31 Q–Q3 Q–R8 32 R×N R–KB1 33 N–Q2 Q–N8!! and there is a threat of mate on KB2.

29 ...	B–R3
30 Q–Q3	B–B1?

Black's nerve gives out. 30 ... R–B7 31 R–KB1 R×B! 32 R×Q+ R×R 33 P×B R–N8+ 34 K–K2 was correct, when Black can either force a draw by perpetual check, or play for the attack with 34 ... R8–KB8. However, here too after 35 Q–B2 Black might anyway have to take the perpetual check.

31 R–KB1	R×R+
32 Q×R	Q–Q1?

Another mistake. 32 ... B–K6 offered better chances.

33 R–B3	B–QN2
34 Q–B2	P–R4
35 Q–N6!	

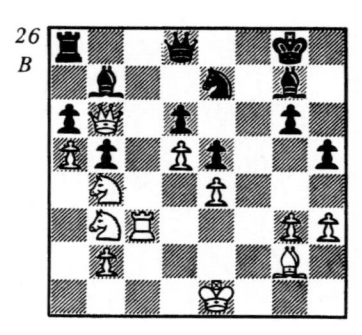

26 B

The winning move. White's will has triumphed.

35 ...	Q×Q
36 P×Q	R–N1
37 R–B7	B–B1
38 N–R5	R×P
39 N4–B6	N×N
40 N×N	1–0

After 40 ... B–QN2 41 N–R5 B–R1 42 R–B8 B–QN2 43 R–N8! White wins a piece.

23 **Petrosian–Pachman**

Bled 1961

King's Indian Attack

1 N–KB3	P–QB4
2 P–KN3	N–QB3
3 B–N2	P–KN3
4 0–0	B–N2
5 P–Q3	P–K3
6 P–K4	KN–K2
7 R–K1	0–0

White's preceding moves constitute not so much a general plan of development, as a concrete mode of play. Black might well have played 7 ... P–Q3 here. As it is, he acts according to the ancient formula:

general development before everything else.

8 P-K5   P-Q3

And here he might have done better to avoid breaking in the centre, continuing 8 ... Q-B2   9 Q-K2 P-N3 with ... B-N2 to follow.

9 P×P   Q×P
10 QN-Q2 Q-B2

Black is experiencing difficulties. For example, if 10 ... N-Q5   11 N-K4 Q-B2   12 B-B4 P-K4?   13 N×KP! B×N   14 N-B6+! and White wins.

11 N-N3   N-Q5

Perhaps 11 ... P-N3 was best, though after 12 B-B4 Black's position is rather 'boring'.

12 B-B4   Q-N3
13 N-K5!

Threatening 14 N-B4 Q-N4   15 P-QR4! Q-N5   16 B-Q2 and so on.

13 ...   N×N
14 N-B4   Q-N4

Black's forces become more and more uncoordinated. In fairness though, after 14 ... Q-Q1   15 RP×N Black is troubled by the threat of 16 B-Q6.

15 RP×N   P-QR4

Directed against the threat of 16 R-R5.

16 B-Q6   B-B3

16 ... R-K1 is refuted by 17 B-B7!

17 Q-B3   K-N2
18 R-K4

White has developed his attack at quite a pace, but fails to divine the correct moment for the decisive sacrifice. He could even here have played 18 Q×B+!! K×Q   19 B-K5+ K-N4   20 B-N7! forcing mate. But in any event, Black is defenceless.

18 ...   R-Q1

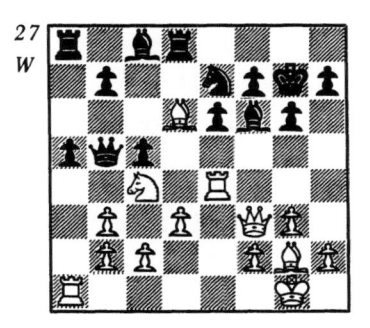

27
W

19 Q×B+!   K×Q
20 B-K5+   K-N4
21 B-N7   1-0

Mate is inevitable after both 21 ... N-B4   22 P-B4+ K-N5   23 N-K5+ K-R4   24 B-KB3 or 21 ... P-K4   22 P-R4+ K-R4   23 B-B3.

Curiously, this was not the only game in which Petrosian sacrificed his queen against Pachman. But whereas in the above example the sacrifice served purely tactical ends, in the earlier game it had a more complex positional character. Here is the score of the game, which was played at Portoroz, 1958:

Pachman-Petrosian, Old Indian

1 P-Q4 N-KB3   2 N-KB3 P-Q3 3 P-B4 B-N5   4 N-B3 P-KN3   5 P-K4 B×N   6 Q×B N3-Q2   7 P-K5(?) N-QB3   8 P×P N×P   9 Q-K4 P-K4!   10 P×P Q×P   11 N-Q5 Q-Q3   12 B-B4 N-K3!   13 B-K3 B-N2   14 0-0-0 0-0   15 **N-N6** White continues to play for material.

28
B

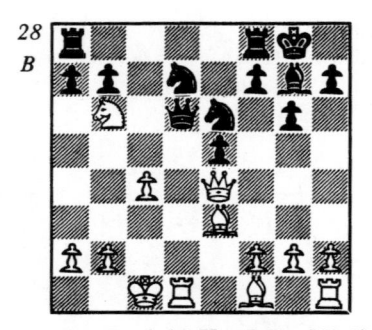

15 ... Q×R+! 16 K×Q P×N! 17
P-QR3 N2-B4 18 Q-B2 P-K5 19
P-B3 QR-Q1+ 20 K-K1 N-Q5 21
B×N B×B 22 P×P N×P 23
B-K2 KR-K1 24 R-B1 R-K2! 25
R-B3 R1-K1 26 R-Q3 B-N8! 27
P-R3 B-R7! 28 B-B3 B-N6+ 29
K-Q1 N-B7+ 30 K-Q2 B-B5+ 31
K-B3 N×R 32 K×N R-K6+ 33
K-Q4 B-R3! 34 P-B5 P-QN4! 35
B×P B-N2+ 36 K-Q5 R1-K3!
0-1. There is no defence against
37. ... R6-K4+.

24 Petrosian–Stein
USSR Team Ch, Moscow 1961
King's Indian

1 P-QB4	N-KB3
2 N-QB3	P-Q3
3 P-Q4	P-KN3
4 P-K4	B-N2
5 B-K2	0-0
6 N-B3	P-K4
7 P-Q5	QN-Q2
8 B-N5	P-KR3
9 B-R4	P-R3

Black rejects 9 ... P-KN4 10
B-N3 N-R4, and tries to carry out
... P-KB4.

10 0-0	Q-K1
11 N-Q2	P-B4

White finds a good answer to this
move. If instead 11 ... N-R2 12
P-QN4 P-KB4 13 P×P P×P? 14
B-R5! or 13 ... R×P 14 Q-B2

followed by 15 B-Q3 and White
keeps his opening advantage.

12 P×Pep	P×P
13 P-QN4	R-N1
14 P-QR3	B-N2
15 N-N3	Q-K3
16 N-R5	B-QR1

Only 5 moves have been played,
yet White has made considerable
progress. He has weakened Black's
pawns and, more important, locked
away the black queen's bishop. This
by no means adds up to a decisive
advantage though, and there is a
lively fight in prospect.

17 P-B3   P-Q4

After this Black's weaknesses become static. 17 ... N-R4 looks better.

18 P-B5	N-R4
19 B×P	N-B5
20 N-K2	P-N4
21 B-B2	P-B4

Sensing the tides of battle running
against him, Stein launches into the
attack on the king's wing.

22 R-B1

White defends coolly, for the time
being strengthening the positions of
his pieces.

22 ...	BP×P
23 P×P	N-B3
24 P×P	N3×P

On 24 ... P×P 25 P-B6! makes
the passed pawn a real danger.
Black pins his hopes on the energy of
his piece attack and the advance of
his KP. But White faces the onslaught
in full array. The hand to hand
fighting begins.

25 N-KN3   P-K5
26 B-Q4

An important move. Exchanging
off the black-squared bishops considerably weakens Black's king's field.

26 ...	R.N1-Q1
27 B×B	K×B

28 Q–Q4+	N–B3
29 Q–B3	K–N3
30 N–B4	N–Q6
31 R.QB1–Q1	N–Q4
32 Q–B2	N–B2
33 N–Q6!	

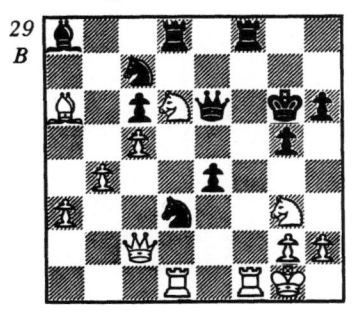

29
B

Played in the grand style. White sacrifices a piece, but breaks up his opponent's K-side.

33 ...   **N × B**

If 33 ... R × R+ 34 R × R R × N 35 P × R N × B 36 Q–K2! and White's attack wins quickly.

34 R × R	R × R
35 N6 × P	N3 × NP
36 P × N	N × NP
37 Q–N1	N–Q4
38 R–K1!	Q–Q2
39 N–B6+!	1–0

After 39 ... K × N 40 N–R5+ K–B2 41 Q–R7 is mate!

8 At the door of The King

Up to the time of the 'Candidates' tournament, which took place in May–June 1962, the isle of Curacao had taken no part in chess history. The only connection it had had with the struggle for the world championship lay in that its shores, and the shores of Cuba were washed by the same Caribbean sea. And Cuba, as is well known, was in its time the field of great chess battles – in Havana Steinitz and Chigorin played, as did Lasker and Capablanca.

Grandmaster Yuri Averbakh, who was present in the capacity of leader of the Soviet chess delegation, described Curacao thus:

'Curacao is a piece of earth, sixty kilometres in length, and width varying from four to twelve kilometres, in appearance remarkably akin to the sole of a boot. Even on large maps, Curacao appears as a tiny spot in the Caribbean sea to the north of the South American land mass, roughly 75 kilometres from the shores of Venezuela. The northern part of the island is very smooth and level, the south very uneven. From an aerial viewpoint (and we flew in by plane) it is clearly visible that one of the deepest indentations into the body of the island, widening appreciably, forms a large inland reservoir. On its banks is an agglomeration of red tiled roofs, tens of smoking chimneys, and hundreds of oil-tanks ... the reservoir, fourth largest in the world, forms a natural harbour. Around the harbour is spread the capital of the island, the city of Willemstad, where the tournament took place.'

The participants lived in a comfortable hotel, with every convenience, close to a pool with running sea water, but all the same the length of the tournament, and the unusual climate presented them with complex problems.

'The tournament was extremely difficult,' said Petrosian afterwards in conversations with correspondents, 'I cannot remember any such complicated tournament previously. Much of the guilt lay with the climate. When the thermometer registered 28–29 degrees, the day was considered cool.'

Petrosian played for first place. Accordingly he had to draw up a general plan of battle, where everything, literally everything, was accounted for. Perhaps he should attend to the advice of Fischer, who declared after the Stockholm tournament that if Petrosian played a little more courageously, he would be the strongest player in the world. Petrosian only smiled when he read these words. Well, he had played rather courageously in the Soviet championships more than once, and the results had not been bad, but was courage really the first requirement in this tournament?

Tigran had grave doubts about this. He knew that a marathon tournament in a tropical climate required stamina rather than bravery, physical and psychological restraint, the ability to distribute energies in such a way that on the final straight one was still running, however slowly, and not crawling. He resolved to conduct the tournament in the manner of a skater, according to a strict graph, trying not to lag behind the leaders too much, but avoiding any sudden, exhausting spurts.

Such a strategy could not succeed in a Soviet championship, nor would have brought first place in the Interzonal tournament at Stockholm; but here in Curacao it had every chance of success. True, there was one indispensable condition – that none of the players set such a burning pace, as had Tal and Keres in the previous Candidates'.

Who might theoretically be capable of doing this? Tal and Keres, and besides them, Korchnoi, Geller and Fischer – Benko and Filip did not enter into it. But shortly before the tournament Tal had undergone a serious operation, and was completely unprepared for an extended struggle, which, by the way, he demonstrated in his very first game. Keres was already 46 years old – for all his fitness, he could not hope to repeat his Yugoslav result on the shores of the Caribbean sea. Geller too was already 37, four years older than Petrosian himself, and could hardly wish to play a sharp tournament variation.

There remained only two – Fischer and Korchnoi. The first would undoubtedly throw himself at the rest; he was extremely ambitious, and after his performance in Stockholm, where he gained first place, $2\frac{1}{2}$ points clear of his nearest rivals, he did not regard himself as anything other than candidate number one. But Fischer was not only ambitious, but excessively self-confident, and besides that he was also very young – 19 years old.

That left Korchnoi. This 'cavalier without fear or reproach' was capable of anything. He would no doubt take up an uncompromising position, but Petrosian was sure that Korchnoi's usually proud motto, 'All or nothing!' would prove suicidal in Curacao.

In round one Petrosian played White against Tal. All their previous meetings had ended in draws, except once, in the 24th championship, when Tal had won. This time there was something nervous, a sort of feverish impatience about Tal's play. Barely having completed piece development, he tried to start tactical operations. Petrosian rebuffed the attempt without particular effort, and, offering a pawn, firmly grasped the initiative. The game was adjourned in a difficult, but hardly hopeless endgame for black. However during the resumption Tal committed a positional error, after which the game could not be saved.

This game already gave indication that the ex-World Champion was not on his best form.

The next partner was another 'gamecock' – Korchnoi. This game was unusually complex and difficult for both sides. Petrosian worked out a deep plan whose main aim was not to cede the centre to White, but he made an inaccurate move, and was forced to go into an inferior variation. Afterwards Korchnoi erred, then the players exchanged mistakes, and finally a position arose where Petrosian had an extra pawn, but with both sides short of time. So when Korchnoi proposed a draw, Petrosian accepted without much deliberation.

This was a typically Petrosianic decision. In the first place, it still seemed to him a long way to victory, especially since he would have to overcome the resistance of a player such as Korchnoi. In the second place, it did not fit into his plans to take the lead too early. As a last resort he was prepared to share the lead with another player, but not to 'call the fire upon himself'. Having this attitude, Petrosian found it relatively easy to overcome feelings of disappointment, when Geller came to the board and showed a pawn move which would have presented Korchnoi with barely soluble problems.

'Why get upset?' Petrosian silently advised himself, 'I saw that move, but did not realize its real strength. That means that I wouldn't have been able to win anyway.' And in fact he didn't grieve very much.

Petrosian was concerned to avoid over-excitement at the beginning of the tournament, and accordingly did not fight particularly hard in the remaining games. He made an exception with Benko, who was generally considered the 'rabbit' of the tournament. All the same, great experience, practical shrewdness and outstanding endurance made the Hungarian player a sufficiently dangerous opponent. Petrosian was one of the first to feel this; in his game with Benko he tried to extract more from the position than was there, and in the end secured the draw with great difficulty.

The players had completed one cycle. First with five points was Korchnoi. He had drawn his first four games, then beaten Fischer with Black in the fifth. In the sixth he overcame Filip in a game lasting over 100 moves, and in the seventh, Tal. In fact he was employing the tactics of the famous Kuts – dash to the front, and let them follow who were able. However, not only Petrosian, but also Keres and Geller were disinclined to follow. All three kept comfortably in the background on four points.

Korchnoi must burn himself out. No man could continue to expend such colossal amounts of physical and nervous energy in every game.

Fifth, to everyone's surprise, was Benko. He had not only been able to take advantage of Tal's temporary fall from form, but had even managed to deal a blow to Fischer! Next with three points came Fischer, then Filip, and finally Tal.

The results of the first cycle were fully satisfactory to Petrosian. If matters could only continue like this to the last phase of the tournament, then his nerves, which until now had never let him down, his patience, restraint – all that went to make up the character of the 'iron Tigan' – would make themselves felt. Only recently, during the Stockholm tournament, Gligoric had called Tigran a 'man without nerves'.

In his second game with Tal, Petrosian carried out a delicate psychological experiment. It was clear to him that after a catastrophic start Tal would throw himself at him. Therefore he chose a rarely met variation of the French defence out of which White obtained a free position, but nevertheless had to tread carefully. On the eighth move Tal thought for over an hour, and began to sharpen the play, ignoring the resultant worsening of his position. Petrosian reacted swiftly and himself sacrificed a pawn. The game did not continue long: on the twentieth move, Tal capitulated. After this meeting, Petrosian finally understood that all was not well with Tal, and mentally erased him from his list of chief opponents.

In round thirteen the French defence brought Petrosian yet another victory – in his game with Fischer. For this meeting he had long ago prepared an old and (for the present day) very rare continuation – the so-called McCutcheon variation. Tigran had travelled to Stockholm with this variation, but there had been no sense unleashing his secret move there, so he stored it for a more serious moment. Petrosian was not only relying on the variation itself, but on its psychological effect, for he knew that Fischer did not orientate very well in unknown situations.

When Fischer saw that Petrosian had chosen an unexpected, but difficult for himself opening, he even glanced reproachfully at his opponent. Petrosian returned this glance, and mentally congratulated himself on his success – the 'secret weapon' was doing its work, even if Fischer should find the strongest answer. But the question of the refutation of the defence did not arise; Fischer went in for a peculiar bishop manoeuvre (a suggestion of Soviet origin) and Petrosian was soon in command of the game, which he carried to victory in the second session.

In the last round of the second cycle Petrosian managed to beat Filip as well. After this he had nine points, and was sharing the lead with Geller, who had also defeated Filip, Fischer and Tal in the second cycle. As for Korchnoi, he had been unable to maintain his sprint and the abyss of disaster yawned before him. In round twelve he had the better position and an extra pawn against Fischer. The win it seemed, was only a matter of time; but Fischer defended dourly and the effects of excess tension began to reveal themselves: Korchnoi put a bishop en prise and suffered a horrible defeat. Next day, it is true, he beat Filip, but then he lost to all three of his main rivals, one after another.

The tournament had now reached the half-way stage, and everything was still going well. Petrosian had won 4 games and drawn the remaining ten, was not particularly tired, nor had his nervous resources been strained up to now. He also took great pleasure in the visit of the Soviet football team, which dropped in at Curacao on its way to Chile. Tigran not only mingled happily with the famous footballers, but also asked for details of the Moscow 'Spartak' team's performance in the championship. There is a large photograph in one of the tournament bulletins – Petrosian, waving his arms, is enthusiastically demonstrating something to Andre Starostin and Igor Netto. We can be sure that the conversation at that moment was not about his games with Tal and Fischer!

For the time being too Geller was playing excellently; in an interview given after the tournament, Petrosian stated that Geller had played 'with great verve and self-control'. But the tension of the finish still lay before him, which, as had happened often before with Geller, might well prove ruinous.

Keres, the third of the grandmasters who had followed a course connected with the retention of energies, was also going well. He was now half a point behind the two leaders. However, he could not continue these tactics and still hope for success. By reason of his age, he could not place too much faith in his finishing ability. So it might be expected that in the third cycle, Keres would try to break away from the field, in order to leave himself with a reserve of points at the end.

Following a five-day breathing-space, which the participants spent on the tiny island of Sint Maarten, Keres returned in truly incisive form: out of seven games he allowed only two draws – with Geller and Petrosian, the remainder he won. This was a phenomenal achievement, and Petrosian would have had every reason for unease, were it not for the game Benko–Keres. Here Benko obtained a winning position, but falling into his usual time-trouble, overlooked a simple combination.

Perhaps weariness had already begun to set in, but looking at Keres one could never tell. He was always calm, unruffled, impenetrable, nor did he ever betray with the slightest gesture his true condition.

Geller, on the other hand, was beginning to show more obvious signs of tiredness. He, for example, incorrectly evaluated his position against Keres, and agreed a draw in a clearly superior position. As well as that, he should definitely have lost his third game with Tal, and only thanks to his partner's time-trouble chalked up a win instead of a loss.

Both his main rivals were tired, but there was no doubt that Petrosian was tired too. When Gligoric had called him a man without nerves, he did not at the time consider this a great exaggeration. He had always felt that self-control was his strongest characteristic. But after 20 rounds, he realized that his spiritual and physical reserves were almost exhausted. For the first time in his life, Petrosian experienced such a condition, whereby every renewal of strength is achieved with enormous difficulty. He was depressed, close to despair, and the only factor which enabled him to take himself in hand, was the knowledge that Keres and Geller must be in a worse state.

For such a conclusion he had not only subjective, but also objective criteria. After the tournament was over, some curious figures came to light; it turned out that in 27 games (Tal did not take part in the last cycle due to illness, and the other players accordingly played one game less) Petrosian had made 839 moves, Keres 924 and Geller 945. Petrosian had expended little more than 48 hours over his games, Keres and Geller, 59 hours each, Korchoni 72 hours and Benko 78!

The fourth and final cycle got under way. In one way or another, this phase must prove decisive – the tension at the end of a two-month-long tournament was by now unbearable. In the third cycle, Keres had made a break, but he was still unable to shake off his pursuers completely – they had themselves managed to accumulate five points. Petrosian had beaten Korchnoi, Benko and Filip; Geller, Filip, Tal and Korchnoi. After 21 rounds the scores were: Keres 14½, Petrosian and Geller 14. Next was Korchnoi with 11.

Now, as never before, Petrosian was convinced as to the correctness of his pre-tournament planning. Returning to Moscow, he was surprised to find that others were of a completely different opinion. V. Panov, for example, wrote at the end of two cycles that the winner would be the one who 'went forth courageously into battle!'. A. Kotov, in an article entitled 'On the finishing straight' wrote that the final meetings between the leaders would have 'decisive importance in the determining of the highest positions'. He then added 'What does T. Petrosian lack, in order to play a match with M. Botvinnik? Courage, above all courage! To receive chances of a match with the World Champion is not at all easy, but now Tigran's chances are excellent. Petrosian must forget about his caution, and play with all his strength, mobilise all his resources. Forward, only forward! . . .'

An accurate assessment of such prognoses was later given by Y. Averbakh: 'It had become clear that the winner of the tournament could only be one of the first three. But who? Quite a few observers, never having played in similar tournaments, and situated quite a distance from Curacao, asserted that the eventual winner would be the player who in the last cycle overcame his rivals. But it would have been sufficient to glance at the candidates to refute such a suggestion:

every victory at the close of the two-month marathon demanded such iron nerves, such strength, of which in the given real situation perhaps only abstract "supermen" were possessed. It was far more likely to suppose that he would retain best chances who preserved the greatest strength, will, and nerves; who played most solidly and with the highest coefficient of reliability.'

The fourth cycle began without Tal; he had fallen ill and dropped out of the tournament. The finishing straight shortened by one eighth, which slightly improved Keres' chances. In the 22nd round Petrosian was free, since he was scheduled to play Tal, so he had the opportunity of observing the play of his main rivals. He did not doubt that his thesis was correct: the winner of the tournament would be, not the one who made a courageous spurt – that variation was definitely excluded – but the player who could make it to the finishing post without suffering a catastrophe. In these circumstances, the main roles were assumed, not by the leaders, but by the remaining participants who, by now having nothing to lose, constituted a deadly danger.

Keres on that day played a draw with Filip, and Geller drew with Korchnoi. Geller played the whole game very actively, sacrificing two pawns. Korchnoi beat off the attack, and Geller had to go into the ending two pawns down, which he nonetheless managed to draw.

If this game already intimated that Geller would find it hard to overcome his nerves, the next round proved it beyond all question.

On that day Geller played against Fischer. Fully realizing, that the latter was addicted to playing one and the same opening, Geller caught him in a variation of the Sicilian worked out by Boleslavsky. Sacrificing a pawn, Geller obtained an excellent attacking position, and wrote down a move on his score-sheet which would have rendered Fischer defenceless. However, thinking about his move, he suddenly changed his mind and played something else. This was a tragic error, and now Geller was losing control of himself, and making more weak moves. Fischer retained his extra pawn and confidently carried the game to victory.

This was the destruction of all Geller's hopes. A destruction which Petrosian had foreseen, and which could in no way have been accidental. Disastrous reversals of form had accompanied Geller in many tournaments, and here it had come again, a definite psychological instability which revealed itself in the most dramatic moments of the struggle. Twenty-two rounds without defeat, and now this failure practically reduced to nought his previous efforts.

Geller's position was worsened in that Petrosian won against Korchnoi on the same day, and with an elegant bishop sacrifice. . Korchnoi had played the opening rather riskily, and then went into a line which gave Petrosian the opportunity of sacrificing a bishop for a dangerous attack. Korchnoi had relied on Petrosian playing 'safety first', and did not seriously consider the latter would undertake any so risky an operation at this stage of the tournament. But Tigran's tactical abilities were capable of allowing him to calculate all the consequences of the sacrifice, and he calmly delivered the knock-out blow. Six moves later Korchnoi resigned.

'It appears that the game of chess does not age,' wrote Taimanov in his notes to the game 'if despite the high level of present-day technique you can still come across a bishop sacrifice on KB7, even between candidates for the world championship!. . .'

The twenty-third round sharply altered the situation. Petrosian caught Keres up – they were now both on 15 points (from a chronological point of view Keres only reached 15 points after he won his adjourned game against Fischer from the third round, but in any event, Keres and Petrosian had identical scores four rounds before the end), and Geller was factually out of the race for first place – he could not catch two at once. The triumvirate had broken up – the challengers were now two!

The next round saw all the games drawn, and then Keres and Petrosian met. Petrosian was out for a draw, but nevertheless he chose an active defence, the Sicilian, against Keres' 1 P-K4. The game followed a previous one of Keres' down to move twelve, and on move 14 Petrosian proposed a draw; Keres asked first to see Black's next move, considering that in the event of almost any move except one he would have the advantage. Petrosian thought for some time and then played the one move, and Keres quickly agreed: in the interim, both players had realized that the one move led to Black's advantage. . . .

The games of the next round were again draws. As White against Benko, Petrosian obtained a minimal advantage from the opening, and quickly affixed the draw. Keres was even more cautious against Geller. On this day Keres, for all his mask of urbanity, seemed more strained than before, not so much by this game perhaps, but by the prospect of playing Benko on the following day. On the face of it there was no cause for alarm; up to now in Candidates' tournaments Keres had a fantastic score against Benko – 7–0! Yet for this very reason, if the gods of war were out to create a 'Greek tragedy' for Keres, they could hardly have chosen a better time. What was more, Benko had worked out a nasty opening system (nasty especially for a player of Keres' style) for this tournament, and in the second cycle had held the advantage, in the third had had equality in his game against Keres. Whatever the reason, Keres sat down to play against the 'lunatic' of the tournament in a state approaching mental paralysis.

In the penultimate round Petrosian was Black against Fischer. As Black in a Sicilian defence, he stood slightly worse, but not so bad that he was unable to follow the events of the Benko–Keres game. Keres was deprived of this possibility, his game was so bad that he was unable to tear his gaze from the board.

At one point Petrosian proposed a draw, but Fischer proudly declined it. Then the position evened out, and soon the initiative passed into the hands of Petrosian, but he was so taken up with following Keres' game that he did not pay much attention to this, and agreed a draw.

Benko meanwhile, having obtained a large positional advantage, as usual got short of time and lost a part of it, but still managed to adjourn in the better position. During the resumption Keres might still have complicated his opponent's task, but he was so demoralized by the turn of events that, after a few moves, he committed an irreparable blunder. . . .

For Keres this meant probably the end of the struggle. He understood that in such conditions, he could hardly beat Fischer in the last round.

And so, with one round to go, Tigran was in the lead by half-a-point! He was loath to believe his good fortune, but it was so: Petrosian, who in his youth was prepared to worship before Keres, was now close to victory in a difficult competition with his previous idol. In a tournament where the prize was a match with Botvinnik. . . . Only one step separated Tigran from triumph. However, that step still had to be made.

In the final round, Tigran had to play his most accommodating opponent – peace-loving Filip. Added to that, Petrosian was White, so a draw, almost guaranteed, would give him at the worst a share of first place. But why not try to win? Surely if Keres suddenly managed to beat Fischer, then Petrosian would have to play a hard match against the 'eternal challenger'.

Petrosian weighted this up carefully, and decided to act according to circumstances, bearing in mind only one thing – that to take risks would be to place in danger all that he had worked for years to achieve. Especially, to alter his tournament strategy at this late stage would be a very dangerous thing.

Although Filip, realizing how much depended on this game, played extremely accurately, Petrosian's position after 14 moves was clearly the more promising. Keres' game looked even better: he had seized the initiative and had very real chances of victory. It appeared that just such a situation had arisen, where Petrosian had to play for a win. But then something occurred which completely stunned the assembled audience: thinking on his move for forty minutes, Petrosian suddenly offered a draw. Filip at first gazed at Petrosian in surprise, then shrugged his shoulders and with obvious pleasure accepted it; it was for him the ideal solution of the problem.

At the door of The King   117

Many, no doubt, condemned Petrosian for this apparently weak-hearted step. I overheard one such remark to this effect: 'Okay, if Keres can't beat Fischer, then everyone will start to praise Petrosian's far-sightedness. But if Fischer loses, then they will say Petrosian showed timidity.'

This assessment outwardly appears very logical, but it slides over the surface of things. We already know that Petrosian, when necessary, could show daring – he had proved this more than once before Curacao. And therefore, that if he had come to the conclusion that he had to beat Filip, he would immediately have begun active operations. But Petrosian had reached the opposite conclusion, and his decision had not been instinctive, but based on the consideration of many circumstances.

The position in his game with Filip was such that Petrosian would have been forced to develop active play on the king's side, whilst his opponent would have advanced on the queen's flank. And play on opposite flanks, as is well known, carries with it a certain amount of risk, which Petrosian was trying to avoid. It would be another matter if Filip were to refuse the draw, then Petrosian's psychological situation would have been alleviated; it was as if Tigran were telling Filip: 'Decline the offer, and you will force me to fight!'

But there was little likelihood of Filip refusing, so had not Petrosian lightened Keres' task by offering the draw?

In actual fact he had not eased Keres' task, rather, complicated it. For no sooner did Keres realize that he had very real chances of catching Petrosian, than he began to agitate inwardly, and if the psychological pressure of the previous round had been difficult to overcome, now it became unbearable.

'An irony of fate!' wrote Averbakh later on, 'The oldest competitor in the tournament, 46-year-old Keres must in the very last round score a victory over the youngest player – 19-year-old Fischer.'

In his calculations Petrosian had foreseen this 'irony'. And in reality, Keres, having achieved an excellent position, did not withstand the tension, and fearing to dissipate his advantage, began to play more cautiously. Fischer, with rather less on his mind, reasserted himself and the game ended in a draw.

There was yet another, extremely vital detail, which influenced Petrosian's decision. Suggesting the draw to Filip, Petrosian was aware that in the final games of the Candidates' tournaments, Keres frequently behaved uncertainly. In 1950, in the first Candidates' tournament, he had lost to Bronstein, in 1953 had had a difficult position against Najdorf, in 1956, had only by a miracle saved himself against Petrosian, and in 1959 suffered a reverse in his game with Olafsson.

And all the same – what if Petrosian's remarkably common-sensical decision had met with disaster, and Keres, against all the odds, had won the game, what then? It was precisely this question that I gave to Petrosian, and he answered:

'That would have meant only that Keres had not played worse than me in this tournament, and that it would only have been just that a match should take place between us.'

The honesty of this remark does not occasion the slightest doubt. In this we hear the voice of the young Petrosian, who believed in the unshakeability of the laws of chess, and of the Petrosian who was later to say, 'I believe only in logic in chess. . . .' In the last round of the Candidates' tournament, Petrosian, as always, played according to position, and considered just and reasonable any result to which his decision might lead.

Fortunately for Petrosian, the result was the most propitious. Finishing his game with Filip, he, trying to stay calm, went out for a walk. From time to time he came back and glanced into the hall. The first time he saw that Keres' position was marvellous, the second time – that the game was almost equal. When he returned a third time, he saw Keres, irreproachably restrained, elegant, smiling as much as was natural, as much as was humanly possible, Keres, coming toward him with outstretched hand: the chess cavalier without fear or failing was hurrying to be the first to congratulate his rival on victory in the tournament. . . .

25 **Petrosian–Tal**

Candidates', Curacao 1962

Reti

1 P–QB4	N–KB3
2 P–KN3	P–B3
3 N–KB3	P–Q4
4 P–N3	B–B4
5 B–QR3	P–KN3
6 P–Q3	B–N2
7 QN–Q2	Q–N3
8 B–KN2	N–N5

A typical Tal thrust. Unfortunately, White is too well developed for it to have any force. Black rapidly finds himself driven back, so he might have done better here in playing 8 . . . Q–R4 followed by . . . QN–Q2, and if White plays 9 B–N2 then . . . 0–0.

9 P–Q4!

The correct reaction. It is very dangerous for Black to accept the pawn sacrifice.

9 . . .	N–QR3
10 0–0	N–N5
11 B–N2	0–0
12 P–QR3	N–QR3
13 R–B1	QR–Q1
14 P–N4	N–N1
15 Q–N3	N–B3
16 P–QR4	

White is very single-minded at this stage of the game. For the moment Black is not threatened directly, but the space disadvantage forces him into passivity.

16 . . .	N–K5
17 KR–Q1	N–Q2

At the door of The King 119

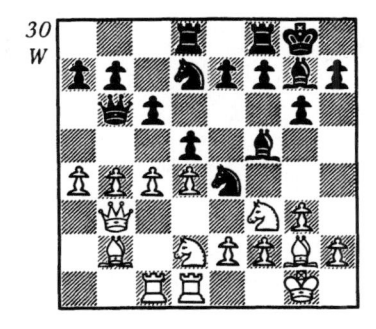

30 W

18 P × P

White prefers the 'bird in the hand', though it was objectively better to preserve the central tension by playing 18 P–R5! Petrosian clearly wished to avoid the complex positions arising from 18 ... P × P 19 Q × P! (19 P × Q P × Q 20 P × P deserves consideration) 19 ... Q–B2 20 P–N5! Q × RP 21 P × P and if now 21 ... R–B1 22 N × N B × N 23 B–B3 with P–Q5 to follow.

After the move chosen by White the number of concrete variations for calculation sharply decreases, but so does the immediate danger to Black.

18 ...	P × P
19 P–R5	Q–Q3
20 P–N5	N × N
21 R × N	R–B1
22 N–R4	R × R+
23 B × R	Q–B2
24 N × B	P × N
25 B–QR3	Q × RP
26 Q–N4	

White gradually develops his positional advances on the Q-side and in the centre. Black could take an endgame by 26 ... Q × Q 27 B × Q, but in that case he has to withstand uncomfortable pressure against his pawns on Q4 and K2. However, the endgame is not to be evaded.

26 ...	Q–N3
27 B × P	P–K3
28 B–B3	R–B1
29 Q–R4	R–B2
30 K–N2	P–QR3
31 P × P	Q × RP
32 Q × Q	P × Q
33 P–K3	

The character of the endgame has crystallized out. White can fairly hope to capture Black's QRP eventually, but whether this will be enough to win is another matter. Black should try to exchange one of White's bishops off.

33 ...	P–QR4
34 R–R2	R–R2
35 B–QN4	P–R5
36 B–B6	B–B1
37 B × B	K × B
38 R × P	R–B2
39 B × N	R × B
40 K–B3	

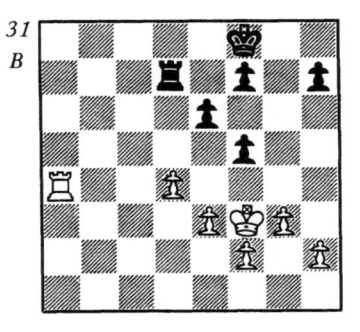

31 B

The game has transposed into a very instructive rook-and-pawn ending, where it is very hard for White to realize his material advantage. However, a few moves later Black considerably lightens his task.

40 ...	K–N2
41 K–B4	K–B3
42 P–R3	P–R4?

An incautious advance. The rook pawn becomes fixed and vulnerable to attack. Black should have continued his waiting tactics. It would have been very hard for White to exploit his extra pawn.

43 R–R8	R–N2
44 R–KN8	R–N7
45 K–B3	R–Q7
46 P–R4	K–K2
47 R–N5	K–B1
48 R × RP	

With the win of a second pawn the win becomes a matter of simple technique. The concluding moves were:

48 ... K–N2 49 R–N5+ K–R2 50 P–R5 R–R7 51 P–N4 K–R3 52 R–N8 K–R2 53 R–K8 P × P+ 54 K–N3 K–R3 55 R–K7 K–N2 56 R–B7 R–N7 57 R–B5 K–B3 58 P–Q5 R–N5 59 P–R6 P × P 60 R × P K–N3 61 R–Q6+ K–N4 62 P–R7 R–N1 63 R–Q1 R–KR1 64 R–KR1 1–0

26 Fischer–Petrosian

Candidates', Curacao 1962

French

1 P–K4	P–K3
2 P–Q4	P–Q4
3 N–QB3	N–KB3
4 B–KN5	B–N5

A surprise. Up till then Petrosian had never played the McCutcheon variation. He later revealed that he had prepared it as a secret weapon for use against Fischer in the Interzonal tournament in Stockholm, but decided to hold it back for the Candidates'. It soon becomes clear what Petrosian had 'detected' in his young opponent. Fischer was clearly unbalanced by the unexpected choice of opening, and instead of following the main line tried out a very dubious Soviet suggestion. As a result the game somewhat loses its theoretical interest, but Petrosian lost nothing from this!

5 P–K5	P–KR3
6 B–Q2	B × N
7 B × B	

Undoubtedly 7 P × B N–K5 8 Q–N4! was both stronger and more thematic, beginning an energetic advance on the K-side. The McCutcheon variation is a rare guest in international tournament play, and though theory has yet to demonstrate a clear plus for White in the main variation, it is generally recognized that Black's game is not an easy one. The positions arising are often very sharp, and require very good preparation from both sides, which in this case Fischer evidently did not have. He therefore 'passes' which constitutes a great psychological victory for Black.

| 7 ... | N–K5 |
| 8 B–R5 | |

The author of this strange move was the Soviet master N. Kopayev, the idea being that after 8 ... P–QN3 9 B–N4 P–QB4 10 B–R3! White keeps his queen's bishop, at the same time the black queen's outlet onto QR4 is blocked. Playing an immediate 8 B–N4 is met by 8 ... P–QB4. However, Petrosian's next move reveals the seamy side of the whole conception.

8 ...	0–0
9 B–Q3	N–QB3
10 B–B3	N × B
11 P × N	P–B3

Very sound. Backed by his superior development, Black begins active operations at once. White has already lost the initiative, and added to that has pawn weaknesses on the K-side.

| 12 P–KB4 | P × P |
| 13 BP × P | N–K2 |

A good manoeuvre, which opens the path of the QBP. Black's knight is very flexibly placed.

14 N–B3	P–B4
15 0–0	Q–R4
16 Q–K1	B–Q2

Black is gradually increasing the Q-side pressure, and now threatens both 17 . . . QR–B1 and 17 . . . B–R5 followed by . . . P–B5. Fischer opts to go into an endgame, though his pawn weaknesses give him the prospect of a long and arduous defence.

17 P–B4	Q × Q
18 KR × Q	QP × P
19 B–K4	

White did not like the variation 19 B × P QR–B1! and gives up a pawn instead.

19 . . .	P × P
20 B × P	QR–N1
21 B–R6	R–N3
22 QR–Q1	P–Q6!

Black could have tried to hold on to his pawn, but he prefers to return it in order to keep the initiative and good piece deployment. If instead 22 . . . R–R5 White takes the initiative with 23 R × P!

23 P × P	P × P
24 R × P	B–B3
25 R–Q4	R × R
26 N × R	B–Q4

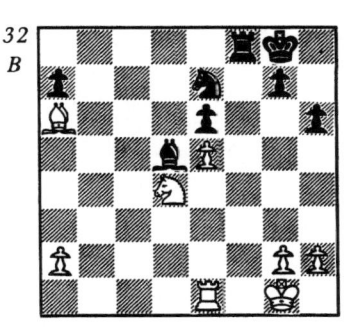

32
B

This is the position Black had aimed for when he sacrificed the pawn back. White has difficulties due to the weakness of his pawns on QR2 and K5. The majority of commentators have passed over this position in silence, considering it unsatisfactory for White. According to Petrosian, however, 27 B–B1! gives White real chances of salvation. If now 27 . . . B × RP 28 R–R1 and 29 R × P. At the same time White has threats of R–N1 and N–N5. After the move played Black's advantage becomes decisive.

| 27 P–QR4? | R–B5 |
| 28 R–Q1 | N–N3 |

White must lose material.

29 B–B8	K–B2
30 P–R5	N × P
31 P–R6	R–N5
32 R–Q2	

32 P–N3?? is refuted by 32 . . . R × N.

32 . . .	N–B5
33 R–KB2+	K–K2
34 N–N5	N–Q3
35 N × N	

The win is not easy. Black has still to play accurately.

Fischer could have tried 35 N × P, which would be answered by 35 . . . R–QB5!, forcing 36 B–N7 N × B 37

P × N B × QNP which is hopeless for White.

35 ...	K × N
36 B–N7	B × B
37 P × B	K–B2

The rook ending is technically won for Black.

38 P–R3	R–N4
39 R–N2	K–N1
40 K–B2	R–Q4
41 K–K3	R–Q2
42 K–K4	R × P
43 R–KB2	0–1

A little premature, but Black's technique proved so convincing that it convinced even Robert Fischer!

A brilliant game, one of Petrosian's best at Curaçao.

27 **Petrosian–Korchnoi**

Candidates', Curaçao 1962

English

1 P–QB4	P–QB4
2 N–KB3	N–KB3
3 P–Q4	P × P
4 N × P	P–KN3
5 N–QB3	P–Q4
6 B–N5	P × P

6 ... N–K5!? was worth consideration. After 7 N × N P × N 8 Q–R4+ B–Q2 9 Q–B2 N–B3! 10 Q × P B–N2 11 N × N B × N Black has sufficient compensation for the pawn.

7 P–K3	Q–R4

Black's opening strategy is very risky. Here it would have been safer to continue 7 ... B–N2 8 B × P 0–0 9 0–0 P–QR3 as in Smyslov-Korchnoi, 20 USSR Ch, 1952. After 10 P–QR4! QN–Q2 11 Q–K2 Black's game is not easy; but now he falls 'out of the frying pan into the fire'.

8 B × N!	P × B
9 B × P	

The simplest. White gives up the supposed advantage of the two bishops in favour of quick development, simultaneously weakening Black in the centre and on the queen's wing.

9 ...	B–QN5
10 R–QB1	P–QR3

Black is unaware of danger. He should have castled here.

11 0–0	N–Q2

Now 11 ... 0–0 would be strongly met by 12 N–Q5!

12 P–QR3

Unnecessarily slow. White should have played 12 N–Q5! at once, and the knight would have been rather stronger than the black bishop. So Black could now have taken the opportunity to simplify the position by 12 ... B × N 13 R × B N–K4! Missing this chance, Black can no longer save the game.

12 ...	B–K2
13 P–QN4	Q–K4

13 ... Q × RP is no good after 14 N–Q5! 13 ... Q–Q1 is dealt with combinatively by 14 B × BP+ K × B 15 Q–N3+ K–K1 16 N–K6!

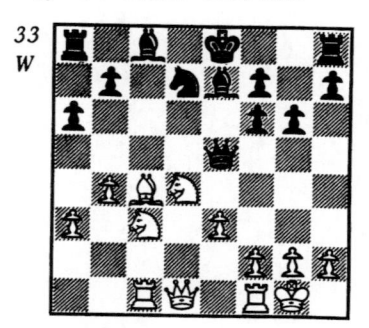

33
W

14 P–B4!

From now on White plays the attack faultlessly. If 14 ... Q × KP+

15 K-R1 there is no answer to the threats of 16 R-K1 and 16 N-Q5.

14 ...	Q-N1
15 B×BP+	K×B
16 Q-N3+	K-K1
17 N-Q5	B-Q3
18 N-K6	P-QN4
19 N5-B7+	K-K2
20 N-Q4!	

A courteous invitation to capture on B7; 20...B×N 21 N-B6+ K-B1 22 N×Q B×N 23 Q-K6! or 20...Q×N 21 R×Q B×R 22 Q-K6+ K-B1 23 Q-QB6! R-R2 24 N-K6! and so on.

| 20 ... | K-B1 |
| 21 N×R | 1-0 |

Black cannot avoid further material losses.

28 Dückstein-Petrosian

Olympiad, Varna 1962

Caro-Kann

1 P-K4	P-QB3
2 P-Q4	P-Q4
3 N-QB3	P×P
4 N×P	B-B4
5 N-N3	B-N3
6 N-B3	N-Q2
7 B-Q3	P-K3
8 0-0	Q-B2

Intending an interesting plan connected with castling long. If 8... KN-B3 9 R-K1 B-K2 10 P-B4 0-0 11 B×B RP×B 12 B-B4 R-K1 followed by...P-QB4, the play becomes very symmetrical. Now the game noticeably sharpens.

| 9 P-B4 | 0-0-0 |
| 10 B×B | RP×B |

After this exchange, Black's attacking chances noticeably improve.

| 11 Q-R4 | K-N1 |
| 12 P-N4 | |

White is consistent. The cause of his defeat is not to be found in tactical errors either. Quite probably, the plan begun on the 10th move was faulty.

12 ...	N-R3
13 Q-N3	N-KB4
14 P-QR4	P-K4

A timely central thrust. Black initiates very curious and instructive play over the whole board.

15 P×P	N×P
16 N×N	Q×N
17 B-N2	Q-B2
18 P-B5	P-R4!

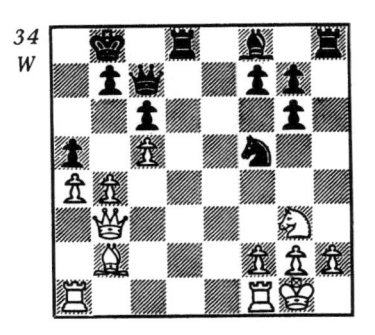

34
W

Seemingly anti-positional – but very strong. 'Surely if Black willingly opens up the lines against his own king, he only plays into White's hands?' However, it is important to remember that the main factor in a chess game is possession of the initiative, and it is precisely thanks to this that Black can transcend the established rules of play.

| 19 QR-Q1 | R×R |
| 20 R×R | R-R5! |

The second link in Black's plan begun on the eighteenth move. The rook fires down the KR-file, as well as along the 5th rank.

21 P×P

If 21 B–B3 P×P 22 B×QNP N–Q5 followed by ... N–K3 and Black's advantage is obvious.

21 ...	B×P
22 P–R6	P–N3
23 R–K1	K–R2
24 B–K5	Q–Q2
25 N–K4	B–Q5
26 P–N3	B×B!

The exchange sacrifice is fully sound, and is the most exact method available for exploiting Black's advantage.

27 P×R	N–Q5
28 Q–Q1	

If, for example, 28 Q–K3, the check on N4 is very unpleasant.

28 ...	Q–Q4
29 R–K3	N–B4!

A new surprise. If 30 Q×Q P×Q and Black regains the exchange 'with interest'.

30 R–K1   N–Q5

Black repeats the position in order to gain time on the clock. 30 ... B–Q5 was also strong.

31 Q–Q3	P–KB4
32 N–N5	P–B4
33 R–K3	P–QB5
34 Q–Q1	K×P
35 R–QR3	B–B3
36 P–R3	P–B5
37 Q–N4	

The endgame is hopeless for White after 37 N–B3 N×N+ 38 Q×N Q×Q 39 R×Q B–K4 and 40 ... K–R4.

37 ...   K–R4

This most royal intervention decides the game shortly!

38 N–B3	K–N5!
39 N×N	K×R
40 N–B2+	K×P
0–1	

9 Ninth Champion

Petrosian's victory in Curacao, for all its narrowness, did not appear accidental: in the 68 games he played on the way to the title match, he had suffered only one defeat. The only argument against this was that he had not beaten any of his main rivals; but by the same argument they had not beaten him either, so if Petrosian was not a worthy challenger, nor was anyone else.

'Tigran Petrosian has been one of the world's leading players for about 15 years,' wrote Alexander Kotov, 'His exceptional talent is recognized even by those who do not particularly like his style of play. Few outstanding players could show such a "level" graph of results as he has done. . . .

'Tigran did not lose a single game at Curacao: his matches with the two leaders were drawn, and he beat the remaining participants. Iron logic, elevated into a system! One important factor which enabled him to pass through 27 dangerous trials unscathed was his unfailing mastery of the opening. It is difficult to say whether this was the result of excellent preparation, or whether he managed to solve the problems at the board, but at any rate, he simply could not be caught in the early stages of the game. All his opponents' efforts to lure him into their lines ended in failure; at the required moment Petrosian selected a completely different opening. . . .'

Petrosian had reached the top of his profession, and achieved the right to challenge the World Champion. The champion was indeed a lofty figure. Botvinnik had been playing in Soviet championships before Tigran was born, and his shadow had lain over chess for more than 30 years. But his achievement had been far more than this; he had altered the whole face and balance of the chess world. In the pre-war years, it was the names of Lasker, Alekhine, Capablanca and to a lesser degree, Euwe, Reshevsky, Fine and Flohr who had a magnetic appeal to chess-players. The 'chess fever' at the time of the 1925 Moscow tournament, the crowds of thousands in the Museum of Fine Arts building during the 2nd Moscow international tournament were largely occasioned by the participation of Lasker and Capablanca, by now almost legends in their own lifetimes.

Yet this hypnosis had no effect on Botvinnik! Quietly yet confidently, he closed on Olympus, and forced the chess gods to bow before him. In order to secure this important psychological victory, he had to share first place with Flohr at Moscow 1935, with Capablanca at Nottingham 1936 (leaving behind Reshevsky, Fine, Euwe, Alekhine, Lasker, Flohr) and take second place in the Moscow 1936 tournament. Curiously, Botvinnik met – and very successfully – all the World Champions over the board, with the exception of Steinitz.

Botvinnik was a fearless fighter with an iron will. His strategy was deep and original and his analytical powers unequalled. Whole generations of Soviet chess-players learnt from his creations, and in that number Petrosian. 'I studied Botvinnik's games when I was twelve years old,' he said before the match 'and I am still learning from them.'

Beyond all doubt, Botvinnik was the most dangerous, the strongest and the most uncompromising of all the players he might have to face. Naturally, before such an opponent Petrosian would sooner have worshipped than fought, but fate had cast him in the role of fighter. . . .

After the Candidates' tournament, Petrosian stated, in interviews with correspondents, that he had begun preparations for his match with Botvinnik even in Curacao. Or perhaps even earlier? Petrosian had minutely commentated Botvinnik's last four world championship matches – with Tal and Smyslov – in the columns of *Sovietsky Sport*. In the press-room during the games he attracted the other commentators to him like a magnet, for they unconditionally recognized his authority. The sergeant-major of the press-room, he was once jokingly called; he could briskly and accurately delineate all the complex plots of both players, and almost every time give an accurate assessment of the position arising.

Tigran gladly undertook this complicated and demanding work. He discovered a side of himself which enjoyed not only analytical, but also journalistic work. At first he was not too confident in himself, but this passed with the gaining of a degree of experience. After four of these championship matches, he found that he had so penetrated to the essence of the play that he could correctly guess beforehand nine out of ten of Botvinnik's moves. (There was of course a difference, as Petrosian himself realized in the very first game of his match, between finding these moves in the noisy and gay atmosphere of the press-room, and doing the same sitting at the table, on the stage, before thousands of watching eyes. . . .)

Commenting on Botvinnik's four matches, Petrosian was not only an observer, a witness, but also to some degree a participant in the matches. He understood that his evaluation of whole games, separate moves, especially, his judgements on the tendency of the match must have some effect on the course of the struggle itself. Accordingly he felt a great responsibility, and did not permit himself to release one unguarded word in print. Later on, when he was playing his first match with Spassky, this gave him the moral right to criticize a few commentators who were not guided by similarly delicate impulses.

Tigran had not only been an observer to the tragedy of Smyslov, and the tragedy of Tal, he had also to explain the events as they took place to millions of chess fans. 'The intelligent man learns through the experiences of others'. Before he could explain these two collapses to others, he had first to explain them to himself.

Smyslov, that 'cold-blooded Russian', as one Dutchman called him, had much in common with his great opponent. The same unhurried judgement, the same logic and depth of thought, the same virtuosity in the endgame. In addition to this, phenomenal intuition and the ability to concentrate on the essentials of a position. The contests between Botvinnik and Smyslov were without parallel in chess history: from 1954 to 1958 they played three matches – 69 games – at the end of which they remained in their initial places.

Why was it that Smyslov, tasting the sweetness of a champion's cup, was unable to maintain his throne?

Possibly, a very simple answer could be given to this question: in the third match (the first had ended in a draw, the second, in 1957, in victory for Smyslov) everything did not depend on Smyslov; Botvinnik had turned out to be stronger and that was all. Yet there was a further consideration: Smyslov had lost the last match not only at the board, but even before the match had begun.

In an article entitled 'Analysis or improvisation?', published after his other revenge match – against Tal – Botvinnik, allocating himself to the 'analytical' school of chess-players, wrote: 'Players of this type begin preparations for a contest long before its inception. This is understandable; if improvisation at the board is always connected with a degree of risk, then painstaking preparation constitutes a solid basis for success'.

Smyslov, of course, knew of his opponent's unusual ability to prepare for games, unerringly seeking his and other's mistakes. An ability of this sort requires, first of all, great strength of character. Only a player able to look upon himself with the eye of an unimpassioned observer could hope to return to the arena of his disgrace, confident of victory. The combination of strength of character and the impartial objectivity of a scientist, allowed Botvinnik to place absolute trust in the analytical data acquired regarding himself and his opponents.

Many chess-players have been able to surmount the difficulties of defeat, but few can withstand the sweet effects of victory; as it turned out in the third and last match, Smyslov began play, secretly hoping that he would not need to expend a great deal of energy here. In the first games of the match, Botvinnik hammered him in one game after another, and the revenge took place. . . .

Next it was Tal's turn. He literally flew towards the summit, overturning the ordered ranks, hierarchies in his path. Not surprisingly, one of the articles greeting his victory over Botvinnik was headed 'Revolution in the chess kingdom'. It was precisely a revolution, and not just a change of kings.

However even the most successful revolutions have to be consolidated. In the first match Botvinnik had been beaten by Tal's unusual 'guerrilla' tactics, to which he had no answer at the time. Yet the fact that he decided to utilize his right to a return match indicated that he had analyzed all the games of the first match, and worked out a deep plan of revenge.

Both Tal and Smyslov made the same error regarding Botvinnik; they underestimated his recuperative powers, and his ability to learn from his defeats. At the end, 25-year-old Tal, at the zenith of his powers, was beaten by 50-year-old Botvinnik!

When I asked Tal after the match, what he considered to be the main reason for his defeat, he answered immediately:

'Botvinnik's resoluteness! I never could have imagined that Botvinnik could be so resolute in play....'

Tigran had before him the sorrowful experiences of his predecessors, but even without it, he would not have made a similar mistake to them. It was not in his nature to underestimate the opponent, rather the opposite. In this he had an appreciable advantage over both Tal and Smyslov.

Tal's victory over Botvinnik in 1960 had been so convincing that both the public at large and the experts believed that Botvinnik would most certainly be beaten in the return match, and many thought that he would waive his right to a return match completely. On this account, many of his friends urged Petrosian not to take part in the next zonal tournament (the 28th Soviet Championship). The reason was this, that according to the ruling of the international chess federation (FIDE) the first two players in the Candidates' tournament automatically qualified for the Candidates' tournament of the next cycle. If Tal were to retain his title, Petrosian would become the second candidate, and together with Keres would receive the right to play at Curacao.

However, Tigran only smiled at those who believed in Tal's undoubted victory. Even if he had done so himself, he would nonetheless not have taken the chance, but played in the qualifying tournaments. And in actual fact he was convinced that Tal had little chance of success in the return match, basing this opinion on his knowledge of Botvinnik's iron will, and Tal's artistic temperament.

After the Curacao tournament there was once again talk of Botvinnik relinquishing his title without a fight. Botvinnik himself had said something to this effect after his second match with Tal. Petrosian did

Tigran Petrosian (Photo: Bozidar Kazić)

Tigran with his wife Rona and his younger son Vartan

(Photo: Bozidar Kažić)

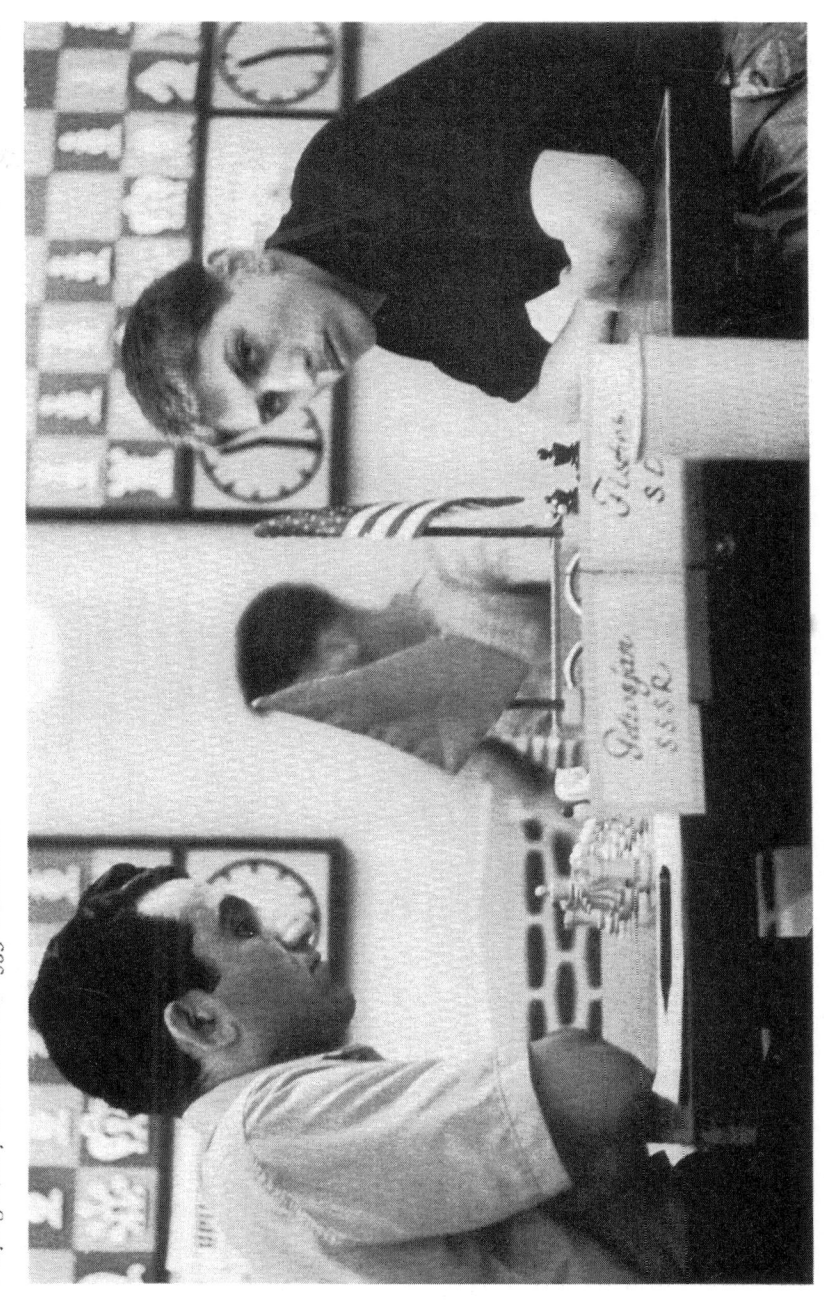

Playing Bobby Fischer in the 1959 Candidates

(Photo: Božidar Kažić)

Playing in the 1968 Moscow Championship

(Photo: Camera Press Ltd)

At the 1966 Havana Olympiad, with Fidel Castro *(Photo: British Chess Magazine)*

Concentration

(Photo: Camera Press Ltd)

At the Match of the Century 1970

Playing top board in the 1972 Skopje Olympiad (*Photo: D.N.L. Levy*)

In pensive mood at a Soviet championship

not put much trust in these reports. He was prepared to accept that Botvinnik had considered the possibility, in much the same way that one considers a bad move on the chess board, prior to its dismissal.

However, according to Flohr, Botvinnik did hesitate a long time before deciding to play the match.

'Botvinnik and I were walking together on the banks of the river' wrote Flohr.

'Do you know what a world championship match entails?' he asked.

'Unfortunately, I've never had to play one, but I have a rough idea.'

'I don't have a rough idea, but an accurate one. It means terrific tension, it takes a year off your life.'

'A serious consideration' continued Flohr, 'but surely any chessplayer would willingly give a year of his life just to play for such a title? And yet: Mikhail Botvinnik has already played 8 times for the world championship!'

After consultation with his doctors, who confirmed his physical well-being, Botvinnik declared that he was ready to play against Tigran Petrosian. Five years later, on the isle of Mallorca, and at Monaco, Botvinnik was to achieve dazzling tournament successes. These results were perhaps the best answers to those who considered that Botvinnik was no longer 'what he had been', and could not play a gruelling match against Petrosian.

Petrosian's next pre-match problem, which allowed for many possible solutions, was, 'How to play?'. Here he had a selection of opinions, besides his own, many of them contradictory to one another. In an article entitled 'Similarities and differences' published in *Ogonyok*, ex-World Champion Euwe compared Petrosian to Capablanca, and Botvinnik to Lasker. Mentioning that Petrosian's losses were as rare as Capablanca's, he continued: 'The resemblance between Capablanca and Petrosian does not lie only in their impenetrability, but also in their style. Both have solid styles, but not dry. Together with positional games of the highest quality, both Petrosian and Capablanca have produced very beautiful attacking games, with sacrifices.

'Both feel at home in all the nooks and crannies of the chessboard. Both prefer simple positions, and are accurate and deep in calculation. And both of them have a dislike of wild play in chess. A sacrifice is either correct or incorrect. A semi-correct sacrifice does not exist in Petrosian's vocabulary. In this Petrosian differs from Botvinnik in the same way that Capablanca differed from Lasker. This is not to say that Lasker and Botvinnik play wildly, but they are more willing to allow a role to the accidental in their games.'

Comparing Botvinnik to Lasker, Euwe wrote later on: 'Botvinnik is a great tactician, an accurate positional player, a jeweller of the endgame and an all-round fighter. I expect a very tense duel in the forthcoming match, but cannot refrain from comparison with the Lasker–Capablanca match of 1921. There is a great deal in common here. Even the ages of the contestants coincide! Lasker, when he defended his title, was 51 years old, as is Botvinnik now. The challenger Capablanca was then 33 years old, the same age as Petrosian. . . .

'In conjunction with their dissimilarities, Botvinnik and Petrosian also have much in common. They both have a preference for solid play, only Botvinnik shifts the balance of the struggle to the region of tactics, Petrosian, to the region of strategy.'

This last assertion of Euwe's was very curious, and had direct relevance to the question – how to play? For it was somewhat at variance with the traditional opinion that Botvinnik felt rather uneasy in tactical situations. This opinion the World Champion had not tried to refute. In his comments on the 7th game of his revenge match against Smyslov, Botvinnik wrote: 'Here my ancient weakness came into play – poor combinative vision.' Quite probably, both Smyslov and Tal shared the same opinion of Botvinnik's tactical capacities, and conducted their match strategy accordingly.

This opinion had such wide currency before the match, that many leading authorities, among them Tal and Korchnoi, suggested that the challenger might do well to alter his style somewhat, and play in a sharper vein.

Not long before the start of the match Tal said the following in an interview: 'It seems to me, that the conflict between the penetrative force of Botvinnik, and the impenetrability of Petrosian will prove one of the most important problems of the match. Botvinnik will no doubt try to achieve his aims by strategical means, avoiding direct struggle, that is tactical complications. . . . As regards Petrosian, his main task will be to refute the strategical ideas of his opponent.

'To sum up, I would like to say, that in all probability the strategical initiative will belong to Botvinnik, the tactical – to Petrosian.'

In the same interview, Tal stated that Petrosian would 'have to come to grips with the necessity of playing in a somewhat different style. Therefore it is likely that the creations of chess artist Petrosian, 1963 model, won't be a reproduction of his games of the last ten years.'

'Of course,' Tal continued reasonably, 'it is one thing to deliver useful suggestions, and another to carry them out. It is very hard to change one's style, as hard as to change one's character, particularly before the most important competition of one's life. . . .'

In this last sentence there was already enough weight to persuade Petrosian against making any alterations in his play. There was another reason in that he was extremely sceptical of Botvinnik's so-called tactical weakness. It seemed to him that Euwe had been nearer to the mark in his evaluation, and accordingly, he decided to play 'according to position', allowing no room whatsoever for fantasy, in fact to play in the way he liked best.

This was at the very least a logical decision, and it was one which had the approval of his new trainer, grandmaster Isaac Boleslavsky. This peaceful, even phlegmatic man had accompanied Petrosian to the Candidates' tournament in 1959. Himself a challenger for the world title in the not-too-distant past, a player of universal style, Boleslavsky recommended himself to Petrosian by his perpetual calm, self-criticism, his ability to soberly judge his own achievements and short-comings. Tigran appreciated these qualities in men, and particularly in chess-players.

The main decision had thus been taken. Tigran considered that in the playing of simple, strategically clear positions, and in the endgame, where Botvinnik was exceptionally strong, he was in no way inferior to the World Champion. He decided to avoid tactical complications, and not only that, but to avoid strategical complications as well. He would play in the style of Capablanca.

As Black he placed his trust in his defensive powers, and on the suggestion of his openings' advisor, grandmaster Alexei Suetin, chose the Queen's Gambit Accepted. This was risky, in that the opening gives White freer play, even the initiative, but on one vital condition: the decisive offensive must be launched at once, otherwise Black would be able to simplify the position, and the weakness of the isolated pawn would begin to tell (as the reader may recall, Petrosian was able to win isolated pawns even in his very early youth).

It was true that in his youth Botvinnik had won a number of games with the isolated pawn, but now he was no longer inclined to hurry, and preferred to prepare his onslaught in length and depth. So there would occur a pause between the ending of the opening and the beginning of White's attack, which the black side might be able to use to its advantage.

In Botvinnik's terminology, Petrosian carefully programmed himself for an exhausting struggle with the World Champion, taking into consideration concrete problems relating to play, psychological factors, and also the difference in age. Before the onset of the match, he read with great curiosity all that was being written by his colleagues about the match. He was gratified to see a definite reservedness about the forecasts, which was a good sign. If Botvinnik's chances were rated in any way higher, this would have showed somewhere. Spassky even stated frankly 'Petrosian has the better chances'. Taimanov commented ingeniously: 'Botvinnik will play better, Petrosian, more accurately.' Tal, however, was inclined to favour the World Champion, even though his prediction came in a sufficiently oblique manner:

'... I hope readers will forgive me, if instead of a forecast, I refer to the recent past and say that a match with Botvinnik is a very difficult business. You may believe me here. ...'

Quite a few observers, among them Euwe, pointed out a paradoxical fact, in no way harmful to Petrosian, that no World Champion had ever managed to win a match against an opponent equal in strength to him. In general, starting from the year 1935, the title-holder hadn't won a single match – Botvinnik had beaten both Tal and Smyslov as an ex-champion! ...

All the experts, in making their forecasts, took into account three main factors: the strength of the contestants, their ages, and their sporting form at the moment of play. Botvinnik's chess biography seemed rather more impressive, but the strengths of the players were reckoned as roughly equal. The age factor was not easy to evaluate. A difference of eighteen years was quite substantial, but the champion had always shown great health and stamina. At the age of fifty he had beaten twenty-five-year-old Tal! But then Petrosian's health was not bad either, so the age difference should have significance, especially towards the end of the match. Finally, both players would undoubtedly be in excellent sporting form when they met each other.

Besides these three criteria, there were others which could affect the course of the struggle. Petrosian was a player of enormous experience, in fact before the match Flohr called him 'the most experienced of all contemporary players'. In the region of match play, however, he was something of a novice, at a time when Botvinnik said of himself that he was more of a match player now. Botvinnik had so far played 6 matches for the world championship, which made a total of 135 games, even if the games of the 1948 championship, where he had played four mini-matches of five games each, are not counted.

Experience had made Botvinnik into a match player, but here Petrosian was not at a disadvantage, for he was a natural match player. He had an unusual ability to sense danger in advance, which meant he need hardly ever lose, though at the price of conceding a large number of draws. In tournament play, too many draws can be harmful, especially if one is aiming for first place. In match play the effect of a draw may be far less detrimental, since the relative scores of the players are not altered. (This is not to say that a draw has *no* effect in match play; towards the end of a match, the player with the higher score can 'threaten' his opponent with a draw, hoping to reach the finishing post in half-points, cf. Spassky-Fischer, 1972. Before the war, matches were played with 'draws not to count', in which case a player had to score a certain number of victories to be adjudged the winner. The 1972-75 cycle of world championship matches will also see this system put into effect.)

Nonetheless, there was another side to match play, far less inviting.

This was the tension involved, and the fact that it was continuous. In tournament play, it was always possible to relieve the strain by demolishing some of the weaker players, or having a quick draw with one of your equals, but in a match there was little opportunity for this.

It was with especial unease that Petrosian's supporters awaited the beginning of the match. At this point the challenger would need to acclimatize himself, so it was to Botvinnik's advantage to try and deliver the heaviest blows possible before his opponent could find his feet. The very first game of the match confirmed these misgivings.

As soon as Tigran entered the variety theatre with Rona, he felt the paralyzing novelty of the situation. This was the same theatre where, two years ago, at the time of the Tal-Botvinnik match, he had spent two months in the press-room. Then he had felt only curiosity on his visits to the hall: what would today's game offer? Now his legs felt so heavy he had difficulty in mounting the stage....

He understood that a great deal depended on the first game. Many commentators had already written of this. He approached the board in a state of inescapable alarm. He had always been a slow starter, had needed to play himself into form, and here was a player opposite him who was able – and willing! – to deliver the first blow himself.

Petrosian was White in the first game. He selected a quiet variation of the Nimzo-Indian defence, where he could set up a very solid position. Tigran did not doubt that he had no possibility of losing such a position. And to avoid loss – this was his main aim at the beginning of the match. Yet making his first moves he suddenly felt a strange condition, akin to that of a somnambulist, settle over him. He little understood what was happening to him. He saw good moves, yet made bad ones. If it had been Tal sitting opposite, Petrosian would have believed the stories about hypnotism.

Botvinnik was playing with shattering confidence. Every one of his moves was logical and followed a single strategical plan. On move 13 Petrosian's position had already become difficult, though not hopeless. Then he made a pawn move to which Keres gave the following annotation 'This despairing thrust is equivalent to resignation, since White's position is broken in a few moves....' Petrosian was routed.

The first game had a sensational effect. 'If there happened to be a "chess stock exchange", similar to the ones in capitalist countries, panic would have set in by now', wrote Panov in connection with this game, 'the players on the upgrade the "bulls", would have thrown themselves at Botvinnik's shares. The "bears", or players going down, would be trying to jettison Petrosian's shares at any cost.'

Tigran considered that he had played this game roughly at first category player strength, not even at candidate master strength. Psychologically, the effect of this game was such that very few, excepting his fans in Armenia, believed he could successfully fight Botvinnik for the world title. These few were those who remembered Petrosian's steadiness, most of all perhaps, his patience. It was this characteristic, very important in match play, that Petrosian was to demonstrate now. In Euwe's aforementioned article there was a very accurate, if somewhat lurid description of the challenger's play: 'Petrosian is not a tiger, who leaps at his prey, more he is a python, who strangles his victim, or a crocodile, waiting for the moment to deliver the decisive blow. . . .'

Having received a painful buffeting, Petrosian did not intend to seek immediate revenge. Long before the match had begun, he had already instructed himself that in the event of dropping one or two games at the start, he would not attempt to make up the difference at once – with Botvinnik such a tactic would be an unforgivable error. So in the second game he had the same intent as in the first – not to lose. All the same, the opening seemed to foreshadow the worst possible outcome. Botvinnik received an isolated queen's pawn from the opening, a Queen's Gambit Accepted, but also strong pressure on Black's position. This pressure threatened to be transmuted into a direct attack on the black king. Many of Botvinnik's energetic moves were greeted by warm applause from the audience, to whom it appeared that Black's position was on the verge of disintegration.

Petrosian was already unable to think of exploiting isolated pawns – he was rebuffing direct threats. Yet despite the thanklessness of his position, despite the relentless pressure from Botvinnik's side of the table, despite the noise in the hall, Petrosian was no longer in a daze. The initial fright was over, and he was defending his bastions stoutly. This time he saw good moves and played them as well.

Black's position continued to worsen. But on the 28th move Botvinnik did not withstand the tension, and agreed to an exchange of queens. This was an error; a lot of the steam went out of the attack, and the pressure decreased. Perhaps there was the germ of a misapprehension in this decision; Botvinnik placed great hopes in his endgame prowess. Petrosian was of another opinion. After the exchange of queens, he quickly and easily brought the game to a drawn result.

Though Tigran had managed to save the game, he felt bad, very bad. Botvinnik had struck at him right from the start, and Petrosian, who had hardly yet begun to fight, could quite believe that a world championship match took a year off your life. It would have been more difficult for him, were it not for the many friends and fans who came to his aid at this difficult time.

Petrosian had many followers in Moscow, Tiflis, and in many other cities of the Soviet Union, but without a doubt his most devoted ones were to be found in Armenia. At the time of the match I happened to be in Yerevan, and saw with my own eyes the crowds of thousands of people who gathered in the square in front of the 'Moscow' cinema, to watch the games as they were relayed on vast demonstration boards. The waves of this enthusiasm reached even to Moscow, where an endless stream of letters and telegrams arrived from Yerevan. How many of them is unknown. Men flying to Moscow on business brought Tigran fruit, fresh vegetables and national delicacies. Rona was relieved of many of her household cares, in order that she might be by her husband's side when needed. And though all this fuss was somewhat embarrassing to Petrosian, it could only warm his heart and ease his melancholy.

He was particularly delighted in the arrival of his friend, Loris Kalashian. Tigran told him about his strange condition during the first game. Loris understood that Tigran must be kept calm at all costs, and lifted out of all feelings of demoralization. And though we may believe that Petrosian would have stayed resilient in any case, the assistance of his friend could hardly have been superfluous. . . .

In the third game it was Botvinnik's turn to agitate. The World Champion may have been under the impression that playing White, the challenger would try to attack him. Referring to the events of the third game, Kotov wrote:

'Petrosian lost the first game. This was a terrible blow to the young pretender. How many grandmasters cannot remember the shock of the first defeat? It requires great will-power to avoid total collapse in the next games.

'And now the third game. Would Petrosian try to strike back? Would he initiate a sharp struggle in order to obtain revenge at all costs? These questions were debated not only by ordinary supporters, but also by the chess experts.'

On the third move Kotov gave the following annotation: 'The most peaceful of peaceful variations, the Queen's Indian defence. No excitement, not a trace of revenge. . . .'

Petrosian as White played the 'quietest of the quiet' Queen's Indian defence, did not avoid simplication, exchanged queens and went into an ending.

However, the endgame proved difficult for Black. Petrosian finally had the initiative and forced the champion back into defence. Botvinnik conducted the defence brilliantly, and though the game lasted a total of 70 moves, secured half-a-point. Despite this, Tigran was fully satisfied with the course of the game. It had not eluded his attention that Botvinnik had been clearly anxious, especially in the opening stage of the game. Of a warlike nature himself, he might have expected Petrosian to play more hotly. What was this – timidity? Or cunning? In any event, such a show of caution was not to Botvinnik's liking, he would have preferred the decisive events to come in the first half of the match.

In the next game the champion once again took the initiative in the opening. But once again Petrosian showed his defensive artistry after an innocuous start. At one time Black's position looked extremely dubious, but in order to increase the pressure, White would have to take a slight risk. Having a point in the bag, Botvinnik did not wish to endanger it, so after some exchanges a draw was agreed on move 24.

Commenting on this game, Panov appended Smyslov's words, delivered at the end of the game: 'A match for the world championship is not for timid souls!' Rona tried to hide this particular number from Tigran, but all the same he got hold of the paper. He took the words of the ex-World Champion at their worth, and grinned with satisfaction. He knew that in his situation, to play quietly, and not attempt to hurry forward – this was true courage. Many people were capable of short, albeit heroic, efforts. But let them try to 'mark time', as he was doing. . . .

He was sure that his restraint would soon have its reward. In fact it came in the very next game. The opening here was very similar to the opening of the third game. Playing White, Petrosian did not resist simplifications. But as in the third game, his artless play had its merit in that Botvinnik was placed in a situation where he could not initiate active counterplay. And for Botvinnik, perhaps, there was no greater torment than to be left in a position of waiting passivity.

A little while after the game had gone into the ending, Botvinnik committed an error. This was already substantial in itself, but, according to Petrosian, it also annoyed the World Champion still more since it arose from incorrectly evaluating the position. Tigran understood that precisely errors of positional assessment were depressing to Botvinnik, for this was one of his strongest sides. Besides this, the position had appeared beforehand on the board at Petrosian's house.

'If Botvinnik goes into this line,' said Tigran to Boleslavsky, 'he will lose.'

Eventually Black had to part with a pawn, not receiving any compensation for it. Tigran felt a tremor of excitement. It was not simply the first game in the match which he stood to win, thus equalizing the score. It would also be the first victory he had ever scored over Botvinnik in official competitions (not counting training games, they had so far played 3 times against each other, all games drawn). When Botvinnik ignored the opportunity of going into a rook ending, Petrosian's confidence rose further. The rook ending was hardly inviting for Black, but nonetheless Tigran was happy that besides a rook, he still had a knight left.

At that moment a dilemma arose, either to maintain the pawn plus, or return it in order to advance up the centre with his king and strengthen the position. Petrosian could hardly bear to part with the fruit of all his efforts, but the position required it of him. He gave the pawn back, but afterwards left his opponent with no chance of escape.

The game was adjourned, and after seven moves of the resumption Botvinnik stopped the clocks. The score was 2½ all.

This game was deeply inspiring for Petrosian. After the match he said that he considered it one of his best games of recent years.

In the sixth game Petrosian once again accepted the Queen's Gambit, and once more Botvinnik perseveringly pursued a decisive advantage. In vain, the game was agreed drawn on move 27. After the next meeting, the initiative in the match went over to the side of the challenger. Here Black went into a not too advantageous, but complex variation of the English opening. Petrosian once again came out of the opening with a definite advantage, without permitting his opponent any real chances of counterplay. Black's forces were gradually stifled, and White's bishops struck directly at the pawns on Black's queen's flank.

White's positional pressure became so immense that even after move 25 there could be no doubt about the outcome. There was one moment when Botvinnik could have complicated the issue, but he preferred to go into a rook ending, which turned out to be hopeless. Botvinnik's uncertain play in the ending came as a pleasant surprise to Petrosian.

What had happened? How could it be explained that Botvinnik, a veteran of match play, should suddenly be found to be lagging behind right at the start? The answer to this could only be that the strategy adopted by the challenger was contrary to the champion's expectations.

Botvinnik sought positions with a clear strategical plan, and Petrosian willingly constructed them. Botvinnik did not fear simplification, and Petrosian freely exchanged pieces. Botvinnik saw the endgame as a desirable stage of the game, but Petrosian also placed his main hopes there. It seemed precisely there, on the World Champion's home ground, that Petrosian was scoring major successes.

However, this apparent symmetry of champion and pretender was only approximate. For in every game, and every part of every game, Petrosian was trying to limit the strategical and tactical possibilities of his opponent. Using terms borrowed from football, he had assigned himself to 'mark' a potentially dangerous player. For an active, energetic nature there is nothing more trying than forced inactivity, and Botvinnik wearied in positions where technique alone was important, whilst Petrosian continued faultlessly and implacably.

With the tide running against him, Botvinnik once more showed his capacity for deep analysis. He had become convinced that playing quietly he had little chance of overcoming his opponent. Accordingly, he sharpened his play, aiming for complex positions, even at the expense of creating weaknesses in his own position. In the 7th game too, it seemed he was bent on this course, for many commentators had expressed surprise that he had opened with such a difficult variation.

During the contest, many people remarked that the champion seemed to be playing as if he were the challenger. The players had exchanged roles.

Tigran understood that he had scored a psychological success. He also realized that Botvinnik was now changing to 'plan no. 2', which he had himself prepared in case the first part of the match went against him. He understood that he could now expect a vicious onslaught from the champion, and, like a seaman who jettisons ballast before the storm, Petrosian attempted, most often by means of exchanges, to weaken the force of the hurricane.

Botvinnik did indeed begin the storm. But, suffering defeat in the seventh game, he had to take into account that another zero against a player who lost so rarely would make his situation almost irreparable. Beginning the game courageously, he would then seem to recollect something, and at the sharpest, most responsible point of the battle, withdraw into manoeuvring, or even from previously prepared positions.

Petrosian sensed this immediately, and tried to make use of his opponent's fatal indecision. Averting the danger, he strove to lengthen the struggle, as a rule into the adjournment. He understood that a continuous and risky attack, in a situation where defeat was equivalent to catastrophe, cost Botvinnik a great deal of nervous and physical energy. Botvinnik, of course, understood this as well, but he already had no other course of action. . . .

In the eighth game, the Queen's Gambit Accepted was once more employed, and once more Botvinnik's initiative petered out before Petrosian's iron defence. The ending even developed in Black's favour, and Botvinnik was forced to find the draw. Petrosian had so programmed himself in the role of the defender, that when in the ninth game Botvinnik gave him the possibility of working up strong pressure he completely unnecessarily exchanged queens, thus letting slip a good portion of his advantage. However, Petrosian was not very annoyed by this; his main problem at this stage of the match was – not to lose.

Quite a few commentators read great significance into Petrosian's slip in the ninth game. B. Wainstein, for example, in the bulletin of the event, suggested that the move whereby the challenger offered the exchange of queens, 'marked a turning point in the first half of the match'. This opinion he backed very logically. Playing 'according to Botvinnik' Petrosian had 'achieved staggering results . . . but this could not continue for long . . . very likely, Botvinnik guessed his "programme". From one point of view, it was very flattering to the World Champion that the challenger was reproducing his style, but it was not for this that he agreed to play a match without revenge, in order that he should lose to himself!

'So Botvinnik switched over to another variant of the programme, which might in simplified form be taken as: seize the initiative ignoring a few weaknesses, and even material losses (not exceeding, naturally, one pawn!).'

Botvinnik had gone over to 'plan no. 2', and this should have caused Petrosian, if not to alter his match tactics, at least to make some correction. But he considered that he might withstand the onslaught, continuing with his original plan. This persuasion was encouraged by the tenth game, where Tigran obstinately producing his Queen's Gambit Accepted, lost a pawn, but without much difficulty secured the draw.

After this game, he caught himself thinking that in general he would not lose another game, that in every difficult position he would find the saving resource. This had occurred to him occasionally in the past – after he had not lost for some time. Always dangerous, against Botvinnik particularly such self-confidence was a treacherous state of mind. Tigran rebuked himself sharply for conceit, but somewhere in his soul he continued to believe in his invincibility.

The eleventh game came near destroying this illusion. Continuing his plan, Petrosian did not expend any great effort to secure the initiative, but at the same time did not manage to paralyze his opponent's energies. Botvinnik laid out his game brilliantly and gradually took control of the board. Petrosian retained his self-control, and defended coolly. The champion erred slightly, but all the same his rooks found their way to the seventh rank, and when the game was adjourned, the assembly in the press bureau almost unanimously judged Petrosian's position to be indefensible. Yet the game was not resumed: analysis showed that White had sufficient resources for a draw.

This was already a serious warning, but Petrosian still considered that everything was going in the best possible way. In the next game, after the World Champion's energetic start had petered out, Tigran seized the initiative, and only let this slip on the move after the time control. The situation was fully to his liking, where, as one observer put it 'despite the World Champion's powerful strategical storm, Petrosian, as the song goes "sinks and rises, and calmly swims on . . . ".' Here Petrosian was not only considering his point lead; the match had now reached the half-way stage, and the champion should soon begin to tire. Furthermore, he remembered the first Botvinnik-Tal match. Then his same opponent, on losing the first game, had pursued his enemy for the next four games, and finally achieved success. But by then he was so bewildered that he straightaway lost two games running. In other words, the attacker sometimes suffers more than the defending side.

This agreeable state of affairs extended only up to the thirteenth game, drawn after a relatively quiet struggle, and then it was the turn of the challenger to switch to 'plan no. 2'. Botvinnik worked up a degree of pressure in the fourteenth game, and the game was adjourned in a position which Petrosian, quite probably, could draw. But on the resumption he committed a few mistakes, and had to resign.

After resigning the game, Petrosian went straight to the press-room: he wanted to convince himself that he had erred, not in the analysis, but during the resumption. He realized that now, when the match had passed the half-way mark, it was necessary to keep a clear head. He had analyzed the adjourned position with Boleslavsky until three o'clock in the morning. Naturally he came to the hall tired and started making mistakes. He should rest more, distract himself from chess. As if guessing his thought, Rona took his arm and almost dragged him out of the press-bureau:

'Hurry – there's just time to catch the football!'

After the fourteenth game, Tigran and Rona travelled to the Sukhanova rest home on the outskirts of Moscow. Tigran went for long walks in the woods, played billiards and table tennis, which never failed to help him when he needed a rest from chess. Besides this, there was always football. This particular brand of sport meant so much to Tigran that he would even permit himself the luxury of considering the chances of the Moscow 'Spartak' team in the league, when it was Botvinnik's turn to move.

Football and music – these were his two joys. He not only liked to listen to good singers, but sung fairly well himself. Sometimes the desire to sing would seize him as he and Rona were returning home on foot from the stadium. The character of the song, whether sad or gay, would depend basically upon how 'Spartak' had played that day. . . .

The fifteenth game was to play, perhaps, the decisive role in the match. Drawing conclusions from his loss in the previous encounter, Petrosian decided that his earlier, negative tactics had outlived their usefulness. Both sides, then, sat down at the board with the same plan in mind – without avoiding risk, to seek victory. But if Botvinnik did not guess his opponent's intentions, then Petrosian understood all, hardly had the first moves been made: Botvinnik selected the complex Grünfeld defence. Petrosian was gladdened; in this opening there was no necessity to create complications artificially, they were part of its very nature.

As never before in the match, Petrosian played the white pieces dynamically. He 'invited' Botvinnik into an extremely sharp variation, but the latter, fearing prepared analysis, led the play along less well-analyzed paths. Petrosian castled on the queen's side and threw forward his king-side pawns. Black's king began to feel uncomfortable, and Botvinnik offered the exchange of queens, notwithstanding his obvious disadvantage in the endgame. The day was far from won, but Petrosian led the attack very enterprisingly and artistically. His knight, causing a diversion on one wing, suddenly switched to the other. Botvinnik could not defend against the rising barrage of threats, and gave up the ghost in the second session. The equality of scores, for which he had striven so long and hard, was destroyed at the first touch. . . .

The game left a very favourable impression. The arbiter of the match, the English master Golombek, stated: 'the fifteenth game is undoubtedly one of the finest creations of modern chess'. Konstantinopolsky wrote: 'Taking into account Botvinnik's sturdy defence we could say that in this vital encounter the challenger showed mastery of the highest order'. However Petrosian liked Bronstein's appraisal most of all: 'T. Petrosian conducted the whole game with great energy'.

Not unnaturally, general opinion underwent sharp alterations during the fourteenth and fifteenth games. After game 14, many considered that the challenger was oppressed, confused, and that now Botvinnik would begin to reap the rewards of his long attack. A. Kotov, for example, judged the situation in this way: 'Petrosian has difficult problems to resolve. Receiving an extra point, the challenger went over to "blanket defence". He undertook nothing decisive, and only awaited the approach of his opponent's army. Such tactics could only end in disaster.'

If an experienced grandmaster could count as a 'disaster' the fact that the World Champion had managed to equalize the scores, then it may be assumed that belief in the success of the challenger was definitely wavering. This was why so many people were startled by Petrosian's show of strength in the concluding part of the match, especially in the fifteenth game. And yet it need not have been so surprising: in previous years Petrosian had more than once showed remarkable resilience. Let us recall the 28th championship.

'After I had missed a win in the first round against Simagin, and then lost in round 6 to Stein,' Petrosian said after the tournament, 'I felt a renewal of energies, and played with greater verve than at the start.' (After his defeat by Stein, Petrosian scored $4\frac{1}{2}$ out of his next five games.)

The fifteenth game had effect even on those who did not rate Petrosian's chances. After this game, where the champion was beaten by all the canons of classical play, the final contours of the match could be discerned.

In the sixteenth game the World Champion created a very promising position. Nearly all his minor pieces were aimed at the king's side. Black's king was sufficiently well protected, but only one or two careless moves from Petrosian, and White's attack would become very dangerous. At a decisive moment, Botvinnik baulked at sharp continuations and started to exchange pieces. Though he still maintained the advantage after that, the worst was over for Black.

Then it was Petrosian's turn to slip, and once again he was up against it. But in this game no one could have accused him of passivity. On move thirty-three Petrosian rejected an exchange, bringing his rook to the seventh rank. Panov gave the following assessment of this move: 'Risky move! Black is hoping for purely tactical chances . . . in effect, the rook is shut out from play'.

In his match with Botvinnik, Petrosian had made very few risky moves, and moves calculating only on tactical chances he had so far not indulged in. Maybe, taken by itself, this move was a bad one, but as part of 'plan no. 2', it was fully justified. Botvinnik made an error, now there were two black rooks on the seventh, and in the second session it was the World Champion who was defending. . . .

The score now stood at $8\frac{1}{2}$–$7\frac{1}{2}$ in favour of the challenger, it was still a long way to the end of the match, but the brutal nature of the previous three encounters indicated that the general battle was now taking place, whereby the outcome of the combat would be decided.

Petrosian held the initiative throughout the seventeenth game. In the previous game he had clearly sensed that the tension of the match had become exhausting for Botvinnik. Added to this the seventeenth game had always been fatal for Botvinnik: in six matches for the world championship he had drawn two 17th games, and lost four. It seemed that 17 was to be Botvinnik's unlucky number again. Petrosian obtained greater freedom of movement, and his central pawn threatened to move forward. However, Petrosian did not notice the strongest continuation, and in one move dissipated all his advantage.

In the eighteenth game Botvinnik gained a large positional advantage out of the opening, but dallied with the attack; he still wanted to build up his advantage bit by bit, and advance without risk. But the extended manoeuvring turned in favour of Black, and when Botvinnik finally advanced his central pawn, Petrosian had already arranged his defences. The game was adjourned. As Bronstein wrote, 'objectively the position was level, but it required extremely accurate and concrete calculations'. Petrosian similarly judged the position, and wanted to offer a draw, but Boleslavsky advised him to play on: surely Botvinnik was tired, and besides, he did not have his Boleslavsky!

Perhaps Botvinnik now regretted that he had (as in the revenge match with Tal) declined the aid of a second. The resumption showed that Petrosian's and Boleslavsky's analysis had been more accurate than the champion's. Botvinnik manoeuvred extremely unsuccessfully, and made a few blunders as well.

By a cruel irony of fate, Botvinnik lost the eighteenth game on the anniversary of his becoming champion, fifteen years earlier. After Botvinnik had resigned, Petrosian went into the press-room, where his puzzled colleagues asked him, what was his opinion of Botvinnik's play during the second session? Petrosian only shrugged his shoulders.

He understood very well Botvinnik's condition, and the reasons for his blunders. Only modesty prevented him from saying angrily to the inhabitants of the press-room: 'I would like to have seen how you would have continued the eighteenth game in Botvinnik's shoes!' However, in fairness he recalled that he had spent months in the press-room himself, and never clearly comprehended what a world championship match entailed.

The events of the next game showed that the World Champion was not only tired, but psychologically injured by his failures. Botvinnik conducted the game in a numbed condition, made a few unsuccessful sallies, and once more went down to defeat. The score stood at 11–8.

This was the finish. The remaining three games carried only formal significance: the twentieth game finished on move 21 in a draw, the next two were drawn in ten moves. On the day of the twenty-second game, which was clearly to be the last, Tigran was extremely nervous. From the morning he was locked in his study with Rona and Boleslavsky, and did not let them out of his sight for a moment. It was obvious that Botvinnik, who had practically made no attempt to fight in the preceding two games, would not alter his decision, and it was precisely this which agitated Petrosian. He was unable to believe that today he would become World Champion.

They could hear doors opening and closing in the corridor, and sounds of muffled voices; this was Tigran's sister Vartoosh, and Rona's friends, who in the absence of the masters of the house, were preparing to receive the innumerable guests about to descend on the home of the new champion.

Long before the actual appearance of Botvinnik and Petrosian, the fans were already crowding the entrance to the variety theatre. These were, of course, Petrosian's supporters. Today they were particularly noisy and excited. But in the foyer and in the hall there was tense silence.

In the two previous games, Botvinnik had shown nervousness. But in the final encounter Petrosian was clearly agitated as well. Making his ninth move, he offered a draw. He might have waited for the suggestion to come from his opponent, but it seemed for the first time in his life he was impatient. Botvinnik thought and thought, for eight minutes. Petrosian could not cope with his nerves, he would rise from the table, take a few steps, then sit down again. It was ten long and tortuous years that had brought him to this. . . .

Botvinnik was thinking. Sometimes with a characteristic movement he would straighten his tie or his glasses. The great Botvinnik. For all his wisdom, he was still only a man, and it was difficult and painful for him to do now what he had to. Suddenly, awakening, he stretched out his hand to the new champion of the world. This was on May 20th, at 17 hours 06 minutes.

An explosion of applause, a torrent of jubilation – and hundreds of fans swarm to the stage, brushing aside the assembled photographers. Even Tigran's personal bodyguard, Sergo Hambartsumian was unable to restrain them. Neither his trainer, neither Petrosian's wife, nor his closest friends were able to leave with him. He was swept away, and only rejoined them near his house.

Entering the flat, Tigran immediately went toward the record player. There already awaited him the pre-selected record: Wagner, prelude to 'Nibelung'. This music associated him with victory in titanic contests. Before each game he unfailingly listened to Tchaikovsky – concert for piano with orchestra. Now had come the turn of Wagner.

After a television appearance, Tigran devoted the rest of the evening to his friends and staunchest supporters, though he frequently had to leave them unattended: an uninterrupted flow of phone calls was coming from Yerevan. Tigran never forgot to thank his supporters – they had indeed raised him up by their attention. Even in the most difficult days of the match he read absolutely all the letters and telegrams, and they came in thick bundles. Rona specially asked the post office not to present the telegrams separately, but to put them all in the post box, otherwise Tigran would be signing for them all day.

Not only Armenia, but all parts of the Soviet Union sent Tigran letters. In Vitebsk, a student Yegorov sent Tigran greetings almost every day. Tigran became so used to his interesting and good hearted letters, that he was disappointed when the daily post did not bring a letter from Yegorov. However, this happened rarely.

But it was by no means a surprise that Armenia in particular was rejoicing for him. In one interview Tigran proudly stated that Armenian babies coming into the world at the time of the match were being christened Tigran or Petros.

The new World Champion received masses of souvenirs. One of them, which was his particular favourite, was made by a musician in the Yerevan symphony orchestra, Kasparian. This was the figure of a chess knight carved out of onyx. If you looked into the tiny eye of the knight, you could see a miniature chess board, and on it the final position from the fifth game, Petrosian's best game in the match.

He had ascended, a feat he would not even have dreamed of attempting five or six years ago. Now, with the excitement all behind him, he was interested to see how the chess world reacted to their new leader. Kuprin wrote: 'A remarkable chess-player, who has overcome the strongest opponents the world could offer, and who may proudly and justly bear the title of the king of chess play.' Petrosian knew that his victory had been just, but what did his colleagues think about this?

The greats of the chess world respectfully bowed before their new master. Bronstein wrote in *Pravda* that 'in the person of Tigran Vartanovich Petrosian the chess world has found a leader who is almost unbeatable in a competition of extended length. He is a fully legitimate successor in the line Steinitz–Lasker–Capablanca–Alekhine–Botvinnik.'

In another article Bronstein expressed the opinion that 'Petrosian became World Champion thanks to exceptional chess gifts and enormous abilities for hard work. An important role was also played by another facet of his talent – a rare chess imagination, which enabled him to foresee and thwart the most veiled intentions of his opponent. An unwillingness to risk even in minimal amounts sometimes gives Petrosian's play a rather dry outward appearance, but to the true connoisseur of chess creativity, a finer champion could not be found!'

Alongside the happiness in his triumph, Tigran also realized that his responsibilities had also considerably increased. Now every game he played would be put under the microscope by chess fans the world over. He was not intending to shirk these responsibilities. He saw it as his duty before all else to play, perhaps even more frequently than before. In a number of interviews he touched on this theme, as if conducting a dialogue with an invisible partner.

'Naturally, a World Champion's appearances often present difficulties to him, since he is always expected to be at his best. Many consider that frequent appearances even endanger the champion's reputation. There is no doubt that nobody is guaranteed against accidental reverses, and not even the very highest of titles can defend a man from this. But I believe in the old saying: "If you are afraid of wolves – don't go into the woods . . .".'

Thus spoke Petrosian. And he believed that he would act in just such a way. But he still did not realize indeed how heavy was the cap of the king. For the time being he was swimming in happiness, and did not suspect what severe, and even unjustified demands would be made upon him by the chess world. All this would be a future discovery. . . .

29 **Petrosian–Botvinnik**

5th match game, Moscow 1963

Grünfeld

1 P–QB4	P–KN3
2 P–Q4	N–KB3
3 N–QB3	P–Q4
4 N–B3	B–N2
5 P–K3	0–0
6 B–K2	

A little-analyzed and peaceful variation. But as the further course of the game shows, it is not altogether harmless.

    6 . . .   **P × P**

6 . . . P–QB4 was worthy of attention, beginning the central struggle immediately.

| 7 B × P | P–B4 |
| 8 P–Q5 | P–K3 |

It appears that this simplifying continuation leads quickest to equality. But . . . the appearance is deceptive. Sometimes the most far-reaching decisions are other than those which lead to combinative melées.

9 P × P	Q × Q+
10 K × Q	B × P
11 B × B	P × B
12 K–K2	N–B3

Black continues with Olympian

detachment to see to the development of his pieces. Yet the time may have arrived to penetrate the position more concretely. Thus 12 ... N–Q4   13 N×N   (13 N–K4 N–R3)   13 ... P×N   14 R–Q1 R–Q1   15 N–N5 N–R3   16 N–K6 R–Q2 would have maintained the equilibrium.

13 R–Q1   QR–Q1

Another casual move. Better was 13 ... K–B2. Now White manages to transfer his knight to the K4 square.

14 R×R	R×R
15 N–KN5	R–K1
16 N5–K4	N×N
17 N×N	P–N3
18 R–N1	N–N5
19 B–Q2	N–Q4

Not 19 ... N×P   20 R–QR1 N–N5   21 B×N P×B   22 R×P B×P   23 R–QN7 with advantage to White.

20 P–QR4

An instructive move. Giving up the QN4 square does not have great significance, and White manages to check the advance of Black's Q-side pawns with this move.

20 ...   R–QB1
21 P–QN3   B–B1

Creating a tactical threat of 22 ... P–B5   23 R–QB1 P×P!   24 R×R P–N7   25 R–B1 P×R=Q   26 B×Q, and White has to take a draw.

22 R–QB1   B–K2

This makes the defence more difficult. Better was 22 ... R–B2, or even 22 ... K–B2, forestalling White's next.

23 P–QN4!

Petrosian vigilantly exploits every chance offered.

In matches between players of the highest class a great advantage is secured if one can discover the 'Achilles' heel' of one's opponent. The Botvinnik–Petrosian match demonstrated that one small weakness in Botvinnik's play was his defence of inferior, simple endgames. This was revealed not only here, but also in the 15th and 19th games of the match.

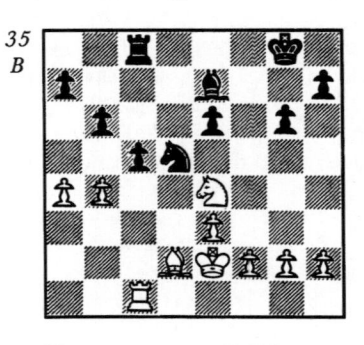

35
B

23 ...   P–B5

Where did Black make the fatal error, here, or on the next move? Grandmaster Stahlberg considered that by continuing 23 ... R–B2 or 23 ... K–B2 Black might have retained chances of saving the game. But it seems fairly clear that by playing 24 P×P P×P (if 24 ... B×P then 25 N–N5 or even 25 N×B) 25 K–Q3 followed by 26 P–R5 and 27 K–B4 White has every chance of winning.

24 P–N5   K–B2

Grandmaster Yuri Averbakh was probably correct in saying that the decisive mistake was made on this move. Continuing 24 ... B–R6!   25 R–B2 P–B6! Black could save the game. Now if 26 B×P (26 N×P and 26 B–B1 are both answered by 26 ... N–N5)   26 ... B–N5   27 K–Q2 (not 27 K–Q3? B×B 28 N×B N–N5+!)   27 ... R–B5   28 B×B (or 28 K–Q3 R×N!)   28 ... R×N   29 B–Q6 R×RP with equality.

25 B–B3!

A clever rejoinder, which Black had underestimated.

25 ...	B–R6
26 R–B2	N×B
27 R×N	B–N5
28 R–B2	K–K2

28 ... P–K4 does not help matters. Tal analyzes the following variation: 29 N–Q2 P–B6 30 N–K4 K–K3 31 P–B3 P–KR3 32 K–Q3 R–Q1+ 33 K–B4 R–Q7 34 K–N3 R×R 35 K×R K–Q4 36 K–Q3!, and the endgame is lost for Black.

29 N–Q2   P–B6

After 29 ... B×N 30 K×B K–Q3 31 K–B3 K–B4 32 R–Q2! White also wins.

30 N–K4	B–R4
31 K–Q3	R–Q1+
32 K–B4	R–Q8

32 ... R–Q7 is answered by 33 K–N3.

| 33 N×P | R–KR8 |
| 34 N–K4! | |

33 P–KR3 was also possible, though the line chosen is more direct. White returns the pawn, but improves the placing of his pieces.

34 ...	R×P
35 K–Q4	K–Q2
36 P–N3	

The most reliable move. 36 P–N4 P–R4 is not so clear.

36 ...	B–N5
37 K–K5	R–R4+
38 K–B6	B–K2+
39 K–N7	P–K4
40 R–B6	R–R8

The game was adjourned here. White is clearly winning, but he still has to be fairly careful.

41 K–B7

Undoubtedly the strongest, which unexpectedly called forth a protest from the opponent. Here Botvinnik turned to the match arbiter and claimed that White had sealed the impossible move 41 K–B8?? (into check!).

One of Petrosian's 'small weaknesses' is that he has a habit of writing the number 7 with a round tail ... in a word, the mediation of the judge was called for, and after the truth of the matter was established, play continued. The nervous strain of a hard match sometimes produces the most unexpected conflicts!

| 41 ... | R–R8 |
| 42 R–K6! | B–Q1 |

White wins quickly in the event of 42 ... B–B4 43 R×KP R×P 44 N×B+ P×N 45 R×P.

| 43 R–Q6+ | K–B1 |
| 44 K–K8 | |

White wins by gradually forcing back the black king.

| 44 ... | B–B2 |
| 45 R–QB6 | R–Q8 |

If 45 ... R×P, 46 N–B3 and 47 N–Q5 decides.

46 N–N5	R–Q1+
47 K–B7	R–Q2+
48 K–N8	1–0

Petrosian's first victory in the match, and one of his best games.

30 Botvinnik–Petrosian

18th match game, Moscow 1963

Queen's Gambit Declined

1 P–Q4	P–Q4
2 P–QB4	P–K3
3 N–QB3	B–K2

3 ... B–K2 is a cunning move, designed to avoid the 'Carlsbad' variation after 3 ... N–KB3 4 P×P P×P 5 B–N5 P–B3 6 P–K3. Now if 6 ... B–KB4 7 Q–B3!, as occurred

in the game Petrosian–Barcza, USSR–Hungary match 1955. Black has to accept the weakening of his pawn structure on the K-side – 7 . . . B–N3 8 B × N!

3 . . . B–K2 side-steps this line; if 4 P × P P × P 5 N–B3 P–QB3 6 B–B4 B–KB4 or 5 Q–B2 P–QB3 6 B–B4 P–KN3 Black successfully develops his queen's bishop.

4 P × P	P × P
5 B–B4	P–QB3
6 P–K3	B–KB4
7 P–KN4	B–K3
8 P–KR3	N–B3

This variation received its 'christening' in the present match.

White's counter-plan is an idea of Botvinnik's, which definitely sets Black a lot of problems; at the same time it is very committal for White. Unusually for this opening, the problem of castling has great significance for both players. There is nothing to prevent either side from carrying out this manoeuvre at once, but it is a case of 'Measure the cloth seven times before cutting!'. In the present game, neither side 'succeeded' in castling.

| 9 N–B3 | QN–Q2 |

9 . . . P–B4 was rather more active, to be followed by 10 . . . N–B3. Black was quite probably put out by the order of moves chosen by Botvinnik (up till now White had played 9 B–Q3), and in order to avoid pre-analyzed lines in the opening, chose to make simple developing moves. Alas, Black's simplicity of play in the opening does not exempt him from the difficulties of the middle-game.

10 B–Q3	N–N3
11 Q–B2	N–B5
12 K–B1	

12 N–KN5 B–Q2 13 P–K4! was more active.

| 12 . . . | N–Q3 |
| 13 N–Q2 | |

13 N–KN5 B–Q2 14 P–K4 or even 14 N × RP was once again worth considering. However, White intends to take advantage of Black's cramped game by preparing the advance P–B3 and P–K4.

| 13 . . . | Q–B1 |
| 14 K–N2 | |

Continuing his plan and at the same time parrying the threat of 14 . . . P–KR4! 15 P–N5? B × P+.

14 . . .	N–Q2
15 P–B3	P–KN3
16 QR–QB1	N–N3
17 P–N3	

On the preceding move, and even more so now, 17 P–K4 was a very serious alternative. Botvinnik seems to lose the rhythm of the struggle here, which eases the defender's tasks.

| 17 . . . | Q–Q2 |
| 18 N–K2 | N.Q3–B1 |

An important defensive resource. Black vacates the Q3 square for his bishop, and the knight can be redeployed on K2.

19 P–QR4	P–QR4
20 B–N3	B–Q3
21 N–KB4	N–K2
22 N–B1	P–R4
23 B–K2	P–R5
24 B–R2	P–N4!?

Black has grown tired of passive defence, and from now on perseveringly tries to sharpen the play.

In contests between the strongest of the world, striking victories and, what is more, easy wins are almost totally excluded. The outer heat of the battle is subdued, replaced by a tense struggle of ideas. What is seen on the surface is nothing, the players pass like sleep-walkers through a maze of underwater labyrinths. And yet at every step the fullest accuracy is demanded, for one slip can be the cause of eventual ruin. The game in question is a typical example of this. Throughout its long course the chances of both sides rise and fall like an apothecary's scales. The end is catastrophic. But . . . we will not divert the reader from the further course of events.

25 N–Q3

25 N–R5 was also possible, to which Black would have to reply 25 . . . N–N1.

25 . . .   Q–B2!

A precise answer. 25 . . . B × B, with . . . Q–B2 to follow, appeared simpler, but it would have given White an extra tempo for his K-side attack: 25 . . . B × B 26 N × B Q–B2 27 P–B4! with N–B3 to come.

26 Q–Q2

White had the opportunity of playing 26 B–K5!, and if 26 . . . B × B (on 26 . . . R–KN1   27 P–B4! is possible) then 27 P × B, threatening P–B4–B5. However, Black could sacrifice a pawn in reply by 27 . . . P–Q5! 28 P × P 0–0–0! and obtain satisfactory play. Striving to limit Black's counterplay as much as possible, White gradually loses his positional superiority.

26 . . .	N–Q2
27 B–N1	N–KN3
28 B–R2	N–K2
29 B–Q1	P–N3
30 K–N1	P–B3
31 P–K4	

The long awaited pawn advance finally occurs, and the play becomes more lively.

31 . . .	B × B+
32 Q × B	

White should have been in no hurry to exchange queens. Doubtless, time was running out.

32 . . .	Q × Q+
33 R × Q	R–Q1
34 K–B2	K–B2
35 K–K3	KR–K1
36 R–Q2	K–N2
37 K–B2	P × P
38 P × P	N–KB1
39 N–K1	N1–N3
40 N–N2	R–Q2

White's pawn centre at last defines itself. The strategical battle begins, as it were, anew. Black has succeeded in organizing effective piece play against the pawns.

41 B–B2

The sealed move. The simplest course to a draw was, perhaps, 41 N–R2 R1–Q1 42 N–B3, and if 42 . . . N–K4 43 N2–K1!

41 . . .   B–B2!

A fine reply, in connection with the subsequent plan of play against the . . . K5 square. Black makes the best use of the resources of the position.

42 N1–K3   P–QB4!

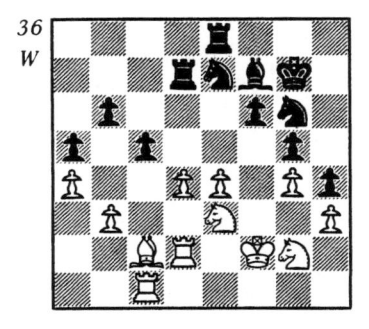

43 P–Q5   N–K4
44 R–B1

The beginning of a faulty plan, which leads to defeat. He should have played 44 N–QB4 N×N 45 P×N B–N3 46 P–K5! or 45 ... N–B1 46 P–K5! after which he could have activated his pieces. In that event he could have fairly counted on getting a draw. But Botvinnik wearies of the struggle, and fails to notice how dangerous his opponent's initiative has become.

44 ...	B–N3
45 K–K1	N–B1
46 R2–B2	R–KB2
47 K–Q2	N–Q3
48 N–B5+	B×N
49 KP×B	

The exchange sacrifice 49 R×B was worth considering, though even then Black's advantage is indisputable.

49 ... **P–B5**

The beginning of the decisive counter-attack. Petrosian plays the last part of the game in full force.

50 R–QN1	P–N4
51 P–N4	P–B6+!
52 K×P	

White has to accept the sacrifice.

52 ...	R–B2+
53 K–Q2	N4–B5+
54 K–Q1	N–R6
55 R–N2	N3–B5

More restless knights!

56 R–R2	RP×P
57 P×P	N×P
58 R–R6	N–B6+
59 K–B1	N×P
60 B–R4	R1–QB1
61 N–K1	N–B5
0–1	

31 Petrosian–Botvinnik

19th match game, Moscow 1963

Queen's Indian

1 P–QB4	N–KB3
2 N–QB3	P–K3
3 N–B3	P–QN3
4 P–KN3	

White could begin immediate operations in the centre by 4 P–K4 B–N2 5 P–K5 N–K5 6 B–Q3, though in that case 6 ... P–Q4 would be sufficient to maintain the equilibrium.

4 ...	B–N2
5 B–N2	B–K2
6 0–0	0–0
7 P–Q4	N–K5
8 Q–B2	

Botvinnik had employed the Queen's Indian three times previously to this, in games 3, 13 and 17, and each time Petrosian had chosen an unanalyzed line of play. Now, having a lead of two points, he resolves to play a 'guaranteed' opening system.

8 ...	N×N
9 Q×N	P–KB4
10 P–N3	B–KB3
11 B–N2	P–Q3
12 QR–Q1	N–Q2

Up to here the game is analogous to the 20th game of the 1960 Tal-Botvinnik match. Then, instead of 12 ... N–Q2, Botvinnik continued 12 ... Q–K2, very quickly equalizing the game. If White wishes, he can now force a draw by 13 N–N5 B×B 14 N×KP Q–K2 15 N×R B×R 16 N×N B×KP 17 N×B+ Q×N 18 R–K1 R–K1 (variation shown by Tal). However, having a minimal advantage, he feels duty bound to continue the struggle.

13 N–K1	B×B
14 N×B	B–N4

14 ... Q–K2 would have been quieter, after which it would have been very hard for White to make anything of his tiny advantage.

Botvinnik gives preference to

another plan, whereby he intends to create counterplay on the K-side. The further course of events indicates that this was a dubious decision.

15 Q–B2	B–R3
16 P–K4	P–B5
17 N–K1!	

17 P×P B×P 18 N×B R×N 19 P–B3 followed by B–B1 was also good. But White rightly considers that Black's attack does not present any real danger, and accordingly aims for complex strategical play, with a view to advancing in the centre.

17 ... Q–K2

17 ... Q–N4 would have been more consistent. Now White 'partitions' the black army with an energetic blow.

| 18 P–K5! | QP×P |
| 19 QP×P | QR–Q1 |

Black's game is extremely difficult. Especially bad is his bishop on KR3. All the same he can put up stout resistance. Here 19 ... R–B2 was best.

| 20 Q–K2 | Q–N4 |
| 21 K–N2! | |

A move typical of Petrosian. On N2 the king is very comfortably placed, to a degree covering the weaknesses round the king's field.

21 ... P–R4

This move only serves to weaken the queen's flank. However, it is rather hard to suggest sensible alternatives. In the absence of good moves, Black is forced to make bad ones.

| 22 N–B3 | Q–R4 |
| 23 B–R3! | KR–K1 |

The equivalent of positional capitulation. Yet if 23 ... R–B2 then 24 Q–K4! with an unpleasant pin along the Q-file. For the same reason 23 ... P–QB4 is bad because of 24 R–Q6. 23 ... N–B4 gives a poor endgame after 24 B×N P×B 25 R×R R×R 26 R–Q1! These variations strikingly illustrate the poor placing of Black's bishop on KR3.

| 24 R–Q4 | N–N1 |
| 25 R1–Q1 | R×R |

25 ... N–B3 does not alleviate his game because of 26 R–Q7!

| 26 R×R | P×P |
| 27 RP×P | Q–B2 |

Black hastens to the defence, but he is unable to maintain equality.

| 28 Q–K4 | P–N3 |
| 29 Q–N7 | |

A characteristic moment in the tense conditions of a world championship match. White had probably planned this manoeuvre in advance. Otherwise it is difficult to explain how he could overlook 29 Q–R4! with a very powerful K-side attack. If 29 ... B–B1 30 N–N5! Q–N2 31 B×B or 29 ... B–N2 30 N–N5 Black's game is extremely bad. 29 ... K–N2 is relatively best, but then 30 R–Q1! sets up the irresistible threat of 31 R–KR1!

After the game Petrosian revealed that he had missed this rook manoeuvre.

| 29 ... | B–N2 |
| 30 P–B5 | P×P |

Relatively best. If 30 ... B–B1, 31 P×P and if 31 ... B×B 32 P×P! wins at once. And after 31 ... P×P 32 Q×Q+ K×Q 33 B×B K×B 34 R–Q6 Black has a lost ending.

31 B×P N–Q2

The defence hinges on this move; now Black can still resist stubbornly.

32 Q×P N×P

33 Q×Q+   N×Q

If instead 33 ... K×Q 34 N×N+ B×N 35 R–Q7+ K–N1 36 R–R7, the rook and bishop endgame holds out little hope for Black.

34 R–QR4   B–B6
35 R–QB4

The time-scramble has its say. 35 B–Q4! was the quickest way to win, when Black has to lose a pawn without any compensation.

35 ...   B–B3
36 B–N6   R–R1
37 R–QR4   B–B6
38 B–Q4

Finally! Now White has every hope of victory. But Black can still fight on.

38 ...   B–N5
39 P–R3   B–Q3

A curious possibility is 39 ... B–K2 40 P–QN4 B–Q1!? Then 41 B–B3 does not work because of 41 ... R–B1! However, White can do much better with 41 N–K5! or 41 N–Q2.

40 P–QN4   B–B2
41 B–B3   K–B1

Black sealed the last move. 41 ... R–R3 was a possibility, and if then 42 P–N5 R–R2 43 R–QB4 P–R5 followed by ... R–N2. There is interesting play after 43 R–K4 N–Q3 (43 ... N–Q1 is strongly met by 44 P–R4!) 44 R–K5 P–R5 45 N–N5, and if now 45 ... R–N2? 46 R×P R×P 47 B–K5! with a decisive advantage. (These variations were pointed out by Boleslavsky). But continuing 45 ... N–B2! Black can still offer staunch resistance.

Accordingly, White's best answer to 41 ... R–R3 is probably 42 P×P followed by marching the knight –Q2–N3.

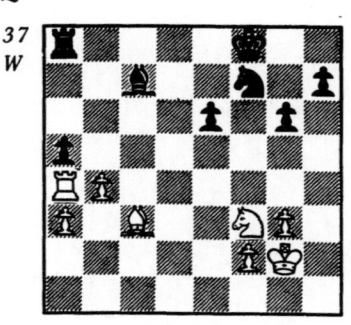

37
W

Against the move played, 41 ... K–B1, 42 P×P is again undoubtedly the strongest move. If now 42 ... K–K2, 43 N–Q4 K–Q2 44 N–N3, firmly supporting the QRP, and threatening R–Q4+ or R–R4! It is extremely unlikely that Black could have saved the position. The move chosen by Petrosian is perhaps a more complicated way of exploiting his advantage.

42 P–N5   K–K1

The play would have been sharper in the event of 42 ... N–Q3 being played. After 43 B–N4! K–K1 (43 ... K–K2 is met by 44 N–K5!) 44 P–N6 B–N1 White is clearly on top, but a forced win is not evident. Now White achieves his positional aim, establishing a defended passed pawn on QN5, which gives him the opportunity of calmly improving the positioning of his pieces.

43 R–QB4   K–Q1
44 P–R4   R–QB1

The white rook cannot be permitted to invade on QB6. 45 R–B6 can be answered by 45 ... B–Q3.

45 N–Q2

Transferring the knight to a new base on K4, White intends to attack Black's weak K-side pawns.

45 ...	N–Q3
46 R–Q4	K–K2
47 R–Q3	N–N2
48 N–K4	P–K4

The threats were 49 B–B6+ and 49 N–B6, which force Black to make new weaknesses in his position.

49 B–N2

Redeploying the bishop on the QR3–KB8 diagonal, White's small force initiates an attack against Black's king.

49 ...	B–N3
50 B–R3+	K–K3
51 N–N5+	K–B4
52 N×P	P–K5
53 P–N4+	

An error in time-trouble, after which White's winning chances become extremely problematical. Instead, 53 R–Q5+! K–K3 54 R–N5 K–B2 55 R–N4 R–B7 56 N–N5+ K–B3 57 N×P+, White achieves a winning position.

53 ...	K–B5!

Quite possibly this neat reply had escaped White's notice.

54 R–Q7

There is nothing better. Now Black manages to exchange off a pair of rooks.

54 ...	R–B2
55 R×R	B×R
56 N–B6	B–Q1

The last move before the time control, and probably the decisive mistake. 56 ... B–Q3! gives Black real chances of a draw. After 57 B×B N×B the knight ending is drawn.

And if 57 B–B1+ K–K4, Black's pieces are very well placed.

57 N–Q7	K×P
58 P–N6	

58 B–B8! deserved serious consideration, threatening to transpose into a winning bishop and pawn endgame by 59 N–B5. If immediately 58 N–B5, Black can defend by 58 ... N–Q3! 59 N–K6 N–N2! and so on.

58 ...	B–N4

Now White's problems are appreciably eased. Black's sole chance lay in the sacrifice of a piece by 58 ... K–B4 59 N–B5 B×P (but not 59 ... P–K6 60 P×P B×P 61 P–K4+!) 60 N×N P–K6! 61 P×P B×P 62 N×P K–K3. White's extra piece is by no means easy to exploit.

59 N–B5	N×N
60 B×N	B–B5
61 P–N7	

61 B–K3 B–K4 62 B–Q2 K–B4 63 B×P K–K3 64 B–Q2 K–Q2 65 P–R5 K–B3 66 K–R3 is simpler, when Black is defenceless against the king march towards the pawns on K4 and KN6.

61 ...	B–N1
62 B–K3	

White also wins after 62 B–N6 K–B4 63 B×P K–K3 64 B–Q8! K–Q2 65 B–R4 K–B3 66 B–N3!

62 ...	P–N4

After 62 ... K–B4 63 K–R3 K–K3 64 K–N4 K–Q2 65 B–B4, a pawn ending arises which Black loses by one tempo.

63 B–Q2	K–B4
64 K–R3	B–Q3

64 ... P–N5+ offered slightly more resistance. After 65 K–R4 B–R2 66 B×P! B×P+ 67 K–R5 B–R2 68

B–N6 B–N1 69 P–R5 Black cannot meet the threat of P–R6–R7! He also loses after 67 ... B–N6 (instead of 67 ... B–R2) 68 B–N6 K–K3 (otherwise P–R6–R7) 69 K×P B–K4 70 P–R5 K–Q2 71 P–R6 K–B3 72 B–K3 followed by K–B5×P and so on.

65 B×RP   P–N5+
66 K–N2   1–0

An enormously exhausting game. The errors committed by both sides are, of course, a direct outcome of tiredness and the nervous tension of the match.

10 And everything back to the beginning again!...

Petrosian had already guessed that the king of chess enjoyed few rights, but a great deal of obligations. Many of these obligations, it is true, proved to be pleasant ones. The most pleasant, and also the most tiring, was his visit to Armenia.

This visit stunned him completely. Even the first meeting with his fans at the aerodrome caused him to re-evaluate the importance of his victory. He was a little frightened by the enthusiasm, and by the responsibility which was now lain on his shoulders. He belonged now, it seemed, not only to himself, but to all those men who had faith in him.

The visit extended over a few weeks. Petrosian appeared in packed stadiums, in factory shops, in towns and villages, before academicians and vine-growers, before men of art and metal-workers. Unable as yet to rest fully after the match, he was tired once again, but the experience of happiness enabled him to forget his physical condition.

Returning from Armenia, Petrosian almost immediately travelled to Los Angeles, to take part in a tournament of 8 grandmasters. His strength seemed undiminished, and he even ended the second cycle with a score of 5/7. In the final table he was first equal with Keres with $8\frac{1}{2}$ points, ahead of Najdorf, Olafsson, Reshevsky, Gligoric, Benko and Panno.

He had already worked out a general programme of appearances. He remembered that whenever Botvinnik had an unsuccessful tournament, it would be blamed on his general lack of practice, especially on the fact that he rarely took part in the USSR championship. Petrosian had no intention of repeating this error, but strangely enough, he wasn't able to take part in any of the USSR finals. The first final happened to be a zonal tournament, and to play when he was not interested in the outcome, as much as the remaining contestants – this would put him under much less nervous tension, it might even be considered that he had an unfair advantage over the others. At any rate, Petrosian felt slightly awkward competing under those conditions, and declined to take part.

At the time of the next championship, history repeated itself. Though he had promised himself that he would definitely take part this time, matters conspired to make this impossible....

True enough, he had many honourable excuses. Becoming World Champion, he discovered it was very difficult to refuse invitations from the most unimportant chess organizations in the Urals or in Siberia, or even from his local polling station on Piatnitskaya Street. He had always considered vanity, conceit, as the most unpleasant characteristics for a man, and did not wish to give cause for anyone to accuse him of this. He took part in discussions, particularly those concerning the problem of draws. He carried out many other duties, both small and large.

He conducted an energetic campaign for the publication of a large number of chess books, and also an all-union, not simply a Moscow, chess newspaper. When eventually the newspaper did appear – *64* – much of the credit for this belonged to the World Champion.

Aware of the fact that his voice had greater weight now, he contributed many articles to the press concerning the current situation in chess. He most frequently returned to a question which concerned him very deeply – to the problem of developing the talents of young stars.

He had his own ideas on this matter. He understood that it was necessary to study seriously with young players. But at the same time he was very sceptical of the measures taken by the chess federation to relieve the young of all cares and difficulties.

'The evil is in this,' said Petrosian in one of his interviews, 'that conditions are artificially created for young and capable chess-players to gain the master title in the fastest possible time. They are permitted to take part in competitions, even international competitions, completely ignoring sporting principles. A sort of open road is placed before these young players, but it is one which leads to their destruction. . . .

'Our strongest chess-players, the pride of the chess world, achieved their successes by the only course possible, through exacting, but just struggle. In chess, as in any form of sport, only fighters can win. Fighters must be forged, not placed in warm ovens. Truly, young masters should be taught mastery of their skill, but this does not entail coddling them, making concessions to youth, to talent. Talent will always find itself a road, as Mikhail Botvinnik, David Bronstein, Vasily Smyslov, Isaac Boleslavsky, Mikhail Tal, Boris Spassky, Victor Korchnoi, Mark Taimanov, Yuri Averbakh and many other grandmasters proved in their youth. . . .'

In mentioning 'many others', Petrosian no doubt had himself in mind. He had never received any coddling, and had forged his character in an 'exacting, but just struggle'.

At the same time Petrosian considered it his duty, as a grandmaster and as the World Champion, to give the more able children practical assistance. This did not prove burdensome: Tigran discovered that he studied with children very happily. At first he taught his son, Vartan, and after that he tested himself out on other children.

And everything back to the beginning again!... 157

Petrosian became a regular guest at the Moscow pioneer palace. He never refused to appear before young chess-players and followed the chess development of the most gifted ones. He was most taken by Seriozha Makarichev – 'Makarchik' as he called him. Even now Petrosian follows 'Makarchik', analyzes with him and helps him with advice.

After one of the 'Spartak' youth tournaments, Petrosian got hold of all the games and spent a week analyzing them. After that he called them all together and gave a detailed analysis of all the games. It can hardly be gainsaid, how useful this seminar was, chaired by the World Champion. . . .

Once Petrosian on his own initiative travelled to Leningrad, where an all-union schoolboys' competition was taking place. There he lived in a hotel with the young chess-players of Moscow, helped them in their analyses and shared their joys and disappointments in the team competitions.

After a loss against the RSFSR team, the trainer of the Moscow team, A. Roshal gave each of the players a slip of paper, on which to write the result of the next match – with the Ukraine team. Petrosian also received a slip. When the match was over and the slips opened, the World Champion's result caused a burst of laughter from all the children – he had written 'Spartak 1 Dinamo 1'. As it turned out, a football match was to take place between these teams on that day.

After Los Angeles, Petrosian took part in quite a few international tournaments. In the 16th chess Olympiad in Tel Aviv he scored $9\frac{1}{2}/13$ on top board – an excellent result. In the powerful Zagreb tournament, which took place in the spring of 1965, the World Champion was third, a point behind Ivkov and Ulhmann, but ahead of Parma, Portisch, Bronstein, Larsen, Matanovic and others. In the autumn of the same year he shared 2nd–3rd places with Stein in the Yerevan international tournament where Korchnoi came first.

All these results were very respectable, but to his surprise Tigran discovered that he was expected to take first place everywhere! And then soon after the Yerevan tournament, he lost twice to Korchnoi in the Moscow–Leningrad match. Quite possibly, he might not have lost both games, but all the same, it was quite possible for such a mighty player as Korchnoi to defeat the World Champion.

Perhaps these relative failures from Petrosian might have been otherwise evaluated, were it not for the brilliant successes of his leading rival, Boris Spassky. The latter had to overcome many powerful opponents on his way to the final, and he not only did this, but succeeded in a manner which could leave no doubt of his superiority.

Beginning with the 31st USSR Championship, where, without losing a game he shared 1st–3rd places with Stein and Holmov, Spassky took first place in the 'tournament of 7', where, besides the three prizewinners of the championship, Bronstein, Geller, Suetin and Korchnoi also took part.

Curiously, in the first three rounds Spassky secured a mere half-point. If we consider his previous psychological instability, this result could only be reckoned a catastrophe. But in the next nine rounds he scored 6½ points, and took first place! In the Interzonal tournament, once more first prize, though this time in a tie with Larsen, Smyslov and Tal.

But the most impressive results were Spassky's victories in the matches with the remaining candidates. The first match with Keres went to ten games. Losing the first, and then drawing the second game, Spassky scored three wins on the trot. In such a short match this proved almost completely decisive. Only Keres' enormous experience and self-control enabled him to prolong the match to the last game. The score of the match was 6-4 in Spassky's favour. At the end of the competition Keres declared that there was no reason for his defeat, other than that Spassky had played better. This was not simply gentlemanliness, but an impartial assessment of what had occurred.

The next in turn was Yefim Geller, who had scored an even more convincing victory over his old rival, Vasily Smyslov (5½-2½). The match was ended in 8 games. Spassky won three games and drew five. Just as in his match with Keres, Spassky excelled his opponent in strategy and tactics. The impression was created that the victor, playing in a universal, and at the same time, aggressive style, had no vulnerable spot.

There remained still one powerful player – ex-World Champion Mikhail Tal. But in this last match Spassky's superiority was also clear. He won 7-4.

This had been very unlike Petrosian's performance at Curacao, where he had drawn both matches with his main rivals. And many people, indeed, came to similar conclusions. . . .

The World Champion at first followed the events of the Candidates' cycle with a sort of aggrieved surprise. How much energy, how many years he had expended in overcoming Botvinnik, and now it seemed everything must begin all over again! And if in the past, as the challenger, he had had nothing to lose, but everything to gain, now the roles were reversed. Tigran had once read an article by Euwe, where the latter recalled how much more difficult it had been for him to play the match as the champion, rather than as the pretender.

Now he remembered this article and experienced a common feeling with the author. It was easier to strive to achieve some new goal, far easier than to retain what had been won.

How deeply was Petrosian affected by Spassky's brilliant victories? He had, of course, followed every move of the Candidates' matches, and even commentated some of the games of the Larsen-Tal match for *Shakhmatnaya Moskva*. At the close of the Spassky-Tal match he took a plane to Tiflis in order to watch the players at first hand, the appearance and manner of his future opponent. At the same time, it would have been hard for Petrosian, reared in an 'exacting, but just struggle', to fear any possible opponent. After the match with Botvinnik was over, he was asked who among his possible opponents he feared most.

'I am afraid of no one on the chessboard, but always hold the greatest respect for all my opponents. . . .'

Before the match, Petrosian studied more than five hundred of Spassky's games, and found therein definite weaknesses which had escaped the eyes of many commentators.

Universality . . . this was the word used to describe Spassky. Petrosian, with his unshakeable faith in his tactical abilities, considered himself worthy of that description too.

'The ideal type of chess-player appears to me,' he later declared, 'one who can do everything equally well. For the time being such a player is an inaccessible ideal. Even such a universal, as Paul Keres, who does better than others, has hidden weaknesses. . . .'

With such an attitude, he might have reacted with open dissatisfaction to the declaration of universality concerning Spassky, but as it happened, he was not irritated.

Before the match began, it seemed that almost the whole of the chess world had acquired tongues, and were 'falling over each other' to deliver prognoses of Spassky's inevitable victory. There were many objective reasons for this; in the first place, the form Spassky was showing. Then, the difference in ages. Petrosian was now 37, seven years older than the challenger. Furthermore, there was the perpetual sympathy which the challenger always wins from the chess public, a sympathy which Petrosian had himself enjoyed when he played against Botvinnik.

If we add to this the relatively modest achievements of Petrosian in the three-year interim, then Panov's enigmatic comment, delivered just before the match, becomes comprehensible:

'The World Champion at present is in essence not one person, but the whole Soviet School of Chess.'

At the end of 1965, in the newspaper *Trud*, an interview with various Soviet and non-Soviet chess players was published. In it appeared a question on the chances of Petrosian and Spassky in a match.

The result of this referendum was not soothing. Keres, Larsen, Gligoric, Reshevsky, Najdorf, all spoke in favour of Spassky. Later on, two ex-champions, Tal and Smyslov, joined them. Botvinnik, Euwe and Fischer withheld their judgement. Only Stahlberg expressed his belief in Petrosian's victory. Seven to one with three abstentions. Say no more. . . .

Tal put the situation very accurately. 'Petrosian has two problems to resolve; one of them, formal – to hold his champion's crown; the other, moral: to unsettle the general conviction that Spassky must win.'

Yet despite the declarations concerning Spassky's 'universality' (in which it was easy to divine a belief in his victory) and the predictions, Petrosian remained unmoved; and not only because predictions are rarely fulfilled. Before the Capablanca–Alekhine match Spielmann forecast that Alekhine would not win a game.

There was a more vital reason; even had Spassky been rather older and more experienced in life, such a run of victories over the leading grandmasters, such a chorus of experts trusting in his final success, must have diverted him from the need to concentrate all his physical and spiritual energies for this match. Let the predictions mount up. . . . When on the eve of the match a book appeared, written by Spassky's second, Bondarevsky, *Boris Spassky Shturmuet Olimp* ('Boris Spassky Storms Olympus'), Petrosian understood that he had found a weak link in his opponent's preparations.

After the match was ended, Petrosian said: 'I consider that one of the reasons for Spassky's failure was the general belief in his victory. Quite a large part was played, perhaps, by the appearance of Bondarevsky's book. The publication of such a book can only be welcomed, but might have been better left till the match was over.'

Who was the opponent who had come to face the World Champion? Where were his strong and weak points?

The Candidate-66 was a very gifted player. He had won the International Master title at the age of 16, and at 18, the title of World Junior Champion. His first trainer was Vladimir Zak, an experienced chess pedagogue, then came Alexander Tolush, and finally grandmaster Igor Bondarevsky. The fact that he was influenced by players of such differing styles in his formative years partly explains his confidence in both simple and complex positions. Precisely for this reason he managed to play a different type of game against Keres, Tal and Geller, creating conditions on the board uncomfortable to each of these players.

At nineteen years Spassky shared 1st and 2nd places in the Soviet Championship, and took part in the Candidates' tournament at Amsterdam, where he took 3rd–7th place.

However, he then revealed a certain psychological instability in important tournaments, and losing the last games of the zonal tournaments in 1958 and 1961, was deprived of the right to take part in the world championship selection series. Spassky's return to the ranks of the Candidates' indicated that he had overcome his psychological problems, and his victories were a witness to his enormous strength.

'It is often considered,' said Tal a little before the match, 'that at one end stands Petrosian, at the other, Tal. And so Spassky is fortunate –

he is in the middle. He has appreciably enriched the 'store-room' of combinations, but at the same time could write books on chess manoeuvring. If the challenger does not quite have the depth of Petrosianic piece-placing, or his patience in defence, then he has his other advantages. . . .'

This advantage Tal saw as, in part at least, the fact that Spassky played the King's Gambit, that is, he had combinative gifts. The course of the match showed that here Tal, and many other observers, underestimated the champion's tactical skills.

In the same interview Tal likened Spassky's style to that of Alekhine, and Petrosian's to Capablanca (adding that comparisons can only be approximate). Reading this, Tigran was reassured that everything, literally everything, was loaded against him; three years previously, Euwe had compared him to Capablanca, and Botvinnik, with Lasker, who Capablanca had beaten. Now he had remained Capablanca, and the challenger had become Alekhine, who had in his time won his match against the Cuban. So much the worse, so much the better!

Panov spoke with even greater conviction of Spassky's combinational mastery. He did not doubt that 'Spassky will lure Petrosian into a whirlpool of unclear complications. In any event, that is the only way to win a match against Petrosian!'

In contrast to the challenger, Petrosian received no advice as to which whirlpools he should drag Spassky into. This was understandable – it was the reverse side of the champion's medal. The champion did not need advice, surely he knew everything, after all, he was the champion.

What did the champion know? First of all, that Spassky's fundamental strength was in positional manoeuvring, in his ability to accumulate tiny positional advantages, and then transmute them into material gains, or – here Spassky showed his many-sidedness – create direct threats against the enemy king. There was no adventurism, no straining of the position; Spassky likewise bowed before the principles of play, and 'forced' decisions were not to his liking.

Perhaps this was exactly how the champion played, and positional manoeuvring was his home ground. In Spassky's place Petrosian would have ignored this circumstance; every man must play 'according to himself'. At least until such tactics were proved clearly unprofitable. He would have played in that way in Spassky's place, and advised Spassky thus in Bondarevsky's position. 'In the final count,' he said before the match, 'the winner will be the one who plays the strongest, independent of such factors as style, psychology and so on.'

If Spassky listened to his advisors, and tried to play for complications, unclear, confused situations, Petrosian would be secretly pleased; in the first place he did not consider himself to be any weaker than Spassky in tactical play, and in the second place, this would mean that Spassky would have to make the running, which would relieve Petrosian of many cares.

However, Spassky's actual choice was still unknown, and must remain a secret until the time of the match. Accordingly, Petrosian and Boleslavsky worked out three possible plans for themselves, one where the champion was in the lead, one for when the score was level, and 'plan no. 3' for that undesirable situation, whereby the challenger led. Fortunately 'plan no. 3' was never needed.

A few months before the match Spassky took part in the Hastings tournament. Although it was a short tournament, Petrosian was astonished. He spoke to his friends roughly in this way: 'I might lose to Spassky if he proves stronger, or if he excels me in the opening, or in positional understanding, or endgame artistry. But I could never lose the match because I didn't prepare properly. . . .'

Knowing Petrosian's character, this should not surprise us. He painstakingly prepared for any opponent. But in this case, taking Spassky's crushing victories over the remaining Candidates into account, and also the general pessimism concerning his chances, he tried to make his preparations particularly thorough.

As in the match with Botvinnik, the role of opening assistant fell upon grandmaster Alexi Suetin. The middle game was dealt with by his trainer and second Isaac Boleslavsky.

When the preparations were over, and only a few minor details had to be added, Petrosian took part in a training tournament, arranged for him by his club, 'Spartak'. His 'testers' were Averbakh, Boleslavsky, Korchnoi, Simagin and Shamkovich. Petrosian scored 8 out of 10, winning all five games in the first cycle. Naturally, a training tournament could not be an accurate criteria of strength and sporting form, but all the same it gave Petrosian confidence.

Physical preparation occupied a great part of the training programme. Tigran was not sure that he was playing better chess than he had done in his match with Botvinnik, but he was quite certain of his improved performances on the skiing slopes.

A few days before the match I met Petrosian in Sukhanova, his usual pre-match residence. When the conversation turned to his preparations for the forthcoming match, Petrosian stated, 'If this,' – pointing to his forehead – 'does not betray me, then everything is in order. At any rate, if the worst comes to the worst, then my conscience is clear – I have done all that I can. . . .'

The match was on hand. But before their appearance on the stage of the Variety Theatre, the players crossed swords in the pages of *Nedeli*. This turned out to be an unusual 'blitz match' between the two. Both were given one and the same question to answer, but were allowed no more than 20 seconds for this.

The interview has great interest, and is presented below.

First question – about chess. What qualities does it develop in a man first and foremost?
T P The ability to concentrate.
B S First of all, in my opinion – perseverance.
Who is the strongest Western chess-player at the present moment?
T P In my opinion, Fischer. But as Tal would say, Larsen does not think so.
B S Fischer.
Who are the most promising young Soviet chess-players?
T P I could give an opinion, but I'm afraid that this would not be to their advantage to do so.
B S I like the play of 16-year-old Yuri Balashov from the Siberian town of Shadrinska.
When did you start to play chess?
T P At the age of 12. But I was playing backgammon, a very popular game in the Caucasus, at the age of four. I recommend it to anyone who wants to develop quick thinking habits and fast reactions.
B S I began to play at the age of 5. But my passion for chess began at 9.
Your favourite writer?
T P Lermontov.
B S I like Shriabin.
Film-actor?
T P My favourite actress? Natalie Wood.
B S I don't have any favourite actor.
Singer or songstress?
T P I can answer that at once: Beniamino Gigli.
B S I like Tito Gobbi best.
Do you like Opera?
T P Very much! Some people consider that opera is a dying form of art, but when I saw a guest performance by *La Scala*, I realized that such opera will live forever.
B S Not yet.
Your favourite musical instrument?
T P Any. It depends who plays it.
B S Piano.
Favourite book?
T P Is it really possible to name a book that always remains under your pillow? At different times and in different moods a man feels the need of different books.
B S I do not have any book which I read all the time, or which I have read many times.

Favourite sport?
T P All types of sport. Basically of course, I am a spectator. But table tennis, skiing, and billiards – these are the type I play.
B S Once it was light athletics. Now, perhaps, it is swimming.

Happiest moment in your life?
T P The first association that comes to mind was the moment I became World Champion. But if you consider it is only given for a time, and then lost eternally, then. . . .
B S . . . (time exceeded)

Most grievous?
T P Every time that 'Spartak' loses.
B S . . . (time exceeded)

Most difficult game?
T P I imagine that this awaits me in the near future.
B S One minute . . . (despite the 20 second allocation). My most difficult game was with M. Tal in 1958 in Riga, the USSR Championship. I lost that game, not being able to overcome the difficulties, and more precisely, myself.

What do you do after defeat?
T P Self-criticism. And after that I try and forget the loss as quickly as possible.
B S Straight after a defeat I am unable to leave off analyzing the events of the game. The main occupation indulged in is self-cursing. Sometimes I praise. Sometimes, losing a game, you win it morally.

After a difficult win?
T P I consider that there will be no less difficult games in the future.
B S After a difficult game I go and lie down. But I don't always sleep.

Does popularity hinder you?
T P Yes, to a degree, yes. . . .
B S It interferes. . . .

What did you dream of becoming as a little boy?
T P Diplomat or warrior. I also dreamt of going to Nakhimovski College, which was created during the war in Tiflis.
B S In childhood I dreamt first of all of being a chauffeur, and then an inventor.

What do you hope your children will become?
T P My elder son has already made the first steps, he is studying in the Moscow State University, and will be a biophysicist. And Vartan? We'll see what he has leanings to most. . . .
B S An unexpected question. I would like to see my children scientists.

Then could you perhaps name what in your opinion is the most respectable profession?
T P Any profession which brings joy and benefit to men.
B S It seems to me that all professions must be respectable.

And everything back to the beginning again!... 165

What are your entertainments, hobbies?
T P Many. Music, books, sport, cinema – and taking photos. I can't say which of them I like best.
B S In my childhood I used to collect records of Chaliapin singing. Recently I have had to collect opening variations.
Do you dance?
T P I even enjoy it very much. But I dance very badly.
B S Badly, but untiringly.
What is your favourite day of the week?
T P If you insist – Sunday. There is always football on Sunday.
B S Thursday. Why? I don't know.
Favourite food?
T P Of course, Shashlik. But also any well cooked meat.
B S Mushrooms.
Time of year?
T P Any, apart from autumn. I don't like slush.
B S Beginning of autumn.
Do you smoke?
T P I tried. I even wanted very much to learn. For 'stability'. But I didn't like it.
B S I am not a smoker. During the Candidates' matches I didn't smoke a single cigarette. But sometimes I smoke 4 or 5 a day. Not to smoke for a few days is not at all hard for me. When I feel that I am beginning to get accustomed to smoking I drop the habit at once.
What part of which city do you like best of all?
T P I like large cities. On warm summer evenings I particularly like Gorky Street (Moscow). And even more – forgive me for immodesty – the summer evenings on the Grand Boulevard of Paris.
B S The old parts of Leningrad.
Your most enjoyable incident from your travels abroad?
T P That happened in 1953. A Swiss newspaper found a likeness between myself and a Persian shah.
B S This was in 1955 at the World Student Olympiad. For some reason I remember a gay party on 8th May, on the eve of the Day of Victory, in a French town called Beaujolais.
What characteristics in man do you consider most worthy?
T P It's hard to select one at once ... of course, integrity, modesty, conscientiousness.
B S Above all, honesty. Secondly, courage.
And on the contrary, the most unpleasant?
T P Conceit.
B S Hypocrisy, sanctimoniousness, impoliteness.
Consider this situation: the decisive game is meant to be played on Monday, the thirteenth of the month, and a black cat crosses your path. How would you react?

T P Let me add: you have left something important at home. Naturally, if the thing was very important, I would return. And if I were late – then I wouldn't notice the black cat. But if there were still time, it would probably be better to cross to the other side of the street . . . you might quite justifiably remark, that I won the world championship title with ticket No. 13. I would reply: I'm surprised till now at that.

B S I am not superstitious.

Is superstition generally prevalent among chess-players?

T P I imagine that most of us suffer from it a little . . . but if we were to speak seriously, things such as black cats and unlucky numbers do not play such a vital role as the psychological make-up of the person himself. I remember in my first official international tournament, in Stockholm 1952. I very much wanted to draw number 7 in the lottery, and play my first game with White against the very weakest player in the tournament. And everything turned out that way! Surely it was impossible to play badly after that? In that tournament I obtained the grandmaster title.

B S I cannot answer for all chess-players.

We return once more to chess. Which colour do you prefer, White or Black?

T P My trainer, grandmaster Boleslavsky has the following saying: 'Love us the little black men, beg the chess pieces, for everyone loves us when we are white.'

B S White, of course. But sometimes I play better with Black.

Chess is an individual or a collective creativity?

T P Deeply individual.

B S Of course, individual. Preparation is collective, but not always. There are chess-players who prepare for games individually.

For what piece do you have a secret weakness (not counting, of course, the king itself)?

T P I have a weakness for any piece in excess of my opponent's numbers – from pawn to queen.

B S At five I liked rooks best of all. At nine I fell in love with the black queen. Now democracy rules in my army.

What is most important in chess, improvisation or analysis?

T P Both are equally necessary.

B S In my opinion it is necessary to find a mean between creativity and precise knowledge.

Will you yourself become a trainer?

T P They tell me that I have a rather heavy character for that.

B S It seems so.

Do you suffer from the phantom of time-trouble?

T P Fortunately, up to now time-trouble is no more than a phantom for me.

B S Thank God, not yet.
  Do you believe in the problem of the 'difficult opponent'.
T P I do.
B S Yes.
  And in accidents in play?
T P It occurs. But mastery, in my opinion, consists in keeping the role of accident to a minimum.
B S I do.
  What is better, to attack or counter-attack?
T P It's better to win.
B S My character is more of a counter-attacker. But attacking is psychologically easier.
  How many hours a day do you spend on chess?
T P I don't have any fixed allocation of time. Everything depends on what has to be done on that day.
B S Sometimes I don't do anything for weeks on end. Sometimes I spend 6–7 hours every day on chess.
  And what significance does regime have?
T P My regime is – going to bed at the right time.
B S That question is a little unclear for me. It seems clear what significance regime has.
  Do the reactions in the tournament hall influence you at the time of play?
T P Of course. Disorderly noise hinders. Approval – gives inspiration.
B S No.
  And the conduct of the opponent?
T P I try to make sure that my opponent's moves, not his conduct, have an effect on me.
B S It doesn't affect me.

. . . remarkable, how similar everything was. The same theatre, the same opening ceremony, no less ceremonial than the previous one, almost the same speeches. But not he, Tigran Petrosian. As before, modest, self-critical, objective, he was prepared to overestimate the strength of his opponents, but now not that much. What ever had been said of Spassky's invulnerability, however highly the experts had rated his chances, he, Petrosian, now knew best of all what was passing through the soul of the challenger.

Three years back he had also sat alongside a famous champion, and hardly believing himself, listened to the official speeches. Now he was calmer, far calmer. Let the debutant agitate, this was his lot. He, the champion, had no right, no need to feel the slightest tremor. This was his privilege as the chess king. He had paid a high price for this, and must now take advantage of it. . . .

Petrosian was so used to putting himself in the place of his opponent at the time of play, to divine his intentions, that he could now even feel for the pretender. In the final count, what was the difference – had it been Spassky, or someone else. Yet the young man was very obliging, and conducted himself irreproachably. He had even publicly declared that he was ready to agree to any demands made by the champion as regards the organization of the match. This was rare generosity. Even Tigran himself, hm, hm, had not shown such reverence in his time. . . .

And generally speaking, he liked this sympathetic Bora very much. His childhood, too, had not been easy. And what that signified none knew better than Tigran himself.

As a youth, Spassky too had been criticized for the dryness of his play, but, despite the influence of grandmaster Tolush, he had not changed, and afterwards had managed, despite the tricks of fortune, which seemed even to deride him, to return to the beginnings and bring everything, if not to a favourable conclusion, at least to a match for the world championship. So all in all this young man was very sympathetic, this Boris Spassky and . . . very, very dangerous.

This was roughly how the champion thought, sitting at the long table next to the challenger.

The start of a match has a colossal significance. It may cast the roles of the players at once, creating a confident rising mood in the one, condemning the other to long and tortuous, often fruitless, labour. Yet if the start is vital, so too must be the very first game.

This time Petrosian did not feel himself lost. Well comprehending the state of his opponent, he began to play calmly. The course of the game was a pleasant surprise for him, and not only in that, playing the black side of a Caro-Kann he quickly equalized; Spassky chose the very same variation that had brought him victory against the Yugoslav grandmaster Matulovic.

Naturally, Spassky understood as soon as Petrosian went in for the line, that he fully intended to avenge the Yugoslav's defeat. Both players move for move repeated the already played game. The silent psychological duel held dubious perspectives for both players. Even though nothing violent was occurring on the chessboard, and both sides were manoeuvring calmly, the inner tension rose.

Spassky diverged first. It seemed that there was nothing concealed in his second arsenal – he simply hoped to succeed with a once profitable variation. Surely he did not intend to win the match merely by repeating moves? For the time being it was a riddle, but at any rate, the opening of the first game had great significance.

The game meanwhile continued. White's diversion had given him no advantage. All the pieces were exchanged, except for the queens. Now in a completely drawn position, Spassky continued to try and make something out of nothing.

Chess, like men, values persistence. Obstinacy, on the other hand, is punished. Suddenly Spassky made a poor move, and Petrosian could win a pawn.

He saw this opportunity immediately and ... then it turned out that he himself was hardly as calm as he had at first thought. Realizing that he had chances of victory, Petrosian – or his evil genius 'the-desire-for-strengthening-of-the-position' – decided to try and see if there were not another, quieter way of winning the pawn. He thought that there was, but overlooked a very obvious retort, and after a few moves a draw was agreed.

Making his incorrect move, Tigran, unnoticed, felt his pulse beneath the table. Instead of the normal 65–70, it was 140! That was how the first game of the world match must be, even if it was not your first match. Interesting to know, what was Spassky's pulse now. . . ?

In the first game both players had felt the agitation of the start, had exchanged errors, but all was normal. The world championship match was under way.

When in the second game Spassky chose a quiet, well-trodden line of the Queen's Gambit, which he rarely used, Petrosian understood what tactics his opponent was employing at the start. For the first few games, while he was still unused to the circumstances of the match, the stage, the partner, he preferred to put his faith on reliable opening systems.

This was of course quite correct, and in his place Petrosian might have done the same thing. At the same time many observers, among them Keres, expressed surprise that the challenger, who was clearly better trained than the champion, had not tried to take advantage of this at once and initiate complexities.

Despite the placidity of the opening, Petrosian managed to gain an advantage. The white rooks, queen and knight held Black's hanging pawns in check. But the advantage was perhaps double edged, for as Bronstein wittily remarked, you never can be sure what they are whispering to each other, these hanging pawns, and which of them is intending to move forward, and which remain behind.

This time the pawns whispered, so it would seem, of their sorrowful state. Petrosian exchanged the queens, obtained the better ending and forced one of the hanging pawns to move forward, upon which they immediately lost their proud appearance. Sensing the onset of a slow but inevitable strangulation, Spassky gave up a pawn to give his pieces breathing space.

At this vital moment Petrosian did not make the most of his possibilities, though he considered that the task involved was far more difficult than appeared from the wings. All the same the game was adjourned in a difficult position for the challenger, but on resumption he defended excellently and achieved a draw.

In the following game too, Petrosian kept Spassky under pressure for a long period of time. Playing Black, the champion soon seized the initiative, and Spassky had to sacrifice a pawn once more in order to give his pieces play, and create some threats on the king's wing.

Strictly speaking, the sacrifice was not correct, but Spassky had already sensed that the tension of the start permitted him to overstep the allowed limits from time to time. For the time being the moment of decision had not arrived, the match was still young, and furthermore Petrosian generally preferred to return the pawn, or decline to make serious efforts to capitalize upon it, if that meant that he was letting himself in for possibly dangerous complications. So while the threat of the first defeat still hung over both players, it was possible to play with fire.

Winning a pawn and obtaining an objectively winning position, Petrosian then committed a series of inaccuracies, but still maintained good winning chances. However, he got into time trouble, and Spassky made excellent use of this to sharpen the play. Petrosian discovered a move guaranteeing him a draw, but did not find the move which maintained the extra pawn in a simple position.

For the third time running the challenger had walked on the edge of an abyss, and for the third time emerged unscathed. How long could this continue?

The fourth game declined to give an answer to this question, since in comparison with the previous one it took a relatively peaceful course. And the fifth was unable to, simply for the reason that the champion, not the challenger, was in a desperate position.

'The first four games showed Spassky's excellent practical preparedness,' said Petrosian later. 'Falling into bad positions, mainly due to inaccurate opening play, he then found the best practical chances available.'

In the fifth game Spassky at last gained the initiative and established a powerful position. But Lasker had quite accurately remarked that winning positions are the most treacherous. The very tension of the match, which had previously aided the challenger, now turned against him. An element of compassion seemed to be present: the psychological tension always benefited the weaker side.

Taking advantage of Petrosian's weak opening play, Spassky severely cramped his opponent's pieces. In view of the threats of inexorable suffocation, it was Petrosian's turn to sacrifice a pawn, in order to free his game slightly. This was a correct and courageous decision, but now Spassky had an extra pawn in a superior position – what more could he ask for?

The press-room was in ferment. 'It's burning,' exclaimed grandmaster Kotov, gladdened that the long row of draws had ended and something could be said about the match. 'It's not burning yet, but at least it's smouldering, Tal corrected him. And Golovko, speaking over the phone to the editors of *Krasnoi Zviozdi*, evaluated the World Champion's position as hopeless.

The evaluation was very near to the truth. Yet at that precise moment when Spassky should have demonstrated technical accuracy, he became nervous. While Petrosian was considering his move, Spassky would pace restlessly, wrinkling his forehead and pursing his lips. He was about to win his first game against the champion, and take the initiative in the match.

Both Spassky's pose, and his gait bespoke his agitated condition. Generally contained, self-controlled, he was now fully in the grip of his emotions. And the main among these was impatience; surely Black's position was ruined.

Capitalizing on an unsuccessful knight manoeuvre of Spassky's, when he should have brought his king to the centre of the board, Petrosian with a few energetic moves created a mini-attack against his opponent's king.

The continuation was bitter; instead of a calm and faultless exploitation of an extra pawn, the challenger had to resort to desperate measures to extricate his king from the attack. The final moves were made in mutual time-trouble, blunders were exchanged, but Spassky still managed to keep his extra pawn. Yet Black's pieces had by then flooded back into the game and were assailing White from front and rear. The game was adjourned, but everyone understood that the champion had saved himself.

That evening, leaving the Variety Theatre, I stood a long while on the embankment, watching the black, disappearing lines of the Moscow river, and listening to the interminable arguments of the chess-fans. Suddenly the noise stopped – and a cry of delight arose from hundreds of throats – it was Spassky coming out of the Variety Theatre. Moody, dark-faced he almost ran up the steps and hurriedly walked along the embankment, greedily and often sucking at a cigarette. He shot past me, leaving an array of forlorn supporters far behind, and disappeared into the gloom of Kammeny Bridge. . . .

The fifth game had opened Petrosian's eyes to much. In life nothing passes without trace, and everything must be paid for in time. How commonly it is said that the challenger has nought to lose in the event of failure. Yet he loses, and loses a great deal! He loses not only the champion's title, but also three years of struggle in the qualifying tournaments.

Spassky in the event of misfortune lost still more. Do you remember with what ease, and at the first attempt Tal overcame all barriers in his path to a match with Botvinnik? And Spassky? Two tragic reverses in the final rounds of the zonal tournament had enforced a six-year period of inactivity upon him; while his colleagues were contending with each other, he was required to begin everything from the beginning. This had not passed without trace, was imprinted on his consciousness and accompanied him at every step.

He could not, must not begin everything again from the beginning, the thought was unbearable; he had to use his chances now, right now. That was why he trembled with excitement and impatience at just that moment when he had to keep a cool head!...

In the sixth game the players tacitly agreed not to play at full strength; the previous game had taken a lot out of them. And the following game was destined to play a decisive role; the chain of draws was broken, and finally the champion took the lead. Petrosian later considered the seventh game as the best he had played in the match.

'It demonstrates my creative attitude,' said Petrosian later, 'limiting the possibilities of the opponent, strategical play over the whole board, surrounding and gradual squeezing of the ring around the enemy king.'

In the seventh game Spassky employed a fairly common psychological ploy: in a Queen's Pawn opening, he employed a variation which Petrosian often played himself. Sometimes this can prove very effective, but in this case its eventual lack of success was clearly foreseeable. Why was this so? Simply because during a game Petrosian would often play 'for his opponent', always evaluate the position through his eyes, look for – and find – the answer to his own intended move. This is why many of Tigran's tactical operations were not carried out; developing a beautiful combination, he would find an accurate and no less beautiful reply for his opponent. The game would continue, and the combination would remain unrevealed.

In this case Petrosian was already used to playing 'against himself', and the choice of opening did not upset him in the least.

The game was also significant from another point of view. Emerging unharmed from the skirmishes of the 2nd and 3rd games, and almost taking the fifth game, Spassky, apparently, decided to attend to the advice of those who considered he should drag the champion into complications. Accordingly he switched his armoury, but the switch was only too welcome to his opponent.

The game had hardly passed the opening stage when Spassky began an advance over the whole board, offering the sacrifice of a pawn at the same time. Petrosian declined the offer, since it was his intent to take the initiative himself. He kept his king in the centre comparatively long, then castled on the queen's wing, precisely on that side where White's pawns were storming. This was a clearly unexpected decision for Spassky, but it soon became apparent that White's attack was still-born, whilst Black's was developing apace.

Petrosian was in his element! Curiously, very few of the experts in the press-room were able to guess his moves, and they gave those moves extremely contradictory evaluations. (Later on the main arbiter of the match, O'Kelly de Galway, who often appeared in the press-room, mentioned that he quite often saw that Petrosian's moves came as a surprise to the assembled grandmasters. He considered this was due to the originality of the champion's style.)

Only one of Petrosian's moves occasioned a unanimous, if stormy, reaction; this was the 17th move, whereby, in combination with other moves, he closed the queen's side. Simagin, Kotov, Holmov, and Flohr immediately condemned the move, seeing in it only a desire of the World Champion to block the position and lead the game to a draw.

Even the far-sighted Tal did not immediately divine the champion's intentions. Tal was then waiting for a phone call, and sat in a corner away from the noisy group of grandmasters.

'Who is better?' I asked him. Casting a glance at the demonstration board and noticing Petrosian's latest move he declared:

'Spassky now!'

This was how firmly rooted was the conviction that the champion would evade complications at any price! Even when Petrosian, fearing for the safety of his own king, added the final defensive touches to his position, before beginning a general advance, this was taken only as a striving for the quiet life.

The illusions were soon dispelled. A few moves later Black's pieces were making inroads on the king's wing. This was the triumph of Petrosian's strategy. Then he sacrificed the exchange and set all his pawns in motion in the centre and on the king's side. This was the triumph of his tactics.

White's pieces were crushed and dislocated under the advancing pawn wall. When the game was adjourned Petrosian sealed a move, whereby he offered up his knight, but simultaneously removed the last white pawn from his path. Finding himself face to face with the naked eyes of the black infantrymen, Spassky accepted his defeat.

The seventh game left a deep impression due to its depth, logic and blend of strategy and tactics. At the same time it gave Spassky his first real grounds for unease. From the game he might perhaps already have realized that he had no hidden reserves of tactical talent to fall back upon.

'You are considered a great strategist, but this match showed that you can also combine brilliantly. Is this not the main surprise of the match?' was a frequent question given to Petrosian by journalists.

'I have never considered myself a poor tactician,' came the quiet, but very proud reply.

As later developments showed, Spassky did not take the warning.

At any rate, one game was not sufficient evidence to sway anyone from his chosen path.

Before leaving the seventh game, we might consider why Petrosian sealed a move by which he sacrificed a knight. Surely he had other, quieter possibilities of finishing the game victoriously?

The question is not quite so unimportant as might appear at first sight. After the match I placed it before the World Champion.

'The knight sacrifice was the most energetic, the most decisive, and as it happened, the best continuation' came the answer.

'And what about the effect?' I continued the interrogation. 'Wasn't it governed by a desire to produce not only the most effective, but also the most beautiful move?' In putting this question I fully realized that the knight sacrifice had been fairly obvious, and could not have therefore been an object of great pride for the World Champion; but at the same time it was the sealed move, and in such cases an experienced chess-player tries to avoid any risk.

Petrosian unhesitatingly rebuffed the suggestion. No, no, never for him! Simply, the position had demanded such a move, and he, as always, played according to the position.

I recall that this answer disappointed me. I thought, as I consider now, that Petrosian had not been entirely frank. A striking move, even if it is only capable of inspiring gasps from the lower rungs of the chess public, should in any event occasion the chess artist some small degree of satisfaction.

Had not Petrosian's second 'I', diligently concealed as it might be, impelled him to sacrifice his knight? I feel that this must have been the case, and that the course of the match demonstrated that the World Champion was not immune to those small joys which make the game of chess immortal.

The chess fans had become so used to world championship matches that many already guessed the character of the next game. The game took place in a half empty, fairly quiet hall, and ended in a quick draw. Spassky needed to recover himself after the shock of the previous defeat, and Petrosian, with a point in the bag, felt no need to force matters.

The ninth game, in which at first it seemed that the champion was in difficulties, was also quickly drawn. Then came the tenth game, after which it became very clear that the challenger was in a bad way, both from the creative and sporting viewpoints.

In this game the challenger employed the King's Indian defence for the first time, which was sufficient indication of his aggressive intentions. The opening was played in a well-known fashion, but then the champion's incautious fifteenth move allowed Spassky to work up dangerous tactical complications.

Once again, it seemed Spassky, in choosing a sharp defence, had lured his careful opponent into complications. This was to many the ideal situation for the challenger. But strangely enough, hardly had the game become tactical when Spassky made an oversight, and with a couple of sharp thrusts Petrosian had seized the initiative, sacrificing the exchange for good measure.

Spassky, who had only just held the initiative, and was preparing to dictate events, suddenly saw to his horror that he must immediately take to defence. This rapid change of roles had a calamitous effect on him, and he was no longer able to put up a cool and stubborn defence. Mentally upbraiding himself for his slip, he committed yet another.

Spassky did not simply lose the tenth game – he was routed. Petrosian sacrificed yet another rook, and noticed with pleasure that he could also sacrifice his queen. This he did, and Spassky immediately resigned.

This was the second serious warning, but Spassky was still not unsettled. . . .

And Petrosian? How gaily his second 'I' danced before his supporters! How proud was Petrosian the tactician that he had finally been able to show himself, and on such an important occasion too! This second Petrosian was gladdened for another reason: in the tenth game, he had won not only because he was stronger in tactics, but also in psychology.

After the match, continuing to uphold the principled correctness of his outlook, Petrosian gave an interview to *Pravda*, where he stated that, in his opinion, 'much harm has been done by the approval given to the so-called psychological or intuitive style of play, wherein objective evaluations frequently give way to unclear, purely sporting factors.'

This was rather harshly spoken. For one thing, Petrosian's own realignment of play in the early 60's had been towards this same intuitive style. For another, even the classical style of play did not totally exclude 'unclarities', or more accurately, psychological factors.

The tenth game had just such an appearance. Petrosian seized the initiative just as much because he presented his opponent with a psychological riddle. At one point in the game, Black's bishop's pawn came forward on the king's side, and Petrosian had to capture it, either with a pawn, or with his rook. The position demanded that he capture with the rook; this was objectively the strongest move, and Petrosian, the principled supporter of the severely classical school of thought, should have played that way.

Yet surely he had not made his intuitive realignment in vain! He clearly sensed Spassky's condition, and his impatient desire to cancel the scores at once, and he intuitively felt that Spassky would answer the pawn capture with a bishop attack which looked at first sight very strong, but was actually a tactical error.

Petrosian made the pawn capture, and the continuation was exactly as he had foreseen. It was a tactical, psychological triumph, a triumph too for the 'intuitive style'.

After 10 games the score was 6–4 in favour of the World Champion. The challenger's position looked extremely difficult, if only because he had not yet discovered a weak link in his opponent's armoury, not a fruitful mode of conducting operations.

From now on the match took a different course. The champion had gained points, and the challenger now had to exert all his strength to make up the difference. For the next few games Petrosian could be sure he would undergo a furious, and very serious, onslaught.

The twelfth game, it is true, almost had a catastrophic outcome for Spassky. But the fates were once again merciful to the defeated, and unexpectedly gave Petrosian a jolt. In between there was the eleventh game, which was also uneasy for Petrosian.

Here Spassky began the attack almost at once, and sacrificed a pawn for a very promising position. However, Black parried all the threats, and on the twenty-first move White offered a draw.

Petrosian thought about the offer. He realized that Spassky did not have enough compensation for the pawn. But all the same, if he had offered a draw, it meant that he had seen something perhaps. Petrosian refused the offer, but then found himself regretting it.

After all, he had a reserve of two points. Why take any risk, more so, since a drawn result strengthened his position?

These thoughts so assailed him that he began to make inaccurate moves, and soon offered a draw himself. Not disguising his surprise, Spassky accepted. Even then Black's advantage was evident, and therefore the peaceful outcome came as a surprise to many. Petrosian very quickly came to regret his decision.

The twelfth game, which marked the end of half the match, was the last one in which the challenger tried to rely on tactics. But burning his fingers yet another time, he unwittingly managed to inflict a painful wound on the champion, which the latter did not repair until long after the match itself was over and done with.

As in the tenth game, a King's Indian defence was played, with the difference that the challenger introduced a new move on move 5. According to Shamkovich, this caused some perturbation in the pressroom. For a long time both sides regrouped their forces, preparing for a tactical struggle on the self-same flank – the king's side. And when the fight commenced, it was not immediately clear who was attacking, and who defending: both sides were attacking! On the twenty-seventh move one of the pawns defending Petrosian's king shot forward. Spassky was not to be left behind; he left his knight en prise, and moved forward one of his central pawns, attacking a white bishop. Petrosian captured the knight, and then another Spassky pawn moved forward, attacking White's second bishop.

And everything back to the beginning again!... 177

This murderous battle created an enormous impression. The spectators were watching with a mixture of horror and amazement the drama unfolding on the large demonstration board. Time-trouble was approaching for both, and the atmosphere became even more electric.

What did Petrosian 'the cautious' do? He sacrificed his rook for a bishop. At that moment the outlines of a deep and exquisite combination became apparent. In the press-room the grandmasters noisily hammered down the pieces: a 'windmill' was on the way!

The 'windmill' is one of the most beautiful of all possible chess combinations, the secret desire of every chess-player. The Mexican Carlos Torre would have been famous had he won only one game in his whole life – the one in the Moscow 1925 tournament, when he caught Lasker himself between the millstones.

On the thirty-first move of the game came the culminating point of the struggle – Petrosian not only left his two bishops under attack, but even put his knight en prise! An unusually beautiful chess picture was created, where three white pieces, standing in a row, presented themselves up for sacrifice. It seemed that Torre's triumph was to be repeated, and on an even more important occasion – a world championship match!

At that moment I quietly approached Boleslavsky, who was sitting in the hall. Generally tranquil, he now bent his head over his pocket chess set and feverishly checked through Petrosian's combination. Yes, there was no mistake, the windmill was prepared for action, and now the wheels would be set in motion. And suddenly Boleslavsky, raising his head to ascertain Petrosian's latest move, almost audibly groaned: Tigran, hurrying because of time-shortage, had made a move which ruined everything. No, the move did not actually lose, but instead of an immortal combination, the outcome was to be another prosaic draw.

Despite its sizeable blemish, the 12th game aroused a great deal of enthusiasm. The tone of the commentators, which had altered after the 7th and 10th games, was now completely different. Euwe very briefly and precisely defined the situation:

'The World Champion is not only excelling Spassky, but even himself. We already know Petrosian as a deep strategist, an excellent defender, an expert in the endgame. But in this match we are seeing a new Petrosian. He sacrifices, counter-attacks, attacks. In other words, a dangerous tactician has appeared.'

And here are the remarks of the editor of the English magazine *Chess*, B. H. Wood. 'Petrosian's play in those games which I had the possibility of spectating, along with a group of chess fans, when we visited Moscow, immeasureably increased our respect for his talent. I imagine a similar shift will occur throughout the world. . . .'

A shift did indeed occur. Tal, for example, in an article devoted to the results of the first twelve games, asserted that 'such a mobilization of pawns, as occurred in the 7th game, has not been seen since the time of the Labourdonais-MacDonnell matches'. Of the 12th game, Tal said that for all its incompleteness it undoubtedly enriched the treasure house of chess artistry. And finally the score – 7–5 – was one with which the champion could well be pleased.

But Tigran was dissatisfied. Why hadn't he found the strongest move in the twelfth game, which might have become the greatest creative achievement of his life? Only because he had found a move which guaranteed a draw, and could not force himself to look for another move.

This creative tragedy had not escaped the eyes of the commentators. Tal later wrote: 'In both the 11th and 12th games Petrosian succeeded in obtaining a considerable advantage. But in the 11th, in a position which offered winning chances, he proposed a draw, and in the 12th, carrying out a marvellous combination, transposed moves at the last moment, and once again a draw came about.

'Naturally, from a sporting point of view these draws in no way worsened his position, but from the standpoint of the artist, whose most beautiful conceptions remain unfulfilled, the effect is depressing.'

And how depressing! Generally he never was guilty of 'remorse for the past', but this time Petrosian-the-artist severely castigated Petrosian-the-sportsman. Petrosian-the-tactician complained of the supremacy of Petrosian-the-strategist. In short, there was a splitting of the first and second 'I's.

However much Rona, Boleslavsky, even Kalashian, once more delegated by his friends in Armenia, tried to calm him, Tigran could not be put together again. What was worse, having obtained such a large advantage in the match, the World Champion, with a feeling of horror, realized that he had no desire any more for battle, nor any reserves against the apathy which threatened him.

There were all the signs here of a psychological depression. Petrosian began to feel unwell. With the permission of the doctor, he took a few days off. And when, having rested, he returned once more to the board and found before him a Spassky, smiling gaily, fresh and confident, with not a trace of the oppression of the last few games, Petrosian took his seat with a feeling of foreboding.

He was not in error. The thirteenth game, which followed the first game in the opening stage, saw Spassky introduce an improvement and establish an appreciable advantage. The champion, as he had done more than once during the match, sacrificed a rook for a knight, but this time it was forced. True, Spassky committed an inaccuracy during the first adjournment, and Petrosian obtained good drawing chances, but in his turn he blundered and lost.

This game had serious consequences. A victory was necessary to

Spassky like air to a drowning man. And not only because he was two points in arrears. Before this game Spassky had never once managed to defeat Petrosian.

In his article following the 12th game, Euwe had written not only of Petrosian, but also of Spassky. He said that all was not lost for Spassky, but he must win at least one game to have chances. Spassky had won that game. But worse still for Petrosian was that the depression had not yet been overcome, but had even progressed. And now Spassky, sensing his opponent's weakness, was even more confident and decisive in play. Declining to lure Petrosian into any more complications, he set about creating difficult strategical games, where the crisis of the battle came in the fifth hour of play. If we consider that the champion was beginning more and more to fall into time-trouble, this was a very sound decision.

Petrosian played the 14th game extremely nervously. He was completely unrecognizable. This was perhaps his weakest game in the match, and if we were to compare it with any, it would be with the first game of his match with Botvinnik. With one difference: Spassky allowed Petrosian to escape.

The next game was very similar to the previous one. For a long time a very nervous struggle was waged, with the advantage slipping back and forth, but when the time-control approached (with Petrosian once again short of time) Spassky sacrificed a pawn and obtained a dangerous initiative. The sacrifice was rather feeble, but in time-trouble the champion overlooked a simple bishop move and had to give up the exchange.

After that Black's position was lost, but at the move before the adjournment Spassky eased his opponent's task. The next day Petrosian, not without help from the challenger, managed to save the game.

'This game might well have proved decisive,' said Petrosian later, 'if I had lost the fifteenth game I am not at all sure that I would have been able to withstand the tension anymore.'

Both these games showed, however, that the challenger was also having difficulty in mastering his nerves. Undoubtedly, in another competition, Spassky would have, both times, realized his advantage. Meanwhile, every draw, however tormenting it might be for Petrosian, shortened the match, and made Spassky's attempts to equalize even more desperate. He now had to take into account that another loss would make his position almost hopeless.

This explains why the next games were comparatively quiet, and that in the 17th game Spassky declined to pursue a promising king's side attack. In the eighteenth game Petrosian held a large advantage for most of the game, and Spassky had to play very carefully to neutralize it.

It was quite obvious that the champion's depression had passed, and this was to enable him to escape the clutches of the challenger just when it seemed the latter was bringing the match to a logical conclusion. For in the next game Petrosian lost due to placing rather too much faith in his defensive powers.

In a French defence Black obtained an equal position, whereby his two central hanging pawns were the pride of his position. But if Tigran had been able to overhear what the two pawns were whispering to each other, he would have learnt that they had not liked his offer to exchange queens on the 21st move.

Petrosian did not play according to the position in this game, but according to the position in the match. And the central pawns, which with queens on had been the pride of his position, now became split and feeble.

Having broken the logic of the position, Petrosian began to manoeuvre unsuccessfully, and in addition made a clear oversight on his last move. The adjourned position was already beyond salvation.

At last, the equalizer! Spassky's long pursuit, begun after the 7th game, had brought its rewards. And though the scores were now merely levelled, his victories still left a strong impression.

However much before the match Tigran had protested that psychology would not play a significant role in the match, now, when the tension of the match was concentrated on the next two or three games, psychology emerged from the background and pulled the strings. All the previous excitement, all the herculean efforts, paled before the realities of the next few games.

The culminating point of the struggle had been reached. A harsh moment, demanding from both players all their reserves of energy and fortitude.

'Chess is not a game for timid souls. Chess demands everything of a man...' wrote the first World Champion, Wilhelm Steinitz, in his autobiography. Chess now demanded everything of Spassky and Petrosian. Particular demands were made of the champion. For a long time he had held an advantage in points, and even allowed himself the luxury of dictating an armistice to his opponent. This had occurred in the 11th game. Then came a period of depression, but he had overcome the temporary weakness. And suddenly at the end of the match, at a time when age differences might be said to be important, a new crisis had arrived, wherein any defeat could decide the fate of the contest.

What sort of decision did cautious Petrosian and cautious Boleslavsky arrive at? Both had no hesitation: in the 20th game, where Tigran had White, he must not think for a moment of drawing, even though the path to victory be connected with risk.

Was this decision courageous? In the given circumstances, this did not play a significant role. The decision was above all, intelligent and well-timed.

Strangely enough, Petrosian felt extremely cool-headed at the approach of this crisis. He received numerous telegrams, telling him not to lose heart. In distinction to his match with Botvinnik, when the majority of telegrams came from Armenia, now many fans all over the country supported him. There were also telegrams from abroad. One of these was particularly dear to Tigran. 'Nothing serious has occurred,' counselled his friend, 'you will win the match.' The sender was Max Euwe.

How did Spassky and Bondarevsky behave at this very important moment? I do not know what they decided, but in the 20th game Spassky selected a very well-analyzed variation, which led to a solid but passive position for Black, in which he could at best count on a draw.

This was hardly a wise choice. Did Spassky really consider that his opponent would agree on a quick draw, knowing that the following day he would have to withstand a furious attack on the black end of the board? Perhaps Spassky reckoned that the World Champion would be glad of a day off? If that was how he judged, his calculations were mistaken. Petrosian had managed to distribute his energies so well that at the finish he amazed everyone with his stamina and capacity for work.

Perhaps there was another possibility, in that Spassky, having finally caught his opponent up, now felt himself washed out, listless? If that was so, why did he not use up one of his free days? When the match was over, Spassky gave an interview in which he stated '. . . I now know what was my biggest mistake in the match. I made it before the 20th game. I should have taken "time-out" before that game. At precisely that moment a new stage of the match had begun, and I should have done all I could to rest and concentrate my energies.'

But perhaps there was an even larger mistake committed by Spassky – that of underestimating the opponent. If this last supposition seems unlikely, it does explain much, and makes Spassky's conduct at the closing stages of the match at least logical. The triumphal storm of the chess Olympus, described and commentated in the book by his trainer, the multitude of experts forecasting his victory, the general belief in his universality, not to say, invincibility – all this, cast into the background as a result of an unsuccessful beginning to the match, reappeared once more in glowing colours.

Had Spassky been rather more experienced in life, he would have forced himself during the course of the match to realize his faulty evaluation of Petrosian. And then he would definitely have taken a rest before his next game, worked out a plan of battle for the last 5 games, meanwhile leaving the champion anxiously awaiting events.

But it was precisely Petrosianic patience and reserve which Spassky did not have. He, undoubtedly, considered taking time-out, but could

182   *And everything back to the beginning again!...*

not wait to finish the rout of, as he thought, his demoralized opponent. Accordingly he seems to have decided on the following: easy draw in the 20th game, and then launch the attack in the 21st.

... when Petrosian saw that his opponent had chosen a variation of the Nimzo-Indian defence, analyzed through and through, he could hardly believe his eyes. White obtained a small, but lasting initiative, without the trace of counter-play from the other side – this was far more than he had dreamt of before the game began. Calmly, but incisively, Petrosian built up his position, broke into his opponent's queen's side and won a pawn. Now in a hopeless position, Spassky sacrificed a piece, then a rook for a bishop, but this only hastened the end.

All so easily the status quo was reaffirmed, and the score stood at 10½–9½.

In the last four games it was enough for Petrosian to take 1½ points, Spassky had to score 3, no less.

That alone, without any reference to psychological imaginings, was enough to correctly forecast the outcome of the match. But psychology, as if seeking to prove to the World Champion that he undervalued and disparaged it, once again entered the lists, and once again on his side.

After a draw in the twenty-first game, when Spassky was unable to begin an advance, long prepared, the twenty-second game saw Petrosian White and in the better position right out of the opening. He was not forcing matters, and seemed ready to steer the game to a draw. In fact he knew that Spassky had to make a break somewhere, and was prepared to deliver the counter-blow.

On the twenty-fifth move the so-called three times repetition occurred on the chess-board. Petrosian could have called the main judge, O'Kelly, to the board, and claimed the draw.

Petrosian considered. Perhaps it was safest to take the draw, but the position was such that if Spassky refused to contine repeating moves, his position could only worsen. So let Spassky say the final word, since he could also call the judge over. Petrosian made a move, once more repeating the position.

Now it was Spassky's turn to think. Affix a draw? But then surely he would have to win the last two games – an almost impossible feat. Diverge from the repetitions? But then he would clearly stand worse. But after all, what else was there to do? And so Spassky made a move which altered the situation on the board. The hall applauded this courageous gesture. Alas, it was the courage of despair. After a few moves Black's game was hopeless.

I will never forget how sorrowfully Spassky parted from his last hopes. Petrosian had just made his 35th move, and was leaving the stage with a characteristic Petrosianic shrug of the shoulders. This levity, this bounce as he all but danced off the stage, this unshakeable confidence in himself – from all this, and without a glance at the board, the spectator could understand that the game was won, and the match therefore, practically over.

Spassky was fidgeting in his chair, resting his head in one hand, then the other. He would bend over the board, then jerk back suddenly. Sometimes, tearing himself from the position, he would direct a long tormented glance to the corner of the hall where, gloomy and drawn, sat Bondarevsky. Many of the spectators, holding their breath, followed this silent pantomime.

Unable to withstand the gaze, Bondarevsky rose and left the hall. And then slowly, for it was obvious that he was forcing himself, Spassky directed his hand towards the board and made his next move. Petrosian returned to the board and put his head between his hands, beginning to think out his reply, but at that moment, once again slowly, Spassky's hand went towards the clock, whose ticking he stopped.

As if on a signal, the hall erupted in applause, and the supporters of the World Champion gave vent to their joyful emotions (in all this commotion few heard a quiet rustle – it was the turning of another page of chess history. . . .).

With the score at twelve–ten, the match could have been ended there and then, as the champion had retained his title. But Spassky did not lay down his arms, and instead of agreeing quick draws, as Botvinnik had done, did his best to at least draw the match. Naturally, Petrosian could not be expected to play at full strength any more, and he lost the 23rd game fairly easily. The 24th was a stern struggle, which eventually ended in a draw, so the final score was $12\frac{1}{2}$–$11\frac{1}{2}$ in favour of the champion.

Once again Wagner triumphantly resounded through Petrosian's apartment, once again he and his friends celebrated to the early hours of the morning, once again the phone rang incessantly with calls from Yerevan, and Tigran Petrosian felt himself the happiest among men.

The closing ceremony, which took place on the very same stage, was no less touching than the previous one. To this at least, one did not grow accustomed! The FIDE vice-president John Prensis proclaimed Petrosian World Champion, the laurel wreath was placed on his shoulders, and speeches were read in praise of his mastery, his will and his perseverance. The head of the Yerevan Institute of Physical Culture, Loris Kalashian, one of Tigran's most loyal friends, also delivered a heart-felt speech, and presented him with a painting by Martiros Sarayan.

Nor did his home town Tiflis forget him. Dramatist Archil Begiashvili, grey-haired but agile, congratulated the twice times champion in the name of Georgia, birth place of two World Champions.

'We know that the people of Yerevan would give much that the

World Champion be born in their city', said Begiashvili, to the friendly laughter of people in the hall, 'But Tigran knew even then what the friendship of nations means!...'

The victory over Spassky was in certain respects even more impressive than that over Botvinnik. Then it had been possible to speak of the differences in ages, that the veteran would find it hard to play a match over a long distance.

Now Petrosian had faced an opponent who was younger than him, athletic, prepared to play, possibly, two matches running, who had crushingly defeated the other candidates; finally, an opponent who had the majority of pre-match forecasts in his favour.

Petrosian had ended a thirty-year tradition: this was the first time since the Alekhine-Boguljubow matches that the champion had won a title fight. Now Petrosian was compared with Capablanca, but not with that Capablanca who had lost the match with Alekhine, but with the Capablanca who had ruled the chess world for six years. By beating Spassky, Petrosian had assured himself at least as long a period as champion.

At the time of the match, particularly at the beginning and middle, there was some talk that the draws were too frequent, that there were few theoretical novelties, that the creative level of the match was lower than might have been expected. There were also discussions begun about the general level of play of the leading grandmasters, and as to whether their predecessors of forty years back had played better.

The key to the situation was given perhaps by Tal, who stated that 'from the sporting aspect, this match was one of the most interesting in the history of chess.'

In an interview, which took place a few days after the match, Petrosian spoke in connection with the assertion of many commentators, that the course of the match had been fully dictated by sporting, not creative considerations. He replied:

'Perhaps I should not be giving an evaluation of my own play, but frankness remains as it is. In the last resort I very rarely recall that I hold the title of World Champion, and that, probably, brings harm.

'First of all, I believe that from a creative point of view the match was sufficiently rich. There were striking combinations with piece sacrifices, as well as examples of stubborn defence, ultra-modern opening systems, and delicate endgames.

'But if it is true that chess is at once an art, a science and a sport, then it is impossible to separate the creative and sporting aspects in this instance. It is quite obvious that in the first and third Botvinnik-Smyslov matches, when Botvinnik scored 3½ out of the first four games, this sporting circumstance largely determined the creative character of the remainder of the matches.

'In our match the score was level up to the 7th game, from the 13th I had a minimal advantage, and after the nineteenth game the score was level. Is it really possible to ask of the contestants, in these extremely tense circumstances, that they sacrifice purely sporting considerations to creative? Surely sport, struggle, the hunger for victory, lies in the nature of chess? If anybody should seriously declare, that when he sits at the chess-board he thinks not of victory, but only of creativity, I should call him a hypocrite.

'I made it very clear to myself that the struggle with Spassky would be decided at the finish. I therefore consciously played down many games, in order to keep my strength up for the decisive moment. If I had listened to many of the severest critics, then I would hardly have been able to win the 20th and 22nd games and, accordingly, the match. . . .

'I should recall that I commentated four world championship matches in the newspaper *Sovietsky Sport*. Understanding, as it seemed to me, the situation of Botvinnik and of his rivals, Smyslov and Tal, I always tried to avoid categorical criticisms. I always remembered that for me as a commentator, it was a thousand times easier than for the players in this most difficult match. . . .

'It may happen that I shall some day have to return to the pleasurable, but responsible role of a commentator. I can quite definitely state that my credo will be objectivity, adherence to principle, and goodwill. . . .'

In order to take leave of the match, I would like to present an excerpt from Bronstein's article. During the course of the contest, Bronstein permitted himself extravagant and often contradictory remarks, but in the present article, published when the result was known, he showed himself an irreproachable and objective critic.

'The World Champion had an extremely difficult problem to solve – to withstand the onslaught of a powerful challenger. He had many difficulties to overcome in preparation, and he did so brilliantly. He had to make a hard decision, either to play combinatively, which I believe was deeply attractive to him, or defend his purely sporting situation. The decision made, – not to diverge from a hard sporting position – was correct if only for one reason: in a world championship match it was up to Spassky to sharpen the play.

'The challenger went in for complications a number of times, but each time suffered heavy losses. Examples were the seventh, tenth, twelfth and eighteenth games. The champion was better orientated in complicated positions, played more beautifully, and in many cases did not balk at sacrificing pieces or pawns.

'Was this a metamorphosis of style? No, deep and many-sided preparation, physical fitness and well-hidden reserves of chess fantasy! . . . Closing my article, I must say that Petrosian scored a worthy and memorable victory. Chess-players will long wonder how despite Spassky's tremendous wins in the Candidates' series, Petrosian won so convincingly that one almost begins to doubt that the matches Spassky-Keres, Spassky-Geller, Spassky-Tal had ever occurred! . . .'

32 **Petrosian–Tal**

3 USSR Spartakiad, Moscow 1963

English

1 P–QB4	N–KB3
2 P–KN3	P–K3
3 B–N2	P–B4
4 N–KB3	P–Q4
5 0–0	N–B3
6 P×P	N×P
7 P–Q4	B–K2

7 . . . N–B3 was possible, putting the . . . Q5 square under fire.

8 N–B3	0–0
9 N×N	P×N

Transposing into lines of the Tarrasch defence. The answer to 9 . . . Q×N was not 10 N–K5 – which is refuted by 10 . . . Q×QP!, but 10 B–K3 Q–KR4 11 R–B1, developing pressure on the Q-side.

10 P×P	B×P
11 P–QR3	P–QR4
12 B–N5	P–B3
13 R–B1	

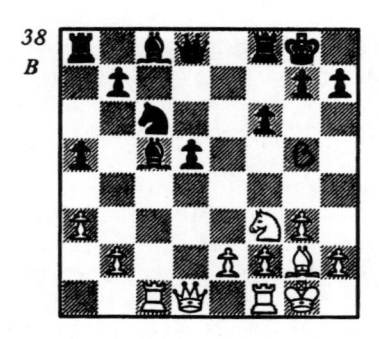

38
B

White's initiative grows step by step. Now 13 . . . B×BP+ 14 R×B

P×B 15 N×P! R×R 16 Q×P+ is bad for Black. At this stage of the game – the transference from the opening to the middle game – White is conducting a positional battle by tactical means, accordingly the game has a very concrete character; but at the same time he never for a moment forgets his positional aims, and is guided by his overall assessment of the position.

13 . . .	B–R2
14 B–B4	B–K3
15 N–K1	R–K1
16 N–Q3	Q–K2
17 P–QN4!	

Black is experiencing difficulties, the cause of which reside in his unsuccessful opening play. Employing a Tarrasch defence after an exchange of knights is no doubt disadvantageous for Black. In that case he is deprived of counterplay and forced to go into passive defence.

17 . . .	P×P
18 N×P	N×N
19 R–B7	

An important in-between move. White's rook makes a decisive invasion on the seventh rank. All these operations have a concretely tactical nature.

19 . . .	Q–Q1
20 P×N	P–KN4?

Black's defensive possibilities were strictly limited, but all the same he would have done better to remain passive by 20 . . . R–N1 and . . . B–N3. Now his K-side is irreparably weakened.

21 Q-Q3

The only move. Quite possibly, White had to foresee this move as early as the seventeenth move.

21 ...	R-K2

Forced

| 22 R×R | Q×R |
| 23 B-K3 | P-Q5 |

Black does not fancy passive defence, and tries to relieve the position at the price of his weak pawn.

| 24 B×QP | R-Q1 |
| 25 P-K3 | B×B |

25 ... Q×P is no good because of 26 Q-K4!

| 26 P×B | Q×P! |
| 27 P-Q5 | |

Black has managed to simplify the position considerably, at the same time maintaining material equilibrium. Nonetheless, the strength of the passed QP, and the weakness of Black's K-side give White real winning chances. Meanwhile the pawn on ... QN2 fulfils the role of an onlooker. So White has a large, if not decisive, positional advantage.

| 27 ... | Q-N3 |
| 28 B-K4 | B-B2 |

Black resolves to give up a pawn. If 28 ... P-R3, 29 R-N1! squeezing the ring tighter round Black's cramped and weakened position.

29 B×P+	K-N2
30 B-K4	Q-B4
31 R-N1	R-Q2
32 Q-KB3	B-N3

The pawn on Q5 is for the moment untouchable. If 32 ... B×P?, 33 Q-B5! and Black is in a bad way.

33 B×B	K×B
34 Q-Q3+	K-N2
35 R-N5	Q-K2
36 Q-B5	R-Q3
37 K-N2	Q-Q2
38 Q×Q+	

The simplest. The rook ending is won without too much difficulty.

38 ...	R×Q
39 K-B3	R-K2
40 R-N6	

When the opportunity arises, White significantly improves the positioning of his rook. Naturally, Black's rook cannot meet the demands made upon it: in limiting the activity of White's king, it simultaneously drops its guard on the QP, and this releases the white rook.

40 ...	P-B4
41 P-Q6	R-Q2
42 P-R4	K-B3
43 P×P+	K×P
44 K-K3	K-B3
45 K-B4	K-K3

Now White has no winning problems. The final moves were:

46 P-B3	K-B3
47 R-N5	K-K3
48 R×BP	K×P
49 P-N4	K-K3
50 R-B8	P-N4

1-0

33 Petrosian-Taimanov

All-Union Central Council of Trade Unions' Ch, Moscow 1964

Nimzo-Indian

1 P-QB4	P-K3
2 N-QB3	B-N5
3 N-B3	N-KB3
4 Q-B2	P-Q3
5 P-Q4	0-0
6 B-N5	QN-Q2
7 P-K3	Q-K1

A little pretentious. 7 ... Q-K2 was simpler, and if 8 B-Q3, then 8 ... P-KR3.

8 B-R4

Useful prophylaxis. 8...B×N+ can be answered by 9 Q×B! (keeping the pawns intact) 9...N-K5 10 Q-B2 P-KB4 11 B-Q3 Q-N3 12 R-KN1! followed by 0-0-0 and P-KN4, with a K-side attack.

8...	P-K4
9 0-0-0	P-B3
10 N-Q2	P-QR3
11 P×P	

A characteristically clear strategic solution from Petrosian. Taking Black's coming Q-side counterplay into account, he decides to play in the centre. In this respect, his 17th move is very noteworthy.

11...   P×P

11...Q×P was probably better.

12 N2-K4   Q-K3

It was not an easy decision to go into the line commencing 12...N×N 13 N×N P-KB4 since after 14 N-Q6 14...Q-K3 is bad after 15 P-B5! and B-B4. But all the same, continuing 14...B×N 15 R×B Q-R4 16 B-K7 R-K1 17 B-K2 Q-B2 18 B-R4 N-B4, Black could have maintained a rough equality.

13 N×N+	N×N
14 B-Q3	P-R3
15 N-R4	P-K5
16 B-K2	N-Q2?

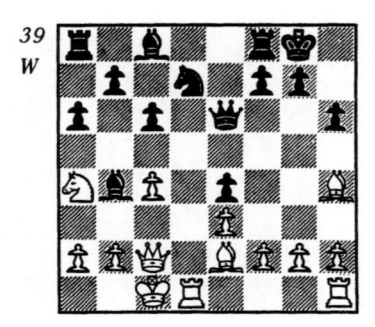

39 W

A serious slip, after which Black falls into Petrosian's iron grip. 16...P-QN4 was necessary, when White should not continue 17 N-N6 R-N1 18 N×B KR×N 19 B×N Q×B 20 Q×P P×P, which gives Black good attacking chances, but simply 17 N-B3! keeping the advantage.

17 R-Q4!

An original manoeuvre, which Black obviously did not take into account. Generally a very clumsy piece in the middle of the board, here the rook acquires burning energy. The K4 square is put under attack, and...P-QN4 is made more difficult (the bishop on QN4 would be attacked in the event of P×P!). White gains a valuable tempo for doubling his rooks on the Q-file.

17...	R-K1
18 R1-Q1	P-QN4

Bad are 18...B-B1 19 R×N B×R 20 N-N6 QR-Q1 21 B×R R×B 22 Q-Q2! or 20...P-KN4 21 B-N3 QR-Q1 22 B-B7 B-B4 23 Q-Q2 B×N 24 B×B P-QB4 25 B×R R×B 26 Q-Q6. In this last variation, Petrosian points out that Black might play 22...B-K2, when it is not so easy for White to exploit his advantage.

19 N-B3

Sidestepping 19 P×P RP×P 20 R×B P×N 21 R×RP R×R 22 Q×R N-B4, when Black's pieces become active.

19...	B×N
20 Q×B	P-N5

A sharp-witted, but nonetheless insufficient counterchance. All the same, White has to work very hard to overcome his opponent's resistance.

21 Q-Q2	P-N6
22 P×P	N-B4

23 Q–N4   N–N2

The only resource. Though the knight is very passively placed, it nonetheless guards the important Q1 and Q3 squares.

**24 Q–N6   P–QR4
25 B–N3   P–QB4
26 Q×Q   R×Q
27 R4–Q2**

The endgame is won for White, so the rest of the game requires little commentary.

27... R–QN3 28 K–B2 B–K3 29 R–QR1 P–B3 30 P–R3 K–B2 31 B–N4 P–B4 32 B–K2 R–N5 33 B–K5 P–R5 34 R×P R5×R 35 P×R R×P 36 P–QN3 R–R7+ 37 K–B1 R–R6 38 K–N2 R–R3 39 B–QB3 P–N3 40 R–Q1 K–K2 41 P–R4 P–R4 42 B–B1 N–Q1 43 B–K5 N–B2 44 B–B4 K–B3 45 B–K2 N–K4 46 R–QR1 R–N3 47 K–B3 N–B3 48 B–B7 1–0.

34 Petrosian–Ivkov

European Team Ch, Hamburg 1965

Queen's Gambit Accepted

1 P–Q4	N–KB3
2 N–KB3	P–Q4
3 P–B4	P×P
4 P–K3	B–N5
5 B×P	P–K3
6 N–B3	P–QR3
7 P–KR3	B–R4
8 P–KN4	B–N3
9 N–K5	QN–Q2
10 N×B	RP×N

Petrosian's favourite system of development against the 4... B–N5 variation. White's strategical plans seem very double-edged. Pawn moves cannot be taken back, and White has already appreciably weakened his K-side. Against this White obtains the two bishops, and a degree of initiative in the centre. It is not easy for White to take advantage of the defects of Black's position. But Black has his problems too. It is difficult for him to find a plan of active counterplay, and without that even the strongest of chess fortresses must become vulnerable. In short, there is a complex and exacting strategical battle in prospect.

**11 P–N5   N–Q4
12 N×N**

In an earlier game Petrosian–Polugaevsky (3 Spartakiad, 1963) 12 Q–N4 N2–N3 13 B–N3 P–QB4 14 N×N N×N 15 P×P B×P 16 B–Q2 R–QB1 17 R–Q1 R–R4 18 P–KR4 N–K2 19 B–B3 was played, with a small advantage to White. In the present game White slightly alters this plan.

12...	P×N
13 B×QP	P–QB3
14 B–N3	Q×P
15 Q–B3	

This is the position Petrosian had aimed for, exchanging his flank pawn for Black's central pawn. Black was probably advised to play 15... Q–KB4, offering an ending where White would have great difficulty in exploiting his two bishops, or, if White refused, after 16 Q–N2 B–N5+ 17 K–K2 (or 17 K–B1) 17... N–B3, obtaining sufficient counterplay.

15...	N–B3
16 B–Q2	Q–KB4
17 Q–N2	P–R4
18 0–0–0	B–N5
19 B×B	P×B
20 P–KR4!	

Coolly played. White gradually establishes an advantageous strategical situation, ignoring the existence of 'local activities'.

20 ...   R–QB1

White would have maintained his pull after 20 ... 0–0 21 P–B3! N–Q4 22 P–K4 Q–B5+ 23 Q–Q2 Q×Q+ 24 K×Q N–B5 25 K–K3, as the ending is not easy for Black. If 21 P–B3 P–B4 22 P–K4 Q–B5+ 23 K–N1 White's advantage is in the middle game, since the threats along the KN-file are obvious enough. On the other hand, after 20 ... 0–0 the direct onslaught is bad: 21 QR–N1 P–B4 22 Q×KNP?? Q×Q 23 R×Q P–B5! and Black wins a piece.

21 P–K4

Now, due to threats of 21 ... P–QB4 White has to deal with concrete matters of business. The positional sacrifice of a pawn gives him the opportunity of creating, with small resources, a very attractive attack on the king. The events take on a forced character.

**21 ...   Q–B5+
22 K–N1   R×P
23 P–K5!   R×R
24 R×R   N–R4**

Bad is 24 ... Q–K5+ 25 Q×Q N×Q 26 R–R8+ K–Q2 27 P–K6+! P×P 28 B×P+ and White wins.

25 B–B2

This 'quiet' move is the beginning of the decisive attack. The threats are both 26 B×P! and 26 P–K6!

25 ...   K–K2

Not 25 ... Q–R3 because of 26 P–K6!

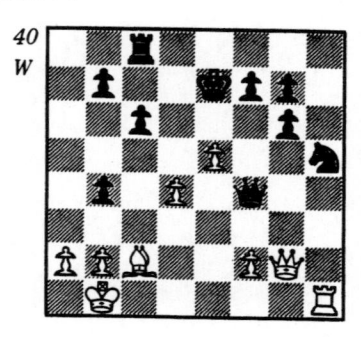

26 B×P

An unusual sacrifice. Paradoxically, Black has no reasonable defence.

**26 ...   P×B
27 Q×NP   Q×QP**

There is a beautiful finish after 27 ... R–KR1 28 Q–Q6+ (but not 28 R×N R×R 29 Q×R Q–K5+ etc.) 28 ... K–K1 (28 ... K–B2 29 P–K6+ K–N1 30 Q×Q N×Q 31 R×R+ K×R 32 P–K7!) 29 Q–N8+ K–K2 30 Q×P+ K–K3 31 Q×BP+ K–B4 32 Q–Q7+ K–N4 33 R–N1+ K–R3 34 Q–K6+ K–R2 35 Q–KN6+ K–N1 36 R–QB1 and White wins.

**28 Q×N   Q–Q6+
29 K–R1   R–Q1
30 R–KN1!**

Simple and elegant. Black's king is in a mating net.

**30 ...   R–Q2
31 R×P+   K–Q1
32 R–N1**

'The Moor has done his work – the Moor may depart.' At the same time White parries the transparent threat of mate on Q1.

**32 ...   K–B2
33 P–K6   R–Q4
34 Q–N4   P–N6**

If 34 ... R–K4 there follows 35 Q–N7+ K–Q3 36 Q–Q7+ etc.

35 P-K7!	R-K4
36 Q-N7	K-Q3
37 Q×R+!	1-0

35 Filip–Petrosian

Yerevan 1965

King's Indian

1 P-Q4	P-KN3
2 P-KN3	B-N2
3 B-N2	P-QB4
4 P-QB3	

If White intends to play for the initiative, he should continue 4 P-Q5. Filip selects another plan, aiming to set up a solid position. Objectively such a plan cannot be bad, but in itself passivity is a faulty method of playing a chess game. This game is a good illustration of this theme.

4 ...	Q-B2

5 P×P was threatened.

5 N-B3	N-KB3
6 0-0	0-0
7 P-N3	P-Q3
8 B-N2	N-B3
9 P-B4	P-K4
10 P-Q5	

A questionable decision. More in the spirit of White's cautious strategy so far would have been 10 P×BP or 10 P-K3, though even here Black has few difficulties.

10 ...	N-QR4

10...N-Q5 was also good. On the other hand 10...N-K2 would lose to 11 N×P! P×N 12 P-Q6.

11 N-K1	R-N1
12 N-B2	B-Q2
13 N-Q2	N-R4
14 P-K4	B-R3!

A typical ploy. Black increases the scope of his black-squared bishop, at the same time hampering the thrust 15 P-B4.

15 R-K1	R.N1-K1
16 N-K3	P-N3
17 B-QB3	N-KN2
18 Q-K2	

More active was 18 N-N4 engendering either the exchange 18...B×N or 18...B-KN4, after which 19 P-KR4 B-K2 20 N-R6+ is possible.

18 ...	P-B4
19 P×P	P×P

Having achieved the advance... P-KB4, Black holds the initiative on the K-side. Now Black transfers the knight to that side.

20 N2-B1	N-N2
21 P-KN4?	

Misplaced activity. Petrosian recommends 21 P-KR3 here.

21 ...	B×N
22 N×B	P×P
23 N×P	Q-Q1!

Black takes full advantage of his opponent's every slip. Carrying out some useful exchanges, Black now shifts his queen to the centre of battle.

24 P-B3	N-KR4
25 B-Q2	N-B5
26 B×N	R×B

White's planless play has led to a positionally hopeless situation. Even without his attack, Black has excellent prospects in the ending.

27 N-B2	Q-R5
28 N-K4	K-R1
29 N-N3	N-Q1

The time has arrived for the long-awaited knight manoeuvre. It is characteristic of Petrosian that he never, even in the heat of the most sharply combinative battles, forgets about his fundamental strategical plans.

192   And everything back to the beginning again!...

30 Q–KB2	Q–R3
31 R–K4	N–B2
32 K–R1	R–B3
33 R–KN1	N–N4
34 R–K3	

41 B

Now comes a brilliant forced finale.

34 ...   Q×P+!!

Similar queen sacrifices are a rarity in the practice of modern grandmasters. It is curious that Petrosian sacrifices his queen most regularly in meetings with Czechoslovak grandmasters.

35 K×Q	R–R3+
36 B–R3	

There is a forced ending too after 36 N–R5 R×N+ 37 K–N3 R–KN1! and mate is inevitable.

36 ...	N×B
37 N–B5	

Leads to a fast finish. Resistance could only have been prolonged by 37 K–N2 N×Q 38 K×N, though here too the ending is won for Black.

37 ...	B×N
38 Q–B1	N–B5+
39 K–N3	R–KN1+
40 K–B2	N–R6+
0–1	

36 **Spassky–Petrosian**

7th match game, Moscow 1966

Queen's Pawn

1 P–Q4	N–KB3
2 N–KB3	P–K3
3 B–N5	

It is curious that Petrosian himself likes this variation, and often plays it. Accordingly Spassky's decision is psychologically dubious. As grandmaster Bronstein put it, Spassky is asking Petrosian to play in the yard of the house ... where he was born.

3 ...	P–Q4
4 QN–Q2	B–K2
5 P–K3	QN–Q2
6 B–Q3	P–B4
7 P–B3	P–QN3
8 0–0	B–N2
9 N–K5	N×N
10 P×N	N–Q2
11 B–KB4	

Only in struggles between players of super-class can it be demonstrated that such a natural move constitutes an inaccuracy. 11 B×B Q×B 12 P–KB4 was quieter, though it cannot be said to bring White any particular advantage.

11 ...	Q–B2
12 N–B3	

12 Q–N4? is bad on account of 12 ... P–KN4 13 B×NP (if 13 B–N3 P–KR4!) 13 ... R–KN1 14 P–KR4 P–KR3 winning a piece.

12 ...	P–KR3
13 P–QN4	P–KN4!

A precise strategical decision. Black is not interested in capturing a pawn – by 13 ... P×P 14 P×P B×P 15 N–Q4 – which gives White a strong initiative. Instead he begins a pawn advance on the K-side, castling himself on the Q-side, 'into the attack' of White's own pawns.

14 B–N3   P–KR4
15 P–KR4

There is interesting play after 15 P–KR3 P–N5 16 RP×P RP×P 17 N–R2 N×P 18 B–N5+ K–B1 19 N×P B–Q3 20 P–KB4 N–B5!– Black has the better chances. Tal suggested 17 N–Q4!? (instead of 17 N–R2) sacrificing a piece after 17 ... P×N 18 P×P for an enduring initiative. But understandably, such extreme methods are not to everyone's taste in a competition for the world chess championship!

15 ...   NP×P

Far more energetic than 15 ... P–N5 16 N–Q2 N×P 17 P×P P×P 18 B–N5+ K–B1 19 P–K4 or 19 Q–R4 when White has reasonable counterplay.

16 B–KB4   0–0–0
17 P–R4?

In the heat of the battle White forgets about his opponent's strategical plans. He should have played 17 P×P P×P 18 R–N1 opening up a line on the Q-side. Here too, Black's game is better, but White's attack would have been rather more lively.

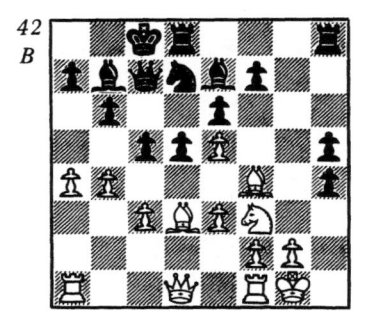

42
B

17 ...   P–B5!

A brilliant move. Black cedes the Q4 square, but comfortably closes the Q-side.

18 B–K2

There were better chances in 18 B–B5. Then if 18 ... P×B 19 P–K6 B–Q3 20 P×N+ followed by 21 Q–Q4, blocking in Black's queen's bishop. If the sacrifice is declined, White can drop the bishop back to KR3.

18 ...   P–R3!
19 K–R1   QR–N1
20 R–KN1   R–N5
21 Q–Q2

21 N–R2 R–N2 22 Q–Q2 was perhaps a little better.

21 ...   R1–N1
22 P–R5   P–N4
23 QR–Q1   B–B1!

Threatening both 24 ... P–B3 25 P×P P–K4 and 24 ... B–N2 25 Q–Q4 N–N1! and ... N–B3.

24 N–R2   N×P!

The exchange sacrifice just begs to be made. But if it is considered, this was thought out long before, Black must be accredited with high creativity.

25 N×R   P×N
26 P–K4   B–Q3

Only not 26 ... P×P 27 B×N Q×B 28 Q–Q8 mate!

27 Q–K3   N–Q2

A paradoxical manoeuvre. 27 ... P–N6 seems natural, trying to open the lines on the K-side, or else 27 ... P×P, aiming for material gains; no doubt both these moves gave as much as was obtained from the move actually played. At the same time, the move chosen is probably the most unpleasant for the opponent. Black has faith in his position, and, forcing the exchange of bishops, increases the weight of his central pawns.

194 And everything back to the beginning again!...

28 B×B	Q×B
29 R-Q4	

29 R-Q2 was more stubborn, when Black likewise continues with 29 ... P-B4. The 'pseudo-active' 29 P-B4 is answered by 29 ... P-B4.

29 ...	P-K4
30 R-Q2	

30 R×QP B×R 31 R-Q1 N-B3 32 P×B K-N1 is also good for Black.

30 ...	P-B4!

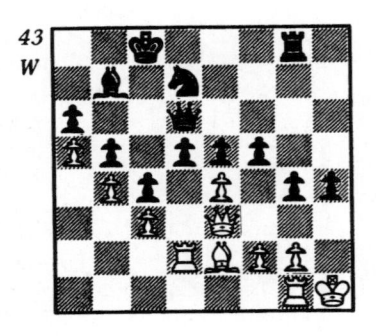

43
W

A dazzling strategical blow. White cannot withstand the central phalanx of pawns.

31 P×QP

31 P×BP N-B3 32 P-B3 N-R4 33 P×P N-N6+ 34 K-R2 P-Q5! or 32 Q-R6 P-R6 33 P×P P-Q5+ 34 K-R2 P-N6+ 35 R×NP R×R do not improve White's situation. (Variations by Tal).

31 ...	P-B5
32 Q-K4	

32 Q-R7 is answered by 32 ... P-K5!

32 ...	N-B3
33 Q-B5+	K-N1
34 P-B3	

If 34 Q-K6 Q×Q 35 P×Q N-K5! is decisive.

34 ...	B-B1
35 Q-N1	P-N6

Now the break ... P-R6 cannot be stopped.

36 R-K1	P-R6
37 B-B1	R-R1
38 P×P	B×P
39 K-N1	

Bad is 39 B×B Q-Q2!

39 ...	B×B
40 K×B	

Or 40 R×B Q-Q2, with threats of ... Q-R6 or ... Q-QR2+.

40 ...	P-K5
41 Q-Q1	N-N5!

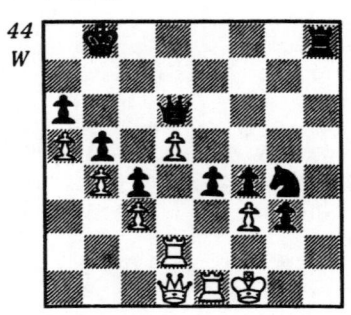

44
W

The sealed move, which leads to an effective finale. And from the point of view of the aesthete, it is the most economical, the shortest route to victory.

42 P×N	P-B6
43 R-KN2	P×R+
0-1	

On 44 K×P or 44 K-K2, 44 ... Q-B5 decides.

In my opinion this game was the best game played by Petrosian in his match with Spassky. Its fundamental worth – faultlessness of play.

37 **Petrosian–Spassky**

10th match game, Moscow 1966

King's Indian

1 N-KB3	N-KB3

2 P-KN3	P-KN3
3 P-B4	B-N2
4 B-N2	0-0
5 0-0	N-B3

In all the post-war world championship matches, with the exception of Botvinnik-Petrosian, 1963, the player lagging behind would invariably employ the King's Indian defence. Yet all the same this line, brought into practice by Borisenko, is seen here for the first time in a world title match.

6 N-B3	P-Q3
7 P-Q4	P-QR3
8 P-Q5	N-QR4
9 N-Q2	P-B4

The play follows well-known paths. Black avoids symmetry, and strives above all for counterplay. Here his knight on QR4 functions by attacking the square ... QB5. Naturally, White tries to thwart Black's plans on the Q-side, and to isolate the knight on QR4. In that event, White would have every chance of winning the strategical battle. He can then play his 'trumps' – space advantage in the centre, and possibility of advancing on a wide front.

10 Q-B2   P-K4

10 ... R-N1 followed by ... P-QN4 is a common alternative, withholding the thrust in the centre. It is then possible to plan ... P-K3 later on, increasing the pressure on White's QB4.

11 P-N3

Tal recommends 11 P-QR3 here: 11 ... P-N3 (11 ... Q-B2 is bad because of 12 P-QN4 P×P 13 P×P N×BP 14 N-N5!) 12 P-QN4 N-N2 13 R-N1, organizing active play on the queen's wing.

11 ...   N-N5
12 P-K4

And here 12 P-QR3 P-N3 13 P-N4 N-N2 also deserved consideration.

12 ...	P-B4
13 P×P	P×P
14 N-Q1	

Objectively better, and more cautious was 14 B-N2. But Petrosian's idea is very interesting from a strategical, as well as a psychological point of view; he invites his opponent to attack him.

14 ...   P-N4

14 ... P-B5 an apparently risky move, might well have been played. But 14 ... P-K5 15 B-N2 B-Q5? 16 B×B P×B 17 P-N4 loses a piece.

15 P-B3

Played in the same 'provocative style'. From the point of view of limiting Black's counterplay, 15 B-N2 was better.

15 ...   P-K5

At the time of the game, and right up to its end, it was thought that this advance was both natural and strong. Surely it does not pay to dally in developing counterplay in the King's Indian. What is more, to seize the initiative in such circumstances must be reckoned as a great success for the black side. Apparently, the outward passivity of White's play should enable Black to undertake decisive operations. Yet there are matters for consideration: what resources does Black have for obtaining his aims?, how far has White's position been weakened? The course of the struggle demonstrated that to penetrate White's position is more difficult than appears at first sight. At the same time it is difficult to criticize the challenger for plunging straight into complications. He was behind in the match, and had to play for a win.

Objectively more circumspect would be to retreat the knight to ... KR3, aiming to develop a gradual initiative on the Q-side. But all this is easy to say! ...

16 B–N2

The exchange sacrifice is hardly to be recommended after 16 P×N B×R 17 NP×P B×P 18 N×P. Maintaining his important bishop, Black has every chance of withstanding White's further attacks.

16 ...   KP×P
17 B×P

17 N×P is bad after 17 ... B×B 18 Q×B or 18 N×B N–K6.

17 ...   B×B

It was probably better to keep the black-squared bishop with 17 ... N–K4. After the opening of the KN-file (by ... P–B5!), he would have had a degree of cover against any White counter-attack.

18 Q×B   N–K4
19 B–K2   P–B5

A very enticing move, but all the same it would have been better to bring up reinforcements by 19 ... R–R2 20 N–K3 Q–B3 (20 ... R–KN2 is also quite good) 21 Q–B2 R–KN2 22 N–N2 N–N3 after which the threat ... P–B5 is appreciably stronger. Tal indicates the variation 23 K–R1 P–B5 24 N×P N×N 25 P×N B–R6 with good counterplay to Black. After 19 ... R–R2 20 N–K3, 20 ... P–B5 again looks strong, but the variation 21 R×P R×R 22 P×R R–KN2+ 23 K–R1 Q–R5 24 P×N Q–B7 25 N–B3! Q×N.K6 26 P–K6 B–N2 27

Q–B6 shows that the opening of the knight file is here in White's favour.

20 NP×P

An error? Surely 20 R×P R×R 21 P×R N–N3 22 N–K4 N×KBP 23 N–K3! R–R2 24 N–B6+ K–B2 25 R–KB1 Q×N 26 Q×Q+ K×Q 27 R×N+ gave White the clearly superior ending. Tal correctly points out that the variation 21 ... R–R2 22 N–K3 R–KN2+ 23 K–R1 B–R6 24 P×N Q–N4 25 N–N4 B×N 26 N–K4 is also in White's favour.

Yet White's decision cannot be declared mistaken, since he is consciously playing on the psychology of his partner, and sets a cunning trap. ...

20 ...   B–R6?

This is it, the psychological crisis of the struggle. Almost without thinking, Black embarks on a previously worked out plan, forgetting for the moment concrete analysis. And in such positions, concrete analyses spell death for general considerations.

Correct was 20 ... R×P 21 R×R Q–N4+ 22 K–R1 Q×R or 21 N–K3 Q–N4+ 22 K–R1 R×R+ 23 N2×R B–R6 and Black's position is in no way inferior.

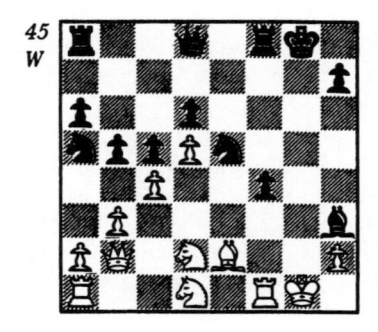

45
W

21 N–K3!

This, in essence, completely forced (21 R–B2? R × P is very bad) reply was clearly underestimated by Black. If 21 ... R × P 22 R × R Q–N4+ 23 R–N4! B × R 24 N × B N × N 25 B × N Q × B+ 26 K–R1 the initiative unexpectedly goes over to White's side. Here is where the isolation of Black's knight on ... QR4 makes itself felt! All Black's play starting right from 19 ... P–B5 hung on tactical calculation, and here one move made from general principles leads to a fiasco.

21 ...   B × R
22 R × B   N–N3

22 ... N–Q2 offered more resistance, though here too after 23 B–N4 N–KB3 24 B–K6+ White has a powerful initiative.

23 B–N4!

White carries out the final attack in great style. 23 N–N4 is not so convincing due to 23 ... P–R4!

23 ...   N × KBP

23 ... P–R3 was rather better. If 23 ... Q–B3 24 B–K6+ K–R1 25 Q × Q+ R × Q 26 P–B5 N–K4 27 N–K4 Black suffers heavy losses.

24 R × N

Yet another exchange sacrifice. To a specialist, perhaps, the finale is elementary, but to the wide circle of chess lovers, the concluding stages are beautiful, as they are instructive.

24 ...   R × R
25 B–K6+   R–B2

25 ... K–B1 26 Q–R8+ K–K2 27 Q × P+ wins for White.

26 N–K4   Q–R5
27 N × QP

The events develop forcibly. 27 ... Q–K8+ 28 K–N2 Q × N 29 B × R+ K–B1 30 Q–R8+ K–K2 31 N–B5+ K × B 32 Q × P+ and 33 N × Q or 31 ... K–Q2 32 B–K6+ only succeed in losing Black's queen.

27 ...   Q–N4+
28 K–R1   R1–R2

If 28 ... Q × N 29 B × R+ K–B1 30 Q–R8+ K–K2 31 N–B5+ K × B 32 Q–N7+ and 33 N × Q.

29 B × R+   R × B
30 Q–R8+!   1–0

The final position deserves a diagram.

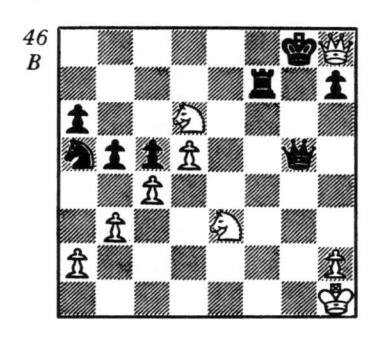

46
B

The ending of this game is very similar to one that took place between Petrosian and Simagin in a match for the Moscow championship, 1956. In the decisive 5th game, the following position arose:

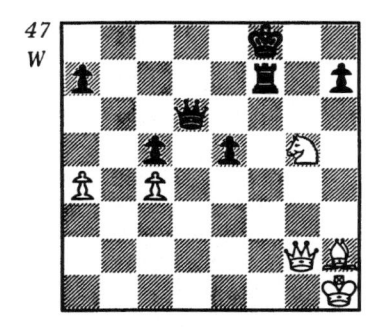

47
W

Petrosian, playing White, finished the game thus: **44 Q–R8+ K–N2 45**

B×P+!! Q×B 46 Q-R8+ K×Q
47 N×R+ K-N2 48 N×Q 1-0.

The tenth game was one of the shortest games of the match, but was also one of the richest, both in content and in dramatic psychology.

38 Petrosian–Spassky

20th match game, Moscow 1966

Nimzo-Indian

1 P-Q4	N-KB3
2 P-QB4	P-K3
3 N-QB3	B-N5

Considering Petrosian's regular match repertoire, 3 N-QB3 comes as rather a surprise. From the time of his first (disastrous) match game with Botvinnik in 1963, he generally replied to 2 ... P-K3 with 3 N-KB3, leading the play into the quiet lines of the Queen's Indian defence.

The very choice of opening shows that Petrosian was intending to alter his cautious opening approach, and was prepared for a theoretical struggle. The previous game had seen Spassky equalize the scores at 9½ all, and this game was to prove the decisive one of the match.

4 P-K3	0-0
5 B-Q3	P-B4
6 N-B3	P-Q4
7 0-0	N-B3
8 P-QR3	B×N
9 P×B	QP×P
10 B×BP	Q-B2
11 B-Q3	P-K4

The general assessment of this extremely well-analyzed position: dynamic equilibrium. White has the two bishops, and a pawn superiority in the centre, and Black has free play for his pieces, and full chances of fighting for the initiative. Deeper investigation has shown (this is however, the opinion of the writer) that White has the better chances here.

12 Q-B2	B-N5

Black's desire to effect exchanges in the centre is fully justified, but all the same 12 ... R-K1 might have been better, not fearing 13 P-K4 because of 13 ... P-B5!

13 N×P	N×N
14 P×N	Q×P
15 P-B3	B-Q2
16 P-QR4	

A new and strong idea. White forestalls Black's likely pawn advance on the Q-side, brings the QN5 square under control, and, finally, widens the sphere of influence of his QB.

16 ...	KR-K1
17 P-K4	P-B5

In many analogous variations, White expends quite a lot of energy trying to encourage this advance, which opens a line for his black-squared bishop. Perhaps Spassky wanted to divert his partner from what might have been already prepared analysis. At any rate, the strategical decision looks dubious. 17 ... B-B3 would have been in the spirit of the position, with ... R-Q1 to follow, creating piece pressure against the centre, and intending when required the manoeuvre ... N-R4-B5.

18 B-K2

Not, of course, 18 B×P on account of 18 ... Q-QB4+.

18 ...	B-K3

More energetic and consistent seems 18 ... Q-QB4+, forestalling the manoeuvre B-K3-Q4. Now Black obtains a prospectless and extremely difficult game.

19 B–K3   Q–B2
20 QR–N1   N–Q2
21 R–N5!

An excellent manoeuvre. White intends to double rooks on the knight file, and, where necessary, transfer his heavy artillery to the K-side by R–KN5 or R–KR5. This is where the move 16 P–QR4 is useful. If the pawn were still on QR3, Black could reply 21 ... P–QR3 and 22 ... P–QN4. Now on 21 ... P–QR3 White simply replies 22 R–N4, and bringing up the reserves with 23 R1–N1, further increases the pressure on the knight's file, and on the pawn at QN7.

21 ...   P–QN3
22 R1–N1   Q–B3
23 B–Q4   P–B3
24 Q–R2   K–R1
25 B–B1

25 R5–N4 looks strong, but then Black has an interesting counter-blow in 25 ... N–B4, and if 26 B×QBP N–Q6, and Black wins.

25 ...   P–KR3

Black has no good plan, and must await events.

26 P–R3   QR–N1
27 P–R5

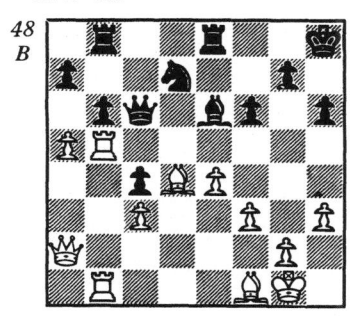

48
B

Initiating the breaking-up process.

The main variation involves an exchange sacrifice: 27 ... P–R3 28 R×P N×R 29 P×N!, and Black must lose another pawn, either on ... QR3 or ... QB5. White would then have very good winning chances, without taking any risk. Black has no possibility of counterplay on the K-side, for example 29 ... P–B4 30 P–K5! P–B5 31 Q×RP B–B4 32 R–N4 Q–N3 33 Q×P B×P 34 P–N7 where Black stands badly. (30 Q–Q2 K–R2 31 P×P B×P 32 R–N4 B–K3 33 Q–R2 is also strong for White).

For the time being Spassky prefers passive defence.

27 ...   R–N2
28 P×P

There was no need to hurry with this exchange. 28 R5–N4! is very strong, as is the following 29 Q–KB2. In that case Black is denied active play.

28 ...   P×P
29 Q–KB2

An inaccuracy: he should not have left the rook file. A K-side advance was in order, with 29 P–N4 followed by B–N2 and P–B4. With his permanent weaknesses on the Q-side, Black would be hard put to find a defence.

29 ...   R–R1
30 Q–N2   R2–R2

Black goes into complications, sacrificing the pawn on QN3. Even though 30 ... R–R3 appears uninviting, White would not have had an easy task breaking through Black's defence.

31 B×NP   R–R7

31 ... R–R6 was worth consideration. If 32 B–Q4 R–N6 33 R×R P×R 34 P–QB4 B×BP 35 Q–B3

R–R5 36 R × P (or 36 R–B1 N–N3! 37 Q × NP B × Q 38 R × Q R × B 39 R × N B–B2 with fair drawing chances) 36 ... Q–R3 and White's advantage, though evident, is hard to exploit.

32 Q–N4   R–QB7

Quite probably the decisive blunder. This move is only in appearance aggressive. Meanwhile, 32 ... R1–R6 33 B–Q4 R–N6 34 R × R P × R 35 P–QB4 R–QB7 36 Q × P R × BP 37 Q–N2 R–B8 or 32 ... R7–R5 33 Q–K7 R–QN1 34 R5–N2 N × B 35 R × N R × R 36 Q–Q8+ B–N1! 37 Q × R Q × Q 38 R × Q R–R6 or 37 R × R Q–B4+ 38 Q–Q4 Q × Q+ 39 P × Q P–B6 40 P–Q5 P–B4 gave Black good drawing chances.

33 B–B2

A manoeuvre characteristic of Petrosian. Getting ready to attack, he nonetheless is concerned about the safety of his own king, intending to provide cover with 34 B–N3. 33 B–Q4 was also quite good. For example: 33 ... R1–R7 34 Q–K7 Q–B2 35 P–K5! with a winning attack.

33 ...	Q–B2
34 Q–K7!	B × P

A desperate sacrifice. Black is defenceless against White's attack e.g. 34 ... R1–R7 35 R–N8+ K–R2 36 Q × B R × B 37 Q–B5+ P–N3 38 Q–Q5 N × R 39 R–N7! and White wins.

35 P × B	R × B
36 K × R	Q–R7+
37 B–N2	N–K4
38 R–N8+	R × R
39 R × R+	K–R2
40 R–Q8	

Parrying the threat 40 ... N–Q6+.

40 ...   N–N3

Here the game was adjourned. When it was revealed that White had sealed 41 Q–K6, Spassky resigned.

11 Instead of an Epilogue

On that memorable evening, the evening of the 22nd game, Tigran allowed himself to drink a small glass of cognac. When they tried to fill his glass a second time, he refused and filled it with apricot juice instead, saying:
'I have to think of the next match, you know.'
Although this was spoken in jest, with a smile, it struck a sympathetic chord inside me. This was a champion's fate. Hardly ridding himself of one match (of which he had thought, for which he had waited, for three years), his mind was already occupied with the forthcoming one.
The inevitability of the next meeting, which could neither be postponed nor brought forward, this battle of the strongest with the strongest – this would colour the next three years of Petrosian's life. And time itself was now measured not in years, but in blocks of three years. . . .
Before the Petrosian-Spassky match, Leonid Zorin wrote:
'It is possible to disagree with the widely held opinion, that the awaiting of joy is greater than the joy itself, but in my opinion it is indisputable that waiting for a battle is harder than the battle itself. . . .'
It is possible to disagree with this opinion too. Rephrasing the expression, it may be said that a match is only a continuation of the 'waiting', but with more direct means. But in any case it is true that the waiting costs a great deal of nervous energy.
A match takes a year off your life – so Botvinnik had said. How many months (or years?) does the waiting account for? . . .
'Every champion prepares himself for the day in accordance with his character,' wrote Zorin in the same article, 'here the most varied shades of mood are possible, from fatalism to carelessness (which is also a form of psychological defence). The player in the best position is the one who most harmoniously balances responsibility with inner freedom.'
How truly this is stated! But how difficult, finding the delimitations of this responsibility and freedom.
I once related the following episode to Petrosian. Not long before his match with Botvinnik, I was leaving the Central chess club in company with Tal, headed in the direction of Arbatskaya Square. As

we were passing a gateway, leading to the yard of the club building, Tal suddenly nodded in the direction of a box of rubbish and laughed; there, on top of a pile of papers and amid other rubbish, lay a board with the inscription 'Tal-Botvinnik'. The workers of the club had been cleaning out the store-rooms before the start of the next match.

Tigran, hearing this story, only spread his hands; you had to be as light-hearted as Tal, with his desire to find something amusing in everything, to laugh at that moment. Tigran also had his share of humour, but it had not been funny to him when he listened to that story.

Inner freedom . . . if he were to speak frankly, then, after becoming champion, he had never yet felt that freedom. With his self-criticism and the increasing demands he made on himself, Tigran could not for one hour forget the measure of responsibility.

Sometimes this so burdened him, that it was with secret grief he thought of his friends, for whom chess-playing remained only a pleasant hobby. For example, Vitia Bravinsky, the curly-headed teenager, who had been evacuated from Harkov to Tiflis, and who frequently had played friendly games with young Tigran. Surely he had not given his life to chess, and now he was a talented scientist, a winner of the Lenin prize.

And what about Loris Kalashian, the head of an institute and a candidate of philosophical science? He had become a chessmaster, but played, as is said, for enjoyment. And yet how insistently Tigran had tried to prove to Loris, in Yerevan, that a man who had shown himself gifted in chess, must undoubtedly be able to succeed in science. . . . Why had he not trusted himself, and devoted himself seriously to something worthwhile?

Would he not one day share the same fate as those famous players of the past, who at the end of their lives felt disappointment in chess? Of Chigorin himself, who was said to have burnt his chess pieces before he died?

These and similar painful thoughts assailed Tigran rather infrequently, but it was difficult to dispel them. Generally they coincided with unpleasant occurrences: an unsuccessful tournament performance, or the conviction that most of the experts spoke in favour of his opponent; or when during a long and difficult match he heard reproaches that his play had low creative content. . . .

But such times passed, and Petrosian overcame the onset of weakness. In the last resort, every champion had to go through this! Every champion came up against the fact that the sympathies of the chess world were generally given to his younger opponent. This was chess life. . . .

And so the desire to resign his title without a fight, 'according to personal wish', disappeared without a trace. Whenever this desire came to him, he would always remember the disbelief he had displayed when it was suggested to him that Botvinnik would refuse to play him, Petrosian. No, no, Botvinnik was too much the fighter to take this way out.

Yet surely he too, Tigran Petrosian, had a will of iron! He had formed himself in 'difficult, but just struggle', and, if you like, was a product of stern natural selection, so let no one think that he would give up his place without a struggle.

Nor did he yet feel any weakening of his chess abilities. True, at the time of the next match he would be forty years old, a critical age for a chess-player, but had not Botvinnik and even Keres kept their strength into their fifties?

This was roughly how Petrosian assessed the situation, when he was left alone with his thoughts.

Very well, the reader may say, but surely it is undeniable that Petrosian has had less than simply modest results in tournaments after his victory over Spassky.

Definitely, yes. But we should not overlook that in his match with Spassky Petrosian expended a lot of nervous energy, which he was not at once able to recuperate. So is not this decline in the champion's fighting spirit a form of defensive reaction of the organism? Maybe precisely this 'creative leave' will give Petrosian, when he once again returns to his sacred calling, the possibility of reuniting all that enabled him to win the title, and later preserve it?

I believe in this. And for that reason I have entitled this chapter 'Instead of an Epilogue'. Petrosian himself must write the epilogue.

But however this epilogue may be, the ninth champion – in creativity complex and contradictory – will remain in the history of chess as an example of a man, a chess-player, a fighter, who, overcoming his desire for excessive caution, stayed true to himself, to his own individuality; who by his modesty and self-critical attitude was ready to overestimate his opponents, but never to fear them; who, finally, whilst paying due attention to practicality in life as in chess, remained in his heart a romantic and a dreamer.

39 Petrosian–M. Johansson

17 Olympiad, Havana 1966

Sicilian

1 P–K4	P–QB4
2 N–KB3	P–Q3
3 P–Q4	P×P
4 N×P	N–KB3
5 N–QB3	P–QR3
6 B–K2	P–K3
7 P–B4	N–B3
8 B–K3	Q–B2
9 0–0	B–Q2

Black plays the Scheveningen system according to the old methods. Practice has demonstrated that Black has a fairly difficult game in prospect. Korchnoi's newer line of play seems to give better chances: 1 P–K4

P-QB4 2 N-KB3 P-Q3 3 P-Q4
P×P 4 N×P N-KB3 5 N-QB3
P-K3 6 P-B4 N-B3 7 B-K3 B-K2
8 B-K2 0-0 9 0-0 B-Q2 and if 10
Q-K1 then 10 ... N×N 11 B×N
B-B3.

10 N-N3

The approved continuation here is 10 Q-K1 followed by 11 Q-N3 etc. But the plan chosen is also good. Indeed, it is even better against the modern variation with 9 ... B-Q2. This was demonstrated, for example, in the game Suetin-Polugaevsky, 34 USSR Ch 1967.

10 ...	P-QN4
11 P-QR3	**B-K2**
12 R-B2	

A 'quiet' but quite playable move. White not only gradually prepares for a storm on the K-side, but also defends his QB2 pawn. In certain positions the rook is ready to switch to Q2, for example, when the weight of the struggle is transferred to the centre.

A long-forgotten game Levenfish-Kotov (12 USSR Ch 1940) also included the move R-B2, though it is true, in a slightly different situation. The play went: 1 P-K4 P-QB4 2 N-KB3 P-Q3 3 P-Q4 P×P 4 N×P N-KB3 5 N-QB3 P-QR3 6 B-K2 Q-B2 7 0-0 P-K3 8 P-B4 B-K2 9 B-K3 N-B3 10 Q-K1 0-0 11 Q-N3 B-Q2 12 R-B2 P-QN4 13 P-QR3 KR-Q1 14 R1-KB1 P-N5 15 P×P N×NP 16 P-B5 P-K4 17 B-R6 B-KB1 18 N-K6! P×N 19 P×P B×P 20 R×N and White obtained a threatening attacking position. Since then the move R-B2 has almost disappeared from tournament practice, and perhaps, in vain. ...

12 ...	P-N5

13 P×P	N×NP
14 B-B3	**R-QB1**
15 P-N4	**P-R3**

Black's game is not easy, but the decisive action is still far away. It would have been more logical to have continued development with 15 ... 0-0. But Black chooses an unreliable strategical plan, forgoing castling, which leads to a rout.

16 P-N5	P×P
17 P×P	**N-R2**

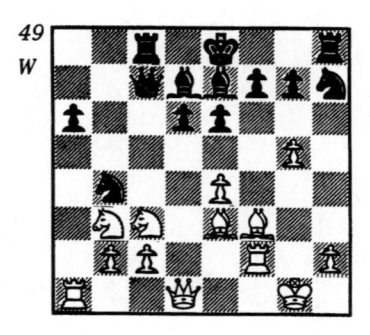

49
W

18 Q-Q2

It was very tempting to play 18 Q-Q4 here, with a double attack on the points QN4 and KN7, but the actual variations involved are not so inviting. After 18 ... B×P 19 B×B N×B, 20 Q×N is not good because of 20 ... N-R6+ 21 K-N2 N×R 22 K×N R×P+ and Black has a dangerous counter-attack. 20 Q×NP N-R6+ 21 K-N2 K-K2 or 21 K-B1 K-K2 22 B-N4 N×R is also good for Black. 20 B-N2 P-Q4 21 Q×N Q×P+ 22 K-B1 N-R6 leads to more problematical positions. However Black's counter-attack is very unpleasant here too, and White has no need to get involved in such adventures in the first place.

18 ...	N-B1

The decisive error. 18...0–0 was a necessity.
19 Q–Q4
Now this double attack is appreciably stronger.
19 ...	N–B3
20 Q×NP	R–R2
21 Q–N8!	

Taking up a dominating position right in the heart of Black's game. Black finds it hard to defend the KB2 square. Petrosian indicates an interesting variation: 21 ... B–Q1 22 R1–KB1 N–K2 23 Q×R N×Q 24 B–R5! and Black is defenceless.

21 ...	N–K4
22 B–K2	B–QB3
23 R×RP	R–QR1
24 R×B!	N×R
25 B–N5!	1–0

40 Petrosian–Bronstein

Moscow Spartakiad 1967

Queen's Gambit Declined

1 P–Q4	P–K3
2 P–QB4	N–KB3
3 N–QB3	P–Q4
4 B–N5	P–B4
5 P–K3	

White avoids the sharp theoretical lines arising from 5 BP×P BP×P 6 Q×P B–K2 7 P–K4 N–B3 8 Q–Q2 N×KP etc. Soon the game transposes into a typical Caro-Kann, Panov variation.

5 ...	BP×P
6 KP×P	B–K2
7 R–B1	0–0
8 N–B3	N–B3

Black employs a very complex plan of defence, by which he allows White to advance on the Q-side, and hopes to obtain counterplay in the

Instead of an Epilogue 205

centre and on the K-side. 8... P–QN3! is probably more elastic, as was played in the game Taimanov–Keres, Candidates' 1953. After 9 B–Q3 N–B3 10 0–0 N–QN5 11 P×P N3×P 12 B×B Q×B 13 B–K4 B–N2 14 R–K1 QR–B1 Black had equalized.

9 P–B5	P–KR3

Here, too, 9 ... P–QN3 was more exact. Now Black gets a difficult game.

10 B–B4	N–K5
11 B–QN5	

By thus indirectly defending the K5 square, and therefore the structure of pawns on Q4 and QB5, White completes his strategical plans, and enters the middle-game with excellent prospects.

11 ...	B–Q2
12 0–0	P–N4

The weakness of his K-side eventually proves ruinous to Black, but at the present stage of the game it has to be accepted, if counterplay is to be obtained.

13 B–N3	P–R3

This only helps White. Relatively better was 13 ... N×B 14 RP×N B–B3. Bad is 13 ... P–B4? 14 B×N B×B 15 B–K5 P–N5 16 N–K1.

14 B×N	B×B
15 N–K5	B–K1

The exchange on ... QB3 was hardly a threat. But Black has difficulty in finding useful moves, and has to await events.

16 R–K1	N×B
17 RP×N	B–KB3
18 P–QN4	B–N2
19 R–N1	

19 P–R4 P–N3 20 P–N5 RP×P 21 RP×P P×P 22 P×P looks tempting, but meets the reply 22 ... Q–N1!, after which the position is

unclear. White's plan is simpler and clearer.

19 ...	P–B3
20 N–B3	B–B2
21 P–N5	Q–B2
22 P×P	P×P
23 R–N6	

This is the position Petrosian had aimed for playing 19 R–QN1. The rook exerts great pressure on Black's game. Realizing the hopelessness of passive defence, Black makes a despairing attempt to unleash the power of his bishops. Unfortunately, this only hastens the end.

23 ...	P–K4
24 P×P	P×P

Bad is 24 ... Q×BP 25 N–QR4 and 26 P×P.

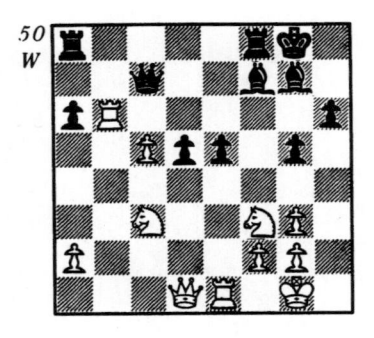

25 N×KP

A finely calculated sacrificial stroke, by which White destroys his opponent's centre and begins the attack on the king.

25 ...	Q×P

If 25 ... B×N 26 N×P! Q×P 27 R×B QR–Q1 (or 27 ... B×N 28 Q×B+ Q×Q 29 R×Q with an easily won ending) 28 N–B6+ K–N2 29 Q–N1! is immediately decisive.

26 R–QB6

An important zwischenzug, which cuts across Black's plans. White's rook on the sixth rank is very mobile.

26 ...	Q–R2
27 N–N4!	K–R1

Black's bishops, not finding any objects of attack, prove to be useless in defence as well. If 27 ... P–KR4 28 N–R6+ B×N.R3 29 R×B, the threat of 30 Q–Q2 decides.

28 N×RP	B–K1
29 R×B!	

White plays the concluding stages of the game with great elan.

29 ...	Q×P+
30 K–R2	QR×R
31 Q–R5	Q–K8

Not, of course, 31 ... R–K8? 32 N–N4+.

32 N–B5+	K–N1
33 N×B	R–KB8
34 Q×R+	1–0

41 Petrosian–Larsen

Palma de Mallorca 1968

Modern Benoni

1 P–Q4	N–KB3
2 P–QB4	P–K3
3 N–KB3	P–QN3
4 P–QR3	

Petrosian's patent, with which he defeated Smyslov in the 1961 USSR championship (see game 20). Larsen's next is an attempt to prove the move a waste of time.

4 ...	P–B4
5 P–Q5	

If 5 N–B3 P×P 6 N×P B–N2, and if then 7 N4–N5 P–Q3 8 B–B4 P–K4 and 9 ... P–QR3 shows up the weakness of P–QR3– no flight squares for the knight.

5 ...	P × P
6 P × P	P–N3

Reaching a modern Benonɪ with White having wasted a move.

7 N–B3	B–KN2
8 B–N5	0–0

Black should not have allowed White the possibility of P–Q6.

9 P–K3

If 9 P–K4 R–K1 threatening ... N × KP!

9 ...	P–Q3
10 N–Q2	P–KR3
11 B–R4	N–R3

At the post-mortem the players thought that 11 ... B–R3 12 B × B N × B 13 0–0 Q–Q2 was better. Now Black gets a rather cramped game.

12 B–K2	N–B2
13 P–K4	

Apparently a further loss of time.

13 ...	P–QN4
14 0–0	Q–Q2
15 Q–B2	R–K1
16 KR–K1	

Preparing systematically for the advance P–K5.

16 ...	B–N2
17 P–R3	P–R3

O'Kelly, who sat in on all the relevant post-mortems, gives in the bulletins as better and necessary 17 ... P–B5 18 P–B4 P–QR4 19 B–B3 N–R3 20 P–R4 N–QN5 21 Q–N1 N–Q6 22 P × P N × BP with a complicated game – this came from Petrosian. Larsen in *Informator* suggests 17 ... P–N4 18 B–N3 R–K2.

18 P–B4	P–B5
19 B–B3	P–KR4

Black wishes to play ... N–R2, which is at present answered by 20 B–N4.

20 QR–Q1	N–R2
21 P–K5!	

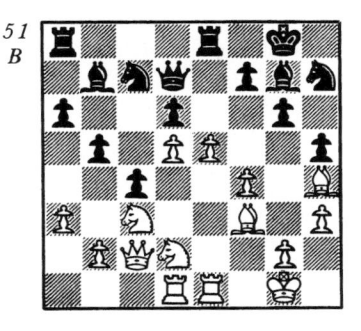

51 B

At last! And this thrust is a decider.

21 ...	P × P
22 N2–K4	Q–B4

Larsen in *Informator* queries this move, and suggests 22 ... B–KB1! 23 P × P R × P 24 N–B6+.

23 Q–B2

Threat 24 N–Q6.

23 ...	QR–Q1
24 B × R	R × B
25 Q–N6	Q–B1
26 N–B5	

If 26 N–Q6 R × N with some counter-chances.

26 ...   **P–K5**

Or 26 ... N–R1 27 Q–R7.

27 Q × B	P × B
28 Q × Q	R × Q
29 P–Q6	B–B1
30 N–N7	N–K3
31 P–Q7	R–N1
32 R × N	

(Notes by Wade in *The Chess Player* book of the event.)

42 Petrosian–Gligoric

Palma de Mallorca 1968

King's Indian

1 P–Q4	N–KB3
2 P–QB4	P–KN3
3 N–QB3	B–N2
4 P–K4	P–Q3

5 P-B3	0-0
6 B-K3	P-B3
7 B-Q3	P-K4
8 P-Q5	P×P
9 BP×P	P-QR3

Preferable is 9...N-R3, as in Petrosian-Reshevsky, Tel Aviv Olympiad 1964.

10 KN-K2	QN-Q2
11 0-0	

White usually plays 11 Q-Q2 here, reserving the option of castling either side. Petrosian keeps open other possible plans for his queen instead.

11 ...	N-R4
12 K-R1!	

A precise move, which serves two aims. In the first place, the king moves off the dangerous KN1-QR7 diagonal, in the second, the KN1 square is freed for the rook, which is particularly important in the struggle against... P-KB4.

12 ...	P-B4

Now a waiting move like 12... K-R1 would be met by 13 P-KN4, and if 13...N-B5 by accepting the pawn sacrifice.

13 P×P	P×P
14 Q-N1	

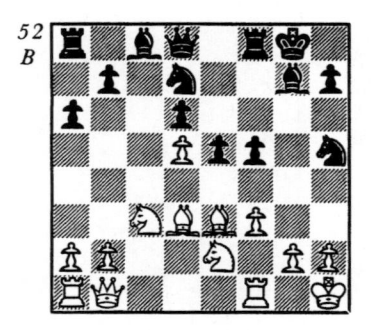

52
B

This move assures White a positional advantage in a relatively quiet position. Black's knight has to go to ...QB4, when it would rather have stood on...K4. All the same, more in line with the previous moves (see note to 12 K-R1!) was 14 P-KN4, and if 14...P-K5 15 P×N P×B 16 N-B4 N-K4 17 P-R6 with a large advantage to White.

14 ...	N-B4
15 B-QB2	P-R4
16 P-B4	P×P

Now the pawn on KB4 is left weak. After 16...Q-R5 17 Q-K1 and the exchange of queens Black may have had a more tenable game.

17 N×P	N×N
18 B×N	R-R3

A very odd manoeuvre – rather like the Duke of York – and on a parallel with a similar idea in Gligoric's game against Gheorghiu. The rook is bound via QN3 to QN5.

19 Q-K1	R-N3
20 R-QN1	Q-B3
21 P-QR3	B-Q2
22 R-B3	P-R5
23 B-K3	Q-K4
24 Q-B2	R-R3

The sacrifice 24...R×P must have been rejected.

25 R-Q1

Naturally, White does not wish to give his black-squared bishop (25 B×N) to win a mere pawn. He intends B-Q4, exchanging bishops and weakening Black's K-side.

25 ...	Q-K2
26 B-Q4	B×B
27 Q×B	Q-B3
28 Q-QN4	

A small surprise. White withholds the exchange of queens for the time being.

28 ...	R3-R1
29 R1-KB1	

White's pressure has brought forth its first fruits – an extra pawn.

29 ...	Q–K4
30 Q–R4	QR–K1
31 P–R3	P–N4
32 R–B4	R–K2
33 P–KN4	Q–B3

White was threatening 34 Q–N5+.

34 Q×Q	R×Q
35 P×P	

In the post-mortem 35 B×BP was thought to win easily. For example, 35 ... B×B 36 P×B N–Q6 37 R–KN4+ followed by 38 N–K4.

35 ...	R–K6
36 K–N2	K–B1
37 R1–B3	R–K2
38 N–K4	N×N
39 B×N	R–K4
40 K–B2	B–K1
41 K–K3	B–R4?

The sealed move. According to O'Kelly, Gligoric thought that 41 ... B–B2 would draw! However, this is not so, since the rooks can invade decisively via QB3.

42 R–B1	B–K1
43 R–QB1	B–Q2
44 K–Q4	K–K2
45 R–B7	K–Q1
46 R–R7	P–R4
47 R–B1!	

If 47 ... B×P 48 B–Q3.

47 ...	R–B2
48 B–Q3	B–K1
49 R–R8+	K–Q2
50 P–B6	R–B1
51 P–B7	1–0

12 Losing the World Championship

In the absence of anything to translate on the 1969 match, I (the translator.) have decided to write on it myself.

The match was in many ways similar to its predecessor. Spassky white-washed his opponents in the Candidates' series, whilst Petrosian produced a crop of undistinguished tournament results. The main difference was that Spassky was much more determined this time, and Petrosian rather less so. This was brought out particularly in the later stages of the match.

If the 1966 match had begun and continued rather cautiously, then the 1969 match was marked by very sharp play right from the start. Petrosian abandoned his French and Caro-Kann, and placed his main hopes on the Sicilian, backed by the Petroff and even the Ruy Lopez. Spassky likewise jettisoned his fianchetto extravaganzas, and relied on the Queen's Gambit Declined. His 'secret weapon' proved to be the Tarrasch defence, and at first sight this appears an almost suicidal decision. Surely Petrosian must be a master at the art of exploiting weak central pawns? The reader need only turn to game 10 (*v* Geller in the Amsterdam Candidates') of this book to be convinced of this. Spassky later explained in an interview that he chose the Tarrasch because it gave lively piece play; true, White had a probable advantage, but (according to Spassky) it was the type of positional advantage which needs to be exploited by precise, concrete moves every time. And this did not suit Petrosian's cat-and-mouse style. At any rate, these tactics met with reasonable success; Petrosian time and again got advantages, fell asleep on them, and allowed his effervescent opponent to crawl out.

Later on in the match, Spassky reverted to the Makogonov-Bondarevsky defence, when he was ahead and needing safe draws.

The beginning was inauspicious for Spassky: he lost the first game, which was very well played by both sides. But as the match progressed it appeared that Petrosian was strangely out of form. He lost the fourth game from an equal position, and in the eighth game even blundered away the exchange. This, combined with a loss in the fifth (where he fell into a bad line and was demolished – no blame attaches here!) put him two down before the ninth game.

The ninth game, with Petrosian as Black, saw him gain the advantage by the subtlest of play; he had winning attacks on both sides of the board. But then uncertainty set in, and Spassky established a probably winning advantage at the adjournment. As a rule in this match, it was Petrosian who let slip his golden opportunities; but here for once Spassky faltered and missed the win. In the next two games Petrosian regained his best form and scored two crushing victories; the tenth game, which saw Spassky unwisely adopt the Nimzo-Indian defence, was almost a replica of the 20th game of the 1966 match. The eleventh game was (for Petrosian) the high point of the match. He played brilliantly and energetically, and demolished his opponent completely. So the scores were again level, but the initiative in the match was with Petrosian.

Perhaps at this point Petrosian could have pushed things through to victory . . . as he should have done in the first five games against Fischer in 1971. For Spassky was thoroughly demoralized, almost a corpse, if a stubborn one, and Petrosian could do what he liked with him.

The 12th game closely resembles game 10 of the book *v* Geller, only White's position was even more won this time. Yet Spassky, by dint of tortuous and tormented defence, and helped by Petrosian's indirectness, managed to scrape a draw.

The fourteenth game was Spassky's favourite of the match; indeed, the middle and late middle-game saw the most subtle and intricate positions arising. On the move before adjournment Spassky blundered. It was said that Smyslov came into the hall and pointed out Petrosian's winning sealed move; but the move was also discovered by a local Armenian while the game was being demonstrated in one of Yerevan's parks. Petrosian found the move as well, and Spassky had to give up the exchange. The win was still a little tricky though, and somehow Petrosian allowed his opponent to escape again (according to Petrosian, he had come to the board in a daze after analyzing the adjourned position until 4 o'clock in the morning. He remarked that the endgame had been a lot more difficult to win than most people had imagined).

While Petrosian was failing to win as White, Spassky as White was coming up against a brick wall in the shape of the Petroff defence. Perhaps Petrosian would have been advised to stick to this defence. rather than play for wins with more aggressive black openings. At any rate, in the next three games as White, Spassky stormed through to three straight wins, whilst Petrosian could only reply with one white win in the twentieth game. Though Petrosian fought to the last, a two point lead was enough, and Spassky became the tenth World Champion.

The defeat had not been a disgrace, and above all Petrosian had shown that he was still capable of developing; and though he became the number 3 world player after the 1969–1972 cycle, I am still optimistic. If he does not succeed in regaining his title, he should show the world such an example of chess longevity that even Lasker or Botvinnik might envy.

43 Spassky–Petrosian

11th match game, Moscow 1969

Queen's Indian

1 P–Q4	N–KB3
2 P–QB4	P–K3
3 N–KB3	P–QN3
4 P–QR3	

Spassky employs a typical Petrosian move – unwisely, as it turns out.

4 ...	B–N2
5 N–B3	P–Q4

Black wishes to develop his bishop on Q3, though the move played allows White to develop his bishop on KN5, outside the pawn chain.

6 P–K3   QN–Q2

More accurate than 6 ... B–K2, after which might follow 7 P × P P × P 8 B–N5+, forcing Black to block his queen's bishop, since 8 ... QN–Q2 is answered by 9 N–K5. After 8 ... P–B3   9 B–Q3   0–0   10 P–QN4 QN–Q2   11 0–0, P–K4 is in the air.

7 P × P

White defines the central position rather early. 7 P–QN4 was more elastic, holding in reserve the plan P–B5, as well as the pawn exchange. In that case 7 ... P–B4 would not be to Black's advantage after 8 NP × P NP × P 9 R–QN1 when the bishop on QN7 is embarrassed.

7 ...	P × P
8 B–K2	

Another slight inaccuracy. The bishop should go to K2 only if Black had played ... P–B4, and thus permitted White to open the Q-file. Against the plan selected by Petrosian, the bishop is better placed on Q3, where it defends the K4 square, and may be transferred to KB5.

If White had feared 8 ... P–B4 in answer to 8 B–Q3, he might have prefaced this move by 8 P–QN4.

8 ...	B–Q3
9 P–QN4	0–0
10 0–0	P–QR3
11 Q–N3	

The opening stage is over, and has been very satisfactory for Black. Now if White plays passively, his king is liable to fall under attack. Spassky's intention is to place his pawns on QR4 and QN5, fixing the QB6 square. After this he will exchange off the black-squared bishops by means of B–QR3. In that case Black's QB2 and his K-side onslaught would be very much weakened. As it turns out, this plan is very difficult to carry out.

11 ...   Q–K2!

Striking at the QN pawn, and simultaneously ruining White's plans.

12 R–N1

After this move White can no longer succeed in exchanging off the black-squared bishops, and without this the advance of pawns on the Q-side becomes pointless, and only assists Black to take the initiative on the queen's wing. It was probably better for White to play an immediate 12 P-N5, though Spassky clearly did not like the variation 12 ... P×P 13 N×NP P-B4! Now if 14 N×B Q×N 15 P×P P×P! and the bishop on QN7 is immune to capture.

12 ... N-K5

A consequence of the move 12 R-N1. White cannot now win a pawn by 13 N×P B×N 14 Q×B because of 14 ... N-B6.

13 P-QR4	N2-B3
14 P-N5	N×N
15 Q×N	N-K5
16 Q-B2	KR-B1
17 B-N2	P-QB3
18 P×BP	B×BP
19 Q-N3	Q-Q2
20 R-R1	P-QN4
21 P-R5	

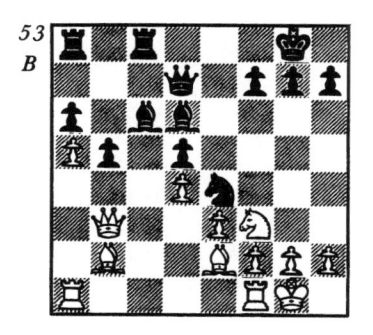

53 B

After this move White's game becomes extremely difficult. Black obtains a strong passed QNP, and a strong base at ... QB5 for a rook. Probably Spassky considered the endgame arising from 21 P×P B×NP 22 B×B Q×B 23 Q×Q P×Q 24 R×R R×R 25 R-R1 R×R+ 26 B×R as dangerous for him. In fact these variations analyzed by Korchnoi show that he need not lose:

a) 26 ... P-N5 27 K-B1 P-N6 28 B-N2 B-N5 29 N-K5 B-B6 30 N-Q3 B×B 31 N×B N-Q7+ 32 K-K2 N-B5 33 N×N P×N 34 K-Q2 P-N7 35 K-B2 P-B6 36 P-K4 with a drawn pawn ending.

b) 26 ... B-R6 27 N-K1 P-N5 28 N-B2 N-Q7 29 B-B3!

This last move, 29 B-B3!, might easily escape attention during preliminary analyses, so this may explain why Spassky preferred to seek chances in the middle-game.

21 ... B-N2

21 ... P-N5 looked very attractive to be followed by 22 ... B-N4. Then after 22 N-K5 B×N 23 P×B B-N4! (not 23 ... N-Q7 24 Q×NP, when the exchange is very hard to exploit) 24 B×B Q×B White's game is scarcely defensible. Petrosian prefers to retain his white-squared bishop, and chooses a more complicated route to victory.

22 N-K5

Seeking to drown his sorrows in complications. If now 22 ... B×N 23 P×B N-Q7 24 Q-N4 N×R 25 B-N4 etc., White's chances are not bad.

22 ...	Q-Q1
23 KR-Q1	Q-R5
24 P-N3	Q-K2
25 P-B3	

White tries to be active, but he is weakening his K-side.

25 ...	N-N4
26 P-R4	N-K3
27 P-B4	P-B3
28 N-B3	N-Q1

Heading for Q3 via KB2.

| 29 K-B2 | N-B2 |
| 30 N-Q2 | R-B5 |

54
W

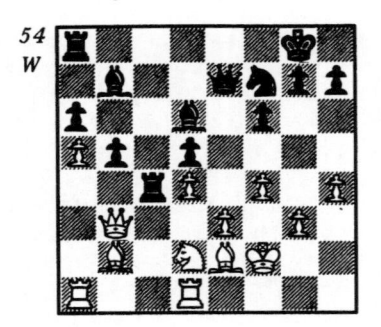

A triumphant entry! Naturally, if the rook is taken, Black has two connected passed pawns and the long diagonal is opened for his bishop.

| 31 Q–Q3 | R–K1 |
| 32 B–KB3 | B–N5 |

The black-squared bishop has served its purpose, and can now be exchanged. At the same time Q3 is vacated for the knight.

33 B–R3	B × B
34 R × B	N–Q3
35 R–K1	P–B4

A far from obvious move, which demonstrates Petrosian's deep penetration into the depths of the position. The weakening of the K4 square is not important, since White's knight can never get there.

Black intends, after the invasion of his knight on K5 and its inevitable exchange, to recapture with the bishop's pawn, opening the way for his queen to invade White's king's position.

36 R3–R1	N–K5+
37 B × N	BP × B
38 Q–N1	Q–Q2
39 R–R2	R1–QB1
40 N × R	QP × N
41 P–Q5	

A last attempt at activity. If 41 Q–N4 Black would play 41 ... P–B6

42 R–B2 R–B5 43 Q–N3 Q–N5 44 R × P Q–B6+ 45 K–N1 Q × NP+ 46 K–B1 Q–B6+ 47 K–N1 B–Q4 48 R1–QB1 Q × KP+! with a quick win.

| 41 ... | B × P |
| 42 R–Q1 | P–B6! |

The sealed move. Black combines a K-side attack with the advance of his Q-side pawns.

| 43 R–B2 | Q–R6 |

Without this move Black would not win.

44 R–N1	Q–N5
45 K–N2	Q–B6+
46 K–R2	Q × KP
47 P–B5	

47 Q–Q1 Q–Q6 48 Q–N4 offered slightly more resistance. Now Black ignores White's demonstration on the K–side, and busies himself with queen making.

47 ...	Q–B4
48 R–KB1	P–N5
49 P–B6	P–N6
50 R2–KB2	P–B7
51 Q–B1	P–K6
52 P–B7+	K–B1
53 R–B5	P–N7
54 Q × NP	P–B8=Q
55 Q × NP+	K × Q
56 R–N5+	0–1

White resigned without waiting for his opponent's reply.

44 Petrosian–Spassky

20th match game, Moscow 1969

Queen's Gambit Declined

It might have been thought that after his defeat in the 19th game the World Champion would be completely demoralized, and only offer formal resistance. However, in this game he once again demonstrates his positional mastery. In my opinion, this was in part due to Spassky, who unexpectedly took 'time out' after the last game, postponed the 20th game, and allowed his opponent to recover his spirits.

But quite possibly Spassky too, seeing the summit of Olympus so dazzlingly close, also needed time to overcome his agitation.

1 P–QB4	P–K3
2 P–Q4	P–Q4
3 N–KB3	B–K2

The Tarrasch defence has already played its part in the match – the part of a not very reliable opening, which provoked White to play for a win. Spassky tries to set up a solid position, and keep the element of risk at a minimum.

4 N–B3	N–KB3
5 B–N5	

The exchange on Q5 gives White nothing, since Black is able to develop his bishop on KB4.

5 ...	0–0
6 P–K3	P–KR3

Spassky played the Makogonov-Bondarevsky system in the second game of the last match, and accordingly, it entered his opening arsenal. He did not manage to equalize the game that time, and the system did not appear again in the match. But then Spassky had excluded all possible forms of the Queen's Gambit. This time, when the Queen's Gambit had become his sole weapon, the Makogonov–Bondarevsky system took its corresponding place. It seems that Spassky intended to play it as early as the sixth game, but instead of 7 P–K3 (the moves ... P–KR3 and B–R4 had already been played)

Petrosian played 7 R–B1, intimating that he was prepared to answer 7 ... P–QN3 with 8 P×P N×P 9 B×B Q×B 10 N×N P×N 11 P–KN3. Spassky did not relish this line, and by playing 7 ... N–K5, he turned the game into a good line of the Lasker defence.

In the fourteenth game Petrosian crossed Black's plans by leaving his knight on QN1 and unexpectedly exchanging on Q5, after which the variation which arose was not the Makogonov–Bondarevsky system, but the so-called orthodox fianchetto.

Now, when Spassky has two points in hand, the Makogonov–Bondarevsky system suits him even better, and side-stepping all his opponent's opening 'machinations', adjusting his move order somewhat, he manages to play that same system.

What could Petrosian do in that circumstance? Following the classical lines would have little point, since it would be extremely hard to realize the minute opening advantage offered. Petrosian decides to part with his black-squared bishop and lead the game along little analyzed paths.

7 B×N	B×B
8 Q–Q2	

This is Korchnoi's move, whose aim is to make ... P–QB4 more difficult. This is achieved by the latent pressure on the pawn at Q5, which White may increase by bringing a rook to Q1. If Black himself exchanges on QB4, and then plays ... P–K4, White can occupy the Q-file.

8 ...   **P–QN3**

The most logical continuation. After reinforcing his Q4 square, ... P–QB4 once again becomes possible.

9 P×P

White would have liked to hold back this move until the bishop had gone to ... QN2, but it is not clear what sort of move he should make instead. There is no sense yet in defining the positioning of his queen's rook, and if he moves the bishop Black can exchange on QB4 and give his bishop a fine diagonal. Likewise on 9 P–QN4 black could play 9 ... P×P 10 B×P P–B4 with an easy game.

9 ...   P×P
10 P–QN4

With this move White forestalls ... P–QB4 for a long time. Later on he places rooks on the QB-file and increases the pressure on QB6.

10 ...   B–N2

10 ... B–K3 was worth considering. Then if 11 B–Q3 P–B3 12 0–0 Q–Q3 13 QR–N1 N–Q2 and ... P–QB4 once again becomes a threat. After White's next move it can never be played.

11 R–QN1   P–B3
12 B–Q3

12 P–N5 is answered by 12 ... P–B4.

12 ...   N–Q2
13 0–0   R–K1
14 KR–B1   P–QR4

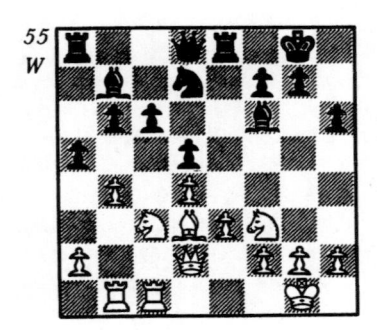

Spassky probably thought that Petrosian would play 15 P–QR3, as he did in the sixth game. After that Black could play 15 ... P×P 16 P×P P–QN4, transfer his knight to the QB5 square via QN3, and obtain a good position. But in the sixth game Petrosian after two losses running was trying only not to lose, and here he has to win at all costs.

Black could have tried another plan, very typical of such positions: transfer the bishop via K2 to Q3, then the knight to K5 via KB3. How might White react to this? Pushing the QRP to R5 gives very little, and P–QN5 is always answered by ... P–QB4. So White would have to think of a break in the centre, by P–K4, which, however, would lead to simplifications and give little chance of a win.

15 P×P!   R×RP
16 B–B5   R–R3
17 R–N3   P–N3
18 B–Q3

White eases his opponent's task. After 18 B–R3 Black's rook would be tied to the QNP, and the bishop on QN2 would be tied to the rook on ... QR3. If 18 ... B–QR1, then 19 P–R4 (not at once 19 Q–K2 because of 19 ... P–QN4) and if 19 ... N–B1 20 Q–K2 B–QN2 21 Q–N2, and Black loses a pawn.

Black could play 19 ... N–N1 instead of 19 ... N–B1, simultaneously defending the rook and the QBP, but this amounts to a positional concession which White could eventually exploit. So in answer to 18 B–R3 Black would probably have to neutralize the activity of the bishop by playing 18 ... B–N2 19 R.B1–N1

P-KB4. But the move ... P-KB4 is a serious weakening of the K-side. White can easily return his bishop to play by 20 P-N3, but, alas, pawns cannot go backwards.

18 ...   R-R2
19 R1-N1

This game was very important for White, so he did not want to play P-K4 unless it led to certain victory. In fact, after 19 P-K4 P×P 20 N×P B-N2 21 N-Q6 R-K3 White has nothing clear, and the game has simplified appreciably.

19 ...   B-N2

This move was criticized by many commentators, and not without reason. True enough, the bishop on KN2 fulfils two functions: guards the K4 square, and protects the pawn on KR3 in case White should play P-K4. But the KRP could be quite sufficiently guarded by the king on KN2, and the bishop should be transferred to QB2, setting up a solid position on the Q-side.

20 P-QR4

The pawn is more vulnerable here than on QR2, but the QNP had to be restrained.

20 ...   Q-K2
21 B-B1   B-R3?

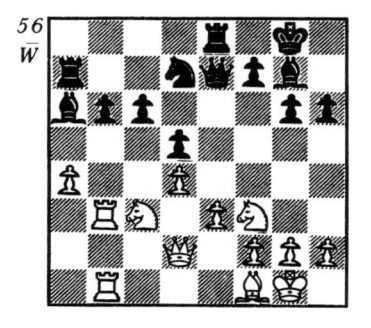

56
W̄

21 B-B1 served two purposes: it freed the Q3 square for the knight, and prepared for B-R3 after 22 P-KN3. Exchanging the bishops does not hinder the first plan, and the second possibility is forestalled at a rather high price. Up till now the pawn on QB3 was practically invulnerable, and Black had just one weakness, at QN3. Now he has to defend two. It is true that White's bishop was a good one, and Black's a bad one, but in this position this was not so important.

21 ... R-R4 was possible. White's threat to transfer the bishop to KR3 could be met easily by ... Q-K3, and Black's position would still be solid.

22 P-R4

All the attention so far has been concentrated on the Q-side, and the exchange of bishops gives White chances on just that wing, so why is this thrust on the K-side necessary?

Before beginning operations on the Q-side, Petrosian stabilizes the position on the K-side. He has decided that the most solid arrangement of pawns is KB2-KN3-KR4, with the king on N2. After the exchange of bishops the white squares on Black's king's wing may need defending, so White may play P-KR5, either forcing a weakening of the king's position, or obtaining KB5 for a knight. For this reason Black played ... P-KR4 himself on move 23.

22 ...   B×B
23 R×B   P-R4
24 R-K1   R2-R1
25 P-N3   Q-Q3
26 K-N2

**57
B**

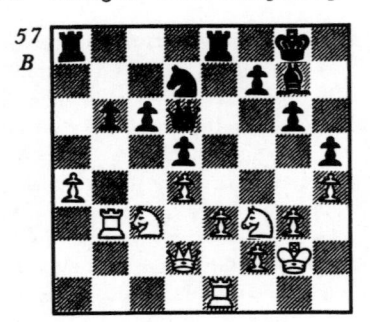

The K-side arrangements are now complete, and it is time to turn to the queen's; for the time being however, Black has everything defended there.

26 ... K-B1

This move indicates that Spassky considers his position sufficiently resilient, and does not see any necessity to change the placing of his pieces. In the 11th edition of the bulletin 'For the chess crown', Platonov suggests transferring the bishop to Q3. But it seems to me that would not solve Black's major difficulties. After the exchange of white-squared bishops Black's main weakness is his QBP, and placing the bishop on Q3 does not help to defend it.

After 26 ... B-B1 the game might continue 27 R-QB1 Q-B3 28 Q-Q1 B-Q3 29 N-K2 R.K1-QB1 30 R3-B3. Black's pieces are tied down, and White's knights are headed for QN4 and KB4 via K1 and Q3.

27 R1-QN1 K-N1
28 Q-Q1 B-B1

It looks as though Black has decided to transfer the bishop to Q3, but in fact it is only the start of another series of repetitions. Black cannot hope to repair the organic weaknesses in his position, but the bishop should have been put on KR3 to defend the ... KB5 square.

29 R3-N2 B-N2
30 R-B2 R-R2

There is a certain indifference about Black's moves, even though Spassky could hardly have been unaware of the approaching danger. 30 ... B-R3 31 R1-B1 R-R4 was still best, in order to answer 32 N-K2 by 32 ... P-QB4. White would then play 33 N-B3, when Black's best is 33 ... B-N2. In that case he would have had better chances than in the game, leaving himself three pawns against four on the king's wing.

31 R1-B1 N-N1

Positional capitulation. Now Black can never move his pawn to ... QB4. 31 ... B-R3 was still the best, but Spassky had little time left, and was thinking only of avoiding immediate material loss.

32 N-K2 R-B2

32 ... R × RP 33 R × P N × R 34 Q × R gave Black no chance of salvation.

33 Q-Q3 R-R2
34 Q-N3 R-R3
35 N-B4

Placing his heavy pieces in the best possible manner, Petrosian turns to the final stage of the operation – the decisive cavalry advance.

35 ... R-Q1
36 N-Q3 B-B1

Black cannot allow White's knight to get to QN4; if 36 ... R-QB1 37 N-N4 R-R4, then 38 N × BP N × N 39 Q × NP and White wins. But now the other knight comes in at K5.

37 N.B3-K5 R-B1
38 R-B3

White is in no hurry, as his

opponent is pinned down. He might have played 38 N-KB4 at once.

38 ...	B-K2
39 N-KB4	B-B3
40 N5-Q3	

If Petrosian had had more time he might perhaps have played 40 N×QBP R×N 41 R×R N×R 42 Q-N5 N-N1 43 R-B8+ K-N2 44 R×N but when you make the last moves with a tottering flag, especially when there is no necessity for the combination, you do not want to have to calculate such variations. Now Black has no defence against the threats of 41 N×QP and 41 N-N4.

40 ...	R-R4

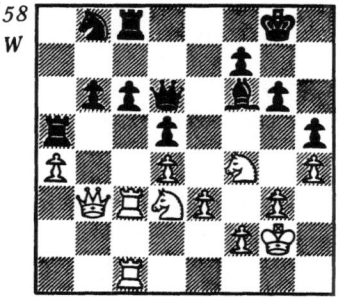

58 W

Here the game was adjourned, and White sealed his move.

41 N-N4 looks the most natural move, when Black loses his QP, but Petrosian prefers another course.

41 Q×NP	R×P
42 R-B5!	

Only this strong move justifies the rejection of 41 N-N4; White not only wins a pawn, but also breaks into his opponent's position.

42 ...	R-R3

If 42 ... N-Q2 White wins by 43 R×BP.

43 R×QP!

The strongest move. 43 Q-N7 R-Q1 44 N-N4 is less good after 44 ... R-Q2, which forces White either to retreat his queen to KR3 (45 Q-B8+ R-Q1 46 Q-R3), losing nearly all his advantage in the process, or go in for a very unclear queen sacrifice by 45 Q×N+.

43 ...	Q×N

43 ... R×Q 44 R×Q or 43 ... Q-B1 44 Q-N7 could not save the game. Black tries to confuse the issue.

44 Q×R	Q-K5+
45 P-B3	Q-K3

If 45 ... Q-K1 46 Q-N7 is sufficient.

46 Q-B4

Stronger than 46 Q-N7, as after 46 ... R-B1 47 R5-QB5 Q×P, Black picks up the pawn on ... Q5.

46 ...	Q×P

The simplest reply to 46 ... R-K1 is 47 R-K5! B×R 48 Q×Q R×Q 49 N×B, and White wins the endgame easily.

47 N-K5	R-B1

On 47 ... R-B2 White could play 48 R-B2, defending the second rank, or 48 R-B5 R-R2 49 R-QR1.

48 R-B5!

This is stronger than 48 R-Q6 K-N2 49 N×QBP N×N 50 R×N B×QP, when White still has great technical difficulties ahead.

48 ...	B-K2

If 48 ... K-N2, then 49 R-B2 followed by R-K2.

49 R-QN1	B×R

Desperation. If 49 ... K-N2 50 R-N7! Q-Q7+ 51 K-R3 Q-Q8 52 Q-B1; or 49 ... B-Q3 50 R-N2 and 51 R-K2.

50 R×N	1-0

(The notes to the last two games are by Boleslavsky in the Soviet book of the match.)

13 The candidates' matches as I saw them
by Tigran Petrosian

After I lost my World Champion's title in 1969, I had to face a new problem. How should I arrange my chess life in the future? The world championship title has never been the main aim of my life. So here I was wondering what to do. Should I simply continue to make periodic appearances in strong tournaments, trying to maintain a reputation as a strong grandmaster, or should I once more try for the champion's crown? There are quite a few examples of sportsmen who, losing their high position, have tried unsuccessfully, even pitifully, to regain what once was theirs. For a chess-player, time is inexorable, and it is impossible to make time stand still.

But when the 1970 Interzonal tournament finished, my hesitations immediately ended. I saw that most of my opponents – Yefim Geller, Mark Taimanov, Bent Larsen, Wolfgang Uhlmann, were players of my own generation. Some of them were only two or three years younger than me, the rest were older . . . so I decided I had no moral right to refuse battle.

There was one other circumstance which impelled me to play in the Candidates' matches: it would be extremely interesting for me to play a third match against Boris Spassky. . . .

Having decided to play in the Candidates' matches, I thought that there would be little point in beginning with only one or two matches in mind. At the same time I realized that the matches were separated from each other by mere 1–1½ month intervals. These short interludes should be used for active rest, rather than chess training. That was why my initial training embraced the quarter-, semi-final, and final stages of the competition.

Factually, the Candidates' matches began before the eight grandmasters sat down at their respective tables; they began as soon as the International Federation had made the drawing of lots.

The drawing of lots was rather a strange affair. One quartet comprised the strongest Soviet grandmasters – Korchnoi, Geller and myself, along with the youngest competitor, Robert Hübner from West Germany. In the other group were the strongest Western players, Fischer and Larsen.

A lottery is a lottery, and anything can happen there. But . . . as I was looking through my papers one day, I came across an interview in a 1966 edition of *Literaturnaya Gazieta*. Among other things, the reporter asked Botvinnik what he thought of Euwe's idea of selecting the challenger in a match between the strongest Eastern and Western chess-players . . . and so, Dr Euwe had had the idea many years ago. And that, which had been only a suggestion when he was an ordinary grandmaster, under his presidentship became a reality.

Last year, when I went to Holland to play in an international chess tournament, I asked Dr Euwe, both as a candidate and a journalist, to say something about the drawing of lots. The FIDE president was unable to communicate any details, and only replied shortly, that everything had taken place normally.

The draw for the world football championships are carried out with the participation of dozens of journalists and spectators; surely the world chess championships are not so insignificant, that no-one should have any precise information about the drawing of lots?

But let us return to the quarter-finals of the Candidates' matches.

It seemed to me, at this stage of the contest, that mine was the most difficult position of all. For the other participants, whatever was the result of their matches, a sensation would not occur. A victory by either Korchnoi or Geller would be considered quite logical. Naturally, Larsen was stronger than Ulhmann, but Larsen is well known for his erratic play. He can crush any opponent, but then he can lose to anybody too. . . . Even Fischer-Taimanov, which everyone expected the American grandmaster to win, left some doubts. For Taimanov was a strong, very experienced grandmaster, who had beaten nearly all the world's greatest players in his time. Even such an expert as Mikhail Botvinnik declared that if Taimanov prepared well, he would have his chances against Fischer.

Coming to my meeting with Hübner, then, it must be said that the whole chess world had no doubt as to the result of this match. On the one side was an experienced grandmaster who had newly lost his champion's title, on the other, a young, inexperienced player, who had carried the grandmaster's title only a few months. Everybody, absolutely everybody expected me to win, and this put me in a very difficult psychological situation.

In the preparatory period, I analyzed Hübner's games, and the results were by no means entirely pleasurable for me; the young German player was developing extremely fast. In 1970 Hübner was far stronger than in 1969, not to speak of 1965, which was the first time we met over the board. Yes, as far back as 1965 I had played Hübner in a simultaneous display in Köln (Cologne), Germany, and, as a matter of fact, I lost.

As a chess-player Hübner was constantly developing. His style of play was purely positional, even classical. So I concluded, in contradiction to most of the commentators, that there was a very difficult struggle ahead of me. At the same time, speaking frankly, I was fully confident of victory.

One of my old trainers, grandmaster Alexei Suetin, travelled with me to Seville as my second. The young Moscow master, Igor Zaitsev, also came to assist us in our work.

The Seville organizers were not very rich, and our playing arena was to be a basement supplied rent-free by an insurance company. Nonetheless, Hübner and I, together with the organizers, surveyed the place and decided it was quite possible to play there.

The match, as is well known, had an unexpected passage, and an even more unexpected end. Six draws in a row, then Hübner lost the seventh game, resigned the match and went home. What was the reason for this strange finish?

In my opinion, before the match began, Hübner was convinced he would lose. To all appearances, he had come to Seville simply to draw a few games with the ex-World Champion, lose a couple, and then go home. But then the first game ended in a draw, then the next, then the next... and however modest a player he might be (and Hübner is a very modest chess-player), he automatically began to think in this way: 'My powerful opponent is completely unable to defeat me. In that case, why shouldn't I be able to beat him?'

As soon as Hübner began to think of victory, he began to get nervous as well. In the sixth game the West German player approached the judges and asked them to move the game into another room, because the conditions were 'very noisy'. The judges rejected this, because the conditions were in fact quite normal. Besides, even if it had been very noisy, the organizers did not have any choice about the playing room. And finally, had we not looked over the hall together before the match and given our assent then?

In the seventh game Hübner gained the advantage, but later on I managed to take the initiative and win the game. Now Hübner's nerves gave way completely. After the game was over, he theatrically tore up the score sheet in front of us and quickly disappeared. Next day we learnt that he had announced his resignation to the judges and gone home.

Independent of the results of the Seville match, Hübner is a very gifted chess-player, and if he works properly at the game, he should have a big future.

The results of the other quarter-final matches are well known: Korchnoi beat Geller, Larsen beat Ulhmann, and Fischer scored 6–0 against Taimanov....

At the end of this last match, which took place in Canada, the chief arbiter, Bozidar Kazic, published a very interesting article, where, amongst other things, he relates the following incident: one day Fischer was spending one of his free hours on the tennis court with the representative of the Canadian chess organization, and made a disparaging remark about the poor playing arrangements. The Canadian was surprised, replying 'Mr Fischer, I cannot understand why you should be dissatisfied. Surely we were not the ones to invite you to Canada. . . .'

Kazic, wittingly or otherwise, had revealed a secret that the initiators and financiers of the Canadian match were Americans. Meanwhile it was the intention that Kazic should be the arbiter in Fischer's future matches. After the publication of the aforementioned article, Kazic's candidature was taken away. . . .

What is more, there was a clause in the Spassky-Fischer match conditions, whereby the arbiter was not allowed to write or publish a single line about the match as long as he lived.

But let us return to the semi-final matches. Once again the American grandmaster did the impossible, winning 6–0, this time against Larsen. This was already something that nobody had expected. A present-day grandmaster simply hasn't the right to be crushed so utterly by another grandmaster. In the previous instance the 'wipe-out' might be partially explained by Taimanov's relatively advanced years, apart from the fact that his chances were not rated very high in the first place. But the Fischer–Larsen result was simply stunning.

In chess there is an unwritten law, that the loser does not generally speak after the match is over. Above all this is because he is to a certain extent seen as having to justify himself, and what he says, therefore, carries less weight. But Larsen nonetheless had the courage to publish an article in which he revealed many curious details. Chess-players had first to accept, with surprise, that Larsen had agreed to play on his rival's 'home ground'. Besides that, it turned out that Larsen himself did not know until the very last moment, where the match was to be held. First he was promised one venue, then another, and so on . . . Larsen writes that the climatic conditions had a very bad effect on his health, and for the first time in his life he landed up in hospital with high blood pressure.

Let us turn to my match with Victor Korchnoi. This, as is well known, had very little excitement up till the ninth game. The first eight games were drawn. Some people even, half serious, half joking, suggested that we were both of us 'afraid of winning and falling into Fischer's hands'. And Fischer himself, when asked, which of us was likely to play more successfully against him, refused to comment, saying his answer might have an effect on the course of the match. . . .

In reality, how is it possible to explain this spate of draws? Imagine two chess-players of equal strength, who have been participating in tournaments together for over a quarter of a century, who know each other down to the smallest detail... in those 25 years, out of all the games played between us, I have only managed to secure a one point advantage, and that point was scored in 1946, when Korchnoi and I met in a junior tournament....

If we keep that situation in view, then it is no longer so surprising that the draws followed one another. And the struggle was in fact not that peaceful. First Korchnoi held a certain initiative, then it passed to me. Finally, I managed to win the ninth game. In the final, tenth game, I obtained a large plus, and offered a draw, but Korchnoi refused. As it turned out, the tension of the struggle was so great that my opponent did not realize how difficult his position had become. Later on Korchnoi's game became hopeless, and when the time for adjournment arrived, he addressed me in the following manner: 'I could resign here or agree a draw.' From a sporting point of view, a draw and a win in this game had the same significance, so I replied 'Of course, a draw.'

It was suggested to hold the Fischer–Petrosian match in either the Soviet Union, America, Yugoslavia or Argentina. As might have been expected, it soon became clear that neither side was willing to play on his opponent's home ground.

It always gives me great pleasure to be in Yugoslavia, I like the country, and its hospitable people. It can even be said that the countryside is very similar to that in the Caucasus, and to my beloved Armenia. Similar too, are men's natures, even the food... in Yugoslavia there would be no language barrier for me, since Serbo-Croat is very like Russian. Finally, it is well known that the Yugoslavs are brilliant tournament organizers.

But I nonetheless declined to play in Yugoslavia, and here is why.

From 1955 up to the match with Fischer, I have played 13 times in Yugoslavia. I have played in official and friendly, team and individual events. I have played as a young grandmaster, as a world championship challenger, and as World Champion; even as ex-World Champion....

Yet in those 17 years, my best results in Yugoslavia have been no higher than 3rd. I have clear memories of terrible blunders in those tournaments, even of putting queens en prise. In such an important competition the memory of these games could have very bad consequences. So I decided that I did not have the moral right to play the match in Yugoslavia.

That left Argentina. From a sporting point of view my results there have been quite good. At the same time I realized that our match would coincide with the extremely damp, suffocating Argentinian spring. I am now no longer so young as to be indifferent to climatic conditions. I can't stand dampness, and I have never been able to rest in our Black Sea resorts. So Argentina was by no means an inviting prospect for me, but there was no alternative. . . .

Just at that moment an unexpected telegram arrived from Greece. The members of that country's chess federation wanted to know why we had not replied to their invitation to hold the match in Athens.

In fact we had never received any invitations from them. As it turned out, it had got as far as Euwe, but he did not think it was necessary to pass it on to us, since he reasoned that Argentina should be given the preference, as chess is very popular there, and, most important, the financial conditions were better.

About that time the Yugoslav grandmaster Gligoric rang me and asked if I didn't want to speak to Fischer over the phone? I said I didn't mind, but that my English was probably insufficient, as was no doubt Fischer's Russian. Gligoric offered to help us here. As a result an unusual conversation came about, on one end, in Moscow, myself, on the other, Fischer in New York, and in the middle, in Belgrade, Gligoric, working as interpreter for both of us.

The conversation lasted quite a long time, and the main topic was the choice of venue for the match. Fischer said that he wanted to play in Argentina, since the money was good, and they prepared good steaks there. I replied that the conditions in general were more important to me, particularly climatic conditions. Gligoric then said 'Fischer says it doesn't matter, FIDE will anyway decide to play the match in Argentina.' I replied angrily that no-one was able to force me to play in Argentina, and in that event Fischer could play with anyone else, but not with me.

Soon the Greek chess federation announced that it was prepared to provide the very best match conditions, and to top anything that Argentina could provide in the way of money. It appeared that, following Euwe's and Fischer's declared principles, their offer should be given the preference.

But matters turned out otherwise. The final decision was referred to the FIDE congress, which once again favoured a drawing of lots.

Another lottery . . . a lottery, which took a strange course. In recent years the international chess federation has generally employed a complex form of lot-drawing – double lottery. First it is decided which of the interested parties should draw the lot, and then the second, decisive draw is made. A double lottery was also made in Canada.

It would have appeared reasonable to have, if not disinterested parties, then at least little children make the preliminary drawing of lots, as generally occurs in such situations. But here it was not to be.

The wife of the representative of the Danish chess federation, Mrs Scholer, was invited to make the first draw. She chose the ticket marked 'USA'. This meant that the main draw was to be made by the representative of the American chess federation, Mr Edmondson. But Edmondson's wife said 'Mrs Scholer, you drew the first lot so well, that I entreat you to draw the second as well'. Mrs Scholer, as might have been expected, drew the ticket marked 'Argentina'. . . .

Accordingly we – myself and my trainers Averbakh and Suetin – had to travel to Buenos Aires. Before the match I realized that I had a very hard task ahead of me, but I thought I had real chances of victory.

The match, as is well known, ended very badly for me. Studying the course of the match carefully, it becomes clear that it divides into two halves, both completely unlike the other. Up to the fifth game, despite the scores being equal, the initiative was on my side. Starting from the sixth game, there seems to be another man playing. . . .

I mentioned earlier on in the article that the loser seems to have no moral right to seek the reasons for his failure in side-issues. I myself have never liked to look for excuses for defeat, and always consider that the decisive factor in a contest will be the relative strengths of the players. But there are times when one has to speak out, in order that certain things be borne in mind in the future. . . .

Just before the match began, something happened that annoyed me very much. An extremely disreputable individual approached me and said insolently: 'Mr Petrosian, we are all waiting for the Spassky Fischer match. So wouldn't it be better if you accepted a nice round sum and went home?'

At the end of the semi-final match, I found a letter waiting for me in the Central chess club, addressed to 'The winner of the Petrosian Korchnoi match'. The writer of the letter, a candidate master from Kishinev, had found an unexpected move in one of Fischer's favourite opening variations. Detailed analysis showed that the move gave Black a more or less won game.

I decided to use the innovation in the very first game. In these matches the first game has great significance. And if we recall how badly Fischer reacts to defeat, then the importance of this game becomes clear. True, I wasn't certain right up to the last moment whether Fischer would fall into the trap. After all, if your opponent willingly goes into your favourite variation, then he must have something up his sleeve. . . .

However, Fischer is a very stubborn chess-player. Everything turned out as I had wished. When I played the innovation, Fischer, who generally very cool at the board, reddened, clasped his head in his hands and began to think.

At that moment the lights went out in the hall. The hall was only dimly lit by small lamps. The arbiter of the match, grandmaster Schmid, approached the board and stopped the clocks. I immediately left the table. It seemed there was nothing strange going on. Light can fuse any time, but what was amazing was that Fischer, that Fischer who had always demanded blazing lights to play by, was now sitting in semi-darkness, deep in thought. I told the judge, by means of an interpreter, that Fischer had no right to be thinking while his clock was not going. Schmid approached Fischer, and suggested he leave the board, but the latter said he preferred to think, and that the judge could start the clocks.

This incident might quite easily be overlooked, had not the same thing happened in the eighth game. This time, when the lights went out, Fischer's game was once more dubious. The only difference was that in the first game, when Fischer's position was worse, the lights were out for about 20 minutes. This time everything was fixed more speedily. . . .

I don't want to draw far-reaching conclusions from these occurrences, but facts remain facts: when Fischer's position was worsening, the lights went out.

Our papers have already reported on the gas-bomb thrown into the hall. I only found out later what was really going on, but at the time I suddenly felt that my eyes were burning, and that there was a bad smell in the air. I decided it must be due to nervous tension, and since my game was extremely bad, even supposed bitterly that the smell was arising from . . . the position. But on the stage the judges, and in the hall, policemen, were running about, and when I approached Schmid, he explained what had happened and assured me that matters would soon be put right. And Fischer was calmly sitting and thinking, as though nothing at all was happening around him. . . .

There were quite a few other peculiar incidents, but I think I have related enough to give the reader a picture of the match.

As I had guessed, the Argentinian spring had very bad effects on me. While the weather was still dry, everything went well. But in the second half of the match the weather changed completely. The humidity of the air reached such a point that we seemed to be breathing water. I also found the temperature changes hard to bear. One example: one morning, as we were leaving the house, the thermometer showed plus 28. Naturally, I did not take my jacket with me. That evening, I suddenly felt extremely cold. Returning home I immediately looked at the thermometer: it registered plus 5 degrees. . . .

I have to say, even though the match ended so badly for me, that the Argentinian chess-lovers and, particularly, the Armenian colony there, were very friendly towards me. I have frequently been an eye-witness to the warmth with which my supporters greet my victories, but I have never seen the like of what happened after I won the second game. The spectators applauded thunderously for about 5 minutes on end.

Of the many meetings with Argentinian-Armenians, I will relate only one. Among the guests were high-ranking Argentinian officials, grandmasters and masters. The 62-year-old grandmaster Miguel Najdorf, who had seen many things in his time, confessed that it was the most impressive gathering he had yet seen in honour of any chess player. . . .

The Argentinian government, highly valuing the role which our match had played in popularizing chess in their country, presented Fischer and myself with commemorative medallions.

In a word, the hospitality of the Argentinians was unequalled, and I would hold treasured memories of Buenos Aires if only . . . I had not lost.

. . . How do I rate the chances of Spassky and Fischer in their forthcoming match? Fischer's recent brilliant successes speak for themselves, but in my opinion, if Spassky plays as he did in the years 1963–1969, his chances will be the better. But . . . there is one reservation here. On becoming World Champion, Spassky committed an error which I myself was guilty of in my time. In the last three years Spassky has competed in very few strong tournaments, and this has had negative effects on his practical strength. So now everything depends on whether he can regain his best form or not.

I should add that the keenest follower of the Spassky–Fischer match will be me; for I have played against both of them. Since I know the strengths of both extremely well, and have definite opinions about them, and wish to test them in practice.

As to the future . . . well, two more years will pass, and if nothing unexpected happens in those two years. . . .

(This article appeared in the Armenian chess magazine *Shakhmatayin Hayastan* No. 5, May 1972).

45 **Polugaevsky–Petrosian**

1st match game, Moscow 1970

English

1 P–QB4	N–KB3
2 N–KB3	P–K3
3 P–KN3	P–QN3
4 B–N2	B–N2
5 O–O	B–K2
6 P–N3	O–O
7 B–N2	P–Q4
8 P–K3	P–B4
9 N–B3	QN–Q2

Here 9 . . . N–B3 was once the normal move, but after 10 P × P Black is in difficulties.

10 P–Q3

The game Botvinnik–Polugaevsky, Belgrade 1969, went 10 Q–K2 P × P 11 P × P N–K5! 12 N × N B × N 13 KR–Q1 Q–B2 14 P–Q3 B–QB3 but White did not succeed in obtaining an advantage.

10 . . .	R–B1
11 Q–K2	Q–B2
12 P–K4	

White clears up the situation in the centre, and turns the game into a King's Indian with reversed colours.

Perhaps Polugaevsky committed a psychological, as well as a chess error in making this move. It is well known that the ex-World Champion is very happy against the King's Indian defence, whereas Polugaevsky has not employed this opening much as Black.

12 ...	P-Q5
13 N-N1	

An inaccuracy. Better was 13 N-QN5 Q-N1, with N/B3 moves, and P-B4 to follow.

13 ...	N-K1
14 N-K1	P-K4
15 P-B4	P-N3!

A precise move. Black intends to exchange on ... KB5, following up by ... N-N2 and ... P-B4. Polugaevsky's next move looks natural, but his 17th is a mistake.

16 P-B5	B-N4
17 P-KR4?	B-K6+
18 K-R2	P × P

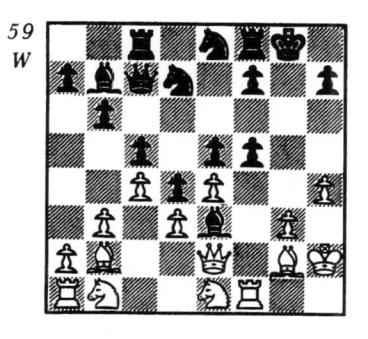

59 W

A critical point. White had originally intended to play 19 B-KR3 here, but then saw that after 19 ... P × P! 20 Q-N4+ N-N2 21 Q × N.Q7 Q × Q 22 B × Q R.QB1-Q1 23 B-R3 P-B4 he would have a lost game, notwithstanding the extra piece. After 40 minutes thought, Polugaevsky rejected the continuation 19 R × P N-N2 20 B-KR3 N × R 21 B × R N-B3, which would have given him compensation for the exchange. If White retreats the rook instead of playing 20 B-KR3, then 20 ... P-B4 gives Black a clear advantage.

19 P × P?	P-K5!
20 B × KP	B × B
21 P × B	N1-B3
22 N-N2	KR-K1

White's position is clearly bad. In order to avoid getting mated, he has to go into an ending a pawn down.

23 N-Q2	B × N
24 Q × B	Q × P+
25 K × Q	N × P+
26 K-B4	N × Q
27 R.B1-K1	N-B3
28 R × R+	R × R
29 R-K1	N7-K5

The only chance of resistance here lay in 30 P-N4, though if Black plays correctly it is insufficient to save the game.

30 R-K2	K-B1
31 K-B3	

Not 31 N-K1 because of 31 ... N-R4+ 32 K-B3 N4-N6.

31 ...	P-Q6
32 R-K3	R-Q1
33 R-K1	

If 33 B × N P-Q7 34 B × R P-Q8-Q+ 35 K × N Q × B, Black brings his king to KB3 and wins.

33 ...	P-Q7
34 R-Q1	N-N5
35 N-K3	N.K5-B7
36 B-B3	R-Q6
0-1	

(Notes to this game by Liberzon in *Chess in the USSR* No. 4 1970).

46 Hort–Petrosian

European Team Ch, Kafenberg 1970

French

1 P–K4	P–K3
2 P–Q4	P–Q4
3 N–QB3	B–N5
4 P–K5	P–QB4
5 P–QR3	B×N+
6 P×B	Q–B2
7 Q–N4	

The sharpest, trying to take immediate advantage of the weakness on KN7.

7...	P–B4

This is a fairly old continuation, which is little played nowadays. At least Black loses no pawns by it!

8 Q–N3	P×P
9 P×P	N–K2
10 B–Q2	0–0
11 B–Q3	P–QN3!

Black exchanges his bad bishop in favourable circumstances, for White cannot easily expand on either wing.

12 N–K2	B–R3
13 N–B4!	Q–Q2
14 B–N4	

Another possibility is 14 B×B N×B 15 Q–Q3 N–N1 16 P–KR4.

14...	R–B2!

Black avoids 14...B×B 15 N–R5! N–N3 16 B×R.

15 P–KR4!?

Slightly optimistic; 15 0–0 is safer.

15...	B×B
16 Q×B	N1–B3
17 R–R3	R–QB1
18 R–N3	N–Q1!

A powerful retreating move. Black intends to place his rook on...QB5 and bring the knight back to...QB3, on the QP.

19 P–R5	R–B5
20 P–R6	N2–B3
21 N–R5	

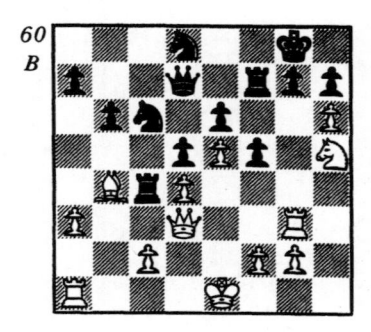

60 B

Setting up an interesting, if fairly transparent, threat: 21...R×QP 22 R×P+ R×R 23 N–B6+ K–R1 24 N×Q. Black decides to give up the exchange, which is very often a strong move in the French defence.

21...	P–N3!
22 N–B6+	R×N
23 P×R	N–B2

Petrosian relates that he was intending to play...N×QP, but was surprised to see a look of confidence on Hort's face. The move played, however, is quite good enough.

24 Q–Q2	R×QP
25 R–Q3	R–R5
26 R–R3	R–N5

The rest of the game sees Black steadily increase his advantage, while White can only look on helplessly; so commentary is superfluous.

27 K–B1 N–Q3 28 R–K1 K–B2 29 B–B3 N–K5 30 Q–Q3 N–B4 31 Q–Q1 R–QB5 32 B–N2 P–QN4 33 Q–K2 Q–Q3 34 K–N1 N–K5 35 R–Q3 Q–B4 36 R–QB1 P–K4 37

Q-K3	P-Q5	38 Q-K2	N×P3	39
R3-Q1	N-Q4	40 Q-Q2	P-K5	41
Q-N5	N-B2	42 R-Q2	N-K3	43
Q-R4	P-R4	44 R1-Q1	R×P	45
R×R	Q×R	46 R-QB1	Q×B	
47 R×N	P-Q6	48 R-R6	Q-Q5!	
0-1.				

47 Petrosian–Mecking

Wijk aan Zee 1971

Torre Attack

1 P-Q4	N-KB3
2 N-KB3	P-K3
3 B-N5	

The Torre attack, one of Petrosian's pet lines. Despite its outward placidity, it promises White a very harmonious development for his forces. Furthermore, it is relatively simple to play, and can be used against almost any possible black formation.

3 ...   P-B4

The sharpest line, aiming to capitalize on White's weakened (by the development of the queen's bishop) Q-side.

| 4 P-K3 | P-Q4 |

4 ... Q-N3 was the consistent move here.

5 P-B3	N-B3
6 QN-Q2	P×P
7 KP×P	

Capturing with the KP gives White a steady initiative down the K-file.

7 ...	B-K2
8 B-Q3	P-KR3
9 B-KB4	N-KR4
10 B-K3	N-B3
11 N-K5!	N×N

An unwise exchange, since the game now takes on a 'French'

character, very favourable to White. Black has the usual bad queen's bishop, and White has control of the Q4 square; nor can Black hope to undermine the white KP. This combination of factors makes the future very bleak for Black.

12 P×N	N-Q2
13 B-Q4	N-B4
14 B-B2	P-QR4
15 Q-N4	

Forcing a weakening of Black's K-side, since 15 ... 0-0 walks into an attack after P-KR4 and R-R3-N3.

15 ...	P-KN3
16 0-0	B-Q2
17 KR-K1	Q-B2
18 P-QR4	N-R3
19 Q-K2	K-B1
20 N-B3	K-N2
21 B-K3	N-B4
22 N-Q4	R-R3
23 B-B1	R3-R1
24 P-KN3	P-N3
25 P-R4	P-R4
26 Q-B3	Q-Q1
27 B-Q2	Q-K1?

This move has been criticized, because it permits White to exchange off the black-squared bishops on his next move. But in the long run such an exchange could hardly be avoided. White adds to his other advantages a crushing grip on the black squares of the K-side.

28 B-N5	Q-Q1
29 Q-B4	R-QB1
30 R-K3	B×B
31 P×B	R-R1

Petrosian decides to delight us with an interesting exploitation of his advantage in the endgame.

| 32 Q-B6+ | Q×Q |
| 33 KP×Q+ | K-R2 |

61
W

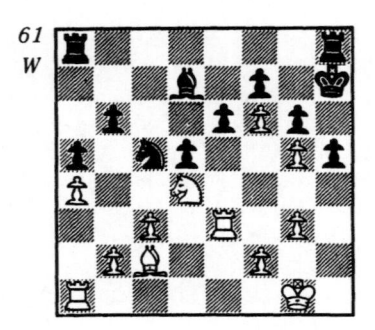

34 K–N2	QR–K1
35 P–KB4	R–QN1
36 R3–K1	N–N2
37 R–R1	K–N1
38 N–B3	N–Q3
39 N–K5	B–K1

White has established complete control. It only remains to open up the lines on the Q-side, and Black is defenceless.

40 B–Q3 R–B1 41 K–B3 B–B3 42 R–KR2 B–K1 43 K–K3 R–B2 44 K–Q4 N–N2 45 P–QN4! N–Q1 46 R–R4 N–N2 47 R–QR2 N–Q3 48 R–KR1 N–N2 49 P–N5 N–B4 50 B–B2 N–Q2 51 R–QR3 N–B4 52 P–B4! The final opening of lines. **52 . . . N–Q2 53 R–QB3 N×N 54 K×N P×P 55 B–K4 R–B1 56 K–Q6 R–B4 57 R1–QB1 P–R5 1–0.**

The game was adjourned here, but Mecking did not manage to resume it.

48 Petrosian–Fischer

2nd match game, Buenos Aires 1971

Grünfeld

1 P–Q4	N–KB3
2 P–QB4	P–KN3
3 N–QB3	P–Q4
4 B–B4	B–N2
5 P–K3	P–B4

The main line here is 5 . . . O–O, followed by 6 . . . P–B4.

**6 QP×P   Q–R4
7 R–B1**

7 Q–N3 was worth considering, and if 7 . . . N–K5?   8 Q–N5+ Q×Q 9 N×Q.

7 . . .   N–K5

A more positional continuation would be 7 . . . P×P   8 B×P Q×BP 9 B–QN3 N–B3. The move played occurred in the game Reshevsky–Hort, Palma de Mallorca 1969, where after 8 N–B3 N×N 9 P×N B×P+ 10 N–Q2 B–K3 the game was sharp and even.

8 P×P

8 KN–K2 is interesting, with the possible continuation 8 . . . P×P 9 Q–R4+ Q×Q 10 N×Q B–Q2 11 R×P B×N 12 R×N.K4 B–B7 13 R–B4 B–Q6 14 R–N4, when White has an extra pawn.

**8 . . .   N×N
9 Q–Q2   Q×RP**

Creating an unanalyzed and completely original position.

10 P×N

10 R×N!? was possible. If 10 . . . B×R 11 Q×B Q–R8+ 12 K–Q2 Q×B 13 Q×R+ K–Q2 14 N–B3! Q×R   15 N–K5+ White has a strong attack. 10 R×N Q–R8+ 11 R–B1 Q×P 12 R–B2 also gives the advantage to White. But, playing 10 . . . O–O!, Black obtains good counter-chances.

**10 . . .   Q–R4
11 B–B4**

If 11 P–K4 N–Q2! (11 . . . Q×P.B4 12 B–KR6! is inferior) 12 B–KR6 B×B 13 Q×B N×P with good play for Black.

**11 . . .   N–Q2
12 N–K2**

But not 12 P–B6? P×P 13 P×P N–B4 14 N–K2 Q–R5 15 B–R2 N–Q6+! with advantage to Black.

12 ...   N–K4

Black is unwise to delay the capture of the QBP. After 12 ... N×P or 12 ... Q×P.4, the opening difficulties would be past.

13 B–R2

More accurate than 13 B–QN3 Q–N4! 14 B–B2 N–B5 followed by ...Q×P.4, establishing a blockade on...QB4.

13 ...   B–B4?

This move, which Fischer made instantaneously, leads to a very difficult position.

14 B×N   B×B
15 N–Q4!

Simple and strong. Now if 15 ... B–Q2 16 P–B6! P×P 17 P×P B–B1 18 P–KB4, and White keeps his extra pawn.

15 ...   Q×P.4
16 N×B   P×N
17 0–0   Q–R4
18 Q–B2!

A precise move, and according to Petrosian, the most difficult one in the game. White brings the KB5 square under attack, and prepares the advance P–B4–5–6!

If now 18 ... B–B3, 19 KR–Q1 R–QB1 20 Q×P R×P 21 R×R Q×R 22 P–Q6! with a strong attack.

18 ...   P–B5
19 P–B4!

More energetic than 19 P×P B×KBP 20 R–N1, though White has the advantage there too.

19 ...   P×P
20 P–B5!   Q–Q7

Realizing that White's attack may soon become decisive, Fischer starts complications.

21 Q–R4+   K–B1

The best chance was probably 21 ... K–Q1.

22 R.QB1–Q1

But not 22 P×P R–KN1.

22 ...   Q–K7

22 ... P–K7 23 R×Q B×P+ 24 K×B P×R=Q 25 P–Q6! is rather bad for Black.

23 P–Q6   Q–R4

If 23 ... P×BP+ the simplest reply is 24 K–R1. If 23 ... B×RP+ then 24 K×B Q–R4+ 25 K–N1 P–K7 26 Q–Q4! with a strong attack. Black's game is already hopeless, and Petrosian plays the final stages brilliantly.

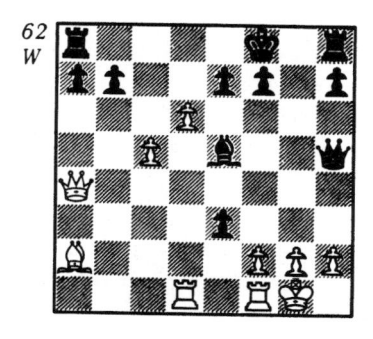

62 W

24 P–B4!

But not 24 BP×P B×RP+ 25 K–B2 R–KN1!

24 ...   P–K7
25 P×B   P×R.Q8=Q
26 R×Q   Q×KP
27 R–KB1!

The attack is irresistible. If 27 ... P–K3 28 Q–Q7! is decisive.

27 ...   P–B3
28 Q–N3   K–N2
29 Q–B7+   K–R3
30 P×P   P–B4

If 30 ... QR–KN1, 31 B–N1! wins at once.

31 R×P   Q–Q5+
32 K–R1   1–0

(Notes by Suetin in *Chess in the USSR*, No. 1 1972).

49 Petrosian–Spassky

Alekhine Memorial, Moscow 1971

Queen's Gambit Accepted

1 P–Q4   P–Q4
2 P–QB4   P×P

Spassky has very infrequently played this opening. Certainly it did not occur in his match games with Petrosian.

3 N–KB3   N–KB3
4 P–K3   P–K3
5 B×P   P–B4
6 O–O   P–QR3
7 P–QR4   N–B3
8 Q–K2   P×P
9 R–Q1   B–K2
10 P×P   O–O
11 N–B3   N–Q4

11 ... N–QN5 is also popular. The tenth match game Botvinnik–Petrosian 1963 continued 12 B–KN5 B–Q2 13 P–Q5 P×P 14 N×P N5×N 15 B4×N N×B 16 R×N B×B 17 N×B P–KR3 18 Q–Q2 P×N 19 R×B Q–B3 and Black, at the cost of a pawn, received sufficient counterplay to draw.

Naturally, there aren't that many chess players who would willingly go into a line which guarantees them at best a draw.

In Vaganian–Kokh, USSR Team Ch 1969, Black instead of 12 ... B–Q2 played 12 ... N5–Q4. After 13 N–K5 N×N 14 P×N N–Q4 15 B×B N×B 16 B–Q3 N–Q4 17 B–B2 Q–B2 18 P–QB4 N–B3 19 R–R3! White had a strong attack.

12 Q–K4

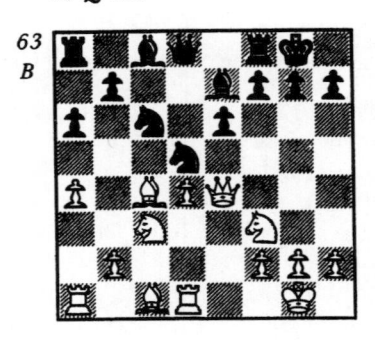

63
B

The sixteenth match game Botvinnik–Petrosian continued 12 B–Q3 N3–N5 13 B–N1 B–Q2 14 Q–K4 P–KN3 15 N–K5 B–KB3 16 Q–B3 B–N2 17 Q–N3 B–K1 18 P–R4 and Black was in difficulties.

Kuzmin played the attack another way in his game with Suetin, Sochi 1970: 12 P–R4!? N3–N5 13 P–KR5 P–R3 14 N–K5 P–QN3 15 Q–N4 N–KB3 16 Q–B3 N3–Q4 17 N×N P×N 18 N–B6! N×N 19 B×QP B–N5 20 Q×B Q×B 21 B×P with advantage to White.

The move played in the game, to the best of my knowledge, has not been met before.

12 ...   N3–N5

It is interesting to consider where the queen would have gone to if Black had played 12 ... N–B3. Very probably K2, since after 13 Q–R4 N–Q4 14 Q–N3 Black could equalize with 14 ... B–Q3. For example: 15 Q–R3 P–K4 16 Q–R5 N–B3 17 Q–R4 B–KN5! 18 P×P N×P 19 N×N B×R 20 N×P R×N 21 N×B B×P+ 22 K×B Q×N 23 B×R+ K×B 24 Q–QB4+ Q–Q4.

Another possibility: 21 B×R+ K×B 22 Q–QB4+ K–B1 23 N×B B×P+ 24 K×B Q×N 25 B–B4 or 25 Q–QN4+.

In both cases, however, White obtains nothing. If 25 B–B4 Q–R4+ 26 K–N1 Q–Q4, and if 25 Q–QN4+ K–N1 26 Q×P Q–R4+, with a draw by perpetual check.

Seeking complications the World Champion rejects 12 ... N–B3, but the position soon becomes difficult.

13 N–K5   R–R2

Black can no longer develop in a normal manner. If 13 ... P–QN3 14 N–B6! is unpleasant, after which I can't find any decent positions for Black – he is worse in all variations. For example 14 ... N5×N 15 N×N P×N 16 B×QP B–KN5 17 P–B3 (17 B×N B×R 18 B×R B–B3 19 B–K3 B×RP 20 R×B Q×B achieves nothing, Black holds on after 20 B–N7 R–K1 21 Q–B4 B–QN4 22 R–QB1 P–R3 23 B–R7 Q×P! and 20 B–B6 B×B 21 Q×B B×P 22 R–Q1 Q–B3! is to his advantage.) 17 ... N×P!? 18 B–K3! with a clear advantage to White, as all Black's pieces are hanging: 18 ... B–KB4   19 Q×N R–N1 (19 ... B–B4 20 Q–B3) 20 Q–K5 B–Q2 21 B–B6 etc.

14 ... N4×N (after 14 N–B6) does not help either: 15 N×B+ Q×N 16 P×N B–N2 17 Q–N4 (17 P–Q5? Q–B3!) 17 ... KR–B1 18 B–KN5! (18 B–R6? Q–B3) 18 ... Q–B1 19 B×KP R×P 20 B–Q2! Now if 20 ... R–Q6 21 B–QB4, or 20 ... R–B7 21 B×N Q×B 22 B×P+!, or 20 ... R–B2 21 Q–B4!

14 B–N3   N–KB3

For some reason Black refrains from transferring his rook along the second rank: 14 ... P–QN3 15 N×N P×N 16 Q–B3 R–B2 17 B–KB4 B–K3 18 QR–B1 B–Q3. Perhaps Spassky did not like the look of this position. White obviously has the advantage, but how considerable is it?

15 Q–R4   P–QN3
16 Q–N3   B–N2

Better was 16 ... K–R1, after which the break 17 P–Q5 would not be dangerous: 17 P–Q5 P×P 18 N×QP N3×N 19 B×N N×B!, but not 19 ... B–K3 because of 20 B–R6! P×B 21 B×B Q–K1 22 N×P+ R×N 23 B×R Q×B 24 Q–QN8+ B–B1 25 R–Q8 K–N2 26 R×B!

If White now plays 20 N–B6 N–B6! is a good reply.

17 B–R6   N–K1

17 ... N–R4 is inferior because of 18 Q–N4.

18 QR–B1   K–R1

18 ... B–R5 19 Q–N4 P–B4 20 B×KP+ K–R1 is no good because of 21 Q–R5! P×B 22 N–N6 mate.

Best was 18 ... N–Q4. After 19 N×N B×N 20 N–B6 B×N 21 R×B R–Q2! the rook makes a timely entrance. If 20 B×B Q×B 21 R–B8 B–B3 22 N–N4 Black can maintain the equilibrium by 22 ... B–Q1!

19 P–Q5!

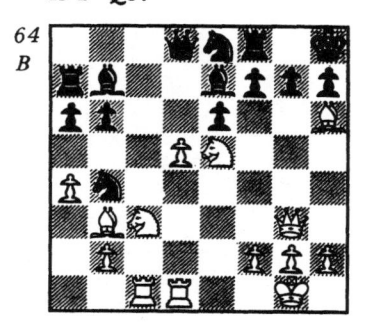

64
B

19 ...   P×P

If 19 ... P×B nothing comes of 20 N×P+ R×N   21 P×P R–N2! 22 R×Q R×Q   23 R×N+ R–N1 24 R×B B×P!, with a draw, since 25 R–K8 R×R   26 K×B N–Q6! is not possible.

But 20 P×P N–Q3   21 P×P! (21 N×P+ N×N!   22 R×Q N×R or 22 P×N Q–N1!) should win easily enough.

19 ... N×P   20 N×N P×N   21 B–K3 (21 B×QP? B×B   22 N–B6 B×N!   23 R×Q B×R   24 R×B P×B is good for Black) 21 ... R–R1 22 N–B6 leaves Black in difficulties.

20 B–K3!

A classic example of Alekhinian strategy. With his diversionary operations on the king's wing, Petrosian has forced Black's pieces into awkward situations, and now he delivers the decisive blow on the Q-side.

20 ...   R–R1

20 ... P–QR4 looks better at first sight, in order to answer 21 N–B4 by ... R–R3. But White has the reply 21 N×QP! N×N   22 B×N B×B   23 N–B6 with great advantage. 20 ... B–B4 is refuted by 21 P–R5 N–KB3 22 N–R4!

21 N–B4

White regains his pawn, maintaining a large positional advantage.

21 ...   N–Q3

If 21 ... B–B4   22 N–R5! is unpleasant.

22 B×P

22 N×NP is bad because of 22 ... N–B4!   23 Q–R3 N×B   24 Q×N B–N4   25 P–B4 B×P!

22 ...   Q–N1

Many commentators considered that 22 ... Q–Q2 was stronger. In my opinion White would answer 23 N–K3, when Black loses a pawn for insufficient compensation: 23 ... QR–B1   24 N.K3×P N×N   25 B×N B×B   26 R×B Q–B3   27 B–Q4! and so on. If 23 ... Q–K3, then 24 B–B5 P–QR4   25 B×N.4 P×B   26 N.B3×P.

23 N–R5

Here too 23 N–K3! is better.

23 ...   N–B4?

Black could have offered sterner resistance by 23 ... R–B1!

24 Q×Q	QR×Q
25 N×B	R×N
26 P–R5	B–N4
27 R–N1	P–Q5

After 27 ... N–K2   28 N×P N2×N   29 B×N N×B   30 R×N Black's game is again hopeless.

28 N–Q5   N–QB3

If 28 ... N×N   29 B×N R–Q2   30 B–K4!

29 B–R4	R–B1
30 P–B4	N3–K2

30 ... B–Q1 is defeated by 31 R.N1–B1!

31 R.N1–B1	R1–QN1
32 P×B	N×N
33 B–B6	R×B
34 P×R	N.Q4–K6

35 P–N7!

White returns the exchange to obtain a completely won position.

35 ...	N×R
36 R×N	P–N3
37 P–N4	N–N2

If 27 ... N–Q3   38 R×P N×P   39 R–N4.   37 ... N–K2 is insufficient after 38 B–B3 K–N2   39 R×P P–B4 40 P×P ep+ K×P   41 R–R4.

38 R×P	N–K3
39 R–Q7	1–0

If 39 ... N×P   40 R–B7 is decisive, and if 39 ... K–N1   40 B–Q5 N–Q1   41 R–B7 wins.

(Notes by Holmov in *Chess in the USSR*, No. 2 1972).

50 Petrosian–Larsen
San Antonio 1972
Dutch

(The notes to this game are by T. Petrosian. They appeared in the Soviet chess newspaper *64*, No. 1 1973).

This game was played at a time when both players were trying to better their tournament position.

Before the start I was tormented by ignorance; it was extremely important to guess Larsen's mood. Was he after the win?

The question was not a frivolous one, and upon it depended the choice of opening move. For after 1 P–QB4, which I frequently play, Black can reply 1 ... P–QB4 or 1 ... P–KN3, and in both cases conceal his intentions and his final choice of opening variation for quite a long time. After 1 P–Q4 it is very much easier to gaze into the heart of your opponent. I should add that for many years my games with Larsen ended only in victory or defeat, but that the last two encounters have been drawn, which shows that Larsen can also be cautious when he feels the need.

1 P–Q4   P–K3

What's this? An invitation to go in to the French defence? Even with 3 N–Q2? No, I thought, Larsen will answer 2 P–K4 with 2 ... P–QB4, offering a transposition into the Sicilian defence, or one of the many forms of the Benoni. And what if 2 N–KB3? Surely a Dutch. Now that's much better!

2 N–KB3   P–KB4

And so a Dutch has indeed come about. One of those openings which, in common with the majority of chess masters, I enjoy playing as White.

3 P–KN3   N–KB3
4 B–N2   P–QN4!?

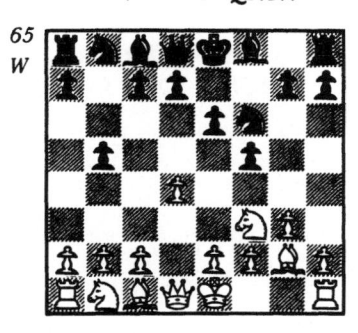

65
W

When the Danish master made this move, Gligoric was passing our table. Always self-controlled, the Yugoslav grandmaster could hardly refrain from bursting out laughing. The move looks very strange. Still, I must admit that I did not manage to solve the unusual problems arising at all well. So if my mood was rosy now, it was not to be for long.

5 N–K5   P–B3
6 N–Q2

It seems that Black is to be quickly punished. It is sufficient only to play P–K4, and whether Black answers with exchanging pawns or not, his position will not bear looking at.

6 ...   Q–N3

Larsen is clearly aiming for concrete play. As it turns out, P–K4 is not so easy to make! If 7 P–QB3 Black plays 7 ... B–N2   8 P–K4 P–B4. True enough, the position looks quite good after 9 QP × P B × BP   10 0–0, or 10 Q–K2, or 9 P–Q5, sacrificing a pawn either temporarily or permanently, but after fairly prolonged consideration I took another decision.

7 P–K4	Q×P
8 N5–B3	Q–B4
9 P×P	Q×KBP
10 0–0	

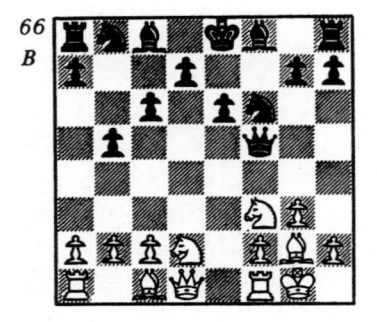

**66
B**

For the sacrificed pawn White has an appreciable advantage in development. If there were something to attack in Black's position, it might be possible to capitalize on this. Unfortunately, there are no vulnerable spots in evidence. At the same time Black's position does not inspire confidence; his queen will be forced to run about, and his Q-side is very tied up due to the action of the bishop on KN2.

10 ...   N–Q4!

An excellent move! Here the knight plays a very important defensive role. At the same time the road home is opened to the queen.

11 N–Q4	Q–B2
12 N2–B3	Q–R4!

Another good move! The queen is engaged in self-defence. Unpleasant moves like N–KN5 and N–K5 are forestalled.

13 R–K1	B–K2
14 R–K5	Q–B2
15 R–K2	0–0
16 N–K5	Q–R4

If 16 ... Q–K1, then 17 N×NP is possible. Now after the preparatory 17 B–B3 Q–K1 18 N×NP, 18 ... R×B is a simple reply. The queen continues to promenade fearlessly. It was precisely this fearlessness, this immunity, which made me feel that somehow White's initiative had dried up, and that he had nothing for the pawn. But then I remembered an ancient truth: many players, sacrificing a pawn, lose because they play as if they had lost it, rather than deliberately parted with it.

While Black has still to complete the development of his Q-side, the initiative remains with White.

17 P–KB4	B–B4
18 K–R1	B–N2

18 ... B×N 19 B–B3 Q–K1 20 Q×B B–N2 deserved serious attention, intending to advance shortly with ... P–QB4, exchanging off the white-squared bishops.

19 N4–B3   B–N3

Black believes in the absolute impenetrability of his position. In the course of time he will play ... P–QB4, without making any positional concessions, such as giving up his black-squared bishop.

20 P–QR4   P–QR3?

If Black's last move was extremely dubious, and I lacked the courage to put a question mark after it, then this one is definitely bad. 20 ... P–N5 was quite playable, since 21 P–R5 B–B2 22 P–R6 is answered by 22 ... B×P.

21 P–B4!

It turns out that 20 ... P–QR3 did quite a lot of damage to Black's game. After 21 ... P×BP 22 N×P.4 there is a very unpleasant threat of Q–N3.

21 ...	N–B3
22 N–N5	P×RP

23 B–B3	Q–K1
24 B–K3	

Here White has a number of good continuations, but time was beginning to run short. As in similar situations, preference is given to 'solid' plans.

24 ...	B×B
25 R×B	P–R3

Black wishes to eject White's pieces at all costs.

26 N–K4	N×N
27 B×N	P–Q4
28 B–N2?	

Missing an excellent opportunity. Naturally, I had thought about making use of the QN1–KR7 diagonal. A queen appearing on KR7 would be definitely disastrous for Black. But how can this be achieved? 28 B–N1 or 28 B–B2, and perhaps B–N6 look very attractive, but I thought that Black could easily defend himself by . . . N–Q2. It did not occur to me that it was not obligatory to place the queen in front of the bishop, but that the reverse formation – bishop before queen – by 28 B–N6 Q–K2(Q1) 29 Q–B2 was quite playable.

It also seems to me that 8 or 10 moves ago, when I was attentively pursuing rather more obscure tactical chances, such an oversight would have been very unlikely. But now when a really good chance appeared, it was overlooked. I should add that I was by no means sure that it was necessary to retreat the bishop to KN2, as the first rank is then badly covered.

28 ...	N–Q2
29 R×P	

The position is gradually becoming simplified, and after 29 . . . N×N 30 R×N it could roundly be stated that White has sufficient compensation for his pawn but no more. The most likely result in that case would be a draw. But this does not suit Larsen, and he begins to create new 'hearths of conflict' on the chess-board.

29 ...	P–B4
30 P×P	N–N3
31 R–R5	N×P

Black's knight has activated itself thanks to tempo-gaining attacks on the white rooks, so it is only proper to return the compliment. 31 R–R5 suggested itself, but where to put the other rook.

32 R–N3	R–Q1

Here my opponent was rather unlucky. I mentioned earlier that I was uneasy about putting my bishop back on KN2, since this left the first rank vulnerable. For just this reason the consequences of the ensuing combination had been precisely calculated by me when I made my 30th move.

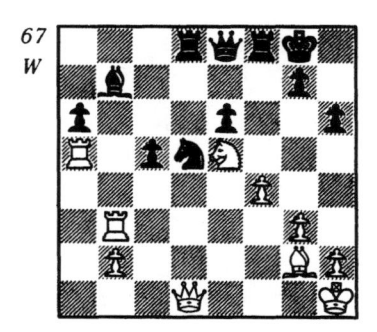

67
W

33 R×B	N–K6
34 Q–K2	R–Q8+
35 Q×R	N×Q
36 R×RP	

Just one more move and the second white rook will be on the seventh rank, with deadly threats against the black king.

36 ...   N–K6
36 ... Q–Q1 37 R6–R7 N–B7+
38 K–N1 Q–Q8+ 39 B–B1 N–R6+
40 K–N2 does not save the game either.

37 R6–R7	N–B4
38 PxN4	Q–Q1
39 P–R3?	

39 B–B3 won immediately. I already realized that I would be winning, or almost winning by playing another move, but I did not want to waste valuable seconds finding it.

39 ...   Q–Q8+

With the flag about to fall 39 ... Q–Q7 had more venom in it, threatening ... Q–B8+, ... Q× BP+ and ... Q×N. I had prepared 40 N–B3, calculating that after 40 ... Q–B8+, when the time control is passed, 41 N–N1 N–N6+ 42 K–R2 would give White at least a draw.

40 K–R2	Q–Q5
41 N–N6	

The adjourned position is not rich in possibilities for Black. The most obvious move – which Larsen sealed – leads to a hopeless ending for Black. Best was 41 ... R–Q1 42 P×N P×P 43 P–N3! P–R4! 44 R×P+ Q×R 45 R×Q+ K×R 46 N–K5 P–R5! when it is not easy for White to exploit his advantage.

41 ...	N–K6
42 R×P+	Q×R
43 R×Q+	K×R
44 N×R	K×N
45 B–B3	

Sooner or later White will produce two passed pawns on the K-side and win. If Black tries 45 ... N–B5 46 P–N3 N–Q7 47 B–Q1 K–K2 (47 ... P–B5 48 P×P N×P 49 B–N3) 48 K–N2 P–B4 to exchange off the Q-side pawns, White can play 49 P–N4, preparing to give up his bishop for the black passed pawn, and win with his remaining disconnected passed pawns, against which, as is well known, the knight is a poor defender.

45 ...   P–R4!

This move deserves an exclamation mark not because it is intrinsically able to change the course of the game, but because it is the only possible move capable of throwing the opponent out of step. At the time when this game was still unfinished, I had two other adjourned games, against Mecking and Saidy, both in very complicated positions. And my attention was mainly directed upon these games, which were practically middle game positions. As well as that it seemed to me that I could resolve practically any endgame which might arise in my game with Larsen over the board. On this account 45 ... P–R4 was almost a complete surprise to me. The natural reaction is 46 K–N3, when White is very happy to exchange the KRPs, thus freeing himself of the fear of being left with a rook pawn and wrong coloured bishop. At the board it seemed to me that after 46 K–N3 P×P 47 P×P N–B5 48 P–N3 N–Q3 49 B–K2 there were technical difficulties in prospect. But, as Larsen pointed out, White wins very easily by advancing his king up the KR-file.

46 P–N5?	P–R5!
47 K–N1	P–K4
48 P×P	N–B5
49 K–B2	N×KP

This is, of course, stronger than 49 ... N×NP 50 K–K3.

50 B–K4	K–N2
51 P–N3	N–B2
52 P–N6	N–N4??

52 ... N–K4 53 K–K3 N × P 54 B × N K × B would have led White to the sorrowful conclusion that the pawn ending is drawn; instead of this Larsen commits a terrible error!

53 B–B5   K–B3
54 K–K3

The bishop cannot be captured, and it was already possible to resign here. Larsen did this after another seven moves.

54 ...	**N–K3**
55 B × N	**K × B**
56 K–K4	**K–B3**
57 K–Q5	**K × P**
58 K × P	**K–B4**
59 P–N4	**K–B5**
60 P–N5	**K–N6**
61 P–N6	**1–0**

Index of Openings

Nos. refer to pages. Bold type indicates that Petrosian was White

1 P–K4 P–K4
Hungarian 48
Ruy Lopez **78**

1 P–K4 Other
Caro Kann 99, 101, 123
French 39, 120, 230, 99
Sicilian 54, 65, 94, **203**

1 P–Q4 P–Q4
Queen's Gambit Accepted **189**, **234**
Queen's Gambit Declined 147, **205**, **214**
Tarrasch **68**, **186**
Slav **52**, 67

1 P–Q4 Other
Benoni **206**

Dutch **40**, **237**
Grünfeld **145**, **232**
King's Indian:
   Panno **194**
   Petrosian **80**, **82**, **83**, **96**, **106**
   Sämisch **103**, **207**
   Other **51**, 191
Nimzo-Indian 64, **79**, **187**, **198**
Old Indian **97**, 105
Queen's Indian **100**, **150**, 212
Torre 192, **231**

Flank/Other
English **122**, 228
King's Indian Attack **104**
Reti **118**

Index of Games

Nos. refer to pages. Bold type indicates that Petrosian was White

A: Complete Games
Bondarevsky **40**
Botvinnik **145**, 147, **150**
Bronstein 99, **205**
Dubinin 39
Dückstein 123
Filip 191
Fischer 120, **232**
Geller **68**
Gligoric **96**, 207
Gurgenidze 101
Hort 230
Ivkov **189**
Johansson M **203**
Keres 94
Korchnoi **122**
Kotov **51**
Larsen **97**, **206**, **237**

Lipnitsky 48
Lutikov **83**
Matanovic **79**
Mecking **231**
Najdorf **103**
Nezmetdinov 65
Pachman **104**, 105
Polugaevsky 228
Reshevsky 64
Smyslov **52**, **100**
Spassky 192, **194**, **198**, 212, **214**, **234**
Stein **106**
Suetin **80**
Szabo 54
Taimanov **67**, **187**
Tal **118**, **186**
Trifunovic **78**
Yukhtman **82**

B: References
Botvinnik–Petrosian (10) 234
   Petrosian (16) 234
   Polugaevsky 228
Bronstein–Panov 78
Geller–Flohr 53, Unzicker 53
Gheorghiu–Gligoric 208
Kuzmin–Suetin 234

Levenfish–Kotov 204
Moiseyev—Boch–Osmolovsky 68
Olafsson–Gligoric 96
Petrosian–Barcza 148
   Polugaevsky 189
   Reshevsky 208
   Simagin 197

Reshevsky–Hort 232
Sakharov–Petrosian 40
Smyslov–Botvinnik 101, Korchnoi 122
Suetin–Petrosian 49,

Polugaevsky 204
Taimanov–Keres 205
Tal–Botvinnik 150
Vaganian–Koch 234

Index – General

Age differential 159, 184
Arbiters
  Golombek 141
  O'Kelly 173
Argentinian-Armenians 227
Bodyguard 144
Books 16, 17, 18, 160
  The Art of Sacrifice in Chess 18
  Boris Spassky Shturmuet Olimp 160
  Chess Praxis 17
Bribery 226
Chess
  disappointment in 202
  no way to earn living 15
Childhood dreams 164
Climatic conditions 223, 224, 227
combinations
  mastery of 161
  '*windmill*' 177
Dancing 165
Draws 156
Drink
  apricot juice 201
  cognac 201
Events (see also World Championships)
  1925 Moscow 125, 177
  1928 Bad Kissingen 49
  1930 San Remo 49
  1935 Moscow 126
  1936 Moscow 126
    Nottingham 126
  1942 Tiflis 19
  1944 Georgian Ch 20, 23
    Tiflis, 1st cat. 20
    Junior tourney 23
  1945 Tiflis Ch 23
    CM tourney 23
    All-Union Youth 23, 24
    Georgian Ch 24
  1946 Georgian Ch 24, 25
    Armenian Ch 27
    USSR Ch ½-final 27, 29, 30
    match v. Kasparian 29
  1947 All-Union CM 32
    USSR Ch ½-final 33, 34
  1948 Trans-Caucasian Republics 34
    Armenian Ch 34

  1949 USSR Ch ½-final 34, 36
    17 USSR Ch 37–39
  1951 Moscow Ch 43
    USSR Ch ½-final 43
    19 USSR Ch 44–47, 59
  1952 Budapest 47
    Interzonal 47, 48, 58, 166
  1953 Candidates 58, 59, 91
  1954 21 USSR Ch 59, 72
  1955 22 USSR Ch 58–60, 72, 73
    Hungary–USSR 61
    Interzonal 60, 61
    Student Olympiad 165
  1956 Candidates 11, 61–63, 72, 91, 160
    Moscow Ch 197
    23 USSR Ch 160
  1957 24 USSR Ch 64, 72, 89, 109
  1958 25 USSR Ch 73–75, 160, 164
    Interzonal 76, 88
    Olympiad 88
  1959 26 USSR Ch 76, 77, 85
    Zurich 88
    Candidates 11, 88, 90–92
  1960 27 USSR Ch 92
  1961 28 USSR Ch 92, 93, 128, 141, 160
  1962 Candidates 11, 12, 93, 108, 109–118, 125
  1963 31 USSR Ch 157
    Los Anglees 155, 157
  1964 Olympiad 157
  1965 Candidates match 158
    Moscow–Leningrad 157
    Simultaneous (v. Hübner) 221
    Yerevan 157
    Zagreb 157
  1965/6 Hastings 162
  1966 All-Union Youth 157
    Moscow Training 162
  1970 Interzonal 220
  1971 Candidates matches 220–228
Food
  mushrooms 165
  shashlik 165
Football 11, 36, 86, 112, 140, 157, 164, 165, 221
Games (see also Sport)
  backgammon 15, 16, 163

244 Indexes

draughts 15
Turkish draughts 15, 16
Impatience 171
Incidents
   gas bomb 227
   lights fusing 28, 226, 227
   sealed move 147
Lenin price 202
Lottery 221, 225, 226
Magazines
   Chess 177
   The Chess Player 207
   Informator 207
   Krasnoi Zviozdi 171
   Literaturnaya Gazieta 221
   Nedeli 162
   Ogonyok 44, 75, 86, 129
   Pravda 144, 175
   Shakhmatayin Hayastan 228
   Shakhmatnaya Moskva 158
   Shakhmaty v SSSR 229, 234, 237
   Sovietsky Sport 21, 126, 185
   Trud 159
   64 156, 237
Music 140, 144, 163, 183
   Gigli 163
   Gobbi 163
   joy of 140
   La Scala 163
   Opera 163
   Piano 163
   Tchaikovsky 144
   Wagner 144, 183
Nakhimovski College 164
Nerves 111, 113, 114, 222
Newspapers (see Magazines)
Openings (see also Index of Openings)
   preparation 111, 114, 131, 162
   Caro Kann 19, 168, 210
   Catalan 33
   French 40, 99, 111, 180, 210
   Grünfeld 25, 140
   King's Gambit 33, 161
   King's Indian 82, 174, 176, 195
   Nimzo-Indian 133, 182, 211
   Petroff 210, 211
   Queen's Gambit 33, 49, 131, 134, 137–139, 169, 210, 215
   Queen's Indian 135, 150
   Queen's Pawn 172
   Ruy Lopez 75, 210
   Sicilian 114, 115, 210
   Tarrasch 210
   Torre 172
Playing conditions 222, 223
Predictions 159, 160

Preparation
   openings 111, 114, 131, 162
   physical 162
   for matches 126, 127, 131, 159, 166, 170
Prophylaxis 17, 22, 54
Psychology 175, 180, 182
Psychological instability/depression:
   Geller 114
   Petrosian 178, 179
   Spassky 160
Pulse 169
Sacrifices 192
Sealed moves 147, 173, 174
Smoking 165, 171
Spartak 34, 36, 157, 162
   football team 86, 90, 112, 140, 164
Sport (see also Games)
   athletics 164
   billiards 140, 164
   ice hockey 86
   skiing 162, 164
   swimming 164
   table tennis 140, 164
   tennis 223
Superstition 165, 166
Time-trouble 95, 112, 166, 167, 170, 171, 177, 179, 219, 240
Trainers 43, 160, 162, 222, 226
World Championship Matches
   age differential 159, 184
   effect of 129, 143, 201
   tension 133, 147
1963 Botvinnik–Petrosian 125–145
   G1: 133–135; *G2:* 134; *G3:* 135; *G4:* 135, 136; *G5:* 136, 137, 144; *G6:* 137; *G7:* 137, 138; *G8:* 138; *G9:* 138; *G10:* 139; *G11:* 139; *G12:* 139; *G13:* 139; *G14:* 140, 141; *G15:* 140, 141; *G16:* 141, 142; *G17:* 142; *G18:* 142; *G19:* 143; *G20:* 143; *G21:* 143; *G22:* 143
1966 Petrosian–Spassky 168–185, 210
   G1: 168, 169, 178; *G2:* 169, 172; *G3:* 169, 170, 172; *G4:* 170; *G5:* 170–172; *G6:* 172; *G7:* 172–174, 177, 180, 185; *G8:* 174; *G9:* 174; *G10:* 174–177, 185; *G11:* 176, 178, 180; *G12:* 176–179, 185; *G13:* 178, 185; *G14:* 179; *G15:* 179; *G16:* 179; *G17:* 179; *G18:* 179, 185; *G19:* 180, 185; *G20:* 180, 181, 185, 211; *G21:* 182; *G22:* 182, 183, 185, 201; *G23:* 183; *G24:* 184
1969 Petrosian–Spassky 210, 211, 215, 216
1972 Spassky–Fischer 132, 226, 228
World War II 20

Index of Names (*See also Index of Games*)

Abramian 36
Abramov 63, 73, 88
Alatortsev 44
Alekhine 12, 24, 25, 31, 49, 77, 86, 125, 126, 145, 160, 161, 184, 236
Antoshin 72
Aronin 29, 44, 72
Aronson 72
Asadoorian 28
Asztalos 61
Averbakh 43, 48, 58, 59, 74, 76, 108, 113, 117, 146, 156, 162, 226
Balashov 163
Bannik 72, 73
Begiashvili 183, 184
Benko 76, 91, 109–112, 115, 116, 155
Blagidze 21, 28
Bogoljubow 12, 25, 184
Boleslavsky 37, 43, 58, 72, 114, 131, 136, 140, 142, 143, 156, 162, 166, 177, 178, 180, 219
Bondarevsky 32, 44, 47, 60, 160, 161, 181, 183
Borisenko 195
Botvinnik 11, 12, 24, 34, 36, 44–47, 59–61, 75–77, 86–89, 113, 116, 125–145, 155, 156, 159, 161, 162, 171, 179, 181, 183–185, 201–203, 211, 221
weakness of 146
Bravinsky 202
Bronstein 19, 20, 37, 43–45, 47, 58–63, 72–74, 76, 77, 117, 141, 142, 144, 156, 157, 169, 185, 192
Buslayev 18
Capablanca 16, 18, 19, 24, 26, 31, 77, 86, 89, 90, 108, 125, 126, 129–131, 145, 160, 161, 184
Chigorin 31, 108, 202
Duz-Hotimirsky 25
Ebralidze 18, 19, 23–25, 28
Edmondson 226
Edmondson, Mrs 226
Euwe 32, 47, 49, 58, 63, 86, 125, 126, 129, 130, 132, 134, 158, 159, 161, 177, 179, 181, 221, 225
Filip 62, 109, 111–114, 116–118
Fine R 125, 126
Fine x 16
Fischer 90, 91, 93, 108–112, 114–117, 159, 163, 211, 220, 223, 225–228
Flohr 37, 38, 44, 45, 47, 52, 59, 77, 125, 126, 129, 132, 173
Furman 59, 60, 72, 73

Geller 11, 13, 36, 38, 43–48, 52, 57–62, 92, 93, 109–115, 157, 158, 160, 186, 220
Gigli 163
Gligoric 47, 58, 59, 76, 91, 111, 113, 155, 159, 225, 237
Gobbi 163
Goldsberg 36
Golombek 141
Gufeld 76
Gurgenidze 72
Hagopian 28
Hambartsurian 144
Hasin 72
Heidenfeld 63
Holmov 34, 36, 72, 73, 157, 176, 237
Hübner 220–222
Ivkov 157
Kalantar A 28
Kalantar K 28
Kalashian 28, 29, 135, 178, 183, 202
Kamishev 33, 34
Kasparian H 21, 23, 27, 28, 34, 36
Kasparian x 144
Kazic 223
Keres 11, 13, 24, 25, 27, 37, 38, 44–47, 58, 59, 61, 62, 72, 73, 76, 90, 91, 109, 110, 112–118, 128, 133, 155, 158–160, 169, 186, 203
Klaman 72
Konstantinopolsky 59, 141
Kopayev 120
Kopylov 44
Korchnoi 25, 59, 60, 72, 77, 88, 89, 92, 93, 109–115, 130, 156, 157, 162, 203, 213, 215, 220, 223, 224
Kotkov 25
Kotov 37, 44, 45, 47, 58, 59, 113, 125, 135, 141, 170, 173
Krogius 25, 76, 92
Kuprin 144
Kuts 110
Labourdonnais 178
Larsen 157–159, 163, 220, 223
Lasker 87, 88, 90, 108, 125, 126, 129, 130, 145, 161, 170, 177, 211
Lekiashvili 16
Lermontov 163
Levenfish 25, 26, 37
Liberzon 229
Lilienthal 37, 38, 43
Lipnitsky 44, 45
Lisitsin 23, 29, 59

246 Indexes

MacDonnell 178
Maizelis 17
Makarichev 157
Makogonov 29, 36
Matanovic 47, 157
Matulovic 168
Mecking 240
Melikan 15, 16
Mikenas 21, 23, 24, 29, 72
Moiseyev 44
Moiseyev-Cherkasky 36
Najdorf 58, 117, 155, 159, 228
Nei 25
Netto 112
Nezmetdinov 67, 72, 73, 76
Nimzowitsch 17–21, 26, 31, 37, 86
Novotelnov 45
O'Kelly 67, 173, 182, 207, 209
Olafsson 90, 91, 117, 155
Panno 155
Panov 47, 60, 73, 113, 133, 136, 142, 159, 161
Parma 157
Petrosian Hmayak 15, 20
Petrosian Rona 86, 133, 135, 136, 140, 143, 144, 178
Petrosian Tigran
  & *'blitz'* 31
  & *blunders* 62, 63
  & *Capablanca* 18, 31, 77, 86, 129
  & *chess books* 16–19, 37
  & *draws* 33, 58–61, 73, 86
  & *logic* 21, 22
  & *Nimzowitsch* 17, 18, 31, 86
  & *psychology* 75
  & *Young chessplayers* 156, 157
  Armenian supporters 134, 135, 144
  bad results in Yugoslavia 224
  caretaker 20
  chess instructor 28
  criticism of 57, 58, 60, 61, 86
  domicile 15, 27, 36, 37
  dryness of play 30
  father's death 20
  first contact with chess 16
  first victory v. Botvinnik 136, 137
  great aunt 20
  hobbies 165
  mannerisms 182
  match player 12, 132
  mother 15
  mother's death 20
  move to Moscow 36, 37
  philosophy of chess 29
  possessions 37
  Sacrifices of Q v. Czech GMs 192
  school 15
  sense of danger 26, 93
  strategist 177, 178
  style 11, 12, 26, 27, 31, 33, 52, 73, 77, 87, 137
  tactician 13, 19, 25, 26, 31, 33, 34, 43, 44, 77, 173, 175, 177, 178
  trainers 43, 162, 222, 226
  unbeatable 74, 125, 139, 178
  World Champion 143
Petrosian Vartan jnr 164
Petrosian Vartan snr 15, 20
Petrosian Vartoosh 15, 20, 143
Pilnik 62
Pirtshalova 28
Platonov 218
Podolny 34
Polugaevsky 92
Portisch 157
Prensis 183
Reshevsky 58, 59, 125, 126, 155, 159
Reshko 23, 24
Romanovsky 26, 59
Rubinstein 49
Saidy 240
Salibegian 16
Sanchez 48
Schmid 226, 227
Scholer Mrs 225, 226
Sereda 28
Shamkovich 19, 162, 176
Shishov 21, 28
Shriabin 163
Simagin 33, 44–46, 141, 162, 173
Sinsads 28
Smyslov 11, 37, 44–47, 58–60, 62, 63, 76, 77, 86, 91, 93, 126–128, 130, 132, 136, 156, 158, 159, 184, 185, 211
Sokolsky 29
Soloviev 23, 24
Sorokin 16, 19, 21, 28
Spassky 12, 13, 19, 21, 59–63, 67, 72, 74–77, 127, 131, 156–186, 201, 203, 210, 211, 220, 228
strength of 161
Spielmann 18, 160
Stahlberg 47, 58, 59, 92, 146, 159
Starostin 112
Stein 93, 141, 157
Steinitz 64, 108, 145, 180
Stoliar 72
Suetin 131, 157, 162, 222, 226
Szabo 47, 58, 59, 62

Taimanov 44–48, 58–60, 72, 73, 76, 77, 115, 156, 220, 223
Tal 11, 13, 32, 67, 72–77, 88–92, 109–114, 126–128, 130–133, 139, 142, 147, 156, 158–161, 163, 164, 171, 173, 177, 178, 184–186, 193, 194, 196, 201, 202
Tarasov 72
Tartakower 21
Tchaikovsky 144
Terpugov 46, 47
Tolush 12, 72, 73, 160, 168
Torre 177
Ufimtsev 29, 30
Uhlmann 157, 220
Unzicker 47
Vasilchuk 24, 25
Vasiliev 29
Vasiukov 77
Veresov 29
Wade 207
Wagner 144, 183
Wainstein 138
Wilde 21
Wood BH 177
Wood Natalie 163
Yegorov 144
Yudovich 11, 93
Zagoriansky 24, 29
Zaitsev I 222
Zak 160
Zorin 201
Zurakhov 25

Index of Places

Amsterdam 62
Argentina 224, 225
Armenia 73, 133, 155, 178, 181, 224
Athens 225
Beaujolais 165
Belgrade 225
Bled 91
Buenos Aires 226, 228
Caucasus 224
Cologne 221
Curacao 11, 93, 108
Georgia 183
Greece 225
Harkov 202
Holland 221
Kishinev 226
Köln 221
Leningrad 23, 157, 165
Leuwarden 62
Mallorca 129
Moscow 177, 225
Arbatskaya Square 201
Central House of Culture for Railwaymen 37
Gorky St 165
Kammeny bridge 171
Piatnitskaya St 33, 156
River 171
State University 164
Sukhanova 140, 162
Variety Theatre 162, 171
New York 225
Paris 165
Riga 74
Seville 222
Shadrinska 163
Siberia 156
Sint Maarten 112
Tiflis (Tbilisi) 15, 20, 27, 28, 158, 164, 183, 202
Palace of Pioneers 17, 18, 28
Urals 156
USA 224
USSR 224
Willemstad 108
Yerevan 23, 27–29, 36, 39, 73, 134, 135, 144, 183, 202, 211
Yugoslavia 224

All Games in Algebraic PGN Notation

[Event "Gorki"]
[Site "It"]
[Date "1950"]
[White "P Dubinin"]
[Black "Petrosian"]
[Result "0-1"]
[ECO "C18"]

1.e4 e6 2.d4 d5 3.Nc3 Bb4
4.e5 Ne7 5.a3 Bxc3+ 6.bxc3
c5 7.Qg4 Nf5 8.Bd3 h5 9.Qh3
cxd4 10.g4 Ne7 11.cxd4 Qc7
12.Ne2 Nbc6 13.O-O Bd7
14.gxh5 O-O-O 15.Bf4 Rdg8
16.Kh1 g5 17.Bg3 Rh6 18.f4
g4 19.Qg2 Nf5 20.Qf2 Rxh5
21.Rfc1 Na5 22.c4 dxc4 23.d5
exd5 24.Qxa7 Nc6 25.Qa8+ Qb8
26.Qxb8+ Kxb8 27.Bxf5 Bxf5
28.Kg1 Rgh8 29.Rd1 Bd3
30.Ra2 d4 31.Rad2 Rd8
32.Rxd3 cxd3 33.Rxd3 Kc8
34.Bf2 Rh3 35.Bg3 Kd7 36.Nc3
Ke6 37.Ne4 Kf5 38.Nd6+ Rxd6
39.exd6 Rh6 40.Rb3 Rxd6
41.Rxb7 d3 42.Rb1 d2 43.Rd1
Ke4 44.Kf2 Kd3 45.f5 Rd4
46.h3 Kc2 0-1

[Site "USSR"]
[Date "1950"]
[White "Petrosian"]
[Black "Igor Bondarevsky"]
[Result "1-0"]
[ECO "A04"]

1.Nf3 e6 2.g3 f5 3.Bg2 Nf6
4.O-O Be7 5.d4 O-O 6.c4 c6
7.Qc2 Qe8 8.Nbd2 d5 9.Ne5
Nbd7 10.Nd3 Ne4 11.Nf3 Nd6
12.b3 b5 13.c5 Nf7 14.a4
bxa4 15.Rxa4 Bf6 16.Bb2 a6
17.Nfe5 Nfxe5 18.dxe5 Be7
19.f4 Rb8 20.Rfa1 Rb5 21.b4

h5 22.Bc3 h4 23.e3 Nb8
24.Ne1 Rb7 25.gxh4 Bxh4
26.Nf3 Bd8 27.h4 Qh5 28.Be1
Bd7 29.Qf2 Kf7 30.Bf1 Rh8
31.Bxa6 Nxa6 32.Rxa6 Be7
33.Ra7 Rhb8 34.Rxb7 Rxb7
35.Nd4 Qh8 36.Qg3 Qb8 37.h5
Ra7 38.Rc1 Qg8 39.Qg6+ Kf8
40.b5 Qf7 41.bxc6 Bc8 {Black
sealed this move and the
next day, in view of the
continuation 42.Qxf7+ Kxf7
43.Nb5 Ra8 44.Nd6+ Kf8
45.c7, he resigned.} 1-0

[Event "Ch URS"]
[Site "Moscow"]
[Date "1951"]
[White "Isaac Lipnitsky"]
[Black "Petrosian"]
[Result "0-1"]
[ECO "C50"]

1.e4 e5 2.Nf3 Nc6 3.Bc4 Be7
4.d4 d6 5.Nc3 Nf6 6.O-O O-O
7.h3 a6 8.a4 exd4 9.Nxd4 Nb4
10.Nd5 Nbxd5 11.exd5 Nd7
12.a5 Bf6 13.c3 Ne5 14.Bb3
Re8 15.Bc2 Bd7 16.f4 Ng6
17.Qd3 c5 18.dxc6 bxc6
19.Nf5 Bxf5 20.Qxf5 d5
21.Bd2 Nf8 22.Qd3 c5 23.Rfe1
Rxe1+ 24.Bxe1 c4 25.Qe2 Qc7
26.Qf3 Rd8 27.Bf2 d4 28.Qe4
g6 29.cxd4 Rb8 30.d5 Rxb2
31.Rd1 c3 32.d6 Qxa5 33.d7
Qc7 34.Qe8 Bd8 35.Qe4 Bf6
36.Qe8 Rb8 37.Kh1 Rd8 38.Ba4
c2 39.Rc1 Qxf4 40.Be3 Qxa4
0-1

248

All Games in Algebraic PGN Notation

[Event "Ch URS Moscow"]
[Date "1951"]
[White "Petrosian"]
[Black "Alexander Kotov"]
[Result "1-0"]
[ECO "E68"]

1.d4 Nf6 2.c4 d6 3.Nc3 e5
4.Nf3 Nbd7 5.g3 g6 6.Bg2 Bg7
7.O-O O-O 8.e4 exd4 9.Nxd4
a5 10.h3 Nc5 11.Re1 Re8
12.Qc2 a4 13.Be3 c6 14.Rad1
Qa5 15.Bf4 Bf8 16.Bf1 Nh5
17.Be3 Nf6 18.Bf4 Nh5 19.Bc1
Ng7 20.Kh2 Bd7 21.a3 Nge6
22.Be3 Nxd4 23.Bxd4 Nb3
24.Be3 Be6 25.f4 Rad8 26.Qf2
Qa6 27.Bb6 Rd7 28.c5 Bc4
29.Bxc4 Qxc4 30.e5 d5 31.Ne4
dxe4 32.Rxd7 Bxc5 33.Bxc5
Nxc5 34.Rd4 Qe6 35.Qc2 b6
36.Rd6 Qc8 37.Qc4 h5
38.Rxg6+ Kf8 39.Rf6 Qd7
40.Rd6 Qf5 41.Rf6 Qd7 42.Rd1
Qc7 43.Qe2 h4 44.Qg4 Rd8
45.Rxd8+ Qxd8 46.Rd6 hxg3+
47.Kxg3 Qc7 48.Qh4 Ke8
49.Qh8+ Ke7 50.Qf6+ Ke8
51.Rxc6 Qd7 52.Qd6 1-0

[Event "Ch URS"]
[Site "Moscow"]
[Date "1951"]
[White "Petrosian"]
[Black "Vasily Smyslov"]
[Result "1-0"]
[ECO "D15"]

1.d4 d5 2.c4 dxc4 3.Nf3 Nf6
4.Nc3 c6 5.e4 b5 6.e5 Nd5
7.a4 e6 8.axb5 Nxc3 9.bxc3
cxb5 10.Ng5 Bb7 11.Qh5 g6
12.Qg4 Be7 13.Be2 Nd7 14.h4
h5 15.Qg3 Nb6 16.O-O a5
17.d5 Nxd5 18.Rd1 Qc7 19.Ne4

O-O-O 20.Bg5 Bxg5 21.Qxg5 a4
22.Qg3 f5 23.Nd6+ Rxd6
24.exd6 f4 25.Qxg6 Qxd6
26.Bf3 Bc6 27.Re1 Re8
28.Bxd5 Qxd5 29.Rad1 Qf5
30.Qxf5 exf5 31.Rxe8+ Bxe8
32.f3 Kc7 33.Kf2 Kb6 34.Ke2
Ka5 35.Rb1 a3 36.Kd2 b4
37.cxb4+ Ka4 38.Kc3 a2
39.Ra1 Ka3 40.Kxc4 Kb2
41.Re1 a1=Q 42.Rxa1 Kxa1
43.b5 Bd7 44.b6 Bc8 45.Kd4
Kb2 46.Ke5 Kc3 47.Kxf4 Kd4
48.Kg5 Ke5 49.Kxh5 Kf6 50.g4
Bb7 51.Kh6 1-0

[Event "Interzonal"]
[Site "Stockholm"]
[Date "1952"]
[Round "15"]
[White "Laszlo Szabo"]
[Black "Petrosian"]
[Result "0-1"]
[ECO "B93"]

1.e4 c5 2.Nf3 d6 3.d4 cxd4
4.Nxd4 Nf6 5.Nc3 a6 6.f4 Qc7
7.Be2 e5 8.Nf3 Be6 9.f5 Bc4
10.Bg5 Nbd7 11.Nd2 Bxe2
12.Qxe2 Rc8 13.a3 Qb6 14.O-O Rxc3 15.bxc3 d5 16.Nb1
Nxe4 17.Rxd5 Nxg5 18.h4 Bc5
19.hxg5 Be3+ 20.Nd2 Bxg5
21.Qd3 Qc7 22.Kd1 Bxd2
23.Kxd2 f6 24.Kc1 Nb6 25.Rd6
O-O 26.Rd1 Qc5 27.Rd8 Qxa3+
28.Kb1 h5 29.Rxf8+ Qxf8
30.Qe4 Qe7 31.Qb4 Qc7 32.Qd6
Qxd6 33.Rxd6 Nc4 34.Rd7 b5
35.Ra7 Ne3 36.Rxa6 Nxg2
37.Kc1 h4 38.Kd2 h3 39.Ra1
Nh4 40.c4 bxc4 41.Rh1 Nxf5
42.Kc3 Nd6 43.Rxh3 Kf7
44.Rh7 f5 45.Kb4 f4 46.Kc5
f3 47.Rh1 e4 0-1

249

All Games in Algebraic PGN Notation

[Event "Zurich"]
[Site "ct"]
[Date "1953"]
[White "Samuel Reshevsky"]
[Black "Petrosian"]
[Result "1/2-1/2"]
[ECO "E58"]

1.d4 Nf6 2.c4 e6 3.Nc3 Bb4
4.e3 O-O 5.Bd3 d5 6.Nf3 c5
7.O-O Nc6 8.a3 Bxc3 9.bxc3
b6 10.cxd5 exd5 11.Bb2 c4
12.Bc2 Bg4 13.Qe1 Ne4 14.Nd2
Nxd2 15.Qxd2 Bh5 16.f3 Bg6
17.e4 Qd7 18.Rae1 dxe4
19.fxe4 Rfe8 20.Qf4 b5
21.Bd1 Re7 22.Bg4 Qe8 23.e5
a5 24.Re3 Rd8 25.Rfe1 Re6
26.a4 Ne7 27.Bxe6 fxe6
28.Qf1 Nd5 29.Rf3 Bd3
30.Rxd3 cxd3 31.Qxd3 b4
32.cxb4 axb4 33.a5 Ra8
34.Ra1 Qc6 35.Bc1 Qc7 36.a6
Qb6 37.Bd2 b3 38.Qc4 h6
39.h3 b2 40.Rb1 Kh8 41.Be1
1/2-1/2

[Event "URS-ch21 Kiev,URS-ch"]
[Date "1954"]
[White "Nezhmetdinov"]
[Black "Petrosian"]
[Result "0-1"]
[ECO "B94"]

1.e4 c5 2.Nf3 d6 3.d4 cxd4
4.Nxd4 Nf6 5.Nc3 a6 6.Bg5
Nbd7 7.Qf3 h6 8.Be3 e5 9.Nf5
g6 10.Ng3 b5 11.h4 h5 12.Bg5
Be7 13.O-O-O Bb7 14.Kb1 Rc8
15.Bd3 Nc5 16.Nge2 b4
17.Bxf6 Bxf6 18.Nd5 Bxd5
19.exd5 Qe7 20.Ng3 Bxh4
21.Ne4 Bg5 22.g3 a5 23.Rde1
Nxe4 24.Bxe4 f5 25.Bd3 Bf6
26.Bb5+ Kf7 27.Qb3 Kg7 28.f3
h4 29.g4 fxg4 30.fxg4 Bg5
31.Bd3 h3 32.Ba6 Ra8 33.Rxh3
Bh4 34.Reh1 Rxa6 35.g5 Qxg5
36.Qc4 Ra7 37.Rxh4 Rxh4
38.Qxh4 Qxh4 39.Rxh4 Rc7
40.Rh1 g5 41.Kc1 Rc5 42.Rd1
Kg6 43.Rd2 g4 44.Kd1 Kf5 0-1

[Event "Ch URS"]
[Site "Moscow"]
[Date "1955"]
[White "Petrosian"]
[Black "Mark Taimanov"]
[Result "1-0"]
[ECO "D46"]

1.d4 Nf6 2.c4 e6 3.Nf3 d5
4.Nc3 c6 5.e3 Nbd7 6.Bd3 Bb4
7.O-O O-O 8.Qc2 Bd6 9.b3
dxc4 10.bxc4 e5 11.Bb2 Re8
12.Ne4 Nxe4 13.Bxe4 h6
14.Rad1 exd4 15.Bh7+ Kh8
16.Rxd4 Bc5 17.Rf4 Qe7
18.Re4 Qf8 19.Rh4 f6 20.Bg6
Re7 21.Rh5 Bd6 22.Rd1 Be5
23.Ba3 c5 24.Nh4 1-0

[Event "Amsterdam ct"]
[Date "1956"]
[Round "10"]
[White "Petrosian"]
[Black "Efim Geller"]
[Result "1-0"]
[ECO "D34"]

1.c4 c5 2.g3 Nc6 3.Bg2 Nf6
4.Nf3 e6 5.O-O d5 6.cxd5
exd5 7.d4 Be7 8.Nc3 O-O
9.Bf4 cxd4 10.Nxd4 Qb6
11.Nxc6 bxc6 12.Qc2 Be6
13.Be3 Qa5 14.Qa4 Qxa4
15.Nxa4 Nd7 16.Rfd1 Rfc8
17.b3 Ba3 18.Bd4 Bg4 19.Rd2
Re8 20.e3 Bf5 21.Bb2 Bxb2

All Games in Algebraic PGN Notation

22.Rxb2 Nb6 23.Nc5 a5 24.Rc1 Rec8 25.e4 Bg6 26.f4 f6 27.Bh3 Rcb8 28.e5 fxe5 29.fxe5 a4 30.bxa4 Nc4 31.Rxb8+ Rxb8 32.e6 Rb1 33.Rxb1 Bxb1 34.Bf1 Nd6 35.a3 Kf8 36.a5 Nc8 37.Kf2 Ke7 38.Ke3 Kd6 39.Kd4 Bf5 40.Be2 Na7 41.a6 Bh3 42.a4 Nc8 43.Nb7+ Kxe6 44.Kc5 Kd7 45.Na5 Kc7 46.Nxc6 Nb6 47.Bb5 Nd7+ 48.Kxd5 Bg2+ 49.Ke6 Bxc6 50.Bxc6 Kxc6 51.a7 Nb6 52.a5 Na8 53.Kf7 g5 54.Kf6 g4 55.Kg5 Kb7 56.Kxg4 Nc7 57.Kg5 Nd5 58.h3 Nc3 59.g4 Ne4+ 60.Kf5 Ng3+ 61.Kf4 Ne2+ 62.Ke3 Nc3 63.g5 Nd5+ 64.Ke4 Ne7 65.Kf4 Nd5+ 66.Kf3 Ne7 67.h4 Kxa7 68.Kf4 Ng6+ 69.Kg4 Ne7 70.h5 Ka6 71.Kf4 Kxa5 72.Ke5 Kb6 73.Ke6 1-0

[Event "Leningrad m"]
[Date "1957"]
[White "Petrosian"]
[Black "Petar Trifunovic"]
[Result "1-0"]
[ECO "C97"]

1.e4 e5 2.Nf3 Nc6 3.Bb5 a6 4.Ba4 Nf6 5.O-O Be7 6.Re1 b5 7.Bb3 d6 8.c3 O-O 9.h3 Na5 10.Bc2 c5 11.d4 Qc7 12.Nbd2 Bb7 13.Nf1 cxd4 14.cxd4 Rac8 15.Bd3 d5 16.dxe5 Nxe4 17.Ng3 Bb4 18.Re2 f5 19.exf6 Nxg3 20.fxg3 Qxg3 21.Bf5 d4 22.Be6+ Kh8 23.Bxc8 Bxf3 24.Qd3 Rxc8 25.Qxf3 Qxf3 26.fxg7+ Kxg7 27.gxf3 d3 28.Rg2+ Kf6 29.Bg5+ Kf5 30.Rd1 Rc2 31.h4 d2 32.Bxd2 Rxb2 33.Rg5+ Ke6 34.Re1+ Kf6 35.Bxb4 Rxb4 36.Re4 Rb2 37.Rf4+ Ke6 38.Re4+ Kf6 39.Rg2 Rb1+ 40.Kh2 Nc4 41.Rge2 a5 42.Rf4+ Kg6 43.Rg2+ Kh5 44.Rf5+ Kh6 45.f4 Ne3 46.Rf6+ Kh5 47.Rg5+ Kxh4 48.Rh6+ 1-0

[Event "Izt"]
[Site "Portoroz"]
[Date "1958"]
[White "Petrosian"]
[Black "Aleksandar Matanovic"]
[Result "1-0"]
[ECO "D38"]

1.c4 Nf6 2.Nc3 e6 3.Nf3 d5 4.d4 Bb4 5.cxd5 exd5 6.Bg5 h6 7.Bh4 c5 8.e3 O-O 9.dxc5 Nbd7 10.Be2 Qa5 11.O-O Bxc3 12.bxc3 Qxc5 13.Rc1 b6 14.c4 Bb7 15.Nd4 Rac8 16.Bf3 Qb4 17.a3 Qxa3 18.Ra1 Qc5 19.Rxa7 Ba8 20.Qa1 Kh7 21.Rd1 Qxc4 22.Be2 Qc3 23.Rxa8 1-0

[Event "26. URS-ch"]
[Site "Riga LAT"]
[Date "1958"]
[Round "01"]
[White "Petrosian"]
[Black "Alexey Suetin"]
[Result "1-0"]
[ECO "E93"]

1.d4 Nf6 2.c4 g6 3.Nc3 Bg7 4.e4 d6 5.Be2 O-O 6.d5 e5 7.Nf3 Nbd7 8.Bg5 h6 9.Bh4 g5 10.Bg3 Nh5 11.O-O a5 12.Ne1 Nf4 13.Nc2 Nc5 14.Ne3 Nxe4 15.Nxe4 Nxe2+ 16.Qxe2 f5 17.f3 f4 18.c5 fxe3 19.Qxe3

All Games in Algebraic PGN Notation

Bf5 20.Rac1 Qd7 21.Rc4 dxc5
22.Qxc5 b6 23.Qe3 Qxd5
24.Rxc7 Qd4 25.Bf2 Qxe3
26.Bxe3 Be6 27.a3 b5 28.Bd2
Rfd8 29.Bc3 a4 30.Re1 Rac8
31.Rb7 Rd5 32.Rb6 Bf7 33.Nd6
Rd8 34.Nf5 Kh7 35.Rb7 R8d7
36.Rxd7 Rxd7 37.Nxg7 Kxg7
38.Rxe5 Kg6 39.Rxb5 Rd1+
40.Kf2 Rc1 41.Rb6+ Kh7 42.g4
Rh1 43.h3 Bd5 44.Rd6 Rd1
45.Rd7+ Kg8 46.Ke3 Bb3
47.Rg7+ Kf8 48.Rg6 Bc2
49.Rxh6 Rd3+ 50.Ke2 Rd5
51.h4 gxh4 52.Rxh4 Kf7 53.f4
Bd1+ 54.Ke3 Kg6 55.g5 Bh5
56.Bf6 Rc5 57.Kd4 Rb5 58.Ke4
Bd1 59.f5+ Kf7 60.Be5 Bc2+
61.Kf4 1-0

[Site "Tbilisi"]
[Date "1959"]
[White "Petrosian,Tigran"]
[Black "Yukhtman,Yakov"]
[Result "1-0"]
[ECO "E73"]

1.d4 Nf6 2.c4 g6 3.Nc3 Bg7
4.e4 d6 5.Be2 O-O 6.Nf3 e5
7.d5 Na6 8.Bg5 h6 9.Bh4 g5
10.Bg3 Nh5 11.Nd2 Nf4 12.O-O
Nc5 13.Bg4 a5 14.f3 Ncd3
15.Qc2 c6 16.Kh1 h5 17.Bxc8
Rxc8 18.a3 cxd5 19.cxd5 Nc5
20.Bf2 g4 21.g3 Ng6 22.fxg4
hxg4 23.Be3 b5 24.Nxb5 Qb6
25.a4 Qa6 26.Nc4 f5 27.Rxf5
Rxf5 28.exf5 Qb7 29.Qg2 Nb3
30.Ncxd6 Qd7 31.Rf1 1-0

[Event "URS-ch26"]
[Site "Tbilisi"]
[Date "1959.01.09"]
[Round "07"]
[White "Petrosian"]
[Black "Anatoly S Lutikov"]
[Result "1-0"]
[ECO "E92"]

1.Nf3 Nf6 2.c4 g6 3.Nc3 Bg7
4.e4 O-O 5.d4 d6 6.Be2 e5
7.d5 Na6 8.Bg5 h6 9.Bh4 c5
10.Nd2 Bd7 11.Nb5 Be8 12.a3
Qd7 13.g4 Nc7 14.Nc3 a6
15.a4 Qc8 16.h3 Rb8 17.Qc2
Bd7 18.b3 b6 19.Nd1 b5 20.a5
Kh8 21.Bg3 Ng8 22.Ne3 Ne7
23.Bh4 Qe8 24.b4 Nc8 25.bxc5
dxc5 26.cxb5 Nxb5 27.Bxb5
Rxb5 28.O-O f5 29.f3 Rf7
30.Ndc4 Rb4 31.Be1 Rb7
32.Bc3 h5 33.gxf5 gxf5
34.exf5 e4 35.Kh2 exf3
36.Rxf3 Bd4 37.Qd3 Bf6
38.Rg1 Kh7 39.Bxf6 Rxf6
40.Qc3 Qf8 41.Rg6 Rf7 42.Rg5
1-0

[Event "Bled ct (11.09.59)"]
[Site "04"]
[Date "1959"]
[White "Paul Keres"]
[Black "Petrosian"]
[Result "0-1"]
[ECO "B39"]

1.e4 c5 2.Nf3 Nc6 3.d4 cxd4
4.Nxd4 g6 5.c4 Bg7 6.Be3 Nf6
7.Nc3 Ng4 8.Qxg4 Nxd4 9.Qd1
Ne6 10.Qd2 d6 11.Be2 Bd7
12.O-O O-O 13.Rac1 Bc6
14.Rfd1 Nc5 15.f3 a5 16.b3
Qb6 17.Nb5 Rfc8 18.Bf1 Qd8
19.Qf2 Qe8 20.Nc3 b6 21.Rc2
Qf8 22.Qd2 Bd7 23.Nd5 Rab8

All Games in Algebraic PGN Notation

24.Bg5 Re8 25.Re1 Rb7 26.Qf2 Bc6 27.Qh4 f6 28.Be3 e6 29.Nc3 Rd7 30.Bd4 f5 31.exf5 gxf5 32.Rd2 Bxd4+ 33.Rxd4 Rg7 34.Kh1 Rg6 35.Rd2 Rd8 36.Red1 Rd7 37.Qf2 Qd8 38.Qe3 e5 39.f4 e4 40.Ne2 Rdg7 41.Nd4 Bd7 42.a3 Qa8 43.Kg1 h5 44.Rb1 h4 45.Rbb2 Rg4 46.Rf2 Qd8 47.b4 Rg3 48.hxg3 hxg3 49.Rfd2 Qh4 50.Be2 Rh7 51.Kf1 Qxf4+ 0-1

[Event "Bled"]
[Site "ct"]
[Date "1959"]
[Round "28"]
[White "Petrosian"]
[Black "Svetozar Gligoric"]
[Result "1-0"]
[ECO "E93"]

1.d4 Nf6 2.c4 g6 3.Nc3 Bg7 4.e4 d6 5.Nf3 O-O 6.Be2 e5 7.d5 Nbd7 8.Bg5 h6 9.Bh4 a6 10.Nd2 Qe8 11.O-O Nh7 12.b4 Ng5 13.Rc1 f5 14.f3 Qe7 15.Kh1 Nf6 16.c5 Nh5 17.c6 b6 18.exf5 gxf5 19.g3 Bf6 20.f4 Ng7 21.Nc4 exf4 22.gxf4 b5 23.Nd2 Ne4 24.Bxf6 Rxf6 25.Bf3 a5 26.a3 axb4 27.axb4 Rg6 28.Ndxe4 fxe4 29.Bxe4 Bf5 30.Bxf5 Nxf5 31.Qh5 Rf6 32.Rg1+ Kh8 33.Rce1 Qf7 34.Qxf7 Rxf7 35.Re4 Kh7 36.Nxb5 Ra2 37.Nd4 Nxd4 38.Rxd4 Re7 39.f5 Ree2 40.Rh4 Rf2 41.b5 Rab2 42.b6 Rxb6 43.Rhg4 Rb8 44.Rg7+ Kh8 45.R7g6 1-0

[Event "Copenhagen"]
[Site "t"]
[Date "1960"]
[White "Petrosian"]
[Black "Bent Larsen"]
[Result "1-0"]
[ECO "A54"]

1.Nf3 d6 2.d4 Nf6 3.c4 Bg4 4.Nc3 Nbd7 5.e4 e5 6.Be2 Be7 7.Be3 O-O 8.O-O Bh5 9.Nd2 exd4 10.Bxd4 Bxe2 11.Qxe2 Re8 12.f4 Bf8 13.Rad1 a6 14.Qf3 c6 15.g4 Nc5 16.Bxc5 dxc5 17.e5 Nd7 18.Nde4 Qc7 19.Rd3 Rad8 20.Rfd1 Nb6 21.b3 Nc8 22.g5 Be7 23.Qh5 Rxd3 24.Rxd3 Rd8 25.Nf6+ gxf6 26.Rh3 Kf8 27.Qxh7 Ke8 28.g6 Bf8 29.g7 Bxg7 30.Qxg7 Qe7 31.Ne4 Rd1+ 32.Kf2 f5 33.Nf6+ Kd8 34.Rh8+ 1-0

[Event "Leningrad"]
[Site "It"]
[Date "1960"]
[White "David Bronstein"]
[Black "Petrosian"]
[Result "0-1"]
[ECO "B10"]

1.e4 c6 2.Ne2 d5 3.e5 c5 4.d4 Nc6 5.c3 e6 6.Nd2 Nge7 7.Nf3 cxd4 8.Nexd4 Ng6 9.Nxc6 bxc6 10.Bd3 Qc7 11.Qe2 f6 12.exf6 gxf6 13.Nd4 Kf7 14.f4 c5 15.Qh5 cxd4 16.Bxg6+ hxg6 17.Qxh8 dxc3 18.Qh7+ Bg7 19.Be3 cxb2 20.Rd1 Ba6 21.f5 exf5 22.Qh3 Qc2 23.Qf3 Bc4 0-1

253

All Games in Algebraic PGN Notation

[Event "URS-ch"]
[Date "1961"]
[White "Petrosian"]
[Black "Vasily Smyslov"]
[Result "1-0"]
[ECO "E12"]

1.c4 Nf6 2.Nc3 e6 3.Nf3 b6
4.d4 Bb7 5.a3 d5 6.cxd5 Nxd5
7.e3 Be7 8.Bb5+ c6 9.Bd3 c5
10.Nxd5 Qxd5 11.dxc5 Qxc5
12.Bd2 Nc6 13.Rc1 Qd6 14.Qc2
Rc8 15.O-O h6 16.Rfd1 O-O
17.Bc3 Qb8 18.Qa4 Rfd8
19.Qe4 g6 20.Qg4 h5 21.Qh3
f5 22.Bc4 Rxd1+ 23.Rxd1 Kf7
24.e4 Qf4 25.Re1 Qg4 26.exf5
Qxc4 27.fxg6+ Ke8 28.g7 e5
29.Qxh5+ Kd7 30.Rd1+ Bd6
31.Bxe5 Nd4 32.Nxd4 1-0

[Event "Team Events of the Spartak Sports Society"]
[Site "Moscow"]
[Date "1961"]
[White "Bukhuti Gurgenidze"]
[Black "Petrosian"]
[Result "0-1"]
[ECO "B11"]

1.e4 c6 2.Nc3 d5 3.Nf3 Bg4
4.h3 Bxf3 5.Qxf3 Nf6 6.d3 e6
7.Be2 Nbd7 8.Qg3 g6 9.h4 h5
10.O-O Qb6 11.Rb1 Bh6 12.Bg5
Bxg5 13.hxg5 Nh7 14.exd5
exd5 15.Kh1 O-O-O 16.f4 Rde8
17.Qf2 Qxf2 18.Rxf2 Nhf8
19.Bf3 Ne6 20.Ne2 f6 21.gxf6
Nxf6 22.b4 Ng4 23.Rff1 Ne3
24.Rfc1 g5 25.fxg5 Nxg5
26.Nd4 h4 27.Nf5 Nxf3
28.Nd6+ Kb8 29.Nxe8 Nd2
30.Re1 Nxc2 31.Nd6 Nxb1
32.Rxb1 Rf8 33.b5 Kc7 0-1

[Event "Bled"]
[Date "1961"]
[Round "08"]
[White "Petrosian"]
[Black "Miguel Najdorf"]
[Result "1-0"]
[ECO "E80"]

1.d4 Nf6 2.c4 g6 3.Nc3 Bg7
4.e4 d6 5.f3 e5 6.Nge2 c6
7.Bg5 Nbd7 8.d5 Nb6 9.Nc1
cxd5 10.cxd5 O-O 11.a4 a6
12.Nb3 Bd7 13.a5 Nc8 14.Bd3
b5 15.Na2 Ne7 16.Nb4 Nh5
17.g3 f6 18.Be3 f5 19.Rc1
Qe8 20.Rc7 Nf6 21.Qd2 fxe4
22.fxe4 Bh3 23.Bg5 Rf7
24.Bxf6 Rxf6 25.Bf1 Bg4
26.Be2 Bh3 27.Bf1 Bg4 28.Bg2
Qf8 29.h3 Bh6 30.Qd3 Bc8
31.Rf1 Rxf1+ 32.Qxf1 Qd8
33.Rc3 Bg7 34.Qf2 h5 35.Qb6
Qxb6 36.axb6 Rb8 37.Rc7 Bf8
38.Na5 Rxb6 39.Nbc6 Nxc6
40.Nxc6 1-0

[Event "It Bled"]
[Date "1961"]
[White "Petrosian"]
[Black "Ludek Pachman"]
[Result "1-0"]
[ECO "A04"]

1.Nf3 c5 2.g3 Nc6 3.Bg2 g6
4.O-O Bg7 5.d3 e6 6.e4 Nge7
7.Re1 O-O 8.e5 d6 9.exd6
Qxd6 10.Nbd2 Qc7 11.Nb3 Nd4
12.Bf4 Qb6 13.Ne5 Nxb3
14.Nc4 Qb5 15.axb3 a5 16.Bd6
Bf6 17.Qf3 Kg7 18.Re4 Rd8
19.Qxf6+ Kxf6 20.Be5+ Kg5
21.Bg7 1-0

All Games in Algebraic PGN Notation

[Event "USSR Team Championship"]
[Site "Moscow"]
[Date "1961"]
[White "Petrosian"]
[Black "Leonid Stein"]
[Result "1-0"]
[ECO "E93"]

1.c4 Nf6 2.Nc3 d6 3.d4 g6
4.e4 Bg7 5.Be2 O-O 6.Nf3 e5
7.d5 Nbd7 8.Bg5 h6 9.Bh4 a6
10.O-O Qe8 11.Nd2 c5 12.dxc6
bxc6 13.b4 Rb8 14.a3 Bb7
15.Nb3 Qe6 16.Na5 Ba8 17.f3
d5 18.c5 Nh5 19.Bxa6 Nf4
20.Ne2 g5 21.Bf2 f5 22.Rc1
fxe4 23.fxe4 Nf6 24.exd5
N6xd5 25.Ng3 e4 26.Bd4 Rbd8
27.Bxg7 Kxg7 28.Qd4+ Nf6
29.Qc3 Kg6 30.Nc4 Nd3
31.Rcd1 Nd5 32.Qc2 Nc7
33.Nd6 Nxa6 34.Rxf8 Rxf8
35.Ndxe4 Naxb4 36.axb4 Nxb4
37.Qb1 Nd5 38.Re1 Qd7
39.Nf6+ 1-0

[Event "Curasao"]
[Site "ct"]
[Date "1962"]
[White "Petrosian"]
[Black "Mikhail Tal"]
[Result "1-0"]
[ECO "A12"]

1.c4 Nf6 2.g3 c6 3.Nf3 d5
4.b3 Bf5 5.Ba3 g6 6.d3 Bg7
7.Nbd2 Qb6 8.Bg2 Ng4 9.d4
Na6 10.O-O Nb4 11.Bb2 O-O
12.a3 Na6 13.Rc1 Rad8 14.b4
Nb8 15.Qb3 Nf6 16.a4 Ne4
17.Rfd1 Nd7 18.cxd5 cxd5
19.a5 Qd6 20.b5 Nxd2 21.Rxd2
Rc8 22.Nh4 Rxc1+ 23.Bxc1 Qc7
24.Nxf5 gxf5 25.Ba3 Qxa5

26.Qb4 Qb6 27.Bxd5 e6 28.Bf3
Rc8 29.Qa4 Rc7 30.Kg2 a6
31.bxa6 Qxa6 32.Qxa6 bxa6
33.e3 a5 34.Ra2 Ra7 35.Bb4
a4 36.Bc6 Bf8 37.Bxf8 Kxf8
38.Rxa4 Rc7 39.Bxd7 Rxd7
40.Kf3 Kg7 41.Kf4 Kf6 42.h3
h5 43.Ra8 Rb7 44.Rg8 Rb2
45.Kf3 Rd2 46.h4 Ke7 47.Rg5
Kf8 48.Rxh5 Kg7 49.Rg5+ Kh7
50.h5 Ra2 51.g4 Kh6 52.Rg8
Kh7 53.Re8 fxg4+ 54.Kg3 Kh6
55.Re7 Kg7 56.Rc7 Rb2 57.Rc5
Kf6 58.d5 Rb4 59.h6 exd5
60.Rxd5 Kg6 61.Rd6+ Kg5
62.h7 Rb8 63.Rd1 Rh8 64.Rh1
1-0

[Event "Curacao ct Rd: 17"]
[Date "1962"]
[White "Robert James Fischer"]
[Black "Petrosian"]
[Result "0-1"]
[ECO "C12"]

1.e4 e6 2.d4 d5 3.Nc3 Nf6
4.Bg5 Bb4 5.e5 h6 6.Bd2 Bxc3
7.Bxc3 Ne4 8.Ba5 O-O 9.Bd3
Nc6 10.Bc3 Nxc3 11.bxc3 f6
12.f4 fxe5 13.fxe5 Ne7
14.Nf3 c5 15.O-O Qa5 16.Qe1
Bd7 17.c4 Qxe1 18.Rfxe1 dxc4
19.Be4 cxd4 20.Bxb7 Rab8
21.Ba6 Rb4 22.Rad1 d3
23.cxd3 cxd3 24.Rxd3 Bc6
25.Rd4 Rxd4 26.Nxd4 Bd5
27.a4 Rf4 28.Rd1 Ng6 29.Bc8
Kf7 30.a5 Nxe5 31.a6 Rg4
32.Rd2 Nc4 33.Rf2+ Ke7
34.Nb5 Nd6 35.Nxd6 Kxd6
36.Bb7 Bxb7 37.axb7 Kc7
38.h3 Rg5 39.Rb2 Kb8 40.Kf2
Rd5 41.Ke3 Rd7 42.Ke4 Rxb7
43.Rf2 0-1

255

All Games in Algebraic PGN Notation

[Event "Curacao ct"]
[Date "1962"]
[Round "23"]
[White "Petrosian"]
[Black "Viktor Korchnoi"]
[Result "1-0"]
[ECO "A31"]

1.c4 c5 2.Nf3 Nf6 3.d4 cxd4
4.Nxd4 g6 5.Nc3 d5 6.Bg5
dxc4 7.e3 Qa5 8.Bxf6 exf6
9.Bxc4 Bb4 10.Rc1 a6 11.O-O
Nd7 12.a3 Be7 13.b4 Qe5
14.f4 Qb8 15.Bxf7+ Kxf7
16.Qb3+ Ke8 17.Nd5 Bd6
18.Ne6 b5 19.Ndc7+ Ke7
20.Nd4 Kf8 21.Nxa8 1-0

[Event "Olympiad"]
[Site "Varna (Bulgaria)"]
[Date "1962"]
[White "Andreas Duckstein"]
[Black "Petrosian"]
[Result "0-1"]
[ECO "B18"]

1.e4 c6 2.d4 d5 3.Nc3 dxe4
4.Nxe4 Bf5 5.Ng3 Bg6 6.Nf3
Nd7 7.Bd3 e6 8.O-O Qc7 9.c4
O-O-O 10.Bxg6 hxg6 11.Qa4
Kb8 12.b4 Nh6 13.Qb3 Nf5
14.a4 e5 15.dxe5 Nxe5
16.Nxe5 Qxe5 17.Bb2 Qc7
18.c5 a5 19.Rad1 Rxd1
20.Rxd1 Rh4 21.bxa5 Bxc5
22.a6 b6 23.Re1 Ka7 24.Be5
Qd7 25.Ne4 Bd4 26.g3 Bxe5
27.gxh4 Nd4 28.Qd1 Qd5
29.Re3 Nf5 30.Re1 Nd4 31.Qd3
f5 32.Ng5 c5 33.Re3 c4
34.Qd1 Kxa6 35.Ra3 Bf6 36.h3
f4 37.Qg4 Ka5 38.Nf3 Kb4
39.Nxd4 Kxa3 40.Nc2+ Kxa4 0-1

[Event "Russia"]
[Site "Match, Moscow"]
[Date "1963.01.06"]
[Round "05"]
[White "Petrosian"]
[Black "Mikhail Botvinnik"]
[Result "1-0"]
[ECO "D94"]

1.c4 g6 2.d4 Nf6 3.Nc3 d5
4.Nf3 Bg7 5.e3 O-O 6.Be2
dxc4 7.Bxc4 c5 8.d5 e6
9.dxe6 Qxd1+ 10.Kxd1 Bxe6
11.Bxe6 fxe6 12.Ke2 Nc6
13.Rd1 Rad8 14.Rxd8 Rxd8
15.Ng5 Re8 16.Nge4 Nxe4
17.Nxe4 b6 18.Rb1 Nb4 19.Bd2
Nd5 20.a4 Rc8 21.b3 Bf8
22.Rc1 Be7 23.b4 c4 24.b5
Kf7 25.Bc3 Ba3 26.Rc2 Nxc3+
27.Rxc3 Bb4 28.Rc2 Ke7
29.Nd2 c3 30.Ne4 Ba5 31.Kd3
Rd8+ 32.Kc4 Rd1 33.Nxc3 Rh1
34.Ne4 Rxh2 35.Kd4 Kd7 36.g3
Bb4 37.Ke5 Rh5+ 38.Kf6 Be7+
39.Kg7 e5 40.Rc6 Rh1 41.Kf7
Ra1 42.Re6 Bd8 43.Rd6+ Kc8
44.Ke8 Bc7 45.Rc6 Rd1 46.Ng5
Rd8+ 47.Kf7 Rd7+ 48.Kg8 1-0

[Event "Moscow Wch-m"]
[Site "?"]
[Date "1963.01.19"]
[Round "18"]
[White "Mikhail Botvinnik"]
[Black "Petrosian"]
[Result "0-1"]
[ECO "D31"]

1.d4 d5 2.c4 e6 3.Nc3 Be7
4.cxd5 exd5 5.Bf4 c6 6.e3
Bf5 7.g4 Be6 8.h3 Nf6 9.Nf3
Nbd7 10.Bd3 Nb6 11.Qc2 Nc4
12.Kf1 Nd6 13.Nd2 Qc8 14.Kg2
Nd7 15.f3 g6 16.Rac1 Nb6

All Games in Algebraic PGN Notation

17.b3 Qd7 18.Ne2 Ndc8 19.a4 a5 20.Bg3 Bd6 21.Nf4 Ne7 22.Nf1 h5 23.Be2 h4 24.Bh2 g5 25.Nd3 Qc7 26.Qd2 Nd7 27.Bg1 Ng6 28.Bh2 Ne7 29.Bd1 b6 30.Kg1 f6 31.e4 Bxh2+ 32.Qxh2 Qxh2+ 33.Rxh2 Rd8 34.Kf2 Kf7 35.Ke3 Rhe8 36.Rd2 Kg7 37.Kf2 dxe4 38.fxe4 Nf8 39.Ne1 Nfg6 40.Ng2 Rd7 41.Bc2 Bf7 42.Nfe3 c5 43.d5 Ne5 44.Rf1 Bg6 45.Ke1 Nc8 46.Rdf2 Rf7 47.Kd2 Nd6 48.Nf5+ Bxf5 49.exf5 c4 50.Rb1 b5 51.b4 c3+ 52.Kxc3 Rc7+ 53.Kd2 Nec4+ 54.Kd1 Na3 55.Rb2 Ndc4 56.Ra2 axb4 57.axb5 Nxb5 58.Ra6 Nc3+ 59.Kc1 Nxd5 60.Ba4 Rec8 61.Ne1 Nf4 0-1

[Event "Russia"]
[Site "Match, Moscow"]
[Date "1963.01.20"]
[Round "19"]
[White "Petrosian"]
[Black "Mikhail Botvinnik"]
[Result "1-0"]
[ECO "E19"]

1.c4 Nf6 2.Nc3 e6 3.Nf3 b6 4.g3 Bb7 5.Bg2 Be7 6.O-O O-O 7.d4 Ne4 8.Qc2 Nxc3 9.Qxc3 f5 10.b3 Bf6 11.Bb2 d6 12.Rad1 Nd7 13.Ne1 Bxg2 14.Nxg2 Bg5 15.Qc2 Bh6 16.e4 f4 17.Ne1 Qe7 18.e5 dxe5 19.dxe5 Rad8 20.Qe2 Qg5 21.Kg2 a5 22.Nf3 Qh5 23.Ba3 Rfe8 24.Rd4 Nb8 25.Rfd1 Rxd4 26.Rxd4 fxg3 27.hxg3 Qf7 28.Qe4 g6 29.Qb7 Bg7 30.c5 bxc5 31.Bxc5 Nd7 32.Qxc7 Nxe5 33.Qxf7+ Nxf7 34.Ra4 Bc3 35.Rc4 Bf6 36.Bb6 Ra8 37.Ra4 Bc3 38.Bd4 Bb4 39.a3 Bd6 40.b4 Bc7 41.Bc3 Kf8 42.b5 Ke8 43.Rc4 Kd7 44.a4 Rc8 45.Nd2 Nd6 46.Rd4 Ke7 47.Rd3 Nb7 48.Ne4 e5 49.Bb2 Bb6 50.Ba3+ Ke6 51.Ng5+ Kf5 52.Nxh7 e4 53.g4+ Kf4 54.Rd7 Rc7 55.Rxc7 Bxc7 56.Nf6 Bd8 57.Nd7 Kxg4 58.b6 Bg5 59.Nc5 Nxc5 60.Bxc5 Bf4 61.b7 Bb8 62.Be3 g5 63.Bd2 Kf5 64.Kh3 Bd6 65.Bxa5 g4+ 66.Kg2 1-0

[Event "Moskva"]
[Site "Moskva"]
[Date "1963"]
[White "Petrosian"]
[Black "Mikhail Tal"]
[Result "1-0"]
[ECO "A15"]

1.c4 Nf6 2.g3 e6 3.Bg2 c5 4.Nf3 d5 5.O-O Nc6 6.cxd5 Nxd5 7.d4 Be7 8.Nc3 O-O 9.Nxd5 exd5 10.dxc5 Bxc5 11.a3 a5 12.Bg5 f6 13.Rc1 Ba7 14.Bf4 Be6 15.Ne1 Re8 16.Nd3 Qe7 17.b4 axb4 18.Nxb4 Nxb4 19.Rc7 Qd8 20.axb4 g5 21.Qd3 Re7 22.Rxe7 Qxe7 23.Be3 d4 24.Bxd4 Rd8 25.e3 Bxd4 26.exd4 Qxb4 27.d5 Qd6 28.Be4 Bf7 29.Bxh7+ Kg7 30.Be4 Qc5 31.Rb1 Rd7 32.Qf3 Bg6 33.Bxg6 Kxg6 34.Qd3+ Kg7 35.Rb5 Qe7 36.Qf5 Rd6 37.Kg2 Qd7 38.Qxd7+ Rxd7 39.Kf3 Re7 40.Rb6 f5 41.d6 Rd7 42.h4 Kf6 43.hxg5+ Kxg5 44.Ke3 Kf6 45.Kf4 Ke6 46.f3 Kf6 47.Rb5 Ke6 48.Rxf5 Kxd6 49.g4 Ke6 50.Rf8 b5 1-0

257

All Games in Algebraic PGN Notation

[Event "Moscow"]
[Site "t"]
[Date "1964"]
[White "Petrosian"]
[Black "Mark Taimanov"]
[Result "1-0"]
[ECO "A17"]

1.c4 e6 2.Nc3 Bb4 3.Nf3 Nf6
4.Qc2 d6 5.d4 O-O 6.Bg5 Nbd7
7.e3 Qe8 8.Bh4 e5 9.O-O-O c6
10.Nd2 a6 11.dxe5 dxe5
12.Nde4 Qe6 13.Nxf6+ Nxf6
14.Bd3 h6 15.Na4 e4 16.Be2
Nd7 17.Rd4 Re8 18.Rhd1 b5
19.Nc3 Bxc3 20.Qxc3 b4
21.Qd2 b3 22.axb3 Nc5 23.Qb4
Nb7 24.Qb6 a5 25.Bg3 c5
26.Qxe6 Rxe6 27.R4d2 Rb6
28.Kc2 Be6 29.Ra1 f6 30.h3
Kf7 31.Bg4 f5 32.Be2 Rb4
33.Be5 a4 34.Rxa4 Rbxa4
35.bxa4 Rxa4 36.b3 Ra2+
37.Kc1 Ra3 38.Kb2 Ra6 39.Bc3
g6 40.Rd1 Ke7 41.h4 h5
42.Bf1 Nd8 43.Be5 Nf7 44.Bf4
Kf6 45.Be2 Ne5 46.Ra1 Rb6
47.Kc3 Nc6 48.Bc7 1-0

[Event "Hamburg"]
[Date "1965"]
[White "Petrosian"]
[Black "Borislav Ivkov"]
[Result "1-0"]
[ECO "D25"]

1.d4 Nf6 2.Nf3 d5 3.c4 dxc4
4.e3 Bg4 5.Bxc4 e6 6.Nc3 a6
7.h3 Bh5 8.g4 Bg6 9.Ne5 Nbd7
10.Nxg6 hxg6 11.g5 Nd5
12.Nxd5 exd5 13.Bxd5 c6
14.Bb3 Qxg5 15.Qf3 Nf6
16.Bd2 Qf5 17.Qg2 a5 18.O-O
O Bb4 19.Bxb4 axb4 20.h4 Rc8
21.e4 Qf4+ 22.Kb1 Rxh4 23.e5

Rxh1 24.Rxh1 Nh5 25.Bc2 Ke7
26.Bxg6 fxg6 27.Qxg6 Qxd4
28.Qxh5 Qd3+ 29.Ka1 Rd8
30.Rg1 Rd7 31.Rxg7+ Kd8
32.Rg1 Kc7 33.e6 Rd5 34.Qg4
b3 35.e7 Re5 36.Qg7 Kd6
37.Qxe5+ 1-0

[Site "Erevan"]
[Date "1965"]
[White "Miroslav Filip"]
[Black "Petrosian"]
[Result "0-1"]
[ECO "A40"]

1.d4 g6 2.g3 Bg7 3.Bg2 c5
4.c3 Qc7 5.Nf3 Nf6 6.O-O O-O
7.b3 d6 8.Bb2 Nc6 9.c4 e5
10.d5 Na5 11.Ne1 Rb8 12.Nc2
Bd7 13.Nd2 Nh5 14.e4 Bh6
15.Re1 Rbe8 16.Ne3 b6 17.Bc3
Ng7 18.Qe2 f5 19.exf5 gxf5
20.Ndf1 Nb7 21.g4 Bxe3
22.Nxe3 fxg4 23.Nxg4 Qd8
24.f3 Nh5 25.Bd2 Nf4 26.Bxf4
Rxf4 27.Nf2 Qh4 28.Ne4 Kh8
29.Ng3 Nd8 30.Qf2 Qh6 31.Re4
Nf7 32.Kh1 Rf6 33.Rg1 Ng5
34.Re3 Qxh2+ 35.Kxh2 Rh6+
36.Bh3 Nxh3 37.Nf5 Bxf5
38.Qf1 Nf4+ 39.Kg3 Rg8+
40.Kf2 Nh3+ 0-1

[Event "Moscow"]
[Site "m"]
[Date "1966.01.08"]
[Round "07"]
[White "Boris Spassky"]
[Black "Petrosian"]
[Result "0-1"]
[ECO "A46"]

1.d4 Nf6 2.Nf3 e6 3.Bg5 d5
4.Nbd2 Be7 5.e3 Nbd7 6.Bd3
c5 7.c3 b6 8.O-O Bb7 9.Ne5

All Games in Algebraic PGN Notation

Nxe5 10.dxe5 Nd7 11.Bf4 Qc7
12.Nf3 h6 13.b4 g5 14.Bg3 h5
15.h4 gxh4 16.Bf4 O-O-O
17.a4 c4 18.Be2 a6 19.Kh1
Rdg8 20.Rg1 Rg4 21.Qd2 Rhg8
22.a5 b5 23.Rad1 Bf8 24.Nh2
Nxe5 25.Nxg4 hxg4 26.e4 Bd6
27.Qe3 Nd7 28.Bxd6 Qxd6
29.Rd4 e5 30.Rd2 f5 31.exd5
f4 32.Qe4 Nf6 33.Qf5+ Kb8
34.f3 Bc8 35.Qb1 g3 36.Re1
h3 37.Bf1 Rh8 38.gxh3 Bxh3
39.Kg1 Bxf1 40.Kxf1 e4
41.Qd1 Ng4 42.fxg4 f3 43.Rg2
fxg2+ 0-1

[Event "Moscow-Wch"]
[Site "Moscow-Wch"]
[Date "1966.01.11"]
[Round "10"]
[White "Petrosian"]
[Black "Boris Spassky"]
[Result "1-0"]
[ECO "E63"]

1.Nf3 Nf6 2.g3 g6 3.c4 Bg7
4.Bg2 O-O 5.O-O Nc6 6.Nc3 d6
7.d4 a6 8.d5 Na5 9.Nd2 c5
10.Qc2 e5 11.b3 Ng4 12.e4 f5
13.exf5 gxf5 14.Nd1 b5 15.f3
e4 16.Bb2 exf3 17.Bxf3 Bxb2
18.Qxb2 Ne5 19.Be2 f4
20.gxf4 Bh3 21.Ne3 Bxf1
22.Rxf1 Ng6 23.Bg4 Nxf4
24.Rxf4 Rxf4 25.Be6+ Rf7
26.Ne4 Qh4 27.Nxd6 Qg5+
28.Kh1 Raa7 29.Bxf7+ Rxf7
30.Qh8+ 1-0

[Event "Moskva"]
[Date "1966.01.21"]
[White "Petrosian"]
[Black "Boris Spassky"]
[Result "1-0"]
[ECO "E59"]

1.d4 Nf6 2.c4 e6 3.Nc3 Bb4
4.e3 O-O 5.Bd3 c5 6.Nf3 d5
7.O-O Nc6 8.a3 Bxc3 9.bxc3
dxc4 10.Bxc4 Qc7 11.Bd3 e5
12.Qc2 Bg4 13.Nxe5 Nxe5
14.dxe5 Qxe5 15.f3 Bd7 16.a4
Rfd8 17.e4 c4 18.Be2 Be6
19.Be3 Qc7 20.Rab1 Nd7
21.Rb5 b6 22.Rfb1 Qc6 23.Bd4
f6 24.Qa2 Kh8 25.Bf1 h6
26.h3 Rab8 27.a5 Rb7 28.axb6
axb6 29.Qf2 Ra8 30.Qb2 Rba7
31.Bxb6 Ra2 32.Qb4 Rc2
33.Bf2 Qc7 34.Qe7 Bxh3
35.gxh3 Rxf2 36.Kxf2 Qh2+
37.Bg2 Ne5 38.Rb8+ Rxb8
39.Rxb8+ Kh7 40.Rd8 Ng6
41.Qe6 1-0

[Site "Laatvia"]
[Date "1966"]
[White "Petrosian"]
[Black "Martin Johansson"]
[Result "1-0"]
[ECO "B85"]

1.e4 c5 2.Nf3 d6 3.d4 cxd4
4.Nxd4 Nf6 5.Nc3 a6 6.Be2 e6
7.f4 Nc6 8.Be3 Qc7 9.O-O Bd7
10.Nb3 b5 11.a3 Be7 12.Rf2
b4 13.axb4 Nxb4 14.Bf3 Rc8
15.g4 h6 16.g5 hxg5 17.fxg5
Nh7 18.Qd2 Nf8 19.Qd4 Nc6
20.Qxg7 Rh7 21.Qg8 Ne5
22.Be2 Bc6 23.Rxa6 Rd8
24.Rxc6 Nxc6 25.Bb5 1-0

259

All Games in Algebraic PGN Notation

[Event "Ol Moscow"]
[Date "1966"]
[White "Petrosian"]
[Black "David Bronstein"]
[Result "1-0"]
[ECO "D50"]

1.d4 e6 2.c4 Nf6 3.Nc3 d5
4.Bg5 c5 5.e3 cxd4 6.exd4
Be7 7.Rc1 O-O 8.Nf3 Nc6 9.c5
h6 10.Bf4 Ne4 11.Bb5 Bd7
12.O-O g5 13.Bg3 a6 14.Bxc6
Bxc6 15.Ne5 Be8 16.Re1 Nxg3
17.hxg3 Bf6 18.b4 Bg7 19.Rb1
f6 20.Nd3 Bf7 21.b5 Qc7
22.bxa6 bxa6 23.Rb6 e5
24.dxe5 fxe5 25.Nxe5 Qxc5
26.Rc6 Qa7 27.Ng4 Kh8
28.Nxh6 Be8 29.Rxe8 Qxf2+
30.Kh2 Raxe8 31.Qh5 Qe1
32.Nf5+ Kg8 33.Nxg7 Rf1
34.Qxe8+ 1-0

[Event "Palma de Mallorca"]
[Site "It"]
[Date "1968"]
[White "Petrosian"]
[Black "Bent Larsen"]
[Result "1-0"]
[ECO "E12"]

1.d4 Nf6 2.c4 e6 3.Nf3 b6
4.a3 c5 5.d5 exd5 6.cxd5 g6
7.Nc3 Bg7 8.Bg5 O-O 9.e3 d6
10.Nd2 h6 11.Bh4 Na6 12.Be2
Nc7 13.e4 b5 14.O-O Qd7
15.Qc2 Re8 16.Rfe1 Bb7 17.h3
a6 18.f4 c4 19.Bf3 h5
20.Rad1 Nh7 21.e5 dxe5
22.Nde4 Qf5 23.Qf2 Rad8
24.Bxd8 Rxd8 25.Qb6 Qc8
26.Nc5 e4 27.Qxb7 exf3
28.Qxc8 Rxc8 29.d6 Bf8
30.Nb7 Ne6 31.d7 Rb8 32.Rxe6
1-0

[Event "Maliorka"]
[Site "t"]
[Date "1968"]
[White "Petrosian"]
[Black "Svetozar Gligoric"]
[Result "1-0"]
[ECO "E81"]

1.d4 Nf6 2.c4 g6 3.Nc3 Bg7
4.e4 d6 5.f3 O-O 6.Be3 c6
7.Bd3 e5 8.d5 cxd5 9.cxd5 a6
10.Nge2 Nbd7 11.O-O Nh5
12.Kh1 f5 13.exf5 gxf5
14.Qb1 Nc5 15.Bc2 a5 16.f4
exf4 17.Nxf4 Nxf4 18.Bxf4
Ra6 19.Qe1 Rb6 20.Rb1 Qf6
21.a3 Bd7 22.Rf3 a4 23.Be3
Qe5 24.Qf2 Ra6 25.Rd1 Qe7
26.Bd4 Bxd4 27.Qxd4 Qf6
28.Qb4 Raa8 29.Rdf1 Qe5
30.Qh4 Rae8 31.h3 b5 32.Rf4
Re7 33.g4 Qf6 34.Qxf6 Rxf6
35.gxf5 Re3 36.Kg2 Kf8
37.R1f3 Re7 38.Ne4 Nxe4
39.Bxe4 Re5 40.Kf2 Be8
41.Ke3 Bh5 42.Rf1 Be8 43.Rc1
Bd7 44.Kd4 Ke7 45.Rc7 Kd8
46.Ra7 h5 47.Rf1
Rf7 48.Bd3 Be8 49.Ra8+ Kd7
50.f6 Rf8 51.f7 1-0

[Event "Moscow"]
[Site "m"]
[Date "1969.01.12"]
[Round "11"]
[White "Boris Spassky"]
[Black "Petrosian"]
[Result "0-1"]
[ECO "E12"]

1.d4 Nf6 2.c4 e6 3.Nf3 b6
4.a3 Bb7 5.Nc3 d5 6.e3 Nbd7
7.cxd5 exd5 8.Be2 Bd6 9.b4
O-O 10.O-O a6 11.Qb3 Qe7

All Games in Algebraic PGN Notation

12.Rb1 Ne4 13.a4 Ndf6 14.b5 Nxc3 15.Qxc3 Ne4 16.Qc2 Rfc8 17.Bb2 c6 18.bxc6 Bxc6 19.Qb3 Qd7 20.Ra1 b5 21.a5 Bb7 22.Ne5 Qd8 23.Rfd1 Qh4 24.g3 Qe7 25.f3 Ng5 26.h4 Ne6 27.f4 f6 28.Nf3 Nd8 29.Kf2 Nf7 30.Nd2 Rc4 31.Qd3 Re8 32.Bf3 Bb4 33.Ba3 Bxa3 34.Rxa3 Nd6 35.Re1 f5 36.Raa1 Ne4+ 37.Bxe4 fxe4 38.Qb1 Qd7 39.Ra2 Rec8 40.Nxc4 dxc4 41.d5 Bxd5 42.Rd1 c3 43.Rc2 Qh3 44.Rg1 Qg4 45.Kg2 Qf3+ 46.Kh2 Qxe3 47.f5 Qc5 48.Rf1 b4 49.f6 b3 50.Rcf2 c2 51.Qc1 e3 52.f7+ Kf8 53.Rf5 b2 54.Qxb2 c1=Q 55.Qxg7+ Kxg7 56.Rg5+ 0-1

[Event "Moscow"]
[Site "m"]
[Date "1969.01.21"]
[Round "20"]
[White "Petrosian"]
[Black "Boris Spassky"]
[Result "1-0"]
[ECO "D55"]

1.c4 e6 2.d4 d5 3.Nf3 Be7 4.Nc3 Nf6 5.Bg5 O-O 6.e3 h6 7.Bxf6 Bxf6 8.Qd2 b6 9.cxd5 exd5 10.b4 Bb7 11.Rb1 c6 12.Bd3 Nd7 13.O-O Re8 14.Rfc1 a5 15.bxa5 Rxa5 16.Bf5 Ra6 17.Rb3 g6 18.Bd3 Ra7 19.Rcb1 Bg7 20.a4 Qe7 21.Bf1 Ba6 22.h4 Bxf1 23.Rxf1 h5 24.Re1 Raa8 25.g3 Qd6 26.Kg2 Kf8 27.Reb1 Kg8 28.Qd1 Bf8 29.R3b2 Bg7 30.Rc2 Ra7 31.Rbc1 Nb8 32.Ne2 Rc7 33.Qd3 Ra7 34.Qb3 Ra6 35.Nf4 Rd8 36.Nd3 Bf8 37.Nfe5 Rc8 38.Rc3 Be7 39.Nf4 Bf6 40.Ned3 Ra5 41.Qxb6 Rxa4 42.Rc5 Ra6 43.Rxd5 Qxf4 44.Qxa6 Qe4+ 45.f3 Qe6 46.Qc4 Qxe3 47.Ne5 Rf8 48.Rc5 Be7 49.Rb1 Bxc5 50.Rxb8 1-0

[Event "Moscow"]
[Site "It"]
[Date "1970"]
[White "Lev Polugaevsky"]
[Black "Petrosian"]
[Result "0-1"]
[ECO "A14"]

1.c4 Nf6 2.Nf3 e6 3.g3 b6 4.Bg2 Bb7 5.O-O Be7 6.b3 O-O 7.Bb2 d5 8.e3 c5 9.Nc3 Nbd7 10.d3 Rc8 11.Qe2 Qc7 12.e4 d4 13.Nb1 Ne8 14.Ne1 e5 15.f4 g6 16.f5 Bg5 17.h4 Be3+ 18.Kh2 gxf5 19.exf5 e4 20.Bxe4 Bxe4 21.dxe4 Nef6 22.Ng2 Rfe8 23.Nd2 Bxd2 24.Qxd2 Qxg3+ 25.Kxg3 Nxe4+ 26.Kf4 Nxd2 27.Rfe1 Nf6 28.Rxe8+ Rxe8 29.Re1 Nde4 30.Re2 Kf8 31.Kf3 d3 32.Re3 Rd8 33.Re1 d2 34.Rd1 Ng4 35.Ne3 Nef2 36.Bc3 Rd3 0-1

[Event "Kapfenberg ETC"]
[Date "1970"]
[Round "01"]
[White "Vlastimil Hort"]
[Black "Petrosian"]
[Result "0-1"]
[ECO "C18"]

1.e4 e6 2.d4 d5 3.Nc3 Bb4 4.e5 c5 5.a3 Bxc3+ 6.bxc3 Qc7 7.Qg4 f5 8.Qg3 cxd4 9.cxd4 Ne7 10.Bd2 O-O 11.Bd3 b6 12.Ne2 Ba6 13.Nf4 Qd7

All Games in Algebraic PGN Notation

14.Bb4 Rf7 15.h4 Bxd3
16.Qxd3 Nbc6 17.h5 Rc8
18.Rh3 Nd8 19.Rg3 Rc4 20.h6
Ndc6 21.Nh5 g6 22.Nf6+ Rxf6
23.exf6 Nc8 24.Qd2 Rxd4
25.Rd3 Rh4 26.Rh3 Rg4 27.Kf1
Nd6 28.Re1 Kf7 29.Bc3 Ne4
30.Qd3 Nc5 31.Qd1 Rc4 32.Bb2
Qd6 33.Qe2 b5 34.Kg1 Ne4
35.Rd3 Qc5 36.Rc1 e5 37.Qe3
d4 38.Qe2 Nxf6 39.Rdd1 e4
40.Qd2 Nd5 41.Qg5 Nc7 42.Rd2
Ne6 43.Qh4 a5 44.Rcd1 Rxc2
45.Rxc2 Qxc2 46.Rc1 Qxb2
47.Rxc6 d3 48.Ra6 Qd4 0-1

[Event "Wijk"]
[Date "1971"]
[White "Petrosian"]
[Black "Henrique Mecking"]
[Result "1-0"]
[ECO "A46"]

1.d4 Nf6 2.Nf3 e6 3.Bg5 c5
4.e3 d5 5.c3 Nc6 6.Nbd2 cxd4
7.exd4 Be7 8.Bd3 h6 9.Bf4
Nh5 10.Be3 Nf6 11.Ne5 Nxe5
12.dxe5 Nd7 13.Bd4 Nc5
14.Bc2 a5 15.Qg4 g6 16.O-O
Bd7 17.Rfe1 Qc7 18.a4 Na6
19.Qe2 Kf8 20.Nf3 Kg7 21.Be3
Nc5 22.Nd4 Ra6 23.Bc1 Raa8
24.g3 b6 25.h4 h5 26.Qf3 Qd8
27.Bd2 Qe8 28.Bg5 Qd8 29.Qf4
Rc8 30.Re3 Bxg5 31.hxg5 Ra8
32.Qf6+ Qxf6 33.exf6+ Kh7
34.Kg2 Rae8 35.f4 Rb8
36.Ree1 Nb7 37.Rh1 Kg8
38.Nf3 Nd6 39.Ne5 Be8 40.Bd3
Rc8 41.Kf3 Bc6 42.Rh2 Be8
43.Ke3 Rc7 44.Kd4 Nb7 45.b4
Nd8 46.Rh4 Nb7 47.Ra2 Nd6
48.Rh1 Nb7 49.b5 Nc5 50.Bc2
Nd7 51.Ra3 Nc5 52.c4 Nd7
53.Rc3 Nxe5 54.Kxe5 dxc4
55.Be4 Rc8 56.Kd6 Rc5
57.Rhc1 h4 1-0

[Event "Buenos Aires m Rd: 2"]
[Date "1971"]
[White "Petrosian"]
[Black "Robert James Fischer"]
[Result "1-0"]
[ECO "D82"]

1.d4 Nf6 2.c4 g6 3.Nc3 d5
4.Bf4 Bg7 5.e3 c5 6.dxc5 Qa5
7.Rc1 Ne4 8.cxd5 Nxc3 9.Qd2
Qxa2 10.bxc3 Qa5 11.Bc4 Nd7
12.Ne2 Ne5 13.Ba2 Bf5
14.Bxe5 Bxe5 15.Nd4 Qxc5
16.Nxf5 gxf5 17.O-O Qa5
18.Qc2 f4 19.c4 fxe3 20.c5
Qd2 21.Qa4+ Kf8 22.Rcd1 Qe2
23.d6 Qh5 24.f4 e2
25.fxe5 exd1=Q 26.Rxd1 Qxe5
27.Rf1 f6 28.Qb3 Kg7 29.Qf7+
Kh6 30.dxe7 f5 31.Rxf5 Qd4+
32.Kh1 1-0

[Event "Moscow Alekhine mem"]
[Date "1971"]
[Round "06"]
[White "Petrosian"]
[Black "Boris Spassky"]
[Result "1-0"]
[ECO "D27"]
[WhiteElo "2640"]
[BlackElo "2690"]

1.d4 d5 2.c4 dxc4 3.Nf3 Nf6
4.e3 e6 5.Bxc4 c5 6.O-O a6
7.a4 Nc6 8.Qe2 Be7 9.Rd1
cxd4 10.exd4 O-O 11.Nc3 Nd5
12.Qe4 Ncb4 13.Ne5 Ra7
14.Bb3 Nf6 15.Qh4 b6 16.Qg3
Bb7 17.Bh6 Ne8 18.Rac1 Kh8

262

All Games in Algebraic PGN Notation

19.d5 exd5 20.Be3 Ra8 21.Nc4
Nd6 22.Bxb6 Qb8 23.Na5 Nf5
24.Qxb8 Raxb8 25.Nxb7 Rxb7
26.a5 Bg5 27.Rb1 d4 28.Nd5
Nc6 29.Ba4 Rc8 30.f4 Nce7
31.Rbc1 Rcb8 32.fxg5 Nxd5
33.Bc6 Rxb6 34.axb6 Nde3
35.b7 Nxd1 36.Rxd1 g6 37.g4
Ng7 38.Rxd4 Ne6 39.Rd7 1-0

[Event "It (cat. 11)"]
[Site "San Antonio"]
[Date "1972"]
[White "Petrosian"]
[Black "Bent Larsen"]
[Result "1-0"]
[ECO "A40"]

1.d4 e6 2.Nf3 f5 3.g3 Nf6
4.Bg2 b5 5.Ne5 c6 6.Nd2 Qb6
7.e4 Qxd4 8.Nef3 Qc5 9.exf5
Qxf5 10.O-O Nd5 11.Nd4 Qf7
12.N2f3 Qh5 13.Re1 Be7
14.Re5 Qf7 15.Re2 O-O 16.Ne5
Qh5 17.f4 Bc5 18.Kh1 Bb7
19.Ndf3 Bb6 20.a4 a6 21.c4
Nf6 22.Ng5 bxa4 23.Bf3 Qe8
24.Be3 Bxe3 25.Rxe3 h6
26.Ne4 Nxe4 27.Bxe4 d5
28.Bg2 Nd7 29.Rxa4 c5
30.cxd5 Nb6 31.Ra5 Nxd5
32.Rb3 Rd8 33.Rxb7 Ne3
34.Qe2 Rd1+ 35.Qxd1 Nxd1
36.Rxa6 Ne3 37.Raa7 Nf5
38.g4 Qd8 39.h3 Qd1+ 40.Kh2
Qd4 41.Ng6 Ne3 42.Rxg7+ Qxg7
43.Rxg7+ Kxg7 44.Nxf8 Kxf8
45.Bf3 h5 46.g5 h4 47.Kg1 e5
48.fxe5 Nc4 49.Kf2 Nxe5
50.Be4 Kg7 51.b3 Nf7 52.g6
Ng5 53.Bf5 Kf6 54.Ke3 Ne6
55.Bxe6 Kxe6 56.Ke4 Kf6
57.Kd5 Kxg6 58.Kxc5 Kf5
59.b4 Kf4 60.b5 Kg3 61.b6 1-0

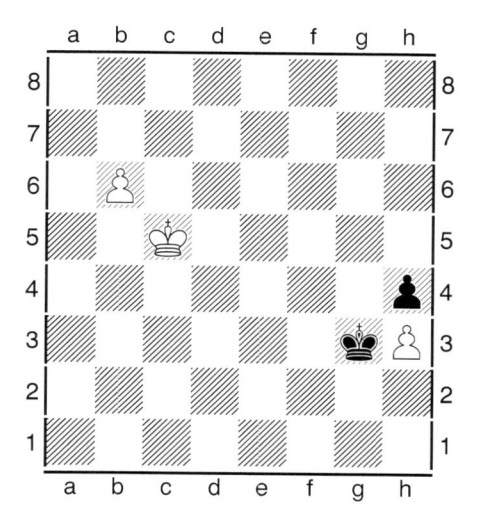

263

Printed in Great Britain by
Amazon.co.uk, Ltd.,
Marston Gate.